PROTECTING HUMAN RIGHTS

Protecting Human Rights

Instruments and Institutions

Edited by

TOM CAMPBELL
JEFFREY GOLDSWORTHY
and
ADRIENNE STONE

OXFORD
UNIVERSITY PRESS

OXFORD
UNIVERSITY PRESS

Great Clarendon Street, Oxford OX2 6DP

Oxford University Press is a department of the University of Oxford.
It furthers the University's objective of excellence in research, scholarship,
and education by publishing worldwide in

Oxford New York

Auckland Bangkok Buenos Aires Cape Town Chennai
Dar es Salaam Delhi Hong Kong Istanbul Karachi Kolkata
Kuala Lumpur Madrid Melbourne Mexico City Mumbai Nairobi
São Paulo Shanghai Singapore Taipei Tokyo Toronto

Oxford is a registered trade mark of Oxford University Press
in the UK and in certain other countries

Published in the United States
by Oxford University Press Inc., New York

First published 2003

British Library Cataloguing in Publication Data
Data available

Library of Congress Cataloging in Publication Data
Data available

ISBN 0–19–926406–6

1 3 5 7 9 10 8 6 4 2

Typeset 9.5 on 12 pt Sabon
by Kolam Information Services Pvt. Ltd, Pondicherry, India
Printed in Great Britain on
acid-free paper by T. J. International,
Padstow, Cornwall

Preface

The chapters in this book were commissioned for the purpose of this publication. They were presented and discussed at a workshop in Melbourne in December 2001, attended by almost all of the contributors and a small number of other participants. The Australian Research Council generously funded the workshop.

The editors are grateful to the contributors, to the other participants in that workshop, to Francesca Casella, Zoe Guest, Sheena Smith, and Shaun Tipson for their assistance with the manuscript, and to Oxford University Press for its support for the project.

Tom Campbell and Jeffrey Goldsworthy wish to thank most enthusiastically their co-editor, Adrienne Stone, who undertook the arduous task of editing the book subsequent to the Melbourne workshop.

Contents

List of Contributors

Larry Alexander is the Warren Distinguished Professor of Law at the University of San Diego School of Law.

James Allan is an Associate Professor of Law at the Faculty of Law, University of Otago.

Tom Campbell is a Professorial Fellow at the Centre for Applied Philosophy and Public Ethics, Charles Sturt University, Canberra.

Steven Curry is a Research Fellow at the Centre for Applied Philosophy and Public Ethics, Charles Sturt University, Canberra.

Julie Debeljak is a lecturer and Associate Director of the Castan Centre for Human Rights Law at the Faculty of Law, Monash University.

David Dyzenhaus is a Professor of Law and Philosophy at the Faculty of Law and in the Department of Philosophy, University of Toronto.

K. D. Ewing is the Professor of Public Law at the School of Law, King's College, University of London.

Jeffrey Goldsworthy is a Professor of Law at the Faculty of Law, Monash University.

Janet L. Hiebert is an Associate Professor in the Department of Political Studies at Queen's University, Kingston, Ontario.

Richard S. Kay is the George and Helen England Professor of Law at the University of Connecticut Law School.

Mark A. Nolan is a lecturer at the Faculty of Law, Australian National University.

Penelope J. Oakes is a Professor of Psychology at the School of Psychology, Australian National University.

Dianne Otto is an Associate Professor of Law at the Faculty of Law, Melbourne University.

Adrienne Stone is a Fellow in the Law Program at the Research School of Social Sciences, Australian National University.

David Tucker is Associate Professor in the Department of Political Science, University of Melbourne.

Mark Tushnet is Carmack Waterhouse Professor of Constitutional Law at the Georgetown Law Center, Georgetown University.

Robin West is Professor of Law at the Georgetown Law Center, Georgetown University.

George Williams is Anthony Mason Professor of Law and Director of the Gilbert and Tobin Centre of Public Law at the University of New South Wales.

Tables of Cases

Australia

Canada

European Court and Commission of Human Rights

The Netherlands

New Zealand

United Kingdom

United Nations Committee on Human Rights

United States of America

Tables of Legislation

Africa

Australia

Commonwealth

New South Wales

Victoria

CANADA

Federal

Quebec

Denmark

Europe

Fiji

Germany

International

Italy

The Netherlands

New Zealand

Norway

South Africa

Spain

Sweden

Sweden

UNITED STATES

Introduction

ADRIENNE STONE

This volume was inspired by the increasing dominance of human rights in world legal and political systems. In political debate, human rights have become the principal means for determining the moral legitimacy of law, and judicially enforced bills of rights as a means for enforcing human rights in the domestic sphere are almost universal in democratic countries. Bills of rights have been adopted in countries rebuilding after periods of turmoil (the two world wars, the 1989 revolutions in eastern Europe, and the collapse of apartheid in South Africa), by stable parliamentary democracies like Canada, New Zealand, Sweden, and the United Kingdom, and in international law.

This increasing dominance exacerbates two enduring problems for human rights theory and practice. The first problem relates to the content and form of human rights: what is and what is not to be counted as a human right, and what does it mean to identify a right as a human right? The second problem relates to the implementation of human rights: what are the most effective and legitimate means of promoting human rights? This volume deals with both problems. It explores the conceptual and moral issues deriving from the expansion of rights discourse, and the institutional mechanisms that may be adopted to protect human rights.

WHAT ARE HUMAN RIGHTS?

Tom Campbell's chapter opens the collection by challenging the idea that the fundamental or essential character of human rights can be defined by abstract analysis, and that the content of human rights can have universal application. In his view, human rights are not usefully defined as those rights that are so fundamental or essential that we can conclude every individual holds them. Nor should it follow from the identification of a human right that every society is required to respect it in all circumstances.

Thus Campbell rejects a 'conceptual' analysis, which seeks a context-free determination of human rights from the idea of what amounts to a 'right' and what it is to be 'human' (p. 20). Although human rights might seem to be more important if they were universally applicable, Campbell objects that such conceptual analyses will, inevitably, be either under- or over-inclusive. There are some rights that can plausibly be said to be universally held but trivial;[1] while others are important but cannot conceivably be said to be universally shared.[2] Such approaches, therefore, result either in a large and disparate set of rights, many of which are of no particular importance, or a narrow set of rights that downplays the diversity among human beings.

Similarly, Campbell dismisses more sophisticated attempts to define human rights by rational, non-empirical philosophical deduction from a single overriding value or small cluster of values. His conclusion is that 'There is no distinctively philosophical ... methodology that can take the place of moral reflection on what constitutes human rights [and] ... direct appeals to moral values do not settle much in the abstract' (p. 29).

The focus of Campbell's chapter is to identify a more satisfactory method for defining human rights. His approach is pragmatic and functional, arguing that human rights are best defined according to the use to which we wish to put them, rather than an abstract idea of what is fundamental to human beings. His approach is also attentive to context, allowing for the concept of human rights to vary according to the particular context in which the question of rights arises (p. 19): 'Once we know the impact of our decisions and what is to be done with them, this sharpens our questions and focuses our minds so that we begin to provide justifiable answers at an appropriate level of specificity. On this approach, "human rights" are conclusions, not premisses.'

Campbell's pragmatic functionalism finds some resonance in Chapter 3, by Mark Nolan and Penelope Oakes (although they do not agree with Campbell's view, expressed elsewhere, that rights rhetoric eclipses claims framed in terms of justice). Their analysis is functional, in the sense that it explicitly defines the use to which human rights are to be put. As social psychologists, they are interested in the psychological harm that injustice causes, and their concern is to consider how that kind of harm can be addressed by the assertion of human rights.

Nolan and Oakes identify two types of psychological harm that might be addressed by human rights. First, there is 'moral exclusion'—the harm caused by unjustified exclusion of some group of persons. In this context, human rights can be used to emphasize the equal moral worth of the excluded sub-group. Nolan and Oakes test the effectiveness of human rights in this context by studying the views of activists opposing attempts by the Australian Government to allow single women and lesbians to be excluded from access to assisted reproductive technology.

[1] Jeremy Waldron makes this point about Art 24 of the Universal Declaration of Human Rights, which recognizes a right to 'rest and leisure, including reasonable limitation of working hours and periodic holidays with pay', remarking that 'it simply seems to lack the moral urgency, the priority, the sense of being an indispensable part of the moral minimum that we usually associate with rights; J. Waldron, *Liberal Rights: Collected Papers 1981–1991* (Cambridge: Cambridge University Press, 1993).

[2] This objection applies particularly to rights that protect marginalized groups defined by their 'differences' from dominant understandings of the human beings and their needs.

However, consistently with their functional approach, Nolan and Oakes are not satisfied with this use of human rights. An emphasis on equality will not psychologically satisfy all harmed claimants. On the contrary, an aggrieved individual or sub-group may demand that decision-makers and others respect difference. In that light they identify a second kind of psychological harm: 'sub-group discrimination'. Human rights can address this harm by emphasizing the 'unequal worthiness' of harmed claimants. To test the assertion of human rights as a response to this problem, Nolan and Oakes investigate the operation of laws imposing mandatory sentences for certain crimes in the Northern Territory of Australia, a policy that had a disproportionate effect on the indigenous community.

The pragmatic functionalism of these two chapters sits in contrast with the contribution from Larry Alexander (Chapter 2). Alexander mounts a startling thesis: that freedom of expression (a central tenet of liberal political theory, a core civil and political right, widely protected in international and domestic instruments) lacks a coherent or principled justification. Instead, he argues, freedom of expression is deeply paradoxical. A free expression principle cannot be applied without the regulator (government) taking a position on the worth or otherwise of the information affected, a position that a liberal concept of freedom of expression would preclude.

His central insight is that all laws have 'message effects'. In other words, all laws affect 'what gets said by whom, to whom, and with what effect'. Alexander starts with a category of laws traditionally thought to be least problematic in terms of freedom of expression: content-neutral laws. These are laws that burden expression incidentally, regulating the time, place, and manner of expression in pursuit of some objective unrelated to the content of the message. Although American free speech law (on which Alexander focuses) has been most concerned with these 'incidental burdens' in symbolic speech and public forum cases, Alexander argues that all laws have incidental message effects. As a result, unless freedom of expression is construed impracticably broadly (so that all laws having incidental message effects are regarded as violating freedom of expression and are invalid) or narrowly (so that no such laws invalidate freedom of expression), there is no choice but to weigh the value of the particular speech at issue against the value of the particular law. Herein lies the paradox: the involvement of government in the process of determining the value of speech itself contradicts fundamental free speech values.

Alexander also identifies the same problem with respect to 'content-based' laws—laws that regulate a message because of its content. Although such laws are usually considered more problematic than content-neutral laws, it still seems necessary to allow some 'content-based' regulation. Thus the paradox repeats itself: unless it is found that freedom of expression is violated whenever government engages in this form of regulation (which would be an extraordinarily broad principle of freedom of expression) or that freedom of expression is *never* violated by such laws (a counter-intuitively narrow principle of freedom of expression), there is no choice but to *weigh* the interest in freedom of expression against the government's interest in regulation. Thus government is again involved in the process of determining the worth of some message, and the 'content-based' principle (like the content-neutral principle just discussed) seems to contradict the basic premiss of freedom of expression.

The root cause, Alexander argues, is a philosophical problem inherent in liberalism itself. Liberalism demands governmental tolerance of the illiberal but, in his words, 'the idea that liberalism cannot take its own side in an argument is an impossibility. Liberal government cannot help but be partisan, which means that liberalism as governmental non-partisanship (neutrality) is an impossibility' (p. 67).

Descriptively, Alexander's chapter thus shares much with Campbell's. Campbell is sceptical of the capacity to find abstract justifications for the content of human rights, and Alexander has demonstrated the impossibility of doing so with respect to freedom of expression (at least when conceiving that right within the bounds of liberal theory). Alexander's reaction, however, is quite different. He is unable to find a principled justification for freedom of speech consistent with the basic tenets of liberalism but (without Campbell's pragmatic functionalism) is unable to abandon a commitment to it. He concludes that: 'The critique is deflationary... It induces, not more toleration... but a sort of normative torpor... In the end, I find my results terribly disquieting, for I count myself as a dyed-in-the wool liberal and a champion of freedom of expression.'

Robin West, the final author in this group, is also both committed to, and troubled by, the traditional liberal conception of rights that so dominates American constitutionalism. Her chapter (Chapter 4) challenges the hostility of the American constitutional tradition to positive rights. This rests, she argues, not only on a misreading of American constitutional text and history, but also on an Americanized neo-Lockean conception of the rule of law, which holds that the democratic political state is untrustworthy. According to this conception, the rule of law, enforced principally through constitutional rights, therefore exists to constrain the state rather than to involve it in actively providing for the citizen.

West offers a reinterpretation of liberal theory drawing on the writings of Thomas Hobbes and Thomas Paine. She identifies in Hobbes's writing a commitment to the right of the individual to the positive protection of the state against private violence. Hobbes's conception of the state thus contains the important insight that the intervention of the state to protect against private violence is essential for the good life in any decent liberal society. Citizens require positive protection by the state, and rights that recognize this need. Thus rights must do more than control or limit the political state. In Thomas Paine's writings she finds a conception of the rule of law as a commitment to representative government—the form of government most likely to act in the interest of the people. The laws produced by that political process are therefore conceived as actions in the interest and on behalf of the people.

She concludes, then, that a commitment to positive rights holds an honourable place in American constitutionalism and the liberal political theory that guides it. 'Positive rights' can be understood, in a Hobbesian way, as protecting us against the dangers of the state of nature and, following Paine, as part of the '"Rights of Man" rightly produced by democratic governance' (p. 114). She advocates a reconceptualization of liberal theory and, consequently, of American constitutionalism that would bring it closer to the more generous understanding of rights seen in public international law.

Democratic foundations

In the second and third parts of this volume the chapters move to considering how rights are to be protected in democratic legal systems. The first group of chapters addresses a central philosophical problem that has dogged the implementation of rights through constitutional bills of rights: that of democratic legitimacy.

A leading defence of constitutional rights has it that such rights operate to *protect* the proper functioning of democratic government and, thus, are not inconsistent with it. Perhaps the most influential versions of this argument are found in the works of John Hart Ely (who argues that the rights entrenched in the United States Constitution protect democratic processes by preventing democratic 'malfunctions' that entrench the powerful or disregard minorities[3]) and Ronald Dworkin (who extends the argument to include judicial review with respect to rights with no procedural aspect but which operate to ensure that citizens are treated with equal concern and respect[4]).

These arguments have recently been subject to criticism by Jeremy Waldron (whom David Dyzenhaus classifies in his chapter as a 'democratic legal positivist', along with James Allan, Tom Campbell, and Jeffrey Goldsworthy). The democratic legal positivist critique, as put by Waldron, relies on the indeterminate nature of rights, and scepticism about the superior capacity of judges.[5] Waldron's most central point is that rights, including those that are necessary for democratic government, are the subjects of ongoing, rational disagreement. Thus, the judge's role cannot be seen as the simple enforcement of democracy, or the mere correction of democratic error, but requires the exercise of judicial choice among competing concepts of democratic government. Thus constitutional rights will only protect democracy if the judge chooses well among those competing conceptions. Since Waldron also argues that judges are not superior decision-makers on such issues, there is no sound basis on which to hand this power to the judiciary. Ultimately, then, he concludes that judicial enforcement

[3] J. H. Ely, *Democracy and Distrust* (Cambridge, Mass.: Harvard University Press, 1980).

[4] R. Dworkin, *Freedom's Law: The Moral Reading of the American Constitution* (Cambridge, Mass.: Harvard University Press, 1996).

[5] J. Waldron, *Law and Disagreement* (Oxford: Clarendon Press, 1999).

of rights always imposes a cost to democratic government and, moreover, that this should be seen as a cost to *rights*: it interferes with the right of participation in government, which he characterizes as 'the right of rights'.

Arguments of this nature feature in a number of chapters in this collection. They are perhaps clearest in James Allan's chapter (Chapter 8), which defends the status quo in Australia, the only remaining Western country with no constitutional, or even statutory, bill of rights. In part, the chapter defends the Australian status quo, relying on the robustness of Australian democracy. It contains a detailed analysis of current Australian voting systems, the institutions supervising federal elections, the process for amending the Australian Constitution, and existing legal protection for rights in Australia. However, Allan also harbours grave doubts about rights and their judicial enforcement in general. He maintains a resolutely utilitarian philosophy of rights, which leads him to the position that 'rights rest ultimately either on the good consequences they generally produce or on the sentiments in their favour that some people happen to feel' (p. 187). Thus Allan concludes (pp. 187–8):

> The main effect of entrenching a bill of rights in a Western democracy is to transfer a significant degree of social policy-making power to unelected judges . . . It is the judges, and no one else . . . who will take these open-textured rights guarantees—the broad and imprecise standards embodied in the language or rights—and apply them to specific situations where legislation passed by the democratically elected legislature has been argued to infringe or conflict with the rights guarantees.

David Tucker's chapter (Chapter 7) provides a precise articulation of these kinds of concern (although he counsels restraint in, rather than abandonment of, the judicial role). His chapter analyses the judicial supervision of elections, a key area in which judges might be expected to act to enforce the necessary conditions of democracy. Following a comparative analysis of the performance of the Supreme Court of the United States and of the High Court of Australia, he is critical of both. The United States Supreme Court has made it difficult to control the influence of wealthy interests on elections, has been disinclined to protect minority parties from a two-party duopoly, and has created unnecessary rigidities in the districting process. The High Court of Australia has been more reticent, but even it has failed, in Tucker's view, to show appropriate deference to legislative judgment in the regulation of political advertising.

Richard Kay, whose chapter (Chapter 1) starts the section, enters this debate with a new defence of bills of rights. His argument focuses principally on competing characterizations of the nature of constitutional judicial review. As he shows, the source of much scepticism of constitutional rights lies in the success of the legal realist critique of adjudication, which has made it impossible to describe the role of judges as simply applying rules made by constitution-makers. It is because the judicial role, under the influence of legal realism, looks more like the legislative role that it is hard to defend judicial authority over that of the elected legislature.

In response, Kay reasserts the idea that, in enforcing rights, courts can plausibly be taken to be enforcing rules (rather than exercising quasi-legislative judgment). First of all, he notes that rights provisions are not necessarily expressed in open-textured terms that leave much room for judicial discretion.[6] Further, even when constitutional provisions are expressed more vaguely, there are important limitations on the power of judges. This part of his defence rests on the role of originalism in constitutional interpretation (pp. 130–1): 'I believe that to follow a rule means to decide in accordance with a judgment made by the maker of the rule at the time of its creation. Rule-application that follows the rule-makers' original design treats the meaning of the rule as fixed.'

Finally, although he acknowledges the limits of the capacity of rules to bind courts, he maintains that, 'in general, entrenched constitutional rules . . . can and do constrain public conduct and protect human rights' (p. 132). The great cases of American constitutional law, so often cited as examples of unconstrained judicial activism, constitute the exceptional, difficult cases. Ordinary cases of rule-application, on the other hand, will never reach the courts. He concludes, then, with qualified support for constitutional rights:

> None of this is to deny that much of what constitutional courts do is unsupportable as rule-application, nor that their actions may have a profound effect on the society involved. Whether these effects are regarded as the justifiable costs of a system of constitutional protection of rights, or whether they appear as intolerable intrusions in a democratic government, will depend on both empirical and value judgments . . . This is a contingent matter—one that will differ in different places and at different times.

The chapters so far have been concerned with bills of rights in their most traditional form—judicially enforced bills of rights fully entrenched in a national constitution. However, the debate over the democratic foundations of judicial enforcement of rights has recently had to grapple with newer constitutional forms which give judges some, but not an exclusive, role in the enforcement of human rights. The Canadian Charter of Rights and Freedoms, enacted in 1982, is the oldest example. It explicitly recognizes that rights may be limited in the pursuit of legitimate goals and, more significantly, allows legislatures to override protected rights for renewable five-year periods. More recent are the New Zealand Bill of Rights Act 1990, which requires judges to interpret legislation to protect the enumerated rights wherever possible, and the Human Rights Act 1998 (UK), which, in addition to an interpretative clause similar to New Zealand's, gives courts the power to declare legislation 'incompatible' with a protected right. Such a declaration does not invalidate legislation, but gives rise to special powers of amendment by legislative or administrative action.

Julie Debeljak, whose chapter (Chapter 6) is motivated by a strong commitment to international human rights, defends these modified, softer forms of bills

[6] Citing Art 1 of Protocol 6 of the European Convention of Human Rights and Fundamental Freedoms, which says, 'The death penalty shall be abolished. No one shall be condemned to such penalty or executed.'

of rights. At a theoretical level she regards opposition to judicial review as unduly concerned with a procedural concept of democracy, preferring a principle of 'democratic inclusion' under which democracy is understood to be a way of improving the *quality* of a citizen's participation in public life. Thus under her conception of the judicial role, as under Ely's and Dworkin's, that role is a corrective to the deficiencies of the majoritarian process. However, Debeljak responds to the positivist criticism that the contested nature of rights concepts requires the imposition of judicial preferences. In light of that criticism, she prefers structural features that allow for judicial determinations on questions of right to be revisited over time and revised by other institutions of government. Thus, rather than deploring the vagueness of rights concepts (in the manner of a democratic legal positivist), she argues that the very vagueness of the concepts allows for careful development over time. Opportunities for such revision are especially likely to occur if judges adhere to judicial 'minimalism', whereby judgments are made on the narrowest possible basis, avoiding the articulation of fundamental principle, and if, as under the UK Human Rights Act and the Canadian Charter, there is a mechanism for a legislative response to judicial finding of rights violations.

In the final chapter in this section (Chapter 9), David Dyzenhaus responds to the increasing influence of democratic legal positivism on this debate. Dyzenhaus notes that there is a measure of agreement between democratic legal positivists and their intellectual opponents. Both groups hold substantive theories of the rule of law. The argument between them is a dispute over whether the law necessarily contains substantive moral values, leaving neglected Lon L. Fuller's procedural account of the rule of law.

Dyzenhaus believes, however, that democratic legal positivism opens the way for a reinvigoration of Fuller's theory. Although the democratic legal positivist objection to bills of rights seems to focus on the institution of judicial enforcement rather than the concept of rights themselves, he is sceptical that democratic legal positivists are really as agnostic concerning the value of rights as they appear to be. Either democratic legal positivists are actually sceptical of the value of 'rights rhetoric' (a position he detects in James Allan's chapter) or they hold a more moderate position (seen in Jeffrey Goldsworthy's chapter in the final section), which accepts that judicial enforcement of rights is legitimate so long as the legislature retains the right to intervene. That latter position, Dyzenhaus claims, relies on the notion of the legislature's tacit consent to that which it does not override (p. 209). But, he objects to that idea:

> Once one understands ultimate legal authority as constrained, the constraints cannot be regarded as the property of the very body that is supposed to be constrained, otherwise the constraints prove illusory. The site of articulation of the constraints must lie elsewhere, even if the legislature can override them . . . In short, all the institutions of legal order are to be understood as involved in a common project, one that seeks to justify exercise of public power by explicit references to the values that make it an authority rather than the 'gunman writ large'.

Institutional designs

The chapters in the final section of this volume each focus, in some detail, on a particular institutional arrangement for the protection of human rights.

Perhaps the most radical response to the recent critiques of bills of rights is the complete abandonment of judicial enforcement of constitutional rights. In his book *Taking the Constitution Away from the Courts*,[7] Mark Tushnet takes this position, at least with respect to abstractly formulated rights such as those that dominate the United States Bill of Rights. That idea is pursued in his chapter in this volume (Chapter 10). Tushnet advocates a 'populist constitutional law of rights'. His vision is of a society in which the principles of the American Declaration of Independence (the equality of persons and inalienability of certain rights) are revered, and inform and inspire public debate and public policy. Central to this vision is the idea that constitutional rights can be faithfully interpreted and implemented by non-judicial actors.

In his chapter Tushnet pursues the idea of non-judicial constitutional interpretation, examining three instances of non-judicial interpretation: the constitutional point of order in the United States Senate, which gives rise to a debate by the Senate on the constitutionality of a proposed bill; review of bills by the United States Office of Legal Council, a division of an executive department responsible for professional legal advice to the administration; and the procedure by which ministers of the British Parliament make statements of compatibility regarding compliance with the Human Rights Act 1998. His conclusion is that these non-judicial actors have some incentives to resist political pressure and engage in reasonably disinterested interpretation. To canvass just one of his examples, senators, like other elected officials, generally seek to develop what they personally believe to be good public policy within the constraints of politics, and may well consider it good public policy to act in accordance with constitutional rights. Further, senators may be accorded some freedom to act on their views by constituents who agree that protecting constitutional rights is good policy or, if the senator has built up a reservoir of goodwill with constituents, by the constituents' respect for the senator's constitutional views. Tushnet acknowledges that senators' constitutional views usually coincide with their public policy positions, but that is consistent with a normative theory of constitutional interpretation, under which the policy preferences of an interpreter are an appropriate influence where other sources of constitutional understanding do not provide a clear answer. Thus, the distinction between judicial and non-judicial actors is blurred. Non-judicial actors can be reasonably disinterested constitutional interpreters and, as Tushnet discusses at length in his book, courts are far from immune from political pressure.

Dianne Otto is also interested in the non-judicial implementation of rights, specifically in the Australian policy of 'indirect implementation' of its

[7] M. Tushnet, *Taking the Constitution Away from the Courts* (Princeton: Princeton University Press, 1999).

international human rights obligations, which usually prevents judicial enforcement of internationally protected human rights in Australia. However, her study (Chapter 14) stands in contrast to Tushnet's. It is conducted in a quite different context, and is more pessimistic about the possibility of effective non-judicial enforcement of rights. Otto examines the implementation of the right to enjoy an adequate standard of living protected by the Covenant on Economic, Social and Cultural Rights, to which Australia is a party. In Australia the obligation to provide housing is implemented through a national programme that provides financial assistance for accommodation and related support services to homeless people. Otto is critical of the programme, and identifies a number of features that may not meet international standards. Those needing housing are accorded contingent 'rights' dependent on them meeting other obligations, and have few remedies available if denied housing or evicted. Otto therefore recommends the establishment of 'independent external mechanisms' able to review the implementation of the programme. Though these may not necessarily take the form of judicial enforcement, she suggests that 'access to judicial remedies... may at some point be necessary... because, ultimately, the courts provide the best guarantee of independent monitoring and of effective remedies' (p. 303).

In between the two ends of the spectrum represented by a populist constitutional law of rights and a fully entrenched, judicially enforced bill of rights sit the new constitutional forms discussed earlier in the volume by Julie Debeljak, which combine judicial enforcement of rights with more democratic forms of decision-making. The next three chapters consider these forms in some detail, with particular emphasis on the Canadian Charter. In a well-known defence of the Canadian Charter, Peter Hogg and Alison Bushell characterize the Charter as setting up a 'dialogue' between the legislature and the courts.[8] Although courts may limit the power of the Canadian parliaments, the limitation clause (s 1) and the override clause (s 33) allow legislatures to achieve their goals by other means or, more rarely, to override judicial decisions. These features, in particular the override, have been much criticized.[9] However, Hogg and Bushell claim that the Charter avoids the counter-majoritarian difficulty because of this combination of legislative and judicial functions.

This claim lies at the centre of the chapters by Jeffrey Goldsworthy, Janet Hiebert, and George Williams. Jeffrey Goldsworthy (Chapter 13), although an opponent of judicially entrenched bills of rights for similar reasons to those advanced by Waldron and Allan,[10] tests Hogg and Bushell's claim against

[8] P. W. Hogg and A. A. Bushell, 'The Charter Dialogue Between Courts and Legislatures', (1997) 36 *Osgoode Hall Law Journal* 75.

[9] Some scholars regard the override as a fatal flaw in the Charter, undermining the judiciary's power to protect rights; J. D. Whyte, 'On Not Standing for Notwithstanding', (1990) 28 *Alberta Law Review*, 347. Others regard even the limited judicial role as leading to an over-judicialization of government; F. L. Morton and R. Knopff, *The Charter Revolution and the Court Party* (Scarborough, Ont.: Broadview Press, 2000).

[10] J. Goldsworthy, 'The Constitutional Protection of Rights in Australia', in G. J. Craven (ed.), *Australian Federation: Towards the Second Century* (Melbourne: Melbourne University Press, 1992), 151.

Waldron's 'rights-based' objection to constitutional rights. His conclusion is that Waldron's objection fails if a bill of rights includes a provision such as the override clause of section 33. The right to decide controversies about rights is not transferred to the judiciary but, at most, is delegated to judges subject to legislative revision, an arrangement quite compatible with democratic government. It is no objection, moreover, that the power to override is, in practice, rarely used. To suggest that citizens are incapable of using the power to override decisions they disagree with, or suffer from 'false consciousness' that leads to excessive deference to the judiciary, is contrary to the premiss of a rights-based objection to bills of rights: that ordinary people are rational beings with a capacity for intelligent moral deliberation.

Goldsworthy therefore concludes that only 'goal-based' objections to constitutional rights—which allege that judicially enforced bills of rights cause 'democratic debilitation'[11]—survive the modifications of the Charter. The claim that judicial review damages the 'spirit and process of democracy' by discouraging robust democratic decision-making in important areas of morality and public policy requires, Goldsworthy insists, careful empirical investigation. However, in the absence of such evidence, he suggests that we should be slow to accept the claim. Democracy requires some faith in the 'intelligence, knowledge, and virtue' of the citizenry (p. 279):

> It is dangerous for any democrat to allege that the electorate is deluded in this way. If the electorate can be duped by the claim that a small group of people possess superior expertise or wisdom, and persuaded to defer unquestioningly to the judgments of that group, then perhaps they might defer as readily to demagogues as to judges. But that would strengthen the case in favour of constitutional rights.

Janet Hiebert (Chapter 11) shares much of the democratic legal positivists' scepticism of fully entrenched bills of rights. Indeed, she expands upon their critique, arguing that the enforcement of rights requires the evaluation of legislative objectives and the proportionality of measures used to achieve them as well as philosophical deliberation about the nature and scope of rights. Legislative judgment is valuable, she argues, on both the issues: 'The idea that only courts can interpret rights represents a cynical and narrow view of a society's commitment to rights. It is cynical because it denies any moral value to parliament's political judgment about how to resolve rights conflicts and is narrow because it confines the meaning and protection of rights exclusively to what evolves from legal rulings.'

It may also undermine the protection of rights by ignoring the many rights claims that never reach the judicial sphere. She therefore defends this legislative role against objections: that it may lead to an unnecessary separation of rights and other policy issues, that principled deliberation is unsuited to a deeply divided and highly politicized body, that it distorts policy decision-making through excessive legalization of political debate, and that it unwisely focuses

[11] Tushnet, n. 7 above.

on an illusory notion of parliamentary intent. Nonetheless, Hiebert defends the judicial role as well as the concept of dialogue between the two institutions. In Hiebert's eyes, the virtue of the Charter is that it allows for both legal and political judgment about the reconciliation of rights claims.

Thus Hiebert reconceptualizes the notion of dialogue: it is not a question of courts asserting rights and legislatures responding in the name of other interests. Both courts and legislatures have a role in determining the *meaning* of rights as well as in reconciling conflicts between rights and between rights and other interests.

George Williams also both defends and reconceptualizes the concept of 'dialogue' in his preferred approach for the implementation of a bill of rights in Australia (Chapter 12). For Williams, dialogue must occur during the process of establishing a bill of rights as well as in the subsequent implementation of those rights. Moreover, the 'dialogue' must include a third institution: 'the community'.

Williams's motivations are partly pragmatic. Having outlined the failure of the Australian bill of rights proposals to achieve the support necessary for constitutional amendment or even legislative enactment, he concludes that the success of such a proposal requires popular engagement. However, Williams's concerns run deeper. His view is that bills of rights are most valuable for their capacity to 'strengthen an existing culture of democratic constitutionalism', and this requires indirect community involvement. For only 'within a community permeated by a culture of rights protection' will a bill of rights be properly maintained (p. 254).

In line with these concerns, Williams proposes 'a community-based bill of rights' model, which requires popular involvement at the drafting process, channelled through a parliamentary committee, and a statutory rather than entrenched constitutional instrument: 'the concept of dialogue suggests that a bill of rights should be susceptible to ongoing development in light of judicial interpretation, changing parliamentary practices, and community input' (p. 256). Thus, he also recommends an override clause, a 'generic limitation clause', like that found in section 1 of the Canadian Charter, an 'interpretative clause' like that found in the New Zealand Bill of Rights, and a parliamentary standing committee to examine all legislation for compliance with protected rights. He prefers, however, to give judges the power to declare legislation invalid rather than to rely upon a declaration of incompatibility like that found in the UK Human Rights Act.

The final two chapters turn to a slightly different (though related) institutional question. They consider the kinds of rights that ought to be protected in a modern democracy. Most of the constitutional models considered in this volume protect traditional 'civil and political' or 'first-generation' rights—freedom of speech and religion, the right to vote, the right to a fair trial, and the like. It is rarer for bills of rights to include protection of 'second-generation' or social and economic rights[12] even though, as Otto's chapter demonstrates, these rights

[12] For one example, see the Constitution of the Republic of South Africa, s 26 (right to adequate housing), s 27 (the right to have access to health care services; sufficient food and water; and social security), s 29 (right to a basic education).

receive extensive protection in international law, and of 'third-generation' or group rights.[13] Keith Ewing (Chapter 16) and Steven Curry (Chapter 15) take up the consideration of these rights.

Ewing's advocacy of constitutional rights is somewhat reluctant. He is convinced of the case against bills of rights but has accepted their inevitability. Since there is no realistic prospect of turning back the tide, Ewing advocates the expansion of bills of rights to 'social rights', such as rights to education, health care, housing, work, and income security, and rights (like the right to associate in a trade union) that ensure the participation of the citizen in the social sphere. These rights are not well protected by legislation and, paradoxically, are overlooked by constitutional measures designed to improve human rights.

This combination of legislative failure to protect social rights and constitutional preference for civil and political rights deeply undermines democracy (p. 331): 'What we have then is a system of government in which two key principles are being further eroded. Both the principle of popular sovereignty (through representative government) and the principle of political equality are being diminished by a constitutional development that gives the courts the power to challenge, if not formally veto, social (and other) legislation.'

The best answer is to extend constitutional protection to social rights and, in this regard, the Human Rights Act 1998 (UK) provides a helpful template. The Act currently operates to incorporate the provisions of the European Convention on Human Rights into British law. That could be extended to the Council of Europe's Social Charter. Moreover, the natural tendency of common law judges to read down or dilute social rights could be mitigated by a provision (like that currently found in section 2 of the Human Rights Act) that requires the domestic courts to have regard to the decisions of the European Court of Human Rights as it interprets the Act.

Steven Curry also argues for an expanded conception of rights to include third-generation, group rights, specifically indigenous rights. The problem he identifies with these kinds of rights is that they appear to undermine liberal democratic principle by according privileges to a special group that are denied to other citizens. Although some group rights, such as language rights, are shared in some form by all citizens, other rights—such as the right of Maoris to remove whalebone for carving, despite a law that forbids the taking of natural items are, by their nature, not accorded to all.

His concern is to justify these special rights within liberal rights theory and according to democratic principle. He does so by drawing on Raz's idea that rights are expressions of 'fundamental human interests' which can be expressed at a high level of generality as needs shared by all persons at all times but, in their specific articulation, will require attention to the cultural and material circumstances of the rights-holder. On this theory, the special position of indigenous

[13] But see Canadian Charter of Rights and Freedoms, s 23 (guaranteeing some minority language and education rights), and the Constitution of the Republic of South Africa, ss 30 and 31 (guaranteeing some linguistic, cultural, and religious rights).

persons entitles them to special rights: 'indigeneity as a category is only possible when one group of people is to be distinguished from another group who arrived later' (p. 311). Moreover, Curry argues, these rights accord with democratic theory because they secure the consent of the governed. The virtue in democracy lies in its capacity to secure the consent of the governed and thus justify legal authority. Thus, he concludes, indigenous rights should be conceived as those rights that indigenous people would have had if the colonizing state had engaged in an open negotiation for a new constitutional state.

Turning to the detail of instantiating his vision, Curry argues that modern post-colonial states must go beyond recognizing the civil and political rights of indigenous people and rectifying their material and social disadvantage. However, these efforts will be incomplete unless indigenous people are also accorded special group rights, which should include cultural rights (such as access to sacred sites), special legal and social rights (such as access to welfare), as well as group rights that recognize the prior sovereignty of indigenous people (p. 319): 'Indigenous people must be able to continue the development of their own communities and cultures within a state formation that embodies their own laws and traditions, and to which they have been able to consent.' This will require that post-colonial states give legal force to the fundamental 'laws of the land' derived from indigenous legal systems (including laws recognizing indigenous land rights), empower bodies having traditional authority to regulate access to culturally sensitive matters like access to sacred sites, recognize the legal status of groups that enjoy self-government, and 'explicitly abolish the presumption of colonial sovereignty'.

This chapter has brought the collection back to where it started. Indigenous rights seem to provide a particularly clear illustration of the complexities involved in moving from fundamental human rights values to the articulation of particular rights. Whatever fundamental or universal values are served by indigenous rights, identifying a precise right requires consideration of more specific objectives of the right and the cultural and political context in which those rights will operate.

The preference for contextual, specific solutions to human rights problems is shared by a number of those writing on the institutional questions raised in the second and third parts of the volume. Even so committed an opponent of bills of rights as James Allan pays careful attention to the particulars of the society (Australia) that he addresses, as does Richard Kay, who, in seeking to restore the balance of opinion in favour of bills of rights, acknowledges how particular contexts will affect the final decision.

CONCEPTUAL BOUNDARIES AND FUNCTIONS OF HUMAN RIGHTS

1

Human Rights: The Shifting Boundaries

TOM CAMPBELL

To investigate the best means of protecting and promoting human rights we first have to identify what we are talking about. Which human rights have we in mind? And why do we select these rather than other possible rights as human rights? What are human rights anyway?

There are many other associated 'which', 'why', and 'what' questions. Why is it that we want to identify, protect, and promote human rights? What is distinctively important about human rights? What are the implications of identifying something as a human right? What are the duties that correlate with human rights? On whom do they fall? What are the consequences of their violation or breach? What is to be done when human rights conflict? What factors, if any, can override human rights? And then there are many 'who' questions.[1] Whose rights and whose duties have we in mind? And, more fundamentally perhaps, who should decide such matters?

Providing answers to such questions raises a host of problems, arising in part because the discourse of rights is multifaceted and diverse in form and content, and in part because the idea of 'humanity' as a normative concept is controversial and contested. Conceptually and politically, both constituents of 'human rights' are in dispute. These issues become all the more difficult to tackle as human rights discourse flourishes and expands. More and more interests are recognized as justifying the protection that flows from being adopted as a human right.[2] This growth is a matter of the form of human rights as well as their content. Thus, even traditional core civil and political liberties are seen as involving positive correlative duties to secure the interests identified in the right, and not, as before, merely negative correlative duties to let people be and leave them alone to go their own way. Human rights are also being put to a wider variety of uses. Human rights feature in challenges to the legitimacy of regimes, in arguments in favour of intervention in the affairs of other states, in

[1] These and other questions are raised in S. Benn, 'Human Rights—For Whom and For What?', in E. Kamenka and A. E. Tay (eds.), *Human Rights* (London: Arnold, 1978). To which may be added 'where' questions; see L. Henkin, 'Rights: Here and There', (1981) 81 *Columbia Law Review* 1582–1610.

[2] These historical developments are usually charted in terms of 'first-generation' civil and political rights, 'second-generation' social and economic rights, and 'third-generation' collective and developmental rights, but there is also continual expansion of the scope of rights within these areas.

demands for important matters to be taken out of the domain of democratic politics and entrusted to the care of judicial institutions, and, more generally, in any calls for reform which can be viewed as having serious import for human well-being.

In all these ways, the boundaries of human rights are expanding inexorably. Faced with such expansion, it is tempting to retreat into a core of apparently incontrovertible human rights with rather limited functions. In this chapter I consider some ways in which we may go about constricting and containing the boundaries of human rights. Although each provides important leads for identifying the domains of human rights, none are deemed to be persuasive in cabining human rights within determinate boundaries. I then take up the challenge of adopting a more expansive approach that seeks not so much to draw the boundaries of human rights as to draw attention to the very different questions that may be raised and answered in the language of human rights. In particular, by concentrating on refining the question as to what distinct functions we want human rights to perform, I suggest that we can articulate some quite specific and more answerable questions as to the what, why, which, and who issues that coalesce around the ideal of human rights. By clarifying the institutional contexts in which we ask the question 'What are human rights?', we avoid floundering in the indeterminacy of human rights discourse while opening the way to manageable expansionist human rights models.

Taking this more contextualized and functional approach to human rights, I suggest that the (largely moral) questions that we should address are of the following kind: What are our overriding criteria for deciding which candidate to vote for in a parliamentary election? Of which rights do we want the content to be defined by judges, not parliaments? The violation of which rights renders a government illegitimate, and what follows from such a judgment? What justifies armed intervention in the internal affairs of a sovereign state? Which crimes should be justiciable before an international court of criminal justice? What fundamental moral duties are incumbent on business corporations and public sector organizations?

Of course, we can answer all these questions, in part at least, in terms of 'human rights' themselves. For instance, perhaps we should vote in accordance with the past or projected performance of a candidate in furthering and protecting human rights. Perhaps the rights we want to be defined and articulated by judges are human rights. And so on. However, this strategy just takes us back to the initial questions about the form and content of these human rights that provide such ready answers to all our questions. I would argue that we cannot make sufficient progress towards answering such questions by reference to an abstract idea of human rights. The generalities that emerge from abstracted and contextless questions about human rights are of relatively little help when we come to settle precise issues of what is to be permitted or required in concrete situations. Further, in practice, when we are pressed to define 'human rights' we want to know what is to be done with such rights, once they have been identified.

Are they criteria for voting, indicators of legitimacy, grounds for intervention, or something quite different? Once we know the impact of our decision and what is to be done with them, this sharpens our questions and focuses our minds so that we begin to provide justifiable answers at an appropriate level of specificity. On this approach, 'human rights' are conclusions, not premisses. We cannot first identify human rights and then work out what we are going to do with them. Rather, we need to identify the roles that human rights are to have in our decision-making processes in particular types of context and then ask ourselves what their form and content should be. In this way human rights expansionism becomes more intelligible and more manageable.

No doubt this is an exaggeration. The discourse of human rights does generate indicators of the sort of interests and issues that are at stake in human rights domains. We do not have a stark choice between human rights as premisses and human rights as conclusions. Rather, it is better to think in terms of a dialectic between definition and use, and between use and definition. Even so, the dialectic is currently unbalanced, with the focus being first on a vision of human rights, and only then on the uses to which they are put and the means for their implementation. To redress this imbalance, I suggest that we need to focus more on what is to be done with human rights. Only then can we arrive at useful answers to the 'which', 'what', 'why', and 'who' questions about human rights.[3]

Cabining human rights

The alternatives for defining and thereby restricting human rights, first as a concept and then in relation to the content of individual rights, may be presented under the labels of conceptualism, empiricism, positivism, moralism, and (despite the linguistic barbarity) philosophism. Each has important insights to offer but, in the end, fail to cabin or contain the expansionism of human rights.

Conceptualism and human rights

By conceptualism I mean the approach that seeks a context-free definition of human rights as, for instance, those rights that are possessed by all human beings. On this approach, to set the boundaries of human rights, we have to determine the meaning of 'rights' and 'human', and put the two terms together, arriving at the definition of a human right as a right that is the possession of any and every human being. This may be presented by saying that human rights are universal rights (at least to persons) in contrast to the rights of particular persons or types of person, or at particular times or places. It follows, more or less as a

[3] Thus, C. R. Beitz, 'Human Rights as a Common Concern', (2001) 95 *American Political Science Review* 269, 277: 'Human rights are meant for certain political purposes, and we cannot think intelligently about their content and reach without taking into account these purposes.'

matter of logic, that such rights are inalienable because, by definition, all human beings everywhere have them all the time.

Such a definition can be used to make a powerful moral affirmation of human equality, but, in itself, it gives us no reason to ascribe any particular significance to human rights because at least some of the rights that are universal to human beings are trivial ones. At this point another definitional characteristic is often introduced. It is contended that human rights are of great or overriding importance.[4] Importance, however, does not flow automatically from universality. Moreover, there are some very important rights that are not universal, even if we restrict the universality in question to all human beings. The criterion of universality can be seen as an unwarranted stress on sameness which plays down diversity to the disadvantage of those individuals or groups who are or are seen as 'different', such as women, persons with mental illnesses, homosexuals, and so on.[5] A strict application of these definitional criteria means that there are few rights that are both important and universal in the sense that they are of equal significance for all human beings. If we take these criteria at all seriously, then not just economic and social rights are at risk, and if we treat the criteria loosely, then we will find ourselves with a very large and disparate set of prima facie claims for all persons which are universal only in the sense that whoever possesses the relevant characteristics in the relevant situation has the right in question. If we take 'universality' and 'importance' seriously, we come out with a highly restrictive view of the boundaries of human rights that is confined to the demarcation of a very limited range of things that it is never justified to do to another person.[6]

Whatever we think about the tension between universality and importance, these issues cannot be settled by conceptual analysis alone. Evidently, conceptual clarification has a great deal to contribute to any study of human rights, but the rigour it may impose cannot be used to disguise the complexity of human rights discourse or pre-empt the moral choices that have to be made in determining what is to count as a human right. Thus the Hohfeldian scheme of the types of rights and their various correlativities, principally with negative and positive duties, have been immensely useful in trying to gain more precision when we talk loosely of rights in general.

This scheme can be used to articulate the view, for instance, that human rights are negative claim rights against government intervention, thus rendering them relatively costless and therefore practicable, and hence promoting the idea of human rights as fundamental liberties protecting a sphere of individual privacy.

4 The classic statement of this position is to be found in M. Cranston, *What Are Human Rights?* (London: Bodley Head, 1973), 63.

5 C. MacKinnon, 'Crimes of War, Crimes of Peace', in S. Shute and S. Hurley (eds.), *On Human Rights* (New York: Basic Books, 1993), 85: 'What happens to women is either too particular to be universal or too universal to be particular, meaning either too human to be female or too female to be human,' so that women's particular experience does not feature in the category of what is important.

6 This may be called the 'torture model' of human rights. See T. Campbell, 'Human Rights and the Partial Eclipse of Justice', in A. Soeteman (ed.), *Law and Pluralism* (Dordrecht: Kluwer, 2001).

But we are now far beyond core libertarian freedoms as identifying the boundaries of human rights. It is widely accepted, without any sense of conceptual incongruity, that governments have costly duties to prevent human rights being violated by persons other than government officials, so that all negative rights against government go along with positive rights which require that government take expansive and expensive measures to see that others do not violate these rights. So, for instance, much of the ever more expensive criminal justice system can be seen as a means for protecting human rights. And, logically, this entails the idea that it is not only government that has duties correlative to human rights. These arguments and their conclusions are also capable of being felicitously expressed in terms of Hohfeldian categories, but the issues involved are not settled by conceptual analysis or definitional stops. Analytical schemes that enable us to categorize types of rights are essential to the process of drawing the boundaries of human rights, but the conceptual analysis involved, although it may help us to present the available alternatives, cannot itself determine these boundaries.[7]

Empiricism and human rights

Another approach to setting boundaries for human rights seeks to identify what counts as a human right by resort to those social, economic, and political ills that are presented in the media and in popular opinion as human rights violations. Thus, in Australia this might mean the plight of aboriginal peoples, treatment of illegal migrants, discrimination on grounds of race, gender, or sexuality, excessive police powers, and maybe abortion, euthanasia, and the protection and education of children, persons with mental illnesses, and so on. In other places, or at other times, public opinion might single out the treatment of migrant workers, victims of preventable epidemics, and acts of terrorism or genocide.

The investigation of the popular consciousness path is important, and work needs to be done about what is perceived as having to do with human rights. It is undeniably true that behind the abstract claims of human rights there have always been important historical events. The Holocaust is the background to the Universal Declaration of Human Rights (1948), the experience of racial discrimination has been central since the 1960s, and recently the atrocities of genocidal civil war are stirring international consciences in a way that clearly fuels the focus and salience of human rights discourse. It is possible, for instance, to investigate which social phenomena prompt people to say that a country's human rights record is deteriorating. Again taking Australia as an example, this approach would lead us to examine which perceived evils of Australian society are generally viewed as human rights evils. This directs us to the deprivations of aboriginal communities, with the shadow of racism, expropriation, and

[7] Indeed, Cranston's preferred analysis itself is clearly driven by a sense of the political significance of being able to identify those governmental duties whose violation can never be justified by practicalities, such a lack of resources. See M. Cranston, 'Human Rights, Real and Supposed', in D. D. Raphael (ed.), *Political Theory and the Rights of Man* (London: Macmillan, 1967).

genocide looming large in this history. More recently it points to treatment of refugees seeking asylum in Australia.

Given the historical role for human rights as a conduit for widespread moral outrage, the empirical study of 'human rights concerns' is appropriate. Yet problems arise here, not simply over the relative lack of hard data, but also over how such data is to be interpreted. We know that the majority of the population are generally in favour of some sort of bill of rights,[8] but we have little information about what particular matters are viewed as typifying human rights and what they take these rights to involve. More seriously, it is not clear what such empirical investigations should be looking for. Is it what the *majority* of people regard as human rights abuses that counts? That must be problematic since one of the bases of human rights thinking is that it is *minorities* who are at risk and whose lives are ignored. What if the majority, for instance, does not regard access to *in vitro* fertilization of single women as a human rights issue: is that decisive? Should we listen only to minorities? But how do we identify these? And how do we test their view that their grievances are properly regarded as human rights grievances? Moreover, popular consciousness of human rights is in a state of flux owing to the exponential increase in human rights discourse that is taking place in what is becoming known as the 'age of rights'.[9] Despite its current popularity, the idea of human rights remains in many ways unformed, obscure, and elusive. It is unlikely that we can expect a coherent, comprehensive, and stable answer to these questions through a study of media reportage, or studies of popular opinion, or more scholarly studies in social psychology.

Another difficulty is the choice of language that is available to groups who wish to protest about their own lot or that of others. Some groups may appeal to justice and others may make use of the language of rights, the choice between the discourses of justice and rights being determined by such matters as the rhetorical appeal to that group or their target audiences, or the sort of remedies which they are asking or demanding.[10]

For such reasons we can see that studies of human rights consciousness, while they may direct our attention to significant human rights issues, cannot settle controversial questions about the boundaries of human rights. Other objects of empirical study, such as what means are available to whom for remedying various types of human ills, are of direct relevance to such important questions as identifying the correlative obligations without which human rights have no immediate moral relevance. And, it may be that empirical studies that

[8] See B. Galligan and I. McAllister, 'Citizen and Elite Attitudes Towards an Australian Bill of Rights', in B. Galligan and C. Sampford (eds.), *Rethinking Human Rights* (Sydney: Federation Press, 1997).

[9] N. Bobbio, *The Age of Rights* (London: Polity Press, 1996); M. Loughlin, *Sword and Scales* (Oxford: Hart, 2000), esp. ch. 15.

[10] See Nolan and Oakes, Ch. 3 below.

identify the minimum social conditions for the survival of human societies may be crucial in selecting a core of human rights for any society.[11] We may also want to give weight to rights that appear to have an important role to play in all known human societies or cultural traditions.[12] Such data are also relevant to, but never fully determinative of, a decision about the proper boundaries of human rights.

Positivism and human rights

Perhaps the most obvious place to go for an authoritative identification of human rights is to human rights law, be it international human rights law or those aspects of domestic law that are known as 'human rights law', such as bills of rights or statutory anti-discrimination law. Thus, it is common to chart the progress of different jurisdictions in enforcing their international human rights treaty obligations as a measure of their human rights credentials. Moreover, we can draw on the activities of the United Nations itself, particularly the work of its Human Rights Committee, to provide our parameters. In theory, this is an easy way forward since it gives us some objective data to deal with, although whether that data would yield a clear picture against which to measure human rights attainments is another matter, especially as we can only get any measure of precision by consulting the vast and ill-defined body of case law interpreting such material in different jurisdictions. International human rights law is the vast supermarket of the precedents to which recourse may be had, there being precedents to suit all tastes available somewhere in its emporium. Moreover, when it comes to asking how far a particular country conforms with international human rights standards, appeal has to be made to a whole array of legal provisions in domestic law that do not go under the name of 'human rights'.[13]

Nevertheless, positivist analysis is a tempting path, for, at the same time as such philosophical and practical issues increase in complexity, it may be claimed that the development of human rights law has made identifying human rights considerably easier. At the end of the Second World War the idea of human rights was barely emerging from the traditional concept of natural rights and loosely associated with great political and constitutional affirmations such as the French declaration of the 'rights of man' and the 'Bill of Rights' amendments to the American Constitution. Since then we have the foundation document of

[11] As suggested in H. L. A. Hart, *The Concept of Law* (Oxford: Clarendon Press, 1962).

[12] See R. J. Vincent, *Human Rights and International Relations* (Cambridge: Cambridge University Press, 1986), 48–9.

[13] Thus D. Kinley (ed.), *Human Rights in Australian Law* (Sydney: Federation Press, 1998), p. ix: 'Human rights may not readily be identified as such in Australian law, but they exist nonetheless. In addition to their express provision, they lie implicit in restrictions on action, and in duties, they may be inferred from the absence of legal regulation or provision. What remains to be done is for these legal provisions to be revealed, recognized and promoted *as* human rights.'

the United Nations, the Universal Declaration of Human Rights (1948), and the subsequent International Covenant on Civil and Political Rights (1966), the International Covenant on Economic, Social and Cultural Rights (1966), the European Convention for the Protection of Human Rights and Fundamental Freedoms (1950), and many other regional human rights instruments. Such documents, and the institutions and case law that have grown up around them, have given a new tangibility to human rights by providing palpable points of reference for definition and analysis. Human rights now have a positive and concrete manifestation that have an empirical objectivity not present in their prior philosophical forms.

The comfort and reassurance that such historical developments may provide is, however, quite spurious when we come to tackle the sort of 'which', 'what', 'why', and 'who' questions outlined above. Positivized 'human rights', either in domestic or international bills of rights, or in the treaties, conventions, and practice of international law, certainly take on a life of their own, and their existence does provide an important empirical focus for philosophical analysis and political activism. But we cannot rely on the fact of their institutional existence to establish the moral bases that may or may not justify that existence. Nor can we rely on the doctrines propounded within these institutions to determine how we should select, analyse, and implement human rights.

The parallel between human rights and religious belief is apt on this point. Religious institutions and the grand buildings often associated with them may help to generate faith in God, but they do not settle theological questions. Declarations and conventions, committees and courts that are created to embody and implement the human rights in which the founders and sustainers of these institutions believe cannot, without circularity, be used to vindicate the truth of these beliefs. Human rights institutions must be seen as the consequences not the creators of human rights.

Indeed, if we come to identify human rights with certain types of positive law, or certain types of institutional mechanisms, such as constitutional and international courts, then we immediately extract human rights from their moral role as the basis for founding, reforming, and developing such human institutions. If human rights do not remain first and foremost a type of moral discourse and become, instead, identified with a certain sphere of law or certain kinds of international institution, then we may make progress in establishing in a historical and sociological sense what human rights are, but to identify 'human rights' with these empirical realities comes at the price of undermining their distinctive and primary role as a powerful and developing moral discourse.

Adequate protection of human rights must (but need not always) involve their positivization in concrete law, international and domestic, but this does not mean that human rights are to be identified with such institutional concretizations. Human rights discourse is first and foremost a moral discourse, and cannot be equated, except contingently, with any part of positive law. The identification of human rights must be a matter of moral judgment.

'Philosophism' and human rights

In terms of most modern, and all post-modern, epistemology the moral status of human rights means that human rights do not exist in any literal sense. Human rights are not 'out there' to be discovered by experience or observation, not even out there in the minds of human beings. They are not the conclusions of rational deduction from matters of fact. They are not the subject matter of cognitive intuitions that can be regarded as either true of false. Their nature, content, and function cannot be revealed to us by any external authority. Human rights are a human creation that can be conceived, defined, reshaped, or abandoned as we choose.[14]

Such a voluntaristic and non-foundationalist approach to moral values in general, and human rights in particular, can, of course, be resisted. One mode of resistance is philosophically based: the idea that there is a method, above moral judgment itself, that can provide answers to our boundary questions about rights. I call this, pejoratively, 'philosophism', because I am picking out just one particular approach within philosophy, an approach that involves sophistical argumentation that arises from the improper extension of this approach from such philosophical terrain as metaphysics, to substantive moral questions that are not distinctively philosophical issues. This approach is particularly significant because of its association with Immanuel Kant, who must be considered the philosophical maestro of human rights, although I do not seek to implicate him personally in the fallacious applications of this method.

By 'philosophism', I have in mind one sort of attempt to provide rational, but non-empirical, grounds for deciding substantive questions in morals. It has to do with working out the essential preconditions of things that we are so sure about that we cannot deny them without contradicting ourselves or calling into doubt our most basic beliefs and experiences. The method, after Kant but much practised by Plato, is usually called 'transcendental deduction'. It starts by getting our agreement to palpable facts of our experience, such as that we are able to make choices that go against our strongest desire, or that we are capable of purposive action, of choosing a goal, working out how to achieve it and acting accordingly. From such indisputable experiences, Kant and others deduce that, for these to be possible, we must have, for instance, freedom of the will, as a contra-causal capacity. On this basis, some philosophers go on to assert that the important fact about human beings is that they have such freedom, and this is then developed into a model of the type of practice consistent with such freedom, namely, that humans as rational creatures must act on principle, legislating morally for themselves, and adopting and following those maxims that they can accept as universal law. With the idea of contra-causal moral freedom is associated the ideas of autonomy and respect for the persons who have this

[14] Thus R. Rorty, 'Human Rights, Rationality, and Sentimentality', in Shute and Hurley (eds.), n. 5 above.

autonomy, together with the prescription that it is wrong to treat human beings merely as means and right to treat them as ends in themselves.[15] This cluster of concepts is then taken to constitute the essence of human rights.

Transcendental deduction can be a powerful philosophical method, particularly in metaphysics. It becomes 'philosophism' only when it is used to perpetrate the fallacy whereby conclusions in one mode of discourse (in this case the metaphysical) are used to draw conclusions in another mode (in this case the moral). A contemporary example of this fallacious extension of transcendental deduction occurs in the work of a highly influential philosopher of human rights, Alan Gewirth. Gewirth builds on the idea of human agency—our experience of voluntary adopting and pursuing objectives—and uses this to identify the necessary conditions for such free and purposive conduct, ranging from freedom from physical constraints to receiving a modicum of education. Gewirth then goes on to claim that because these preconditions are necessary for our existence as agents, and because we cannot deny our existence as agents without engaging in voluntary acts of argumentation which are instances of the very agency we deny, we must accept that we have a right to that which makes our agency possible.[16]

This is a very tempting approach to drawing the boundaries of human rights. It gives a distinctive foundation for human rights values, it accounts for the basic freedoms, and gives a justification for including certain social and economic rights as necessary conditions of human agency in addition to the traditional civil and political freedoms. It is strongest in working out the considerable implications of taking human agency seriously. There are, however, serious flaws in the argument. Its most general weakness is the move from establishing that something is necessary for a person to be a successful agent, to the conclusion that other people have overriding duties with respect to that person's opportunities for agency. This move may be persuasive, but it is not necessary. We do not have to accept it in order to believe consistently in our own agency.[17] And, if we do accept it, we need not give it priority weighting. And even if we are persuaded by these moves, this still does not take us as far as endorsing autonomy as the sole important aspect of human existence. The fact that there happens to be an impressive-looking philosophical argument that applies to agency but not to other features of human experience does not establish a superior moral status or priority for autonomy. Autonomy is a human good, particularly if we are thinking of moral autonomy (although much of the argument applies equally to the autonomy involved in amoral prudential reasoning), but is it the only

[15] This is a crude summary of Kant, *Groundwork of the Metaphysic of Morals* (1785), trans. H. J. Paton as *The Moral Law* (London: Hutchinson, 1953).

[16] A. Gewirth, *Reason and Morality* (Chicago: University of Chicago Press, 1978), ch. 2: 'Since the agent regards as necessary goods the freedom and well-being that constitute generic features of his successful action, he logically must also hold that he has rights to these generic features and he implicitly makes a corresponding rights-claim.'

[17] For critiques of Gewirth, see J. R. Pennock and J. W. Chapman (eds.), *Human Rights (Nomos XXIII)* (New York: New York University Press, 1981), and E. Regis, *Gewirth's Ethical Rationalism* (Chicago: Chicago University Press, 1984).

good? More particularly, is it the only fundamental good? What about human pleasure; what about passive experiences? What about spontaneous and willing love and caring, not undertaken from a sense of duty or the willing of a universalizable maxim? These other values may or may not be captured in a transcendental argument, but this seems irrelevant to whether or not we should accept them as being on a par with autonomy. The idea of the necessary conditions of action is very important, but it cannot claim special moral status simply because it derives from a transcendental deduction.

Moreover, even although Gewirth's paradigm can make room for those social and economic factors that are preconditions of human agency, this does not entirely capture the reasons why we think that these and other rights are important. Consider torture. Gewirth may explain that torture is contrary to human rights because torture undermines a person's capacity to act autonomously. Often it does, and that is bad. But is that all that is wrong with torture? Does torture not hurt? Is the deliberate infliction of pain on anyone not a violation of human rights even if the victim's autonomy is unaffected? Is human suffering not as fundamental a moral consideration as human autonomy? No philosophical argument can defeat moral assessment of such points. Philosophism, like conceptualism, empiricism, and positivism, cannot provide determinate answers to the 'what', 'which', 'why', and 'who' questions of human rights that enable us to bypass moral reflection and choice.

Moralism and human rights

The implications to be drawn from the limitation of the other approaches all suggest that the processes of moral reflection are indispensable for arriving at determinate answers to the human rights questions I have raised. This points to another approach to establishing the boundaries of human rights by identifying the particular moral values that underpin them. It may be argued, for instance, that human rights are, as a result of these moral assumptions, conceptually linked to such values as equality, dignity, autonomy, or respect. This approach gains plausibility from the fact that rights in general and human rights in particular play a role in opposing the free rein that is sometimes given to the idea of utility, that is, the maximization of either happiness or preferences as the overriding value. Human rights, then, become identified with a particular type of moral consideration that characteristically trumps considerations of general utility.[18]

The main problem with this approach is that the justification of the standard list of human rights (and more so in case of the increasingly common longer lists) can be achieved only by reference to a wide and open-ended set of moral criteria.

18 The language here is derived from an exponent of this approach, R. Dworkin, *Taking Rights Seriously* (London: Duckworth, 1978). For other examples, see J. Donnelly, 'The Social Construction of International Human Rights', in T. Dunne and N. J. Wheeler (eds.), *Human Rights in Global Politics* (Cambridge: Cambridge University Press, 1999), and C. Nino, *The Ethics of Human Rights* (Oxford: Clarendon Press, 1991).

Equality is, perhaps, the most promising candidate for adoption as the sole or primary human rights value, especially as non-discrimination plays such a crucial role in human rights discourse. However, while the principal role of equality in human rights discourse, or certainly in declarations and conventions of human rights, is in the affirmation that human rights are to be enjoyed equally by all persons, irrespective of race, nationality, religion, gender, or ethnic background,[19] this does not in itself tell us what the human rights are that are to be enjoyed without discrimination.

Much work has been done on the idea that human beings have equal worth, but this has given rise to a great deal of controversy.[20] On the one hand, there are those who affirm equal worth as a given that cannot be established but must be taken for granted, particularly as an assumption within a political community. On the other hand, there are those who want to identify the properties in virtue of which human beings may be said to have equal worth. The latter is a more rational approach, but inevitably introduces into the debate values other than equality itself, and shifts the focus to those properties that human beings have in common, such as the capacity for moral choice, or the vulnerability to distinctively awful forms of suffering, and capacities for a variety of types of worthwhile activities. All this introduces a maximizing as well as a distributive element and is either very open-ended or highly controversial in the identification of what is to count as human rights values.

If equality cannot serve as the core value underlying human rights, we may turn to another value, one that is entrenched in the Universal Declaration of Human Rights and increasingly popular as the value-basis for human rights, namely human dignity, a value that is often conjoined with the idea of respect.[21] The contention is that, by treating people with respect, we enable them to live dignified lives. This means treating people 'as human beings', or, in Kantian terms, as 'ends in themselves', something that helps to generate mutual respect and self-respect. Again, this approach can be construed in a variety of ways. In a narrow vein it may be seen as an explication of Kant's view that humans are to be highly regarded because they are autonomous beings who 'legislate' for themselves by having the capacity to make morally principled choices. This is enlightening with respect to those many rights that have to do with liberty and choice, but it is too narrow to cover those rights that relate to the minimization of human suffering, and in itself is powerless to distinguish the proper from the improper uses of human autonomy. If, in response, we adopt a broader view of

[19] As in the Universal Declaration of Human Rights, Art 2: 'Everyone is entitled to all the rights and freedoms set forth in this Declaration, without distinction of any kind, such as race, colour, sex, language, religion, political or other opinion, national or social origin, property, birth or other status.'

[20] D. A. Richards, 'Rights and Duties', (1981) 92 *Ethics* 3–20; G. Vlastos, 'Justice and Equality', in R. B. Brandt (ed.), *Social Justice* (Englewood Cliffs, NJ: Prentice Hall, 1962); R. J. Arneson, 'What, if Anything, Renders All Humans Morally Equal?', in D. Jamieson (ed.), *Peter Singer and His Critics* (Oxford: Blackwell, 1999).

[21] The Preamble to the United Nations Declaration of Human Rights affirms 'the dignity and worth of the human person'. For an in-depth study of the concept of human dignity, see N. Rotenstreich, *Man and His Dignity* (Jerusalem: Magnes Press, 1983).

what makes for a dignified life, then, while dignity may clearly exclude some forms of life, it becomes highly contingent as to its possible content in a way that depends on the particular cultural views of those involved.[22]

It seems unlikely, therefore, unless we are persuaded by a purist neo-Kantian line, that all human rights can be identified by reference to a certain distinctive human rights value or very limited cluster of values. Most justifications of paradigm human rights, such as freedom of speech, not only draw on a broad range of values, such as autonomy, self-development, and the acquisition of knowledge, but involve a deal of consequentialist reasoning[23] much of which terminates in utilitarian values, such as pleasure and pain.[24] And so, while there is no doubt that equality, dignity, and autonomy are indispensable concepts with which to explicate human rights, they do not preclude the input of other values to determining the boundaries of human rights or in themselves generate any tolerably clear criteria for deciding which rights are human rights.

Conclusion

It would appear therefore that, in seeking to cabin human rights, there is no one decisive methodology that will enable us to draw or redraw the boundaries of human rights. Analytic and conceptual work is essential for the clarification of alternatives open to us and the elucidation of how current human rights discourse operates. Empirical work can identify the points of contemporary human experience that lend themselves most naturally to the rhetoric of human rights, and this is important in pinpointing the concerns that lead to the deployment of the discourse. Positive human rights law can be seen as an embodiment of aspects of the history of human rights and highlight important enforcement mechanisms. Philosophical methodologies can bring out the hidden implications of basic human experiences. But there is no distinctively philosophical, or other, methodology that can take the place of moral reflection on what constitutes human rights. On the other hand, direct appeals to moral values do not settle much in the abstract, although they may point us in the direction of the types of moral consideration that are central to human rights.

Contextualizing human rights

At this point it is helpful to contextualize our reflections on human rights, both with respect to their moral sources and with respect to the potential practical

22 See, for instance, D. Feldman, 'Human Dignity as a Legal Value', [1999] *Public Law* 682, 682: 'The canon of fundamental rights and freedoms is controversial and inadequate to pin down the meaning of dignity.'

23 See P. Pettit, 'The Consequentialist Can Recognise Rights', (1988) 38 *Philosophical Quarterly* 42–55.

24 Thus, T. Campbell, 'Rationales for Freedom of Communication', in T. Campbell and W. Sadurski (eds.), *Freedom of Communication* (Aldershot: Dartmouth, 1994).

consequences and institutional arrangements that we associate with acknowledging a right as a human right. Broad moral reflection is required to identify the considerations on which the discourse of human rights feeds and reflects, and subject them to a process of critical analysis in the light of the practical political alternatives open to us. This is not something that can be done in a contextless manner through the detached analysis of bare concepts. Nor is it something that is best approached through the generalized affirmations of official texts and grand treatises. Nor does it call, in the first place, for a detailed examination of the case law of human rights courts and administrative agencies, although this body of law, which has its echoes in other areas of law and government, provides many important examples and arguments that can be taken into account in moral reflection, and may be of immense importance when it comes to considering the implementation of human rights. In contrast, I suggest that it is best to start this process by looking directly at the historical and existing situations that trigger what may be called the 'human rights response', that is, a condemnation that is characteristically expressed in terms of human rights discourse, and then seeking to channel these responses into proposals for efficacious institutional design and political action.

To this extent I favour the 'self-evident' rather than the marginal case approach to developing a philosophy of human rights.[25] That is, we should commence our analyses with obvious human rights violations, such as torture, imprisonment without trial, genocide, and deliberate starvation of others, rather than cases where there is controversy about whether a violation of human rights is involved, such as the punishment of hate speech or the practice of capital punishment. This is not because of any naive assumption that because something presents as self-evident, either because we cannot bring ourselves to doubt it or because everyone involved in the debate agrees that it does not require justification, this means that it has the status of 'truth'. This approach does rest on the assumption, however, that when engaged with human rights we are dealing with the practical articulation of certain foundational moral experiences and affirmations about the basic values associated with human life. However complex the idea of human rights becomes as we move towards its positivization in actual political and legal systems,[26] its core foundations lie in some straightforward but profound moral experiences.

[25] Compare B. Williams, 'In the Beginning was the Deed', in H. H. Koh and R. C. Slye (eds.), *Deliberative Democracy and Human Rights* (New Haven: Yale University Press, 1999), 50: 'Fundamental human rights, it seems to me, had better get slightly nearer to being what their traditional defender always took them to be, that is, self-evident, and self-evidence should register more than the convictions of their advocates if the claims to human rights are to escape the familiar criticism that they express only the preferences of a liberal culture', with T. Nagel, 'Personal Rights and Public Space', in Koh and Slye (eds.), *Deliberative Democracy and Human Rights*, 33–4: 'unfortunately the flagrant violation of the most basic human rights is devoid of philosophical interest.'

[26] Nagel is surely right when he goes on to assert that human rights 'require precise argument, definition and adjustment, which will always give rise to controversy, and there is room for very considerable disagreement and development in the details of their design'; Nagel, n. 25 above, 35.

Many points should be made about these foundational moral responses that cannot be adequately explored here. Major issues are involved in turning the perception of importance into judgments about what is overriding or inalienable or absolute. Difficult questions arise about whether foundational moral experiences prompt us to refrain from harming, or to seek punishment or redress, or to take positive action to help victims or prevent harm. Doubts may be raised about whether evocation of powerful emotional responses is itself an adequate test of moral importance. Yet it is clear that we cannot begin to answer our human rights questions without long and careful reflection on moral responses to specific human conditions. In the next section I deal with just one of the ways in which basic moral responses may be directed towards the formulation of concrete practical policy.

Institutional contextualism

Perhaps because the practical force of human rights is so manifest this aspect of human rights discourse has been under-explored in relation to the definition of human rights. The common approach is to seek to determine what human rights are and what rights are human rights and then proceed to see how to implement or protect these rights. This is a natural approach to take given that the logic of human rights builds on the premiss of the existence of morally intolerable situations. It seems sensible first to identify the evil, and then to seek to rectify it.

However, at the current stage of the institutional development of human rights this traditional approach is inadequate because of the wide range of different practical responses to human rights violations that may be deemed appropriate. Some human rights abuses call for priority policing and high criminal penalties, perhaps administered by international courts. Some human rights abuses may require armed intervention without the consent of the governments whose territories are the targets of the intervention. Some abuses of human rights may call for the adoption of a bill of rights administered by constitutional courts. Other abuses call for legislation with civil remedies. Still others call for international condemnation, perhaps through the Human Rights Committee of the United Nations.[27]

While these various practical responses may be regarded simply as alternative, and sometimes complementary, ways of dealing with the same morally unacceptable situations, it is also clear that it is difficult to make determinations about the content of human rights until we know what the practical consequences of so doing are likely to be. Indeed, with some exaggeration, it may be that whether or not we accept something as a human right depends on what that commits us to in practical terms. This means that our list of human rights must vary with the type of remedy or practical response that we have in mind. This form of human rights

[27] See G. Best, 'Justice, International Relations, and Human Rights', (1995) 71 *International Affairs* 775–800.

relativism may seem appropriate given the difficulty of identifying core human rights that apply to all circumstances. What counts as a human right may indeed depend on the practical consequences that flow from adopting it as a human right.

In some ways this is unproblematic, for we already have various categories of human rights that correlate with different modes of implementation. War crimes and crimes against humanity trigger certain types of response, such as trials before international courts. Genocide licenses armed intervention in the affairs of other states. Civil and political rights call for bills of rights which give courts the power to strike down legislation which contravenes these rights. Social and economic rights are associated with reprimands from UN committees, and various forms of discrimination, such as race, religious, and gender, seem to call for civil responses and various types of legislative response.

However, these categorizations are controversial when they are remedy-led. It is often claimed that all human rights are equally important and equally demanding of enforcement. While it is common to talk of 'fundamental' human rights, with the implication that some human rights are not fundamental, this is contentious, particularly when it seems to downgrade some human rights as deserving less protection.

Further, changing our criteria of what is to count as a human right depending on the practical implications we give to whatever is deemed a 'human right' has a remedy-relativism that may seem both philosophically wrong and morally offensive. Surely, it may be argued, we have first to enquire or discover what human rights are. This means what they are everywhere and always. We cannot have some rights as human rights for some purposes and not for others. Whether or not something is a human right is, it may be argued, a moral fact that is independent of place, time, response, and purpose.

Such a robust approach is sustainable, if at all, only by prioritizing a very limited notion of human rights. If, for instance, a human right is associated only with the idea that there are some things that it is never right to do to anyone in any circumstances, such as torturing them, then we may have a lively sense that there is a defensible list of such rights that we can identify independently of context and the practical implications of their adoption. The aim is to eliminate torture, and we then proceed to commend and adopt all available means to this end.

However, human rights discourse has developed far beyond such a 'never-ever' core of rights. Even in the case of the most sacrosanct of human rights it is sustainable only by adopting very restricted definitions of content of the rights in question, such as the right not to be tortured. Moreover, it is philosophically untenable to assume that underpinning the language of human rights there is a metaphysical realm of rights that has a content and function independent of historical circumstances. No doubt such human rights essentialism has its attractions from the point of view of legitimization and rhetoric, but it is certainly unhelpful and unproductive to think of determining what rights are human rights as an exploration of a universal essence rather than something about which we have to decide. Human rights are human creations to serve human purposes.

If we can accept some such human rights relativity with respect to instrumentalities, it is permissible to think of different categories of human rights in relation to different practical implications. In fact, this is not simply a matter of the remedies that we are considering employing, but goes to the question of the conduct we are seeking to justify by means of the discourse of human rights. The suggestion is that it is in fact exceedingly helpful to take this approach, for it provides us with more manageable questions to ask and gives us a clearer basis for examining our answers to those questions.

The advantage of posing limited and precise questions about human rights is neatly demonstrated in the clear-cut approach of Thomas Nagel, using what I have called the 'torture model' of human rights. Confining himself to what he calls 'the most basic rights', such as those relating to torture and racial persecution, Nagel asks, What does it mean to object to these common horrors as violations of universal human rights? His twofold answer comes down to one core implication: 'that these are forms of treatment to which no one should be subjected.'[28] This formulation cannot be rejected as the sort of naive essentialism referred to above. Whatever reason Nagel has for adopting this analysis of basic rights, he does not suggest that it implies the pre-existence of a metaphysical set of rights. Indeed, he is clear that the existence of moral rights depends 'on whether there is a decisive justification for including these forms of inviolability in the status of every member of the moral community'.[29]

However, Nagel cannot succeed in demonstrating that this is all there is to human rights. When he says that the 'idea of rights exempts a core of individual discretion from the authority of others—removes it from the category of conduct that might be regulated if good public reasons so indicated',[30] this cannot be claimed as a deduction from the general idea of human rights. The claim that 'To be exempt from different kinds of invasion is the common denominator of human rights' seems an unduly dogmatic restriction on the scope of human rights, although it does render more manageable the problem of identifying which rights are human rights if 'the definition of specific rights depends on an argument about where these boundaries fall'.[31]

However, we need not lose the advantage of Nagel's methodology for refining questions about human rights when jettisoning his liberalist confines. Instead, we can identify one of the types of question to be posed about human rights in the following hypothetical terms: 'If the consequence of adopting x as a human right is that it is never right to prevent a person from having or doing x, then is this or that a human right?'

[28] Nagel, n. 25 above, 35. The second criterion is really an explication of the first, to the effect that 'wrongness is not a function of the balance of costs and benefits in this case'. Putting the two together, he defines these basic rights as 'universal protections of every individual against being justifiably used or sacrificed in certain ways for purposes worthy or unworthy'.

[29] Ibid. 36. [30] Ibid. 37. [31] Ibid. 40.

An excellent example of how this approach goes is to be found in the recent work of John Rawls, in his essay 'The Law of Peoples',[32] where he provides a definition of human rights closely tied to a particular function. There Rawls states that human rights are not the basic rights of a liberal democratic society. Although there is a very substantial overlap in content between liberal rights and human rights, the latter do not include democratic rights of a Western sort. Rather, human rights are 'a special class of rights of universal application'[33] that

(1) 'do not depend on any particular comprehensive moral doctrine or philosophical conception of human nature, such as, for example, that human beings are moral persons and have equal worth, or that they have certain moral and intellectual powers that entitle them to these rights',
(2) 'express a minimum standard of well-ordered political institutions for all peoples who belong, as members of good standing, to a just political society of peoples', and
(3) constitute a 'minimally decent regime'.[34]

All this sounds as arbitrary as Rawls's dogmatic categorization of justice as the 'overriding' consideration in the distribution of benefits and burdens in society in *A Theory of Justice*.[35] We may wonder where he gets the quite precise idea of what human rights are and what their content is. To decide what these minimum standards are he deploys his own constructivist methodology, based this time on reflection about what independent states, behind a veil of ignorance, would adopt as human rights to bind their actual conduct. It is difficult to know what to make of this, owing to the open texture of the idea of what counts as 'decent', but the focus sharpens considerably when he tells us the implications of these rights in political practice. Human rights are, we are told, 'sufficient to exclude justified and forceful intervention by other peoples, say by economic sanctions, or, in grave cases, by military force'.[36]

Once we know the function that human rights are to perform, we can appreciate why 'legitimacy does not require democracy and is compatible with a hierarchical society, so it is not a test of liberal democracy'. It is the non-intervention principle that is central to the whole enterprise. It is this principle that enables him to say that 'Human rights are thus distinct from, say constitutional rights, or the rights of democratic citizenship, or from other kinds of rights that belong to a certain kind of political institution, both individualist and associationist.'[37] Liberal democracies do respect human rights but human rights do not require liberal democracy, but only 'such basic rights as the right to life

[32] In Shute and Hurley (eds.), n. 5 above.

[33] J. Rawls, *The Law of Peoples* (Cambridge, Mass.: Harvard University Press, 1999), 70.

[34] Ibid. 68.

[35] J. Rawls, *A Theory of Justice* (Cambridge, Mass.: Harvard University Press, 1961).

[36] He gives two other functions from which nothing in particular would seem to follow: they are 'a necessary condition of a regime's legitimacy and of the decency of its legal order' and 'they set a limit on pluralism among peoples'.

[37] Ibid. 70.

and security, to personal property, and the element of the rule of law, as well as the right to a certain liberty of conscience and freedom of association, and the right of emigration. These rights we refer to as human rights.'[38]

All this is, of course, far removed from the list of human rights we would think necessary even in a basic list for domestic use. But then it is far removed from what Rawls takes to be appropriate within a liberal democracy. The crucial thing is that he is talking of those rights that must be respected and secured if the principle of state sovereignty is not to be overruled by the morality of intervention.

Whatever we think of the standards he sets for intervention,[39] there is something very promising in this aspect of his method. It enables us to have different sets of rights for different purposes and we need not, and should not, look for one set of human rights that serves all these purposes.[40] On this approach we do not decide on human rights in a contextless way, considering first which rights are human rights and then thinking of all the many ways that can support and enforce these rights. Rather, we think of different questions, different types of situation, different moral thresholds for action of various types, various ways of going about securing our purposes, and argue backwards to what moral values

[38] Rawls gets to this point through a rather tortuous use of some work by Philip Soper, who argues for a type of natural law position that limits sovereignty by identifying the limits of toleration. Rawls's conclusion is that, to be tolerated, a society must 'be guided by a common good conception of justice', that is 'a conception that takes impartially into account what it sees not unreasonably as the fundamental interests of all members of society... It is not the case that the interests of some are arbitrarily privileged while the interests of others go for naught.' There must be 'a sincere and not unreasonable belief on the part of the judges and other officials who administer the legal order that the law is indeed guided by a common good conception of justice'. This belief must be demonstrated by a willingness to defend publicly the state's injunctions as justified by law. Courts are an efficient way of doing this. These aspects of legal order are necessary to establish a regime's legitimacy in the eyes of its own people. To sum up the second requirement we say: the system of law is sincerely and not unreasonably believed to be guided by a common good conception of justice, takes into account people's essential interests, and imposes duties and obligations on all members, 'adding that the political institutions of a well-ordered hierarchical society constitute a reasonable consultation hierarchy'. They include a family of representative bodies, or other assemblies, whose task is to look after the interests of all elements of society. Although in hierarchical societies persons are not regarded as free and equal citizens as they are in liberal societies, they are seen as 'responsible members of society who can recognise their moral duties and obligations and play their part in social life'. He continues: 'with a consultation hierarchy there is an opportunity for different voices to be heard, not, to be sure, in a way allowed by democratic institutions, but, appropriately in view of the religious and philosophical values of the society in question. Thus, individuals do not have the right of free speech as in liberal society; but as members of associations and corporate bodies they have the right at some point in the process of consultation to express political dissent and the government has an obligation to take their dissent seriously and to give a conscientious reply. The different voices can be heard... because the sincere belief of judges and officials has two components: honest belief and respect for the possibility of dissent.' So it is 'not a purely paternalistic regime'. This secures 'certain minimum rights to means of subsistence and security (the right to life), to liberty (freedom from slavery, serfdom and forced occupations) and (personal) property, as well as to formal equality as expressed by the rules of natural justice' and some toleration of religion and immigration, i.e. human rights. Rawls, n. 35 above, 62.

[39] For criticisms of this aspect of Rawls's position, see A. Buchanan, 'Rawls's Law of Peoples', (2000) 110 *Ethics* 697–721.

[40] Beitz, n. 3 above, 269, 276: 'it is not true that the only role of human rights is to justify coercive intervention.'

are appropriate and how they may be best pursued in this context. We do not ask, for instance, what are human rights and then argue whether these ought to be incorporated in bills of rights, but we ask whether there are any rights we want to see protected by a process of judicial override on the basis of general principles and call these 'human rights'.

I suggest, then, that, to identify the boundaries of human rights, we should first identify the choices that are open to us in the articulation of the practical form of human rights and the institutional settings which may be used to implement various types of human rights. By the practical form of human rights I mean essentially the identification of the possible duties and methods of implementation that are deemed appropriate. By the institutional settings I mean the type of system that may be set up to articulate and implement these duties, be they legislative, constitutional, administrative, or ethical. And so, while we cannot possibly allow Rawls to claim that his human rights are the authoritative and universal type of human rights, we can follow through his method in a number of different contexts and come up with a number of equally valid and different sets of human rights. We will not thereby arrive at 'human right's proper',[41] but we will come closer to achieving an idea of what human rights are appropriate for what contexts.

There are significant dangers in this approach. It could lead to an analysis of human rights in terms of its distinctive mechanisms of implementation, such as through bills of rights, international treaties and how they are monitored, or the work of United Nations committees, so that 'human rights' becomes identified with procedural human rights law and its associated institutions. This, then, can have the unfortunate consequence that everything that is then implemented through such mechanisms comes to be regarded as a human right, even when the interests at stake seem far removed from the moral foundations that can plausibly be attached to human rights. And we lose sight of the fact that some human rights are protected by institutions with a wider range of functions than those we have identified as distinctive human rights protection mechanisms.

To avoid this trap we must be able to make some progress in our first type of contextualization in order to have some idea of the sort of moral considerations that are most closely associated with human rights. This is a vital exercise, if only because human rights are primarily presented as a series of simple abstract claims to the effect that people have rights to such things as to life, or liberty, or health. What meaning we ascribe to such abstract statements depends crucially on the values to which we subscribe. These things are the reasons why we believe that they ought to be given some form of special protection and priority. This is why the interpretation of human rights law is such a variable and subjective matter.

However, what I am suggesting is that this moral reflection has to be done, first, by paying attention to, and trying to get inside and evaluate, the moral

[41] Rawls, n. 35 above, 80.

responses to the evils that are widely regarded as human rights abuses and, most often neglected, viewing these responses in the context of specific issues and mechanisms for remedies and resolutions. This may mean ceasing to talk of human rights in general, or at all, except as an overarching and imprecise identifier of a range of specific spheres of interest and action. This would break the connection between a homogeneous category of 'human rights' and specific institutions, such as bills of rights, or international criminal courts, or specific moral or political questions, such as justified intervention, or obligations of international aid.

This amalgamated approach to human rights boundaries, which comes out with a variety of human rights domains, is a somewhat messy one. It may lose something of the alleged indivisibility of human rights and the symbolic image of a common flag under which to march. However, it is more realistic and potentially more precise than the simplistic and essentialist presuppositions of much human rights discourse. It certainly counters the dangerous assumption that the only effective way of bringing morality into politics is to turn judges into politicians and replace politicians with lawyers through enforcing all human rights through bills of rights, and it may discourage us from moving too rapidly from establishing the occurrence of just any form of human rights violations to launching armed intervention against the alleged perpetrators.

2

Freedom of Expression as a Human Right

LARRY ALEXANDER

Introduction

Everyone reading this chapter I am quite sure thinks of herself or himself—as I think of myself—as an ardent supporter of freedom of expression. For do we not all, every one of us, feel outrage whenever some tinhorn despot jails or executes people merely for speaking against the regime? And do we not get indignant whenever some cowardly university administrator sanctions some professor or student for violating a Stalinist code of political orthodoxy? Or when some Comstockian school board orders removal of *Huckleberry Finn* or *Catcher in the Rye* from the high school curriculum or library? Or when censorious hecklers drown out a speaker whom we have invited because they disagree with her message?

On the other hand, everyone reading this chapter I am also quite sure is, as I am, deeply ambivalent about freedom of expression. For we are all, every one of us, instinctively censorious regarding ideas that we believe to be false and/or dangerous. We would probably like to stop those politicians we oppose from running those thirty-second attack ads on television. (They are misleading or false, and others, less enlightened than we, will be misled by them!) We would like to keep our kids (and perhaps vulnerable adults) from watching and reading, not only pornography (it misportrays sex and women), but the more common, mind-rotting trash of which most popular entertainment consists. And do we really want our tax dollars to fund, not travelling exhibitions of Rembrandt, but the 'performance art' of, say, covering oneself with chocolate as some sort of juvenile political comment? And although we might tolerate the inconvenience of diverted traffic for a civil rights demonstration, must we do so for every crackpot political movement that wants to parade?

Not only are we ambivalent about freedom of expression, but we are quite uncertain of its scope, justification, and force. Does it even cover demonstrations that inconvenience traffic and pedestrians and result in noise and litter? Is dipping oneself in chocolate within freedom of expression, or is it merely bad art and a waste of food? And are false or misleading statements covered by freedom of expression? There is considerable disagreement about the answers to these scope questions and the justifications for the answers.

Even if we can agree about the scope of freedom of expression—the specific activities that it covers—we may disagree about both its moral justification and its moral force. Does freedom of expression reflect a deontological norm, and if so, what is its weight against countervailing moral considerations? Or is freedom of expression merely an instrumental norm justified by its consequences? If so, what should freedom of expression protect despite its short-term negative consequences, and how do we know that we have performed the consequentialist calculus correctly?

The scope of freedom of expression

Freedom of speech has always been thought to cover more than what is literally speech, that is, spoken language. For example, no one disputes that it covers written language as well as spoken language. Moreover, it is difficult to see how it could be withheld from sign language, pictographs, pictures, movies, plays, and so forth, and indeed the legal protection afforded freedom of speech in countries such as the United States has been extended to all of these media of communication and expression, as well as to abstract artistic and musical performances. Usually, then, freedom of speech refers to—and is frequently referred to as—freedom of expression or freedom of communication.

It is a commonplace to distinguish between 'speech' and 'symbolic speech'. As the previous paragraph should make clear, however, that distinction is illusory. All speech employs symbols, whether they be sounds, shapes, gestures, pictures, or any other medium. There is thus no such thing as non-symbolic speech; there is only speech that employs symbols that are less or more conventional. The same point also applies to any purported distinction between speech or expression and 'conduct' or 'action'. All expression requires conduct of some sort, and any conduct can be communicative. The conclusion to be drawn is that freedom of speech or expression should be thought of as freedom of communication.

It is most natural to think that if there is a right to freedom of expression, it must be the right of the speaker. Thus, when the government threatens S with punishment if he attempts to give certain information to A, we are tempted to regard this as a violation of S's right to freedom of expression.

On most accounts of why freedom of expression should be protected, however, it is A whose right is violated whether or not S's freedom of expression is also violated. For assume that S is the author of a book and is now dead (or the citizen of a foreign country). He has no freedom of expression now in A's country. If A's government is violating anyone's rights by prohibiting the dissemination of S's book, it is A's (the audience's) rights. Moreover, if A's government prohibited A from watching sunsets because it feared A would be inspired to have subversive thoughts, freedom of expression would arguably be implicated, *even though there is no speaker.*[1]

Let me elaborate on this point—namely, that government's *purpose* for regulating, not *what* it regulates, is central to freedom of expression—for it is crucial. As I see it, there are the following possibilities for determining the scope of freedom of expression:

(1) Freedom of expression is implicated whenever 'expressive conduct' is suppressed or penalized.
(2) Freedom of expression is implicated whenever conduct that is *intended* to communicate a message is suppressed or penalized.
(3) Freedom of expression is implicated whenever an audience is prevented from receiving a message.
(4) Freedom of expression is implicated whenever an activity is suppressed or penalized for the purpose of preventing a message from being received.

Now it is easy to see that (1) cannot possibly be true. Any conduct can 'express' ideas, even if the one engaging in it does not so intend. For those observing or hearing about the conduct may form certain ideas as a result. If (1) were true, then freedom of expression would be implicated by all laws and thus by both the laws that currently exist and all alternatives to those laws.

Principle (2), which focuses on the intent to communicate a message, is also implausible. I have already mentioned two counter-examples, the dead author and the foreign author. But perhaps these examples are unconvincing. One might argue, for example, that the dead author does have a right to freedom of expression that survives his death and prevents the suppression of his work. Likewise, one might argue, I think plausibly, that freedom of expression should not be viewed parochially as the product of the nation-state and its laws but instead as a right that transcends jurisdictional boundaries and protects speakers and authors wherever located.

So let us move beyond these examples and focus on a speaker who is alive, who is within whatever jurisdiction is relevant, and who intends to express an idea through the conduct that is suppressed. Let us suppose that Alan has the apartment next to Bertha. Bertha is ill and quite sensitive to noise, which impedes her recovery. Alan is rehearsing for a role in a play. Sometimes he reads his lines in a booming voice to practise projecting. He pays no attention to the ideas he is expressing, only to the quality of his vocalizations. At other

[1] In suggesting that the right to freedom of expression is best thought of as belonging to the audience, I do not mean to imply that people have a claim right against the government or anyone else that they be spoken to or provided with information. If the right of freedom of speech ultimately belongs to the audience, it is in the form of a right not to be prevented from obtaining information or ideas that are otherwise available to it.

In saying that freedom of expression is best thought of as a right of the audience, I also am not saying that speakers have no standing to object to having their speech suppressed.

times he practises his swordplay, also required for his part, by clanging a sword against a metal fixture. Both his reading and his swordplay disturb Bertha, who hears them only as noise, and who seeks to have Alan legally enjoined from rehearsing in these ways.

Now if Bertha succeeds in enjoining Alan's clanging his sword, surely Alan's freedom of expression is not implicated. The fact that he is rehearsing for a play is of no importance; he could have been training for a jousting tournament or just enjoying the sound of metal on metal.

Is Alan's reading his lines relevantly different from his clanging his sword? Even if he were intending to express some message, his only audience is Bertha, who neither hears the message nor cares about it. She hears only noise. From her perspective—and from Alan's—the line-reading and the sword-clanging are on a par. Therefore, if freedom of expression is not implicated by suppressing the swordplay, it is not implicated by suppressing the line-reading.

Now if Alan himself were formulating ideas in reading his lines aloud—if he were, in essence, his own audience—things might look different. That brings us to principle (3), which posits that freedom of expression is implicated whenever an audience is prevented from receiving a message. But (3) has the same vice as (1), namely, that it is virtually limitless. For people can derive ideas from almost anything. If the law prohibits driving at 100 miles per hour, then we are not going to be able to form the idea of what it is like to drive that fast. If the law protects freedom of expression, we are not going to be able to form the idea of what the absence of legally protected freedom of expression would be like. All laws preclude certain courses of conduct and experiences. As a consequence, people will have different ideas in different legal regimes, and any legal regime will suppress some ideas, spawn others, and colour all.

Before concluding that (4)—which focuses not on what is being regulated nor on the effect of the regulation, but on the purpose behind it—is the proper principle for delimiting the scope of freedom of expression, let us consider an alternative principle that combines (2) and (3). This principle—(3′)—would hold that freedom of expression is implicated whenever conduct that is intended to communicate a message is suppressed or penalized with the result that an audience is prevented from receiving the message, even if the reason for suppressing or penalizing the conduct has nothing to do with the message(s) intended or received. This principle is definitive of what Laurence Tribe calls Track Two freedom of speech cases, to which I now turn.[2]

Freedom of expression on Track Two

Tribe's Track Two branch of American First Amendment free speech cases covers regulations of expressive conduct enacted for reasons other than to affect what

[2] L. H. Tribe, *American Constitutional Law*, 2nd edn. (Mincola, NY: Foundation Press, 1988), §12–2, p. 792.

messages are conveyed and received.[3] In other words, Track Two regulations are concerned exclusively with the non-communicative impact of the conduct regulated. (Track One regulations, about which more later, are, by contrast, those enacted precisely to affect what messages are communicated; their scope is thus defined by principle (4).)

Track Two cases have traditionally been broken into two sub-categories: the public forum cases and the symbolic speech cases. The former concern access of private speakers to governmental or quasi-governmental facilities, and in some cases to private facilities that the speaker seeks to have treated like governmental facilities.[4] Current First Amendment jurisprudence distinguishes among traditional public fora, such as streets, sidewalks, and parks, public fora created by government designation, and non-public fora.[5] The conventional doctrine in public forum cases is that in traditional public fora and designated public fora, the government may impose narrowly drawn regulations of the time, place, and manner of speech in order to serve significant government objectives unrelated to the speaker's message. The government may not, however, bar speech entirely from such public fora and must leave adequate alternative channels of communication available.[6] On the other hand, if a facility is a non-public forum, the government may bar speech entirely or selectively, so long as it does not discriminate according to viewpoint.[7]

Public forum cases are more complicated, however, than the preceding account indicates. First, alternative channels of communication are never entirely adequate. All regulations of the public fora will entirely suppress speech with respect to some potential audience, and will entirely suppress speech with a particular cognitive and emotive impact. Secondly, the analysis leaves unresolved whether the government must make a certain quantum of traditional public fora available, whether it must construct such fora if few are available or be prevented from razing those that are available, or whether it need only maintain those available as of a certain date or those of a certain vintage.[8] Lastly, the United States Supreme Court has recognized that, with respect to designated public fora, the government may and often has opened fora to speech on a limited basis. The Court has found no First Amendment violation where the government creates fora for speech of all kinds but for only certain

3 For more extensive treatment of the issues in this section, see L. A. Alexander, 'Trouble on Track Two: Incidental Regulations of Speech and Free Speech Theory', (1993) 44 *Hastings Law Journal* 921.

4 Compare *Marsh v Alabama* 326 US 501 (1946) (proscribing regulation of speech in a company town) with *Hudgens v NLRB* 424 US 507 (1976) (allowing ban on picketers at a privately owned shopping centre).

5 *Cornelius v NAACP Legal Defense & Educ Fund, Inc* 473 US 788, 802 (1985).

6 *Ward v Rock Against Racism* 491 US 781, 796–802 (1989). It need not, however, choose the least restrictive means available.

7 *Perry Educ Ass'n v Perry Local Educators' Ass'n* 460 US 37, 46 (1983).

8 The Court in *International Society for Krishna Consciousness, Inc v Lee* 505 US 830 (1992) suggests in dicta that the government may fail to construct public fora and may convert public fora into other facilities; the only restrictions Track Two analysis imposes upon the government in this regard concern public fora that already exist and will continue to exist.

speakers.[9] It has similarly found no violation where the government creates fora for speech on some subject but not others.[10] Lastly, it has upheld the government's creation of fora for only those viewpoints the government favours, as when it runs public schools.[11] This offends the asserted doctrine that even in non-public fora, government may not engage in viewpoint discrimination.

The other sub-category of Track Two cases consists of the symbolic speech cases.[12] Here, the government forbids certain conduct irrespective of whether those who would otherwise engage in that conduct intend their engaging in it to symbolize and communicate some idea to others. The free speech issue arises when someone in fact wishes to engage in that conduct to symbolize and communicate an idea. The accepted doctrine is that government may regulate the symbol on the same grounds and with the same restrictions as it may regulate the time, place, and manner of speech in a public forum. That is, it may do so if it is advancing a significant interest unrelated to the communicative impact of the conduct, if its regulation is narrowly tailored, and if adequate alternative means exist for the speaker to convey his message.[13]

I wish to establish two propositions. The first, and easier to establish, is that the public forum cases and the symbolic speech cases have been, and should be, treated under the same standards. The second is that Track Two analysis applies to any law. In other words, the entire body of laws is subject to Track Two First Amendment analysis.

An examination of both the phrasing and application of the Supreme Court's time, place, and manner test for public forum speech and its test for regulation of symbolic speech reveals that they are essentially the same test. Both tests, as stated, require that the regulation in question be narrowly tailored but not that it be the least restrictive alternative. Moreover, in both tests the government's objectives must be 'significant' (that is, important), and the government must leave the speaker adequate alternative means to convey the message.

Regardless of the test it employs, the Court is correct, from a theoretical standpoint, in employing the *same* test for both areas. Whenever government is regulating conduct that is being engaged in to symbolize some message, government is regulating the 'time, place, and manner' of speech. It is easy enough to see that, for example, burning a draft card or dancing in the nude is employing a particular manner of expression to symbolize a message. However,

[9] See *Minnesota State Bd for Community Colleges v Knight* 465 US 271 (1984). But see *Rosenberger v Rector and Visitors of the University of Virginia* 515 US 819 (1995); *Widmar v Vincent* 454 US 263 (1981).

[10] A public hospital's bulletin board can be limited to posting notices concerning hospital business; and a public school classroom discussion can be restricted to subjects in the curriculum. See S. R. Goldstein, 'The Asserted Constitutional Right of Public School Teachers to Determine What they Teach', (1976) 124 *University of Pennsylvania Law Review* 1293.

[11] See *Hazelwood Sch Dist v Kuhlmeier* 484 US 260 (1988); *Board of Education v Pico* 457 US 853 (1982); Goldstein, n. 10 above.

[12] Given that all speech employs symbols and is thus symbolic, the area should perhaps be redescribed.

[13] See *United States v O'Brien* 391 US 367 (1968).

the time of a speech or demonstration or the place in which it occurs may also be employed symbolically.

The second proposition I want to establish is that, just as there should be no distinction between Track Two regulations affecting the time, place, and manner of speech and those affecting its symbolic or expressive aspects, so too should there be no distinction between Track Two laws directly regulating speech activities and all other laws. All Track Two laws regulate speech only indirectly in this sense: in a Track Two case, government's interest is not in what is being communicated but is in the communication's effects on values unrelated to communication, such as noise, congestion, property, aesthetics, or privacy. Track Two regulations are of First Amendment concern because they affect what gets said, by whom, to whom, and with what effect, even though the regulations are not intended to affect such matters. However, *all laws affect what gets said, by whom, to whom, and with what effect*. In short, all laws have what I shall call 'message effects'. Therefore, all laws, the entire *corpus juris*, should be subject to Track Two analysis.

Track Two includes not only restrictions on obstructing traffic while speaking or demonstrating, using amplifying devices in residential neighbourhoods, posting signs on utility poles, burning draft cards, or sleeping in parks, but also tort, contract, and property law, the tax code, and the multitude of criminal and regulatory laws and administrative regulations. For example, laws determining who owns what property under what restrictions or the price and availability of various resources will also determine what gets said, by whom, to whom, and with what effect—that is, such laws will have message effects. A change in the law of any region of the *corpus juris* will have message effects. Laws equalizing income would surely have dramatic message effects. Elimination of the law against battery would produce a new form of symbolic speech as well as information—for example, what it is like to batter and be battered—and concerns that do not exist while the law against battery is on the books.

The courts cannot, however, apply the ordinary Track Two test to all laws, even though all laws are logically subject to Track Two analysis. For example, the setting of the marginal tax rate affects my income, which, if greater, I might devote to increased speaking. Under the current Track Two test, if the government's interest in the present rate is not a significant interest, and the rate adversely affects my speech, the government would be required to abandon that rate in favour of another rate. But any other rate the government chooses will affect somebody's speech—it may result in lower transfer payments, adversely affecting the communication between poorer speakers and their audience—and thus, *it* will have to serve a significant interest as well.[14] Therefore, the Track Two test cannot be applied universally unless the requirement of

[14] Moreover, all laws curtail the symbolic expression of opposition to the laws themselves through violations, a point that by itself undermines the possibility of requiring a significant interest in order to restrict symbolic speech.

a significant government interest is trivialized either by finding almost any interest to be significant or by being made synonymous with 'the entire *corpus juris* is what it should be'. (The latter trivializes because it tautologizes: Track Two laws are constitutional if they are constitutional.)

This leaves the following problems. First, Track Two covers all laws because all laws have message effects—they affect what gets said, by whom, to whom, and with what effect. Secondly, a Track Two First Amendment challenge to a law or group of laws is a demand that the laws be changed; but every change in the laws will have message effects, so that Track Two First Amendment claims are always aligned against each other. Thus, testing challenged laws by the significant government interest test will entail testing all of their alternatives by that test. Finally, the universal application of Track Two analysis would result in the elimination of all sets of laws except those serving significant interests (as compared to all possible alternative sets). Because of this difficulty, the universal application of Track Two analysis would most likely result in complete abandonment of Track Two protection, with all asserted interests deemed 'significant' so long as they are not a mask for message-related concerns.[15]

What happens if instead of treating all speech interests as having a constant and significant weight, the particular value of the intended speech, given its intended audience, is weighed against the values the particular laws serve? This is the heart of my critique of Track Two analysis. I propose that the value of speech cannot be balanced against the government's Track Two interests in any way that is principled and that respects the very freedom of thought that the First Amendment is thought to protect.

To make Track Two analysis work, we must assign a value to the audience's loss of information due to incidental restrictions on speech. That value in turn must be weighed against the values furthered by the incidental regulations at issue, values such as freedom from noise, litter, congestion, and taxes. Moreover, that value must also be weighed against the information lost to that and other audiences if the incidental regulations are struck down. (Each alternative set of regulations produces a different state of the world, which in turn makes available different information and/or different audiences for the same information. A trivial example: a world without an anti-litter law lacks the information 'what a world with an anti-litter law is like'. A less trivial example: a world in which extra police must be assigned to monitor and control street demonstrations and

[15] How should we classify government's decision to ban conduct *because* it is message-bearing but not because of concern with the messages borne? Theoretically, I believe these should also be regarded as Track Two regulations. If government can build a park exclusively for softball, basketball, and tennis, and not for political rallies, then it can disfavour the activity of communication relative to other activities. Nonetheless, because speech-specific regulations can mask concerns with the messages being conveyed—after all, why would government favour all other potentially littering paper over 'pamphlets' (paper bearing a message) if not out of a desire to suppress certain messages?—they are perhaps justifiably treated as content-related regulations rather than Track Two regulations.

reroute traffic has less money available to hire teachers in public schools than a world in which street demonstrations are prohibited.[16])

In addition to the theoretical difficulties of the balancing process, the Track Two analysis also poses the theoretical problem of placing a value on the information at stake. On the one hand, if we evaluate the information at stake from the position of not knowing yet what it is, we face the theoretically impossible task of placing a specific value on unknown information. On the other hand, if we evaluate the information at stake from the position of knowing or imagining what it is, we risk imposing our evaluation on others through the striking down of the existing set of incidental regulations, thereby pre-empting the very freedom of evaluation by others that is supposedly central to the First Amendment and the value of freedom of expression it embodies. In the name of the First Amendment, we end up imposing an evaluative framework on others and arguably violating the First Amendment. Put differently, the First Amendment is arguably supposed to protect a realm of pure process, the substantive results of which are legitimate only because that process is pure; once substantive results begin guiding the construction of the process itself, the legitimacy of the results of that process is compromised.[17]

The above argument is not one directed exclusively at courts. It applies to all coercive impositions of such valuations of information and thus suggests that legislative evaluation of information gains and losses is equally problematic. It suggests that legislatures should perhaps measure only the strength of the constituents' preferences in deciding, for instance, between open space suitable for speech and alternative land uses. And it suggests that taxing one group because of another group's preference for speech activities—for example, in building a town meeting hall—is illegitimate to the extent its justification depends upon the good the public will derive from the speech. (Building a meeting hall, an auditorium, or a library is non-problematic to the extent it reflects the majority's private good preference for information of a certain type rather than, say, more tennis courts.) Finally, when government itself speaks with taxpayers' resources, it is evaluating specific information—the most problematic of all government activities from a First Amendment standpoint. Public schools and universities, public grants and subsidies for research, public broadcasting, public financing of election campaigns, and a variety of other activities, rather than being extensions of the animating spirit of the First Amendment, are in tension with it.

I shall discuss each of these points at greater length.

[16] It is bootless to attempt to tot up the information gained and lost under alternative sets of incidental restrictions. Information does not come in discrete units such that it would be meaningful to compare states of the world in terms of which state has more information. Maximizing the net stock of information is quite meaningless. All laws have information effects, but that is all one can say.

[17] See R. C. Post, 'Managing Deliberation: The Quandary of Democratic Dialogue', (1993) 103 *Ethics* 654; R. C. Post, 'Racist Speech, Democracy, and the First Amendment', (1990) 32 *William and Mary Law Review* 267, 282–3, 290, 293 (hereafter Post, 'Racist Speech'); R. C. Post, 'The Constitutional Concept of Public Discourse: Outrageous Opinion, Democratic Deliberation, and *Hustler Magazine v. Falwell*', (1990) 103 *Harvard Law Review* 601, 670.

Balancing speech interests against non-speech values served by incidental regulations

The entire *corpus juris*, from the general common law of contracts, property, and torts to the most particular tax regulations, affects what gets said, by whom, to whom, and to what effect. Speech and listening are costly activities. They use resources such as space, newsprint, radio frequencies, presses, and police protection, and impose other costs—noise, litter, and clutter. *Schneider v State*,[18] for example, in which the Supreme Court struck down a municipal ordinance banning pamphleteering on city streets and sidewalks in order to reduce litter, resulted in the imposition on the public of the costs of litter or, alternatively, the extra costs of the state's next-best alternative for eliminating litter. (If a less restrictive alternative is on the order of a Pareto superior move—the alternative does all the good at no greater cost and without affecting speech—then less restrictive alternatives are unlikely to exist; all alternatives will have greater costs in some respects.)

Thus, the Court's decision in *Schneider* constitutionally mandated what can be viewed as a subsidy of pamphleteers. But why such a subsidy of pamphleteers?[19]

Consider Jane, who complains about the high costs of the *New Republic*, cable television, books from Oxbridge University Press, and a college education. Those costs result from laws—laws regarding property rights, laws conserving trees, laws affecting labour costs, laws regarding tax liability, and many other laws. Jane's receipt of speech—which is, after all, what the First Amendment is arguably about—is adversely affected by those laws. Why should her attempt to receive this speech not be subsidized? (Alternatively, if one resists the notion that listeners' rights are central to the First Amendment, why should the *New Republic* and Oxbridge University Press, for example, not receive subsidies or relief from various laws in order to communicate with a wider audience?)

Next, consider John, who wishes to demonstrate on Main Street, which will tie up traffic and require police presence. If, against the city's wishes, a court mandates that he be allowed to demonstrate, then the decision can be viewed as a forced subsidy of John and correlatively a forced imposition of costs on others.

Next, consider Joan, who is denied several outlets for her message that, given her limited resources, would be the most effective: putting graffiti on the side of city hall, using a loudspeaker at night in a residential neighbourhood, or putting up a pamphlet stand on land that, owing to various zoning laws, is currently unaffordable for her. Why should Schneider but not Joan get a First Amendment subsidy here?

Finally, consider Jason, who wants the city to build an auditorium suitable for public lectures and rallies, but who is opposed by Jean, who would like the city

[18] 308 US 147 (1939).

[19] If one objects that the term 'subsidy' is rhetorically loaded in favour of the existing set of entitlements, we can more neutrally ask why we should give the entitlement to the pamphleteer.

to build more tennis courts because she and others prefer playing and discussing tennis to attending public lectures, and Jerry, who wants lower taxes so that he can afford to go to night school.

The *O'Brien* line of cases raises the same questions.[20] If a medium is being regulated for non-censorial reasons, then striking down the regulation under the First Amendment imposes a costly First Amendment easement on others. If Jake wishes to protest inflation by burning an inexpensive work of art in the lobby of the Treasury Building, presumably a court will not protect him, even though he has cost each taxpayer an insignificant amount. Yet, how is Jake different from any other user of a tangible medium that the government wishes to regulate to avoid costs to a variety of values? This question is especially relevant because those values can always be translated into amounts of money that the taxpayers would pay to preserve them.

Track Two also includes such obviously important-to-speech governmental decisions as what resources should be dedicated to the police and courts, and as a component of that decision, to protecting speakers from hostile audiences beyond those dedicated to protecting persons from assault and battery generally. Resources that go to protecting speakers are, of course, unavailable for other public projects, which include such things as public schools and libraries and the ideas they would otherwise communicate. Since Track Two includes *all* laws and governmental decisions, however, it includes these allocations of resources decisions.

Without a theory of proper message effects, non-content-related regulations cannot be evaluated under the First Amendment, except in an arbitrary manner. Schneider did win, of course, as did the Hare Krishnas in *International Society for Krishna Consciousness, Inc v Lee*.[21] But why they and not O'Brien, the sleep-in protesters in *Clark v Community for Creative Non-Violence*,[22] or the many other actual losers? And if Schneider and the Krishnas, why not my hypothetical Jane, John, Joan, and Jason?

As discussed above, assigning the speech value a constant weight in the calculus—for instance, equal to a significant governmental interest—does not help. Without a theory regarding message effects—what gets said, by whom, to whom, and with what effect—assigning any weight will be arbitrary. More importantly, because speech interests are affected regardless of what set of Track Two laws are chosen, the speech 'constant' appears on both sides of the equation and does not produce a winner.

An alternative that might be considered would be straightforward balancing rather than assigning speech an arbitrary constant value. Under this approach, all of the information at stake under all alternative sets of laws would be

[20] *United States v O'Brien* 391 US 367 (1968) (upholding a prosecution for burning a draft card under a statute forbidding destruction of draft cards, despite the defendant's claim that he was burning his card to protest induction for the Vietnam War).

[21] 505 US 830 (1992) (striking down restriction on distributing literature in an airport).

[22] 468 US 288 (1984) (upholding conviction for violation of a regulation banning sleeping in a park).

examined, as well as all the non-speech values, and a determination would be made as to which set of laws is superior.

There are obvious practical and institutional objections to such a balancing proposal. Given that this approach would involve nothing less than a comparison of all possible entire sets of laws, both for their message effects and for their effects on all the non-speech values, the proposal is a practical impossibility for a legislature and surely for a court.

This practical objection should by itself be sufficient to undermine all Track Two judicial decisions and to dictate complete judicial withdrawal from Track Two. There remains, however, a theoretical objection to the enterprise as well. In principle, we cannot evaluate the message effects of Track Two laws: either we assume the viewpoint of one who does not know what the information at issue will turn out to be, in which case we cannot evaluate it at all, or we assume the viewpoint of one who does know what the information will turn out to be, in which case we can evaluate it, but only from a partisan perspective inconsistent with freedom of expression itself.

The latter point is not that an individual cannot have a point of view about the values of the competing types of information, or that one point of view cannot be correct. The point is, rather, that the First Amendment, on its orthodox understanding, requires government to treat any point of view on these matters as just one point of view among many.[23] The only point of view it privileges is its own—namely, that no particular point of view shall be privileged.[24]

Of course, this view of the First Amendment's central value is contestable and contested. For example, some argue that the First Amendment requires only that no 'political' position be privileged, and that only 'political' speech and information are protected.[25] This position, however, is, for related reasons, both unhelpful for Track Two analysis and also wrong. Regardless of what alternative sets of laws we compare in assessing Track Two challenges, political information will be lost and gained under each.[26] Furthermore, the

[23] See *West Virginia State Board of Education v Barnette* 319 US 624, 642 (1943): 'If there is any fixed star in our constitutional constellation, it is that no official, high or petty, can prescribe what shall be orthodox in . . . matters of opinion'; S. M. Gilles, 'All Truths Are Equal, But Are Some Truths More Equal Than Others?', (1991) 41 *Case Western Law Review* 725, 726, 740–4; cf. D. A. Strauss, 'Persuasion, Autonomy, and Freedom of Expression', (1991) 91 *Columbia Law Review* 334, 370.

[24] This is paradoxical. Indeed, the First Amendment has been held to protect anti-First Amendment views, which is also paradoxical. See C. A. Auerbach, 'The Communist Control Act of 1954: A Proposed Legal–Political Theory of Free Speech', (1956) 23 *University of Chicago Law Review* 173; see also Post, 'Racist Speech', n. 17 above, 303–4 (discussing the paradox of public discourse exemplified by tolerating the intolerant). And see pp. 66–9 below.

[25] See, for example, L. R. BeVier, 'The First Amendment and Political Speech—An Inquiry into the Substance and Limits of Principle', (1978) 30 *Stanford Law Review* 299, 300; R. H. Bork, 'Neutral Principles and Some First Amendment Problems', (1971) 47 *Indiana Law Journal* 1.

[26] Consider the effect of *Schneider v State*, n. 18 above, and *International Society for Krishna Consciousness, Inc v Lee*, n. 8 above, on the political proposition that 'streets and airports should be free of pamphleteers', a proposition communicated symbolically by the presence of the laws struck down in those cases.

evaluation of the political information at stake surely will be political and thus inconsistent with governmental non-partisanship. More fundamentally, the question of what information has political relevance is itself political.[27] If that is true, the position that the First Amendment protects only political speech devours itself.

Would Track Two analysis avoid the 'point of view' problem if it sought 'balance' or 'representation' or 'adequate airing' of points of view? This tack is equally unavailing. First, how many issues are there, and how many points of view are there on each? Secondly, whose position 'represents' a point of view? Thirdly, when has that position been 'adequately aired'? The first question, if it is a meaningful one, is not a metaphysical one but one itself referable to points of view. Moreover, the number of points of view per issue is not determinable, since any answer depends on how the 'issue' is described and what information and state of the argument is posited.[28] As for representation and adequacy of airing, no one can represent my point of view except me; and that point of view has not been adequately aired until it is universally accepted. To illustrate, if people disagree with me, they obviously have not listened or understood, or they are intellectually deficient. How else can I explain their disagreement if I still hold my point of view to be correct?

This is the paradox. Track Two laws are extremely important in determining the quality of public debate. Indeed, Track Two laws almost assuredly have a much greater effect on speech than laws covered by principle (4), where government's purpose is to affect messages, if relative effects can be meaningfully measured. Nevertheless, the core First Amendment value that no partisan point of view be privileged precludes government from evaluating information gains and losses, which, in turn, means that Track Two analysis is precluded by the First Amendment itself.

Again, the point is not just an institutional one about the limits of courts. It applies to any institution subject to the First Amendment. Legislative evaluations of information, though democratic (unlike judicial evaluations), are themselves antithetical to the core First Amendment value.[29]

Finally, one might argue that adopting a comprehensive normative theory—such as Rawlsianism, utilitarianism, or libertarianism—as the vantage point for First Amendment analysis provides a basis for evaluating information gains and losses and thus for evaluating Track Two laws. The rejoinder to this position is that although comprehensive normative theories are in one sense

[27] Ninety-nine per cent of us would agree that the *MacNeil/Lehrer News Hour* has more relevance to political choices than do reruns of *Gilligan's Island*. Yet, how do we convince the remaining 1 per cent while remaining politically 'neutral'?

[28] See Strauss, n. 23 above, 349.

[29] Thus, a decision that there shall be public libraries, not public tennis courts, if it is a decision about the relative values of the information provided by libraries and tennis (and not just a weighing up of constituents' preferences *qua* preferences), represents government's endorsement of a partisan political view that is arguably inconsistent with the First Amendment. See nn. 16 and 17 above.

the proper bases for evaluating Track Two laws, they are the proper bases only in so far as they are not distinctly related to free speech. Rawlsianism, utilitarianism, and libertarianism are frameworks for assessing the entire *corpus juris*—to see if it maximizes liberties and wealth, maximizes aggregate or average welfare, or reflects libertarian rights—and in that sense they are important to Track Two analysis. In that same sense, however, they have nothing to do with speech or relative information value as distinct issues apart from liberties, welfare, and libertarian rights. Usually a comprehensive normative theory assumes full information of whatever type the theory makes relevant and then directs that that information be deployed to produce the results the theory dictates. And even if we assume the lack of full information, information effects can only be relevant to the choice of Track Two laws in a very restricted way. We would have to assume that the choice among Track Two laws was entirely neutral with regard to all values made relevant by the theory in question, and that relative information effects were the only ground for choice. The theory would then dictate that we choose that set of laws most likely to lead to the information upon which the theory itself places the higher value.

Yet, even in this extremely restricted way in which comprehensive normative theories would be relevant to Track Two analysis, choosing laws because their message effects are endorsed by a specific normative theory poses a First Amendment problem. Presumably the First Amendment, even if its ultimate justification rests on a comprehensive normative theory, forbids imposing such a comprehensive normative theory on citizens' evaluative decisions. Further, since imposition of a single comprehensive normative theory is the strongest of all governmental intrusions on the citizens' evaluative processes, it is arguably the most antithetical to the First Amendment.

Summary

If we assume the position of ignorance regarding message effects—what would get said, to whom, by whom, and to what effect—under alternative sets of Track Two laws, then we can make no evaluation of those sets in terms of information gains and losses. On the other hand, if we assume the position of knowing the information effects under each alternative set of Track Two laws, we then face the problem that all evaluations of such information are positional and partisan and should not be officially endorsed by government. Even a comprehensive normative theory underlying the First Amendment will be too strong to be a Track Two tool because it will usually endorse a set of Track Two laws on grounds independent of information gain and loss. Moreover, comprehensive theories are nothing more than partisan positions that the government should not endorse in attempting to structure public debate, even if, paradoxically, they themselves provide the justification for the First Amendment and its proscription of their own endorsement.

The implication of the failure of balancing

Track Two First Amendment analysis requires that we balance information gains and losses and all other values furthered by the entire set of laws in question against the information gains and losses and all other values furthered by all the alternative entire sets of laws. We cannot do this as a practical matter. Perhaps more importantly, we cannot do this as a theoretical matter. Even if we knew what information each alternative set of laws would generate, the First Amendment itself forbids government to act on an evaluation of that information. Track Two analysis is not an extension of the First Amendment but a violation of it. Track Two laws can be evaluated on many grounds—but not on First Amendment ones.

There are two major implications for the First Amendment to be drawn from this conclusion. Most obviously, the courts should no longer hear Track Two challenges to laws.

The second implication, however, is directed at legislation, not adjudication, and is quite far-reaching. For if my analysis is correct, the legislature violates the First Amendment if it adopts and imposes through law any partisan evaluation of information, which is to say, any evaluation. Essentially, although the government may enact laws based on a variety of values, it may not constitutionally rely on the value of information gained or lost in choosing which laws to enact or repeal.

This, in turn, suggests that the government's decision whether to build an auditorium to provide a forum for public debates, its decision to fund election campaigns, its decision to expand public education, its decision to fund research, and a multitude of other decisions resting wholly or in part on government's evaluation of information, rather than its aggregation of private preferences, are constitutionally problematic.

The Core of Freedom of Expression: Regulations of Conduct for the Purpose of Affecting Messages Received

Having shown, through an excursion into American First Amendment jurisprudence and its Track Two component, that principles (1), (2), (3), and (3′)—all of which focus on the *effects* of regulations on messages intended and received—are untenable for delimiting the scope of freedom of expression, I shall now turn to principle (4), which has as its focus the regulator's *purpose* in regulating conduct. Principle (4) includes within freedom of expression all conduct that is restricted for the purpose of affecting the messages that audiences receive. It is immaterial under principle (4) whether the conduct is the conventional method of expressing ideas—written or oral language—whether it is intended to express ideas by those engaging in it, or whether most people would receive the message in question from observing or hearing the conduct. All that matters is *why* the conduct is regulated. If it is because of a message that the regulator wishes to suppress, alter, or otherwise affect, freedom of expression is implicated. Thus, if government forbids people from climbing Half Dome in Yosemite National Park—not because of the danger that they might be injured, not because of the harm they might cause the environment, but because government fears that some of them are receiving spiritual messages from the experience that the government wishes them not to receive—freedom of expression is in issue despite the absence of a speaker, an intent to speak, conventional symbols, and perhaps even the meaning most would attach to the experience. The same would be the case if government banned toy guns for children out of fear that a few would get militaristic ideas.

Principle (4) defines the scope of freedom of expression by the purpose of the regulator. (I shall assume for the time being that 'regulator' and 'government' are synonymous, though I shall take up this issue later.) And the purpose that defines a freedom of expression issue is that of affecting the content of messages received.[30]

Content regulations can usefully be subdivided into three types. First, there are regulations designed to affect content where government fears that the message, if unaffected, will cause harm without any further choice by the audience receiving it. Secondly, there are regulations designed to affect content that it is feared will otherwise cause harm through a further choice by the audience, but a choice that the government cannot control because the audience cannot be penalized for making the harmful choice. And thirdly, there are regulations that are like the second type, except that the audience *can* be penalized for making the harmful choice. I take up these three types of content regulations in turn.

Content regulations where the message directly causes harm

The content of messages received can directly cause many types of harms that government may legitimately try to prevent. The content of a message may be a confidence between an attorney and his client, a physician and her patient, or a priest and his penitent. The content may be an embarrassing fact about a private person. The content may be 'owned' by someone who has not authorized its communication; or the conveyor of the message may be under a contractual duty not to convey its content. The content may offend the audience's sensibilities, or cause the audience emotional trauma. Or the content may be received by the audience as a coercive threat.

Now if content regulation of this sort—the sort involved in invoking confidentiality restrictions, the privacy tort, intellectual property law, contractual

[30] For support for the position that principle (4) is the defining principle of freedom of expression, see L. Alexander, 'Free Speech and Speaker's Intent', (1995) 12 *Constitutional Commentary* 21; J. Rubenfeld, 'The First Amendment's Purpose', (2001) 53 *Stanford Law Review* 767, 769, 777–8, 784.

obligations, laws banning offensive speech, the tort of infliction of emotional distress, and the crime of uttering threats—is to be deemed to implicate freedom of expression, there are three possible courses open. First, we might hold that all such laws violate the right of freedom of expression. People should be free to send and receive messages the content of which is confidential, private, created by another, emotionally distressing, and so forth. This would, of course, have very profound implications and would represent a major change in the jurisprudence of all those countries that recognize a legal right of freedom of expression.

The second alternative would be to say that although such regulations implicate freedom of expression, they do not necessarily *violate* freedom of expression. Whether content regulations of the sort we are considering violate freedom of expression will depend upon the results of *weighing* the interest in freedom of expression against the government's interest in preventing harms to confidentiality, privacy, ownership and creativity, emotional peace, and so forth.

If we take this second, less radical course, however, then we are back in the same briar patch we entered with Track Two regulations. For how can we construct a metric for weighing the interests in receiving certain messages against the harms those messages cause unless we assign a value to the ideas or information those messages contain? If we assume ignorance of what ideas and information will be affected, we have an obvious problem in assigning weight to the ideas and information. On the other hand, if we assess the ideas and information *ex post*, with knowledge of what they are, we still must assign them value to be weighed against the harms they threaten; and how can we do that except by reference to a framework that will differ from person to person and that will be partisan and controversial through and through?[31]

To take just one example of this last point, assume that a client reveals to his attorney, in confidence, that he committed a serious crime—perhaps a murder—in his past. Later, the client is a candidate for high office—the Senate or the presidency—and the attorney desperately wants to reveal what he knows about the candidate. Is the attorney–client privilege more important than keeping serious criminals from being elected to high office?

My point here is not that we, individually, cannot do the weighing. We can, or at least we do. My point is, rather, that the results we come up with will be a function of what we believe is true and valuable, and that each of us will differ along these lines. And this in turn means that when content regulations of the sort under consideration get evaluated, first by the legislatures (or courts or administrators) that enact them, and then by the courts that hear the challenges to them on free expression grounds, we shall have governmental officials deciding whether a message is protected by freedom of expression either in complete ignorance of what the message is or on the basis of *their* views of what is true and valuable. And having governmental officials restricting the receipt of messages because they do not regard the messages as true or

[31] See Rubenfeld, n. 30 above, 789, 793, 824, for a similar argument against balancing.

sufficiently valuable seems to be inconsistent with the very idea of freedom of expression. For if freedom of expression does not, at a minimum, prevent government from censoring messages because *it* deems them to be of too little value, what *does* it prevent government from doing?

The Supreme Court generally has upheld regulation of speech when the content of the speech could be deemed to be 'owned by another',[32] or 'subject to another's contractual right',[33] and so forth. What is not appreciated is how radically these decisions undermine principle (4). In all these cases the government wishes to prevent receipt of a message because of its content. Of course, the laws under which the government acts are framed in a content-neutral way in terms of the harms the government is trying to prevent—use of another's property, breach of contract, disclosure of confidences, secrets, or private facts, infliction of emotional distress, and so on. *But in every free-speech case government acts to prevent harms that can be described in content-neutral ways.*

The third alternative would be to hold that content regulations of the sort that we are considering *never* violate the right of freedom of expression, the same conclusion reached with respect to Track Two regulations. The reason would be the same reason for excluding Track Two regulations from the scope of freedom of expression: we cannot have a non-partisan assignment of weight to the value of the messages suppressed that can be compared to the legitimate harms the government wishes to prevent.

My conclusion, then, is that content regulations premissed on the direct harms that specific messages cause present us with a stark trilemma: either we must deem the laws protecting confidential communications, privacy, copyright, and so forth *always* or *never* to be violative of freedom of expression, or we must permit government officials to declare what is true and valuable in the realm of ideas and information. None of the choices seems acceptable, but no fourth way is apparent.

Content regulations where the message causes harm in two steps

The non-regulable second step

Sometimes government wishes to prevent receipt of a message, not because receipt will cause harm directly, but because receipt will likely cause the audience to act in ways that cause harm either to others or to the audience itself. In some cases, the government can attempt to prevent the harm only by preventing the message from being received. In others, the government has two chances to prevent the harm: it can attempt to prevent the audience from receiving the message, and, if it fails, it can attempt to prevent the audience from taking harmful action. I take up the first of these possibilities here, and the second in the next subsection.

[32] See *Harper & Row Publishers, Inc v Nation Enterprises* 471 US 539 (1985); *Zacchini v Scripps-Howard Broadcasting Co* 433 US 562 (1977).

[33] See *Cohen v Cowles Media Co* 501 US 663 (1991).

Here are some examples of the first type of message-induced harm. Bob spreads false and vicious rumours about Brenda that if believed will cause the audience to shun her. Bertha tells Bill, falsely, that her potion will cure his cancer and obviate the need for chemotherapy. Brian prays aloud in the presence of Brad, who is a deranged atheist and prone to go on murderous rampages whenever he hears someone proclaiming the existence of God.

In each of these cases the government may want to prevent the audience from receiving the message because it fears that the audience, in response to the message, will act in ways harmful to others or to the audience itself. Moreover, the only tenable way for the government to prevent the harm is to prevent the audience from getting the message. Once the audience has heard the message, whether it then acts in a harmful way is beyond government's ability to control. Those who hear credible lies about Brenda cannot be punished for shunning her. Nor can Bill be reliably prevented from going off his chemotherapy. And Brad, who's deranged, is totally beyond the law's normative control.

Thus, to prevent harm, government must prevent Bob, Bertha, and Brian from getting their messages out. Such attempts fall squarely within principle (4), but do they violate freedom of expression? Should government be precluded from penalizing defamatory speech, dangerously deceptive speech, or speech that causes irresponsible actors to commit harms? What would justify a right that so restricts government?

The regulable second step

Before answering the questions just raised, let us look at the final set of laws regulating messages, those premissed on preventing harms that government may also attempt to prevent by punishing the acts that directly cause them. For example, when government punishes the incitement or solicitation of crime, it seeks to prevent the harmful act—the crime—by preventing the criminal from receiving the message encouraging the crime. It, of course, also punishes the criminal acts themselves. Therefore, it has two bites at the crime-prevention apple.

Because government can punish the audience for any crimes it commits, should it be able to prevent the audience from hearing the messages encouraging those crimes? Or does so preventing the audience contravene the right of freedom of expression? On the one hand, because the acts that the messages encourage are legitimately forbidden, it may appear that any messages that encourage them must be valueless as messages and equally condemnable. On the other hand, if freedom of expression does not protect the audience's right to assess for itself the truth and value of a message that the government deems false and valueless, then it is hard to see what freedom of expression could mean.

Thomas Scanlon, in 1972,[34] and David Strauss, in 1991,[35] put forward as the core principle of freedom of expression one that forbids government from

[34] T. Scanlon, 'A Theory of Freedom of Expression', (1972) 1 *Philosophy and Public Affairs* 204.
[35] Strauss, n. 23 above.

interdicting messages for the reason that those messages might persuade the audience to act in ways the government deems harmful. Scanlon calls his principle the 'Millian Principle'.[36] Strauss calls his the 'Persuasion Principle'.[37] They elaborate and ground them slightly differently, but for my purposes it is what they have in common that is significant.[38]

The first thing to note about the Scanlon–Strauss position is that it can be given both a very broad and a very narrow reading. On the broadest of readings, it forbids government from penalizing solicitations and other encouragements to crime, and it forbids it as well from penalizing defamations and harmful misrepresentations. For if we take the idea that an audience has a right to make its own assessment of messages—the right that grounds the Scanlon–Strauss restriction on the government—then laws against solicitation of crime, defamation, and misrepresentation all appear to violate the right by attempting to pre-empt the audience's assessment of messages.

One might attempt to pare down the reach of the Scanlon–Strauss principle by exempting intentional (knowing or reckless) defamations and misrepresentations from its scope. For after all, if both the government and the speaker believe that X is false, it is difficult to see how we, as audience, have any interest in being told, with apparent sincerity, that X is true, especially when treating X as true will turn out to be harmful to others or to ourselves.[39]

Eliminating intentional misrepresentations does go some distance in reducing the reach of the Scanlon–Strauss principle. However, the principle still invalidates lots of laws. If Barney really believes that his quack potion cures cancer, then the Scanlon–Strauss principle protects his right to convince Betty to take it, even if government is correctly convinced that the remedy is useless and dangerous. Moreover, ordinary criminal solicitations remain protected expression under the Scanlon–Strauss principle.

[36] 'There are certain harms which, although they would not occur but for certain acts of expression, nonetheless cannot be taken as part of a justification for legal restrictions on these acts. These harms are (1) harms to certain individuals which consist in their coming to have false beliefs as a result of those acts of expression; (2) harmful consequences of acts performed as a result of those acts of expression, where the connection between the acts of expression and the subsequent harmful acts consists merely in the fact that the act of expression led the agents to believe (or increased their tendency to believe) these acts to be worth performing.' Scanlon, n. 34 above, 213.

[37] 'The persuasion principle . . . holds that the government may not suppress speech on the ground that the speech is likely to persuade people to do something that the government considers harmful. Put another way, harmful consequences resulting from persuasive effects of speech may not be any part of the justification for restricting speech.' Strauss, n. 23 above, 335.

[38] Scanlon justifies his principle on the ground that equal and autonomous citizens would not cede authority to government to violate it. In other words, Scanlon's principle is one of the legitimacy of *governmental* acts. Scanlon, n. 34 above, 214. Strauss, on the other hand, views his principle as resting on the right not to have one's autonomy, in the sense of control over one's reasoning processes, violated; it is thus a principle that extends beyond governmental action. Strauss, n. 23 above, 354–6. Scanlon later repudiated his principle—T. M. Scanlon, 'Freedom of Expression and Categories of Expression', (1979) 40 *University of Pittsburgh Law Review* 519, 532–4—a repudiation Strauss attributes to its narrow focus on governmental acts. See Strauss, n. 23 above, 356 n. 62.

[39] Strauss does in fact exclude lying because lying, not its suppression, is paradigmatically a violation of autonomy. Strauss, n. 23 above, 335, 366–7.

One might attempt further to pare down the Scanlon–Strauss principle by eliminating from its purview assertions of 'facts'.[40] Facts in the free expression context are frequently contrasted with opinions, on the one hand, and with values, on the other hand. But neither the fact–opinion nor the fact–value distinction seems capable of producing a tenable and robust domain of freedom of expression.

The fact–opinion distinction, which surfaces occasionally in the Supreme Court's defamation jurisprudence,[41] is particularly problematic.[42] Almost any statement of opinion can be viewed as an assertion of facts of various types. If Bob says, 'In my opinion, Brenda is a drunk', rather than merely 'Brenda is a drunk', his 'opinion' can be interpreted as implying the existence of specific but unmentioned facts (what he has observed or heard, what inferences are warranted from the evidence he possesses, and so on). On the other hand, if Bob lays bare all of these facts and then gives his 'opinion' in addition, his opinion adds nothing. It is surely harmless, but for that very reason, no government would care about suppressing it. Therefore, if government fears harm from expressions of opinion, it must be for the reason that those expressions contain implicit assertions of facts that the audience might believe to the detriment of the audience itself or others.

The same problem infects the distinction between assertions of fact and assertions of value. To the extent that government fears the latter, it does so because it fears the audience may be persuaded to adopt the values asserted—again, to the audience's or others' detriment. But to be persuaded by an assertion of value requires assigning that expression the status of something capable of persuading. If expressions of value had the status of, say, burps, they could not persuade an audience to adopt the values so expressed. One does not have to be a realist regarding the ontology of values to regard expressions of value to be heavily larded with implicit factual assertions. And surely it is these implicit 'is' assertions in the assertions of 'ought' that the government fears will persuade and thereby result in harm. For example, when one states that the existing great inequality of income justifies the overthrow of capitalism by force, the statement contains many 'factual' claims, some explicit, most implicit. Such claims include: (1) there exists great inequality of income; (2) capitalism causes it; (3) inequality is a greater injustice than the use of force required to eliminate it will inflict;

40 Both Scanlon and Strauss make such a move. Scanlon excludes statements of fact that cause harm only by enabling the audience to carry out what it otherwise has decided to do on other grounds—statements such as giving out the combination of the bank's vault or the formula for making nerve gas out of common household ingredients. Scanlon, n. 34 above, 211–13. Strauss, on the other hand, at times appears to be excluding all—but only—*false* factual statements from protection by his principle, although his principle might appear to exclude only *intentionally* false statements of fact. See, for example, Strauss, n. 23 above, 366, for an example of Strauss's ambiguity on this point.

41 See *Milkovich v Lorain Journal Co* 497 US 1 (1990) (discussing the fact–opinion distinction and its relevance to the constitutionality of defamation liability).

42 See, for example, F. F. Schauer, 'Language, Truth, and the First Amendment: An Essay in Memory of Harry Canter', (1978) 64 *Virginia Law Review* 263, 276–81.

(4) when a greater injustice can be eliminated by means of a lesser injustice, it is right to eliminate it. The first two claims could be considered straightforwardly 'factual'. The last two are evaluative. If they contain implicit factual claims, perhaps those are the type about which citizens must be able to deliberate. Such implicit factual claims may be that Scripture supports the claim, that Scripture is an inerrant moral guide, and so forth.

Still, I doubt that it will be possible to justify protecting some factual claims—those implicit in evaluative claims—without protecting others. Are we better able to deliberate about the inerrancy of Scripture than the causes of income inequality? I see little hope in any wholesale distinction between false factual and false value claims.[43]

Moreover, suppose government suppresses the doomsday speech of, say, those who oppose genetically engineered foods on the ground that the speech consists of (unintentionally) false and misleading statements of fact that, if believed by the public, will impair the public's ability to deliberate rationally—its autonomy—and lead it to choose courses of action that cause harms (more expensive, less pest-resistant foods; violations of trade treaties; starvation in the Third World). Would we not consider government to be in violation of the right of freedom of expression? If we say that our verdict depends on the truth about genetically engineered foods, have we not given away the game?

Indeed, is not the prohibition of libelling the government—making false claims about its policies and personnel—the paradigm of a violation of freedom of expression?[44] And does not the libel consist of factual assertions, not assertions of value? On the other hand, if the claims *are* false or misleading and capable of causing great harm, how are they to be distinguished from other false or misleading and dangerous factual assertions?

If neither the fact–opinion nor the fact–value distinction carves out a robust but not too robust realm of freedom of expression in cases where government fears the expression will cause harm in two steps, are there any other distinctions that might do the trick? For example, can and should we not distinguish speech that will cause harm before it can be counteracted by opposing speech from speech that can be effectively so countered? One occasionally sees this asserted to justify the Supreme Court's distinction between 'mere advocacy' of harmful acts and 'incitement' to such acts.[45]

This distinction, however, also fails to withstand close analysis. In ordinary, everyday examples of criminal solicitation—which no one seems to regard as protected by a right of freedom of expression—the speaker is soliciting an undercover police officer who needs no counter-speech to be persuaded not to

[43] For an analysis of the fact–opinion and fact–value distinctions that is sensitive to these problems, see Rubenfeld, n. 30 above, 819–22.

[44] Is that not the reason the Alien and Sedition Act is regarded as a central violation of the First Amendment despite their almost contemporaneous enactments? But see pp. 71–2 below.

[45] See *Brandenburg v Ohio* 395 US 444 (1969) (distinguishing constitutionally protected 'advocacy' from constitutionally unprotected 'incitement').

carry out the crime.[46] On the other hand, abstract advocacy of, say, violent overthrow of all capitalist governments may reach audiences who are beyond the reach of counter-speech, or who are impervious to it, and so forth. The advocacy may be open and notorious, or it may be transmitted to only a few people. Effectively countering such advocacy might require large resource allocations—to the detriment of other rights—which government may understandably not wish to make, especially given that it regards what is advocated as wrong and worthless. And considering every argument pro and con, of which there may be an indefinite number, will outstrip the always finite resources of time and attention.[47]

So if speech that can be *effectively* countered by opposing speech defines the realm of freedom of expression, that realm may be quite small, depending upon what resources we believe government must commit to making counter-speech effective. And because withdrawing resources from other goals in order to devote them to countering advocacy of harms is itself harmful (to those goals), the government is put to committing some harms in order to prevent others. Or at least this is so if the right of freedom of expression requires it to employ only counter-speech, and not prohibitions, to combat advocacy of harms. But that means that advocacy of harm, if not prohibited, will be harmful one way or another. It will either be harmful by forcing government to devote resources to counter-speech—which even then might fail to be totally effective. Or it will be harmful by persuading the audience to engage in harmful acts.

So far, then, my conclusion is that the domain of speech that causes harm in two steps cannot be divided into regulable and non-regulable speech by the fact–opinion, fact–value, or counterable-by-speech/not-counterable-by-speech distinctions.

I am equally dubious about other suggestions for dividing up speech that causes harm in two steps into the regulable and non-regulable. Some, for example, exempt incitement and solicitation of harmful acts from the scope of the right of freedom of expression by deeming them to be so intertwined with the harmful acts they incite that they should be deemed harmful acts themselves, not expression.[48] Others would exempt them by calling them, but not abstract advocacy of harmful acts, 'situation-altering', by analogy to speech acts like promising or taking marriage vows.[49] The idea is that, like these other speech acts, incitements and solicitations change the normative situation of their audience and thus are more akin to acts that tangibly alter the environment than to mere speech. Still others place incitement and solicitation of harmful acts on the harmful act rather

[46] Strauss recognizes that ordinary criminal solicitations fall within his principle. See Strauss, n. 23 above, 338–9.

[47] As Strauss recognizes. See ibid. 336–7, 367.

[48] See, for example, Rubenfeld, n. 30 above, 828.

[49] See, for example, K. Greenawalt, *Speech, Crime, and the Uses of Language* (New York: Oxford University Press, 1989), ch. 3.

than the expression side of the ledger by claiming that they trigger action through bypassing rational deliberation and evaluation.[50]

With all respect, I believe that none of these attempts to sever incitement and solicitation from advocacy succeeds. Incitement and solicitation are no more or less 'acts' than any other speech that may cause a harmful response. Nor do they alter the normative situation except to the extent that the audience's values and receptivity to the message allow them to do so, which is true for all expression. And they bypass audience deliberation and evaluation, again, only if the audience permits them to do so. One may deliberate about and evaluate a request to commit a murder to no less extent than one may do so regarding the proposition that capitalism should be overthrown by force and violence.

Principle (4) and message-driven governmental regulation: a tentative conclusion

When receipt of a message is itself directly harmful, and government wishes to regulate the message for that reason, its regulations are either always or never violative of the right of freedom of expression, or so I have tentatively concluded. Any attempt to carve out an intermediate position would require the *government*—first, the legislature in deciding what to regulate, and secondly, in jurisdictions with a judicially enforceable constitutional right of freedom of expression, the courts in deciding which such regulations to permit or strike down—to weigh the value of the messages expressed against the disvalue of the harms they cause. But such message evaluation by the government seems deeply inconsistent with any conception of freedom of expression.

When receipt of a message causes harm in two steps, but the government cannot effectively regulate the second step, then with the exception of messages that the speakers know to be false or deceptive, which I view as unproblematically regulable, I see no difference in terms of freedom of expression from messages that cause harm directly.

When the second, harmful step by the audience *is* regulable—as with advocacy, incitement, and solicitation of harmful acts—then the choice seems to be between regarding all governmental interdiction as violative of freedom of expression, even if no other regulations of messages are, or treating governmental interdiction of such messages as no different from all other regulations that fall under principle (4). Moreover, even if the first of these alternatives is correct, government might still legitimately regulate messages that cause harm through persuading morally responsible audiences to act harmfully if government's *reason* for regulating were fear that the message might persuade members of the audience who are *not* morally responsible actors—the immature, the insane, and so forth.[51]

[50] Strauss views some acts of incitement as falling outside his principle because they are designed to induce action by bypassing rational deliberation. See Strauss, n. 23 above, 338–9.

[51] For example, even if a television programme depicting a violent act could not be censored because of concern that criminals who are morally responsible for their acts might decide to ape its

We are left, then, with either a right of freedom of expression that is counter-intuitively capacious and covers the entire domain of principle (4), or one that is counter-intuitively narrow and covers, at most, those messages that cause harm by persuading responsible audiences, and *only* responsible audiences, to act harmfully. Paradoxically, finding a right of freedom of expression that feels 'just right' in terms of its scope requires the very evaluations of messages that any conception of freedom of expression would view as its central evil.

A brief look at Track Three: government speech and subsidies of approved expression

If principle (4) defines the core of freedom of expression—governmental regulation of speech because of concern with the messages audiences may receive, or what Tribe labels Track One regulations[52]—how should we view speech by the government itself, or speech by private parties that the government subsidizes, what I call Track Three governmental acts?[53] Track Three consists of all 'expression' by governmental officials that is within the scope of their employment, ranging from propaganda supporting governmental policy, to public education, to message-selection by public libraries, museums, and theatres, and to routine information conveyance by bureaucrats. It also consists of subsidies to scholars and artists who promote governmentally preferred views or pursue governmentally preferred research, or subsidies to governmentally favoured speakers and topics, subsidies that can take the form either of money and similar resources or, importantly, of exemptions from regulations that apply to other messages.[54] (The line between the 'offer' of a subsidy and the coercive, regulatory 'threat' of a penalty is, of course, much controverted; wherever it is located, my concern

content, the concern that some psychotic may do so might take censorship out of the domain of the Scanlon–Strauss principle and render it just another example of message-driven regulations designed to prevent harm. And because *any* message *might* cause those who are not morally responsible for their conduct to act harmfully, the Scanlon–Strauss principle is threatened with total irrelevance.

As an aside, this point connects with a point I made in an earlier article to illustrate why freedom of expression cannot turn on the value of any particular item of expression (as opposed to government's reasons for regulating): any particular item of expression can convey a multitude of messages to different audiences. Thus, a medical textbook might be read most frequently by voyeurs looking for 'dirty pictures', while a pornographic movie might be viewed primarily by persons engaging in serious sociological and psychological research. See L. Alexander, 'Low Value Speech', (1989) 83 *North Western University Law Review* 547.

[52] Tribe, n. 2 above, §12–2, 791.

[53] See Alexander, n. 3 above, 926.

[54] Sometimes the Supreme Court allows regulatory preferences for certain classes of speakers or certain topics. See, for example, *Minnesota State Bd for Community Colleges v Knight*, n. 9 above; *Perry Educ Ass'n v Perry Local Educators' Ass'n*, n. 7 above; *Greer v Spock* 424 US 828 (1976); *Lehman v City of Shaker Heights* 418 US 298 (1974). Sometimes it does not. See, for example, *Carey v Brown* 447 US 455 (1980); *Police Dept v Mosley* 408 US 92 (1972); *Southeastern Promotions Ltd v Conrad* 420 US 546 (1975); and a large number of cases striking down rules disfavouring access by speakers on religious topics.

here is with the subsidy side, not the coercive side, which was the subject of the prior section.[55])

Does Track Three implicate the right of freedom of expression? It surely involves governmental assessments of the truth and value of messages and the government's desire to affect what people believe, so in that respect it resembles Track One. On the other hand, Track Three, unlike Track One, does not involve the restriction of anyone's liberty to produce message effects, or so it might appear.[56]

There are two reasons to think that despite this point of difference from Track One, Track Three does implicate freedom of expression. First, we would think it problematic if public school teachers instructed their pupils on, say, the superiority of the Republican Party or socialized medicine. Likewise, we would think it problematic that a public library purchased only pro-capitalist books.[57] Perhaps the unease we would feel would not arise from concern about freedom of expression, but from concern reflecting some other value. But the unease is some evidence, I believe, that Track Three is not outside the ambit of freedom of expression.

Beyond our unease with these types of governmental partisanship, there is a second reason to think Track Three and Track One are not neatly distinguishable in terms of freedom of expression. That is because governmental speech and subsidies *do* in a real sense restrict liberty. Governmental speech and subsidies employ resources that come, of course, from private citizens and leave them with fewer resources to devote to propagating their own views. Now this may seem trivial in an advanced Western nation where the percentage of anyone's tax bill traceable to governmental speech activities is tiny. Imagine, however, a very poor nation whose citizens have very little in the way of surplus monies available to publish and to broadcast, and assume that the government of that country, fearful of dissent, taxed those resources to support a massive governmental propaganda machine. Would we not in such a case believe that the citizens' liberty *was* being restricted by the taxation, and being restricted to affect what messages were being received?

I shall not attempt to settle the relation between Track Three and freedom of expression. Government could not operate without some governmental speech, a point suggesting that not all of Track Three can be inconsistent with freedom of expression (unless the latter demands anarchy). On the other hand, because governmental speech does require the scarce resources of the citizenry, I think it implausible that *no* Track Three cases implicate freedom of expression.

[55] For recent illumination on the offer–threat distinction and the concept of coercion, see M. N. Berman, 'Coercion Without Baselines: Unconstitutional Conditions in Three Dimensions', (2001) 90 *Georgetown Law Journal* 1.

[56] Whenever, however, the government restricts access to information, not to guard a sensitive secret, but to manipulate the public's beliefs, it *is* restricting liberty to produce message effects and is therefore on Track One.

[57] See, for example, *Board of Education v Pico*, n. 11 above (striking down removal of books from public school library).

A FOOTNOTE ON PRIVATE REGULATION OF SPEECH AND FREEDOM OF EXPRESSION

Does principle (4) apply, not just to governmental regulations, but to private restrictions on others' liberties as well? If Megacorp refuses to hire anyone who supports the Democratic Party—in order that its market clout may affect political messages and bring about the Republican policies it favours—is the right to freedom of expression violated? If Megafarms prevents, through use of the trespass laws, union organizers from gaining access to its farm workers—because it fears the effects of their messages—has it violated the right of freedom of expression of the union and the farm workers? If Mediagiant orders its reporters to slant their stories in favour of the Democrats, on pain of dismissal, is it violating the reporters' or the audience's right of freedom of expression?

On the one hand, such private entities, backed by the laws of property, contract, and so forth, are surely acting like governments within the domain those laws carve out for them. On their property, or within the scope of their employment, others are being restricted from conveying messages in ways that would be paradigmatic freedom of expression violations were the restrictions imposed by government.[58]

On the other hand, the right of freedom of expression against government would be worthless if it did not entitle private persons to affect messages as they want. A newspaper publisher cannot be prevented by government from giving her slant to the news, and this seems to entail that government must permit the publisher to invoke Track Two laws—contract, property, tort, and so forth—to get her views out, even if this means that her reporters, *qua* employees, are denied any right of freedom of expression to ignore her orders with impunity.

There is a dilemma here. Private restrictions on speech, enforced through content-neutral Track Two laws, can have as great or greater a magnitude of message effects—what gets said by whom, to whom, and with what impact—as governmental restrictions on messages. Indeed, this point about private restrictions is just a corollary of the point made earlier that Track Two laws may have more important message effects than the message-targeted laws that fall under principle (4). But if freedom of expression were implicated by the Track Two laws that give private persons, organizations, and corporations the ability to regulate speech within the domains those laws carve out, then freedom of expression would always appear on both sides of every contest. Every set of Track Two laws will produce different private messages and message effects. And every incursion by government into this domain designed to alter those message effects would come under principle (4) and involve government in deciding which messages should be heard more and which less.

[58] See *Marsh v Alabama*, n. 4 above (striking down the trespassing conviction of a religious pamphleteer distributing literature on the streets of a company town); *Lloyd Corp. v Tanner* 407 US 551 (1972) (permitting a private shopping centre to invoke trespass law to ban pamphleteers); *Hudgens v NLRB*, n. 4 above (permitting a private shopping centre to bar picketers).

Perhaps there are some Track Two laws that give so much power to private persons that the latter should be viewed as equivalent to governments for purposes of freedom of expression. Just as the government often acts no differently from how private employers act—and is for that reason permitted by the First Amendment to restrict its employees' speech[59]—so also may private employers (or landowners) at some point look indistinguishable from governments and become subject to similar legal constraints.[60] But the jurisprudence of determining when an otherwise private actor becomes 'governmental' will, I suspect, be quite difficult to rationalize.[61]

PHILOSOPHICAL FOUNDATIONS OF FREEDOM OF EXPRESSION: LIBERALISM, EPISTEMIC ABSTENTION, AND RULE-CONSEQUENTIALISM

The right to freedom of expression appears problematic through and through. Its potential scope is defined by principle (4), which focuses on whether government's reasons for regulating include a concern with what messages audiences receive. But that scope is either too broad, rendering almost all content-based governmental regulations—and perhaps all governmental speech and speech subsidies—violative of freedom of expression, or it is indeterminate and incapable of principled delineation. Moreover, it leaves Track Two laws entirely untouched despite the high magnitude of their message effects, and indeed, paradoxically, it itself prevents government from remedying what it takes to be the untoward message effects of Track Two laws.[62]

In this section I shall attempt to diagnose the cause of the failure to find a cogent and defensible principle defining a right to freedom of expression. I believe that such failure is part and parcel of the failure of liberalism to provide a justification for tolerating illiberal views—which toleration is definitive of liberalism. The great liberal freedoms—freedom of religion, association, and expression—are deeply paradoxical because they rest on the notion of epistemic abstinence[63]—the idea that liberal government cannot impose its views of the

[59] See, for example, *Connick v Meyers* 461 US 138 (1983) (upholding dismissal of a public employee for disruptive speech activities). See generally R. C. Post, 'Between Governance and Management: The History and Theory of the Public Forum', (1987) 34 *UCLA Law Review* 1713.

[60] See *Marsh v Alabama*, n. 4 above.

[61] Compare *Marsh v Alabama*, ibid., with *Hudgens v NLRB*, n. 4 above. See generally L. Alexander, 'The Public/Private Distinction and Constitutional Limits on Private Power', (1993) 10 *Constitutional Commentary* 361.

[62] Any principle that governs the purposes for which actors act but not the effects of those acts presents deep theoretical problems. Just as no account of culpability can be divorced from an account of wrongdoing, neither can a concern for the purposes of actions be divorced from a concern with the effects of actions. See L. Alexander, 'Rules, Rights, Options, and Time', (2000) 6 *Legal Theory* 391. Nonetheless, freedom of expression appears to demand abstinence from the evaluation of message effects, leaving only purposes to evaluate.

[63] The term was coined by Joseph Raz. See J. Raz, 'Facing Diversity: The Case of Epistemic Abstinence', (1990) 19 *Philosophy and Public Affairs* 5.

Good on dissenters; that *qua* liberal government, it cannot know the Good. But the idea that liberalism cannot take its own side in an argument is an impossibility. Liberal government cannot help but be partisan, which means that liberalism as governmental non-partisanship (neutrality) is an impossibility.

Now much has been written on this paradoxical aspect of liberalism as it applies to freedom of religion.[64] And there is a growing body of literature on the paradoxical relation between liberalism and illiberal associations and groups.[65] But with the exception of Stanley Fish, no one seems to have noticed that the same paradox infects that third liberal bulwark, the right of freedom of expression.[66]

Any philosophical account of political morality will, perforce, take a stand on what is true, right, and valuable and what is not. It will be 'partisan' in favour of its own conclusions. Thus, it must regard as error and possibly malign those ideas that it rejects.

Liberalism in any of its renditions is no different. If liberalism is the correct political morality, all positions inconsistent with its tenets are incorrect. There is no neutral ground to stand on in these matters.

So if someone advocates illiberal positions, and the government fears that an audience may be persuaded to adopt those positions and cause wrongful harms as a consequence, government cannot be both committed to liberalism and agnostic about the positions advocated, nor can it view such agnosticism as a justification for refraining from suppressing the expression in question.

On the other hand, if a liberal government were to suppress speech because it feared the audience would be led to illiberal conclusions, in what sense would that government be 'liberal'? For the core of anything recognizable as freedom of expression does seem to be what Justice Jackson said it was, namely, the prohibition of establishing an official orthodoxy on matters of opinion.[67]

What about the autonomy of those whom the government fears will misassess the truth or value of a message? Does not censorship of such messages violate the audience's deliberative autonomy, and cannot a right against such violations of autonomy generate a substantial right of freedom of expression?

[64] See, for example, S. Fish, 'Mission Impossible: Settling the Just Bounds Between Church and State', (1997) 97 *Columbia Law Review* 225; L. Alexander, 'Liberalism, Religion, and the Unity of Epistemology', (1993) 30 *San Diego Law Review* 763.

[65] See, for example, L. Alexander, 'Illiberalism All the Way Down: Illiberal Groups and Two Conceptions of Liberalism', (2001) 12 *Journal of Contemporary Legal Issues* 265; M. D. Rosen, 'The Outer Limits of Community Self-Governance in Residential Associations, Municipalities, and Indian Country: A Liberal Theory', (1998) 84 *Virginia Law Review* 1057; L. A. Swaine, 'How Ought Liberal Democracies to Treat Theocratic Communities?', (2001) 111 *Ethics* 302; N. M. Stolzenberg, '"He Drew a Circle that Shut Me Out": Assimilation, Indoctrination, and the Paradox of a Liberal Education', (1993) 106 *Harvard Law Review* 581. See also B. Barry, *Culture and Equality* (Cambridge, Mass.: Harvard University Press, 2001).

[66] See S. Fish, *There's No Such Thing as Free Speech and It's a Good Thing, Too* (New York: Oxford University Press, 1994).

[67] See *West Virginia State Board of Education v Barnette*, n. 23 above, 642.

I believe that focusing on autonomy merely replays the paradox with a different label attached. First, most regulations under principle (4)—though designed to prevent direct harm (to privacy, secrecy, confidentiality, ownership, contractual rights, and emotional peace)—do not involve violations of audience autonomy. The harms these regulations are meant to prevent will occur no matter how the audience deliberates about the messages.

Secondly, even where government does seek to prevent harm through audience action taken in response to the message, *autonomy is on both sides of the equation*. On the one hand, the government is restricting the audience's ability to receive messages because it fears audience misassessment—arguably, a case of disrespect of the audience's deliberative autonomy. On the other hand, government believes that because the message is wrong (in the facts or values it asserts), it will only be misassessed by the audience because of some defect in the audience's ability to deliberate rationally about the message, a defect that impairs the audience's autonomy. If the message asserts a fact that is untrue, then the audience's ability to assess the situation rationally is no different from a case in which someone deliberately lies to it. For the harm that a lie does to an audience's autonomy is not due to its being a *lie* but rather to its being *untrue*. If the message makes a value claim that is false, then it will only persuade its audience to the extent that the audience is mistaken about matters of fact or matters of logic, which again will suggest defects in the audience's autonomy. Suppression of messages that will cause audiences to misassess what to do then can be seen—and from government's perspective, will be seen—as enhancing rather than violating the audience's autonomy.

Put differently, autonomy, like the liberalism that gives it pride of place, is a Janus-faced value that looks both at the process of belief-formation and at the substance of what is believed. Bypassing the individual's own rational deliberation and brainwashing her appears inconsistent with autonomy, even if she is brainwashed to hold correct views. But the individual who misunderstands his world both factually and normatively also seems to lack autonomy, no matter how independent the deliberations that led him to error.

Of course, even the most developed political philosophy will fail to answer some questions about the world—how safe are the 2001 Toyotas, how many genes are on the chimpanzee's genome, who killed Jon Benet Ramsey, and so forth. And for these questions, it may indeed be the case that government regulation of messages will impede the search for answers. Uncensored exchange of research data, freedom to publish academic articles in peer-reviewed journals, and investigative reporting by the news media all probably usefully contribute to the production of specific, retail truths, at least relative to centralized control by government of all scientific research, academic publication, and investigation of wrongdoing. But these retail truths about the best procedures for answering certain kinds of questions cannot be generalized into anything recognizable as a general right to freedom of expression. They represent practices that have a rule-consequentialist structure of justification specific to particular kinds of questions and to particular cultures, eras, and technologies. Rather than representing a general human right that transcends political, cultural, and historical boundaries and pre-exists any particular institutional arrangements (such as adversarial trials, democratic voting, or university research), retail, rule-consequentialist justifications for particular freedoms of expression have a 'good for this time and destination only' quality.[68]

Some miscellaneous approaches to freedom of expression: governmental fallibility, democracy, and the right to speak the truth

Governmental fallibility and freedom of expression

John Stuart Mill in *On Liberty* famously argued against censorship of false (or immoral) opinions on the ground, among others, that those opinions might turn out to be true, in whole or in part.[69] And given what we know of governments, the chances are quite high that government, in suppressing the receipt of false opinion, will also suppress a lot of well-founded opinions.

There are two points to be made regarding the argument for free expression based on fallibility. First, fallibility does not provide any justification for freedom of expression in cases where messages are suppressed for reasons other than their falsity. For example, no Track Two regulations fall within this justification. Nor do regulations under principle (4) that are aimed at one-step harms such as those to privacy, confidentiality, ownership, and so forth.

Secondly, it would be difficult to argue that those regulations that *do* come within the justification—those designed to prevent harms that require two steps (receipt of the message plus action taken in response to it)—should *all* be immune from government regulation. As Woody Allen in *Sleeper* reminds us, even claims like 'meat larded with saturated fat is good for your health' might turn out to be true.[70] So, too, I suppose, might claims that free trade impoverishes, or that Stalinism is the key to prosperity. Are we supposed to leave all such claims unregulated on the ground that government is fallible in distinguishing the true from the false?

Notice, too, that if government's admitted fallibility regarding which opinions are true is an argument against its regulation of messages, it is also an argument

[68] The same point can be made about other rule-consequentialist theories of freedom of expression. They must first posit some valuable consequence that freedom of expression advances—e.g. better information, better political decision-making, autonomy, etc.—and then show why freedom of expression, appropriately defined, *uniquely* furthers these values. I believe that all such theories fail as *general* theories of freedom of expression, though they may justify specific freedoms of expression in specific cultures and eras. See L. Alexander and P. Horton, 'The Impossibility of a Free Speech Principle', (1984) 78 *North Western University Law Review* 1319.

[69] See John Stuart Mill, *On Liberty*, ed. E. Rapaport (Indianapolis: Hackett, 1978), ch. 2.

[70] *Sleeper* (Metro-Goldwyn Mayer/United Artists 1973).

against all other regulations. For any set of laws expresses government's opinions about the value of various activities and the interests they affect, and those opinions may be wrong. Nor is it a response to this point to argue that regulating conduct and regulating messages are different in that regulation of conduct leaves open the possibility of assessing the regulation and arguing for its repeal, whereas regulating messages interferes with assessment and argument themselves. As I pointed out in discussing Track Two regulations, regulating conduct deprives us of information about how the world would look without the regulation; and the absence of such information may well affect the argument over the wisdom of the regulation. Moreover, regulating conduct has enormous message effects—what gets said by whom, to whom, and with what effect—which means that any set of laws will affect its own assessment.

Is a right of freedom of expression derivable from a right to be governed democratically?

It is commonplace to argue that a right of freedom of expression is a corollary to democratic government.[71] In order to govern ourselves, it is necessary that we be free to discuss all matters that bear upon policy choices and elections, or so it is said. For some who hold such a view, the resultant right of freedom of expression is quite capacious.[72] For others, it is narrowly cabined to 'political speech'.[73]

Now the 'argument from democracy' for freedom of expression has some well-known difficulties, aside from deciding upon its scope. As Frederick Schauer points out, freedom of expression is thought to be a right *against* governmental regulations even when those regulations have been democratically enacted.[74] In other words, freedom of expression is thought to oppose and trump democratic decision-making, at least when the latter concerns freedom of expression itself. Therefore, if freedom of expression is a corollary of democratic decision-making, then it will appear on both sides of the balance whenever democratic governments restrict expression.

Moreover, although the subject is far too large for adequate treatment here, I am sceptical that there *is* a moral right to untrammelled democratic decision-making.[75] There may be a moral right to that form of government that is most likely in fact to enact measures that reflect the moral rights we possess. And in

[71] See, for example, R. Bork, 'Neutral Principle and Some First Amendment Problems', (1971) 47 *Indiana Law Journal*; A. Meiklejohn, *Free Speech and Its Relation to Self-Government* (New York: Harper, 1948).

[72] See, for example, Meiklejohn, n. 71 above; M. H. Redish, 'The Value of Free Speech', (1982) 130 *University of Pennsylvania Law Review* 591.

[73] See, for example, Bork, n. 71 above.

[74] See F. Schauer, *Free Speech: A Philosophical Enquiry* (New York: Cambridge University Press, 1982), 40–4.

[75] See L. Alexander, 'Jeremy Waldron on Democracy and Constitutionalism: A Sceptical Appraisal', Paper presented at the 2001 Annual Meeting of the American Political Science Association (on file with the author); L. Alexander, 'Are Procedural Rights Derivative Substantive Rights?', (1998) 17 *Law and Philosophy* 19, 36–42.

many times and places, that form of government may be democratic, though probably not purely majoritarian. Moreover, some types of freedom of expression may be instrumental in helping some forms of government do what is morally best. But it is a contingent, empirical matter just what form of government, with what rights of freedom of expression, will best realize the moral rights we in fact possess.

Is the right of freedom of expression not a right to spread error, but a right to speak the truth?

The saying, 'I disapprove of what you say, but I will defend to the death your right to say it', commonly misattributed to Voltaire,[76] reflects perhaps the common understanding of the right of freedom of expression—namely, that it is a right to voice error. I have attempted to show that it is difficult to construct a case for protecting false statements, whether they be labelled statements of fact, statements of opinion, or statements of value.[77]

Perhaps, however, freedom of expression is better conceived as a right to express the truth rather than a right to express error. For the principal defence of the Sedition Act of 1798, supported by many of those who had earlier in the decade placed the First Amendment in the Constitution, was that the Act punished only false statements about government malfeasance.[78]

Could it be, then, that a right to speak the truth, rather than a right to voice error, may be the notion that best undergirds freedom of expression? The former is surely an easier right to defend than the latter. Government's motives are no doubt quite a bit less trustworthy when it comes to true statements about its misdeeds than when it suppresses only false statements. And correct information is almost always an aid to autonomous decision-making.

Nevertheless, much of Track One is concerned with regulations of statements that are harmful even if, or in some cases only if, they are true. Harms to ownership, privacy, contractual rights, sensibilities, and confidentiality either do not depend on the truth of what is expressed, or depend upon its being true rather than false.

Therefore, a right to express the truth has some bite to it. However, it is a less robust right than freedom of expression is normally thought to be. Moreover,

[76] The saying was invented as a reflection of Voltaire's attitude by Evelyn Beatrice Hall under the pseudonym of S. G. Tallentyre in *The Friends of Voltaire* (London: Smith, Elder, 1906).

[77] See text accompanying nn. 40–2 above.

[78] The Sedition Act of 1798, which made libelling the government a crime, also provided that truth was a defence. Supporters of the Act's constitutionality expressed the belief that such a defence was sufficient to make the Act constitutional. Opponents believed that the Act would chill valuable speech because the truth of 'opinions' could not be proved. See L. W. Levy, *Legacy of Suppression* (Cambridge, Mass.: Belknap Press, 1960), 258–63. The latter view emerged victorious in 1964 when the Supreme Court found ordinary defamation law violative of free speech when applied to protect public officials; *New York Times Co v Sullivan* 376 US 254 (1964). See generally H. Kalven, Jr., 'The *New York Times* Case: A Note on "the Central Meaning of the First Amendment"', (1964) *Supreme Court Review* 191, 204–7.

even *its* status is problematic when government seeks to protect against harms inflicted in one step by speech, for such harms usually do not follow from the falsity of the speech but only from the fact of it.

Conclusion

I have searched for the scope and ground of a human right of freedom of expression and failed. The scope of such a right must be defined by principle (4), which includes all regulations intended to affect the messages audiences receive. That principle, though capacious, excludes all Track Two laws, which in sum have message effects far greater than laws within the scope of principle (4).

On the other hand, principle (4) could invalidate all laws intended to affect messages that directly cause harm—to privacy, sensibility, confidentiality, and ownership—as well as to laws designed to prevent harms from false or deceptive messages, messages that taken broadly include advocacy of illegal acts and libels of the government in addition to more garden-variety lies and deceptions. And principle (4) would seem to affect as well government speech and speech-subsidies.

Paring down principle (4) so that it invalidates only some but not all regulations within its scope has been the preoccupation of a multitude of free expression theorists, none of whom has come up with a theory that is persuasive. I attribute this failure to the philosophical paradox that bedevils liberalism: liberalism demands, impossibly, agnosticism about its own imperatives. Freedom of expression, one of the flagship values of liberalism, reflects that paradoxical demand.

Stanley Fish famously says of his similar post-modern, anti-foundationalist critique of liberalism and its attendant values that they may leave everything where it was.[79] And, of course, he is correct in the sense that what is true of liberalism is true of any of its opponents. They are as much ideological constructs as liberalism. In one sense, absolutely nothing follows from the post-modern critique.

But, of course, that is not entirely accurate. Something *does* follow. The critique is deflationary. It takes the wind out of liberalism's sails, even if it provides nary a breeze to liberalism's competitors. It induces—not more toleration, as Fish fiercely and correctly denies[80]—but a sort of normative torpor.[81]

[79] See, for example, Fish, n. 66 above, 20–1; S. Fish, 'Almost Pragmatism: Richard Posner's Jurisprudence', (1990) 57 *University of Chicago Law Review* 1447, 1464–9. See also L. Alexander, 'What We Do, and Why We Do It', (1993) 45 *Stanford Law Review* 1885, 1896–8.

[80] Fish, n. 66 above.

[81] See G. Sher, 'But I Could Be Wrong', (2001) 18 *Social Philosophy and Policy* 64, 65: 'My awareness that I would now have different moral convictions if I had had a different upbringing or different experiences . . . makes it . . . *harder* for me to act on my moral convictions when these conflict with the moral convictions of others.'

If the critique were completely inconsequential, it would be hard to see why Fish would so often and fervently push it.[82]

In the end, I find my results terribly disquieting, for I count myself as a dyed-in-the-wool liberal and a champion of freedom of expression. I *know* that those tinhorn despots who jail their opposition are violating the opposition's human right of freedom of expression. On the other hand, I worry that my conclusion reflects only my dislike of tinhorn despots, or worse, only my dislike of their other policies. And I worry even more that if I were in their shoes, and I were quite certain that speech opposing me were both in error and harmful to the common weal, I might shut down opposition speech. Like one of those thirty-second attack ads that do not fool me, speech opposing me may fool others.

[82] See L. Alexander, 'Theory's A What Comes Natcherly', (2001) 37 *San Diego Law Review* 777, 781.

3

Human Rights Concepts in Australian Political Debate

MARK A. NOLAN and PENELOPE J. OAKES

Introduction

In this chapter we report empirical findings that suggest Australians assert human rights as one of a number of possible political responses to felt harm and perceived injustice. Australians' responses to the existence of a mandatory sentencing scheme, and the exclusion of lesbians and single women from using assisted reproductive technology, are reported. Despite the absence of an Australian bill of rights, respondents were motivated to use human rights arguments to press social justice claims. This willingness to use rights concepts challenges us to consider how to best provide mechanisms of human rights protection that remain relevant to the needs of aggrieved persons. The chapter begins by describing human rights use as a psychological response to injustice and is then followed by a discussion of the empirical findings.

Theoretical approach

Human rights as instruments of justice

We consider that asserting human rights is one of many possible political responses to perceived injustice. Reliance on human rights arguments need not take the form of making a formal complaint to a legal institution.[1] Once injustice is perceived, a victim and/or activist faces a variety of decisions regarding how they respond to that injustice.[2] One of these decisions is to determine whether human rights arguments can or should be used at all. When human rights rhetoric is chosen as the means to pursue justice, the use of rights will be shaped further by understandings of the concept and purpose of human rights in society. These understandings of the purpose of human rights help to determine the role

[1] See Otto, Ch. 14 below, regarding indirect forms of human rights implementation.

[2] This argument was initially developed when considering the social-psychological literature on use of justice norms: M. A. Nolan and P. J. Oakes, 'The Selection of Justice Norms in the Human Rights Context: Social Beliefs, Justice Norms and Activist Identity', Paper presented at the Spring Workshop in Social Psychology on Justice and Fairness, School of Psychological Science, La Trobe University, 27–8 Nov. 2000 (copy on file with authors).

human rights will play in social debates over justice. For example, the purpose of human rights may be understood as the protection of individual interests equally within a nation-state. In contrast, human rights could be understood as protections of vulnerable sub-groups[3] within that broader collective.

Campbell has claimed that human rights can be used too much as responses to social injustice.[4] In this work, Campbell suggests that the use of human rights arguments ought not be allowed to 'eclipse' the use of non-rights justice language to press political claims. One reason for this concern is that using human rights arguments risks undermining the role of elected governments by giving too much power to judges as interpreters of rights rhetoric. Or, as Campbell articulates the objection in this volume, there is a 'dangerous assumption that the only effective way of bringing morality into politics is to turn judges into politicians and replace politicians with lawyers'.

However, our claim is that the human rights discourse is a specific example of a broader discourse of justice. We reject the notion that human rights is a discourse of law and that justice is a discourse of politics.[5] Instead, *both* human rights and justice rhetoric can be used as instruments of political and moral influence. The data reported below suggest that activists do not slavishly prefer human rights language to justice language. The decision to claim a rights violation is not an automatic result of perceived disadvantage, even when rights language capable of describing an injustice is available for use. Activists can be shown to consider strategically how best to represent an injustice in a particular political context. In some cases, human rights are judged to be the best means by which to pursue justice.

The studies reported in this chapter cannot answer the question of whether the use of human rights rhetoric undermines the role of elected governments in our political system. However, results of a third study not reported here in full are worthy of mention. This additional research suggests that concerns about restrictions on national sovereignty are not always paramount when people consider the UN's human rights monitoring roles.[6] Instead, values of equality, freedom, dignity, international harmony, and cooperation were endorsed when participants considered the details of the UN human rights protection regime as it operates in Australia. As a result of this value-orientation, participants suggested that the Australian Government was right to submit to international human rights compliance monitoring, and they further believed that this international monitoring of domestic issues was fair.

[3] Here we tend to avoid the term 'collective rights', preferring the term 'sub-group rights'. The latter phrase better describes the way subordinate groups within a national collective may identify and define their sub-group's rights.

[4] T. Campbell, 'Human Rights and the Partial Eclipse of Justice', in A. Soeteman (ed.), *Pluralism and Law* (Dordrecht: Kluwer, 2001).

[5] Ibid.

[6] See Study 1 in M. Nolan and P. Oakes, 'A Study of Australians' Value-Laden and Identity-Mediated Responses to the UN's Treaty Compliance Mechanisms', in preparation.

In psychological terms, this approach to conceptualizing human rights behaviour is consistent with some identity psychology[7] applied to inter-group contexts in which claims of injustice commonly occur.[8] We suggest that asserting human rights is one of many possible strategies that individuals and sub-group members in Australia use to assert commonalities, entitlement, and desert. As such, human rights are socially mediated, justice concepts that people internalize and use in political argument.[9] This approach is shaped by political, legal, and psychological realism, and is similar to the study of human rights by some political scientists.[10]

This is to admit that psychological representations of rights are subjectively constructed to some degree. Representations of rights and understandings of the purpose of rights are shaped by ideologies, circumstance, comparison, and the perceived identity relationships within inter-group contexts. These construals of human rights are debated and may change. Yet, at the same time, they are bounded by social-psychological processes and politico-legal realities. This constraint prevents these representations of rights from spiralling automatically into uncertainty and vagueness. Therefore, such representations of justice concepts (i.e. of human rights) may be at odds with philosophical, legal, and political prescriptions of what makes a good theory of justice and rights—but these are the cognitions Australians use to make sense of injustice.

Why equality is not enough

Human rights may be used by sub-groups seeking to emphasize the moral importance of equality. However, other moral values such as liberty, need, equity, and affirmation can also be pursued by the use of human rights arguments. As Campbell claims, *both* equal worth *and* unequal worthiness are necessary moral values that ground a comprehensive theory of justice.[11] As

[7] A set of social-psychological theories of personal and social identity processes and inter-group behaviour. Principally, social identity theory: H. Tajfel and J. C. Turner, 'An Integrative Theory of Intergroup Behaviour', in W. G. Austin and S. Worchel (eds.), *The Social Psychology of Intergroup Relations* (Monterey, Calif.: Brooks/Cole, 1979); H. Tajfel and J. C. Turner, 'The Social Identity Theory of Intergroup Behaviour', in S. Worchel and W. G. Austin (eds.), *Psychology of Intergroup Relations* (Chicago: Nelson-Hall, 1986); and, self-categorization theory: J. C. Turner, M. A. Hogg, P. J. Oakes, S. Reicher, and M. Wetherell, *Rediscovering the Social Group* (Oxford: Basil Blackwell, 1987).

[8] M. J. Platow, M. Wenzel, and M. A. Nolan, 'The Importance of Social Identity and Self-Categorization Processes for Creating and Responding to Fairness', in S. A. Haslam, D. van Knippenberg, M. J. Platow, and N. Ellemers (eds.), *Social Identity at Work: Developing Theory for Organizational Practice* (New York: Psychology Press, 2003), 261.

[9] See work by social psychologists using social representations theory to demonstrate the cognitive representation of human rights law by the lay perceiver: for example, W. Doise, D. Spini, and A. Clémence, 'Human Rights Studied as Social Representations in a Cross-National Context', (1999) 29 *European Journal of Social Psychology* 1; M. Herrera, M. Lavallée, and W. Doise, 'Human Rights and Politics: A Social Representational Analysis of Political Positioning During the 1995 Quebec Sovereignty Campaign', (2000) 3 *Group Processes and Intergroup Relations* 25.

[10] D. Beetham (ed.), *Politics and Human Rights* (Cambridge: Basil Blackwell, 1995).

[11] See his 'equal worth and unequal worthiness' theory of justice in T. Campbell, *Justice* (Basingstoke: Macmillan Education, 2001), and in Campbell, n. 4 above.

such, human rights, as means towards the end goal of justice, can be used to emphasize both equal worthiness as well as equal worth. Some sub-groups in Australia would no doubt agree that, even when equal treatment occurs, unequal worthiness is often ignored at the risk of creating or perpetuating differential need. In this sense, the equality motive does not completely describe the psychological motivation for pressing sub-group justice claims. Appeal to a sole, abstract, and uncontextualized value such as equality[12] will not psychologically satisfy all harmed claimants or their supporters.

Elaborating here, we suggest that an aggrieved individual or sub-group may demand that the decision-makers and others respect difference, and be prepared to celebrate that difference. Therefore, victims and activists may expect that a system of human rights protection would allow a claim of relative sub-group disadvantage as well as a claim of violated individual rights. This means it is important to understand which values guide the expression of the justice motive in particular contexts; including the use of human rights as 'instruments of justice'[13] aimed at achieving equality, and/or the legitimization of sub-group identities within a diverse society.

We aim to understand these identity processes and motives, and suggest that equality is not enough. This is because there are some sub-group identities that are not, and cannot, be shared by all Australians. If these identities are harmed, a justice response based solely on achieving 'equal treatment for all Australians' may not address the psychological harm caused to the victim's sense of self. We include in this category of non-universal identities, identities such as racial identity, sexuality orientation, and indigenous identity. For example, an equality-driven response to the suffering of, say, an indigenous Australian may risk failing to address the psychological cause of distress: the failure to address harmed 'indigenous' identity since the victim must ignore the harmed identity and be content that they receive the same treatment as all 'Australians'. Equality is not always psychologically fitting in these circumstances. This type of response may neither address the harmed aspect of complex identities (for example, harm as an indigenous Australian), nor work to fulfil satisfactorily Australia's international human rights obligations. We are not all the same in any true universal sense. In some circumstances, descendants of white Australian settlers or migrants to Australia cannot be categorized as the same as indigenous Australians in terms of their psychological needs.

When non-universal sub-group identities are denied expression, these identities are threatened. This may result in greater identification with that sub-group.[14] It seems as though many rights protection regimes regulate sub-group discrimination by providing negative rights (freedom from sub-group discrimin-

[12] Or autonomy: see Campbell, Ch. 1 above.

[13] Ibid.

[14] See identity threat research in social psychology: for example, N. R. Branscombe, N. Ellemers, R. Spears, and B. Doosje, 'The Context and Content of Social Identity Threat', in N. Ellemers, R. Spears, and B. Doosje (eds.), *Social Identity: Context, Commitment, Content* (Oxford: Blackwell Science, 1999).

ation). However, these regimes may fail to provide positive rights and other opportunities to celebrate these identities.[15] In this situation, an equality-driven conception of the purpose of justice and human rights values is operative. At best it can achieve equality and the 'mainstreaming' of important claims of sub-group difference. This psychological mismatch is one reason why, as Steven Curry suggests (in Chapter 15 of this volume), mainstreaming is not appropriate for the protection of indigenous rights. In some cases, for example, indigenous Australians will feel most satisfied when their rights are particularized (for example as native title rights), enabling them to identify as 'indigenous' and to *practise* that identity (for example, by having rights to negotiate as traditional owners and custodians of the land with developers). This is in contrast to being able merely to psychologically recategorize self as an 'Australian' in order to achieve some form of protection that falls short of appropriately realizing an 'indigenous' self-definition.

Linking the justice motive to types of identity harm

The importance of matching available justice responses with perceived harm was outlined by Syroit,[16] a social psychologist writing on justice. Syroit's work suggests that people perceive injustices as violations of either personal identity or social identity (for example, as a member of a sub-group within Australia). As such, people will be motivated to respond to these different types of harm at the most fitting psychological level. For example, if an indigenous Australian felt violated because of their membership of an indigenous group, 'fitting' justice would demand the protection of indigenous identity and the ongoing ability to identify as indigenous. Poor fit may be achieved, however, by only offering a limited range of identity protection (i.e. the right to be protected as a group of individual Australians).

Critics of the United Nations' Human Rights Committee's (HRC) view in the *Toonen* communication[17] have complained of a poor psychological fit between harm and remedy in that case. These critics suggest that violations of rights to sexual privacy were caused by the Tasmanian anti-gay laws, which allowed arbitrary search and arrest on the suspicion of homosexual activity between males. However, the majority view of the HRC was that the laws breached the right to privacy of all Australians, rather than constituting a breach of the freedom from sexuality discrimination. This meant that the HRC missed an

[15] K. Sullivan, *Group Identity and American Constitutionalism*, The Geoffrey Sawer Lecture, Centre for International and Public Law, Faculty of Law, Australian National University, 9 Aug. 2000, discussing this point in terms of American anti-discrimination law.

[16] J. E. M. M Syroit, 'Interpersonal and Intergroup Injustice: Some Theoretical Considerations', in R. Vermunt and H. Steensma (eds.), *Social Justice in Human Relations: Societal and Psychological Origins of Justice* (New York: Plenum Press, 1991), vol. i.

[17] *Toonen v Australia*, Communication No. 488/1992, UN Doc. CCPR/C/50/D/488/1992, 4 Apr. 1994. See, for example, W. Morgan, 'Identifying Evil for What It Is: Tasmania, Sexual Perversity and the United Nations', (1994) 19 *Melbourne University Law Review* 740.

opportunity to legitimize homosexual identity and to protect it from future harm. Such a response would have demonstrated an understanding of which identity was harmed and the importance of providing specific remedies for specific harms.

Two types of perceived injustice caused by two types of psychological harm

In this way, we argue that it is necessary to consider which psychological identity is harmed by decisions and treatment. This approach helps to determine the required scope of a psychologically fitting regime of human rights protection. It can also help to predict which justice response may be preferred by particular victims and their supporters. A complicating factor here, of course, is that perceived political efficacy—as well as the nature of the harm—may influence response preference. So, regardless of whether justice (or human rights) defined as equal worth or unequal worthiness fits the psychological harm best, the interests of the victim may also be determined by the political reality of the situation.

That complication of context aside, we can still attempt to determine possible *types* of harm that lead to differing perceptions of injustice and differing understandings of what constitutes appropriate redress. In addition to a distinction between harm to personal identity and social identity, there may be two additional types of psychological harm resulting in different types of perceived injustice. The first, 'sub-group discrimination', occurs when a legitimate identity is dealt with in an unjustified way according to shared norms, social history, or relevant social comparisons *within* a moral community (for example, a nation).[18] The second type of perceived injustice, 'moral exclusion', may occur when the identity is effectively *excluded* from the set of identities legitimized by a moral community. The person still willing to self-define in terms of an excluded identity discovers that the expression of that identity is neither tolerated nor celebrated.

We suggest sub-group discrimination occurred during the operation of mandatory sentencing laws in the Northern Territory of Australia, as investigated in Study 1 below. The second type of felt harm, moral exclusion,[19] seems to be driving the perceptions of injustice held by lesbians, single women, and their supporters in Study 2 below. Moral exclusion may also accurately describe the felt harm and perceived injustice of indigenous Australians who were denied land rights for the greater part of the history of white settlement in Australia. It perhaps also describes the type of harm and perceptions of injustice felt by women denied the status of legal persons.

Finally, we suggest that human rights, *as well as* justice rhetoric, are available to Australians willing to emphasize either equal worth or unequal worthiness in

[18] See Platow *et al.*, n. 8 above, for a discussion of the psychological perception of the moral community.

[19] See further S. Opotow, 'Deterring Moral Exclusion', (1990) 46 *Journal of Social Issues* 173.

response to identity harm. An important empirical question here is: will human rights be perceived as useful responses to either of these harms (sub-group discrimination or moral exclusion)? If so, will a conception of human rights as unequal worthiness be preferred when addressing sub-group discrimination, whereas human rights as equal worth be preferred to achieve moral inclusion?

Overview of political issues used in the studies

In March and April 2000 we studied reactions to mandatory sentencing laws in the Northern Territory (NT). Incarceration rates for indigenous Australians remained disproportionate in the NT under mandatory sentencing. During this time, disaster struck the remote community of Groote Eylandt. A 15-year-old boy, Johnno Warramarrba, was put into custody for twenty-eight days for his second offence (breaking and entering and stealing stationery) and he subsequently took his own life. The laws also put fellow Groote Eylandter Jamie Wurramara into jail for a year for his third offence—stealing biscuits from the office of mining company Gemco one Christmas Day. The judiciary was also quite concerned that their judicial discretion to sentence freely was taken away in mandatory sentencing cases. Study 1 investigates the operation of these mandatory sentencing laws.

Study 2 investigated reactions to the Howard Government's legislative proposal to restrict access to assisted reproductive technology (ART).[20] The Sex Discrimination Act Amendment Bill 2000 (Cth) was introduced into Parliament the day after Justice Sundberg of the Federal Court handed down his decision in *McBain v Victoria*.[21] The decision rendered the Infertility Treatment Act 1995 (Vic) inoperative by way of constitutional inconsistency with the Sex Discrimination Act 1975 (Cth). The Victorian legislation had purported to deny access to ART to lesbians and single women. The federal amendment proposed to exclude lesbians and single women (those not married or not in recognized de facto relationships) from the protection of the Sex Discrimination Act 1975 (Cth).

Study 1: The mandatory sentencing study

One hundred and two first-year psychology students participated in this study, conducted in March–April 2000. The aim was to measure what Australians perceived the purpose of human rights in Australia to be in the context of the

[20] ART is defined in the proposed legislation as 'in-vitro fertilisation, artificial insemination, gamete, zygote or embryo transfer, or any other services to assist in non coital fertilisation'.

[21] (2000) 99 FCR 116.

mandatory sentencing issue. We sought to determine how Australians perceiving mandatory sentencing as unjust would construe the purpose of human rights law. The construals tested were human rights as ways to ensure equality for all Australians (expressing an equal-worth value), or, as ways to provide protection for vulnerable groups (expressing an unequal-worthiness value). Participants were also asked if they thought twelve human rights (see Table 3.1) were violated by the mandatory sentencing scheme.

We first presented the participants with legally accurate information about the NT mandatory sentencing scheme. The following information was presented:

In the Northern Territory, mandatory sentencing laws oblige magistrates to order the following minimum periods of detention for anyone 17 years and over who is convicted of stealing property of any value: 1st offence = 14 days, 2nd offence = 90 days, 3rd offence = 1 year. For example, Person X, a 17-year-old from the Northern Territory, was convicted for stealing a t-shirt off a clothesline earlier this year. This was Person X's first offence. Under the mandatory sentencing laws, Person X was imprisoned in an adult prison for 14 days.

Table 3.1: Rights violated by mandatory sentencing laws

Human right	*No. (%) who perceive a violation (N = 83[a])*	*Legal source of right*
Right of a child to receive sentence proportionate to offence	75 (90.4)	CROC
Right of a child not to be imprisoned with adults	70 (84.3)	CROC
Right of a child to be imprisoned only as a last resort	69 (83.1)	CROC
Right to a fair trial	63 (75.9)	ICCPR/CROC
Right to be protected as a minor	62 (74.7)	CROC
Right to appeal a criminal conviction	58 (69.9)	ICCPR/CROC
Freedom from arbitrary detention	57 (68.7)	ICCPR/CROC
Right to a imprisonment aimed at reform and rehabilitation	53 (63.9)	ICCPR
Right of child to be imprisoned to promote dignity, respect for law, and reintegration	53 (63.9)	CROC
Right to equality before the law	48 (57.8)	ICCPR/CROC
Right to freedom from racial discrimination	42 (50.6)	ICCPR/CERD/ ICESCR
Right of a child to be protected from discrimination	40 (48.2)	CROC

[a] Missing data in sample of 88 because some participants did not complete the violation and ranking tasks.

Note: CROC = Convention on the Rights of the Child; ICCPR = International Covenant on Civil and Political Rights; CERD = Convention on the Elimination of All Forms of Racial Discrimination; ICESCR = International Covenant on Economic, Social and Cultural Rights.

Perceived human rights violations and the importance of protecting particular rights

Participants were presented with the statement 'Mandatory sentencing laws breach human rights' and asked to rate the extent to which they agreed with this statement on a 7-point scale. Only 14 participants (13.7 per cent) out of a total of 102 surveyed supported mandatory sentencing when asked explicitly 'In general, I support/I do not support the Northern Territory mandatory sentencing laws'. We excluded these 14 supporters of mandatory sentencing from analyses. The sub-sample of 88 participants who were opposed to mandatory sentencing agreed that mandatory sentencing breached human rights.[22] However, on closer inspection of some reasons participants gave for their ratings, it was clear that 15 critics of mandatory sentencing did not think that the laws breached human rights. This is important evidence that felt dissatisfaction, moral outrage, and perceived injustice do not always lead to a willingness to claim that human rights violations have occurred.

Participants were then asked to choose which rights they perceived were breached from a list of rights (Table 3.1), and, which of these rights were most important to protect in the Australian criminal justice system (Table 3.2). The presented rights were found primarily in the UN's International Covenant on Civil and Political Rights, and the Convention on the Rights of the Child, but are also echoed in the International Covenant on Economic, Social and Cultural Rights, and the Convention on the Elimination of All Forms of Racial Discrimination. As can be seen from Table 3.1, most participants perceived that procedural rights were breached by the presented scenario. Notably, freedom from discrimination was not perceived to be violated as often as these procedural rights.

Participants were asked which rights are the most important to protect in the Australian criminal justice system. Most respondents allocated their number one importance ranking to 'right to a fair trial' followed by 'right to equality before the law' and 'right of a child to receive a sentence proportionate to the offence'. It should be noted that two 'equal-worth' rights gained the most number one preferences (see Table 3.2).

The perceived purpose of human rights law

In order to determine participants' perceptions of the purpose of human rights law in this context, we randomly assigned half of the participants to one of two conditions. In the first condition we asked them if they agreed with the following equal-worth construal of the purpose of human rights. We asked them to rate the extent to which they agreed that the presented statement 'captured their own definition of human rights' on a 7-point scale (1 = disagree, 7 = agree):

[22] Mean = 5.19, standard deviation = 1.50, median = 6.

Table 3.2: Importance of protecting particular human rights in criminal justice systems (number 1 rankings)

Human right	*No. (%) who perceive a violation*	*Legal source of right*
Right to a fair trial	37 (44.6)	ICCPR/CROC
Right to equality before the law	14 (16.8)	ICCPR/CROC
Right of a child to receive sentence proportionate to offence	12 (14.3)	CROC
Freedom from racial discrimination	8 (9.9)	ICCPR/CERD/ ICESCR
Right of a child to be protected from discrimination	6 (7.4)	CROC
Right of a child not to be imprisoned with adults	6 (7.1)	CROC
Right of a child to be imprisoned only as a last resort	6 (7.1)	CROC
Right to a imprisonment aimed at reform and rehabilitation	6 (7.1)	ICCPR
Right of child to be imprisoned to promote dignity, respect for law, and reintegration	3 (3.6)	CROC
Right to appeal a criminal conviction	2 (2.4)	ICCPR/CROC
Right to be protected as a minor	1 (1.19)	CROC
Freedom from arbitrary detention	0	ICCPR/CROC

Note: ICCPR = International Covenant on Civil and Political Rights; CROC = Convention on the Rights of the Child; CERD = Convention on the Elimination of All Forms of Racial Discrimination; ICESCR = International Covenant on Economic, Social and Cultural Rights.

Human rights are meant to protect all individuals merely as a result of being human. Human rights provide universal protection for all human beings because all people are born equal and deserve to live in the same state of freedom. Everyone has the same rights regardless of which groups you belong to. That is how to ensure that all individuals enjoy equal rights. No right given to certain group members should discriminate against non-group members. Even as members of different groups we are individuals who deserve equal treatment. If human rights do not equally protect individuals of any group then there is no point in having them.

We asked participants assigned to the second condition to rate the extent to which they agreed with the following unequal-worthiness construal of the purpose of human rights law 'captured their own definition of human rights' on a 7-point scale (1 = disagree, 7 = agree):

Human rights are meant to protect the needs of particular vulnerable groups within society. For example, minority groups, indigenous groups, employees, religious groups, cultural groups, the underprivileged, those without real political representation, those suffering extreme financial hardship, the dispossessed, the economically disadvantaged, racial targets and ethnically disadvantaged groups. Some people do claim that human rights are for protecting all humans within society equally. However, as a matter of reality, human rights are asserted to protect disadvantaged groups. True protection of the individual requires protection of a particular group within the society to which they belong.

In addition, participants rated the extent to which they would be happy for Mary Robinson, the UN High Commissioner for Human Rights, to use the presented view to guide her in an upcoming review of the mandatory sentencing scheme.

We excluded the 14 supporters of mandatory sentencing from analyses as well as 6 participants who misunderstood the intended gist (human rights as providing equality for all versus human rights as providing protection for vulnerable groups) when asked to summarize the meaning of the presented construal. Also, one participant's survey was incomplete. This left a sub-sample of 81 participants. The 37 participants presented with the equal-worth construal of the purpose of human rights said that it captured their own view of the purpose of human rights significantly more[23] than the 44 participants presented with the unequal-worthiness construal of human rights.[24] The participants presented with the equal-worth construal were also happier for the UN's High Commissioner for Human Rights, Mary Robinson, to use this view of human rights in a review of mandatory sentencing laws[25] than were those presented with the unequal-worthiness construal of human rights.[26]

Study 2: the assisted reproductive technology study

In Study 2 we tested whether activists would choose the language of inclusive rights (equal worth) or non-rights language promoting sub-group interest (unequal worthiness) when motivated to campaign for access to ART. We posted the questionnaire and materials on the Internet, and the URL was advertised on email networks of Australian non-governmental organizations (NGOs) advocating liberal access to ART. Participants were randomly assigned to one of two audience conditions by a link on the web site. In each condition, participants evaluated two speeches for potential use in ART issue campaigning. Each participant chose which speech they preferred a spokesperson to deliver to either an in-group audience (fellow women's activists from a group that had campaigned for liberal access to ART) or an out-group audience (Howard Government MPs wishing to restrict access to ART).

The 'inclusive human rights' speech (Speech A) was read first by all participants followed by the 'sub-group interests' speech (Speech B). Speech A (see Appendix 3.1) used arguments based on the right to health and privacy in

23 Mean = 5.30, standard deviation = 1.33.
24 Mean = 5.20, standard deviation = 1.30; $F(1,77) = 10.89$, $p < .05$.
25 Mean = 5.59, standard deviation = 1.20.
26 Mean = 5.18, standard deviation = 1.66; $F(1,77) = 4.69$, $p < .05$.

decisions related to reproduction and family life. In contrast, Speech B (see Appendix 3.1) aimed at justifying the suitability of lesbians and single women as parents and the need to 'respect, protect, legitimate and celebrate' the lives and parenting choices of these women.

Results suggested that activists preferred the inclusive rhetoric of human rights (equal worth) to that of sub-group justice (unequal worthiness). This result confirms earlier social-psychological research on political persuasion. This work suggests that speakers attempt to persuade potentially hostile out-groups by making the audience perceive that the speaker is similar to the audience, and that both the speaker and audience identify as members of the same social group defined in with the same norms and values.[27] However, these results extend that finding, by showing that activists perceive that this rhetorical goal can be achieved by using inclusive human rights arguments defined in line with the same norms and values.

Contrary to predictions, this preference held irrespective of whether participants were seeking to persuade an in-group audience or an out-group audience (see Figure 3.1). The activists still preferred to see the inclusive human rights speech presented to a sympathetic in-group audience as well as to the hostile out-group audience. This suggests that equal-worth construals of human rights may serve the functions of arguing for moral inclusion, *as well as* mobilizing supporters to participate in such campaigns. We had predicted that activists may prefer to use unequal-worthiness rhetoric to in-groups. We had thought that participants may prefer to use this type of rhetoric to fellow activists, since this audience would be expected to prefer rhetoric celebrating difference and legitimizing a marginalized sub-group identity.

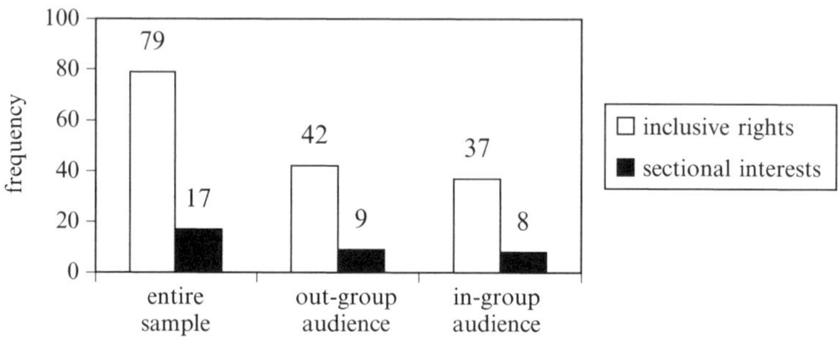

Fig. 3.1. Speech preference for entire sample and by condition

[27] S. D. Reicher and N. Hopkins, 'Seeking Influence through Characterizing Self-Categories: An Analysis of Anti-abortionist Rhetoric', (1996) 35 *British Journal of Social Psychology* 297; S. D. Reicher and N. Hopkins, 'Self-Category Constructions in Political Rhetoric: An Analysis of Thatcher's and Kinnock's Speeches Concerning the British Miners' Strikes (1984–5)', (1996) 26 *European Journal of Social Psychology* 353.

Reasons for preferring inclusive human rights rhetoric

Participants were also asked to give reasons for their speech preference. These reasons were coded and are summarized in Table 3.3. These data suggest that activists tailor their preferred political strategy according to their expectations of how the protest message will be perceived by the audience. For example, participants preferring Speech A for delivery to the hostile out-group audience did so mainly because of its inclusive approach and more diplomatic tone:

Table 3.3: Reasons for speech choice by condition and preferred speech

Respondent	*Out-group*	*In-group*
Inclusive human rights (Speech A) choosers	(N = 42)	(N = 37)
Inclusive	22	24
Tone	30	22
Sophisticated, intelligent	2	2
Diversity message	—	1
Sectional interests (Speech B) choosers	(N = 9)	(N = 8)
Diversity message	7	7
Tone	1	1
Inclusive	1	0

Note: Entries are the number of times these reasons were mentioned by participants and sometimes more than one reason was given by each participant.

> I don't always believe that the most radical line is the most effective. When in Rome, speak as the Romans do . . . talk to them in their speak . . . and maybe they will hear what you have to say. (ID no. 64, out-group audience condition)

> I am a lawyer and the lesbian mother of twin boys. I do not feel the need to banner wave. Only logical arguments make any sense to governments. Change and recognition will only come about by ordered logical argument. (ID no. 83, out-group audience condition)

> Speech A fits with some of the rhetoric of the current government (the individualistic tone does anyway, if not the emphasis on human rights). It is more likely to be heard than Speech B. Speech B will not change the mind of anyone who is proud to discriminate against lesbians. Talk of 'celebrating' the lives of lesbians and single mothers is too challenging for the government. (ID no. 141, out-group audience condition)

> . . . you catch more flies with honey. (ID no. 50, out-group audience condition)

Some activists were also concerned that Speech B's emphasis on the experience of lesbians and single mothers could backfire and work to invite further discrimination against these groups or to justify their exclusion:

> in [the] political context, I am concerned that in seeking to convince conservatives to change a position, emphasising difference may only further alienate them from the decision. This legislation is a classic case of excluding 'the other'. As such it [is] most politically advisable to mainstream the argument so it is closer to home to decision-makers. (ID no. 31, out-group audience condition)

. . . emotive arguments may just persuade [the Howard Government] that lesbians and single women are the difficult people. (ID no. 144, out-group audience condition)

[Speech A is] more mainstream friendly, more reconciliatory and inclusive rather than exclusively about marginalised groups. [Speech B] further entrenches marginalised people in the margins, and makes it difficult to have areas of commonality. (ID no. 145, out-group audience condition)

As well as asking for reasons for speech preference, we also measured 'meta-stereotypes' here.[28] These meta-stereotypes reflect the activists' expectations of how the audience will stereotype the spokesperson upon delivery of the speech. The content of the meta-stereotypes suggested that activists preferred a speech because they thought the resultant impression of the speaker would be positive (i.e. cooperative, constructive, reasonable, community-minded, and inspirational), *rather than* negative (un-Australian, radical, political, divisive, and provocative).

Against expectations, most participants did not prefer presentation of the more radical sub-group justice message (Speech B) to the in-group audience. The majority of participants preferred that Speech A be used to mobilize fellow activists. We interpret this to mean that participants were careful not to overestimate the level of consensus on the issue within in-group audiences. In light of this uncertainty, activists again preferred the inclusive approach expressed in human rights terms. One participant expressed this view in their reason for preferring Speech A:

It would very much depend on the type of women's organization—[with] conservative types such as . . . [group X—name supplied] you'd need to be very careful, as opposed to openly feminist, community-based organizations which would respond better to Speech B. (ID no. 183, in-group audience condition)

Reasons for preferring unequal-worthiness rhetoric

A minority of participants, however, did prefer Speech B. Of these 17 participants (17.8 per cent of the entire sample), 9 of them preferred the presentation of sub-group justice arguments (Speech B) to the out-group and 8 of them preferred that Speech B be presented to the in-group audience. This preference reflected a desire to emphasize the celebration of diversity (see Table 3.3) by personalizing the injustice with descriptions of the excluded women's lives. These participants appeared motivated towards presenting a more radical message, and 11 of them also preferred a statement of broad social beliefs that read:

[28] O. Klein and A. E. Azzi, 'The Strategic Confirmation of Meta-Stereotypes: How Group Members Attempt to Tailor an Outgroup's Representation of Themselves', (2001) 40 *British Journal of Social Psychology* 279; J. D. Vorauer, K. J. Main, and G. B. O'Connell, 'How Do Individuals Expect to Be Viewed by Members of Lower Status Groups? Content and Implications of Meta-Stereotypes', (2000) 75 *Journal of Personality and Social Psychology* 917.

Society should be thought of as a collection of groups, where each group member furthers their own individual interests by furthering their group's interest.

And preferred the following statement less:

Society should be thought of as a collection of discrete individuals, each of whom is free to further their own individual interests in an open system.

In both audience conditions, these activists appeared motivated to seek change by promoting the interests of the disadvantaged sub-groups:

I don't think that there is really a need to beat around the bush on any issue, why waste time namby pambying around the real issues through fear of being labeled, or offending someone. (ID no. 118, out-group audience condition)

The Government needs to know what would the effects be for those who are subjected to their discriminative decision-making. I believe being straightforward is the best strategy in this case because this way they can't hide behind foggy explanations that may avoid the 'hot spot'. (ID no. 150, out-group audience condition)

Conclusion

The results from both studies suggest how Australians assert human rights in response to perceived injustice. Some of these results are worth bearing in mind when making prescriptive statements about the form Australia's regime of human rights protection should take. The responses demonstrate a level of strategic thinking and identity management by aggrieved Australians. Sub-group identity may be actively managed by the use of either justice or inclusive rights-based rhetoric.

It appears that an equal-worth construal of the purpose of human rights is more popular in Australia than a construal based on unequal worthiness. This was the case irrespective of whether participants were responding to examples of sub-group discrimination or moral exclusion. Results from the mandatory sentencing study suggest that Australians perceived the purpose of human rights law in response to sub-group disadvantage to be the provision of equal treatment of all Australians. Similarly, results from the ART study suggested that activists find equal-worth rhetoric desirable when attempting to argue for inclusion of an excluded sub-group. However, not all activists in Study 2 preferred this 'mainstreaming' approach. For some, an emphasis on unequal worthiness was preferred.

It is important to note that, although we designed the 'unequal worthiness' speech in Study 2 to have non-rights arguments, rights language may also be used to advocate a celebration of diversity and sub-group interests. This 'rights way' to emphasizing the unequal worthiness of sub-groups is seen in recent campaigns by human rights NGOs such as Amnesty International. Amnesty has campaigned to protect 'women's human rights' and 'children's human rights', creating a more complex claim of rights protection than campaigns based on equal-worth rhetoric alone.

If human rights are used by activists in political debate to achieve goals such as moral inclusion and to encourage debate over legislative and judicial action, then the danger posed by the use of rights rhetoric to democracy may be minimal. In Campbell's terms, then, any 'eclipse' of justice by human rights may be partial—if an eclipse occurs at all. Responses to injustice may be expressed with a range of justice concepts *including* human rights arguments. However, even if a partial eclipse occurs, will victims, non-victims, activists, and non-activists alike really be blinded by staring into that eclipse? We suggest not. Perhaps what will result is the pursuit of justice with human rights arguments in a way sensitive to the nature of the psychological harm experienced. This would allow different construals of the purpose of human rights to guide the use of rights-based arguments against sub-group discrimination and moral exclusion.

Appendix 3.1

Speech A

In modern Australian society, it is crucial that all Australian women have access to assisted reproductive technology (ART). Denying access to some groups of Australian women denies them universal human rights such as the right to health and the right to privacy in decisions related to reproduction and family life. All Australian women should have a right of access to ART without distinction of any kind. This includes a right of access to ART without discrimination on the basis of marital status.

However, the proposed Sex Discrimination Amendment Bill clearly discriminates on the basis of marital status. If passed, the Bill would allow the discriminatory rules devised by many governments to continue to the detriment of many women. The Bill would allow State Governments to exclude lesbians and single women from ART—denying them the chance to use ART in accordance with their fundamental rights to health and privacy. Therefore the proposed Bill officially sanctions discrimination and violates universal rights rather than protects them.

Supporters of this Bill desperately need to rethink the reality of using ART. The reality is that all Australian women willing to use ART think long and hard about parenting. Lesbians and single women, like other Australian women needing ART, carefully consider the sacrifices involved in being a parent. In addition, all these women think long and hard about the physical and emotional risks involved in using ART. Being forced to do all this thinking means that women willing to use ART, irrespective of their marital status, have already made a significant commitment to parenting when they walk through the doors of an ART clinic. Their universal right to health and their universal right to privacy must be upheld from this point onwards, in order to protect the interests of all of these women and to protect their ability to make a deep commitment to parenting.

All of these women deserve equal access to an ART provider. This means that lesbians and single women with the courage to approach a clinic have a right to be free from discrimination on the basis of marital status. Lesbians and single women, like all other Australian women, deserve an equal chance to accept the challenge of parenting, assisted by the latest reproductive technology, and to demonstrate how good a parent they can be to their children.

ART providers offer a wide range of health services that many women need. All women in need of these services should be able to benefit from ART. However, if these services are not officially available to all, some groups of women will be unfairly denied access to ART and will be denied their fundamental human rights. Of course, with exclusion comes desperation. Those excluded, such as lesbians and single women, can only fulfil their commitment to parent by using unofficial, unhealthy and unsafe methods.

We can avoid the negative consequences of desperation by upholding Australia's promise to protect the right to health and the right to privacy without discrimination on the basis of marital status. If, as Australians, we want these rights to protect all Australian women, we must provide equal access to assisted reproductive technologies to all.

Speech B

In modern Australian society, it is crucial that all Australian women have access to assisted reproductive technology (ART). Denying access to lesbians and single women on the basis of marital status is insulting and discriminatory. On the other hand, governments could acknowledge and legitimize the lifestyles and commitments of lesbians and single women by providing them with access to ART.

However, the proposed Sex Discrimination Amendment Bill insults lesbians and single women rather than includes them. The Bill clearly discriminates on the basis of marital status. If the Bill is passed, it would allow the discriminatory rules devised by many governments to continue to the detriment of lesbians and single women. These women suffer because they are denied access to the ART services they need to assist them with having children while continuing to live a lifestyle consistent with their psychological needs.

Supporters of this Bill desperately need to rethink the reality of using ART. The reality is that lesbians and single women willing to use ART think long and hard about parenting. They carefully consider the sacrifices involved in being a parent. In addition these women think long and hard about the physical and emotional risks involved in using ART. Being forced to do all this thinking means that women willing to use ART, irrespective of their marital status, have already made a significant commitment to parenting when they walk through the doors of an ART clinic. Of course, lesbian and single mothers also face the added burden of prejudice, such as the criticism that they live in dysfunctional families. So lesbians and single women must make a significant commitment to parenting in order to cope, not only with the reality of ART, but with the reality that marital status discrimination may confront them wherever they go as parents of their children.

There is enough prejudice in society already that causes unnecessary harm to lesbians and single women. We do not need the proposed Bill to further blind some to the functional nature of non-traditional family structures. The prejudiced must be prevented from ignoring the available support from, say, a lesbian partner, from a partner other than a husband or male *de facto*, from extended family members and from friends. Much research shows that lesbians and single mothers are effective and loving parents, so they deserve the chance to have access to an ART provider to have their special health needs serviced.

ART providers offer a wide range of health services that lesbians and single women need. However, if these services are not officially available to these women, we can conclude that the Government is full of homophobes who wish to deny the existence of functional and loving, although non-traditional, family units. Of course, with exclusion comes desperation. If lesbians and single women are excluded from using ART, then they can only fulfil their commitment to parent by using unofficial, unhealthy and unsafe methods.

We can avoid the negative consequences of desperation by being willing to respect, protect, legitimate and celebrate the lives of lesbian and single mothers. To do this, we must shamelessly provide lesbians and single women with access to assisted reproductive technology.

4

Human Rights, the Rule of Law, and American Constitutionalism

ROBIN WEST

Human rights discourse in the United States, like US rights discourse more generally, typically proceeds on the assumption that, at least in this culture, rights are non-positivistic, principled, legal limits to what states, state actors, and state agents can do to their citizens. Rights, that is, impose constraints on what states can do; they do not *obligate* states to do anything. This view, widely held by American rights critics and theorists alike, underlies the common critical claim that 'second-' or 'third-generation' positive 'welfare rights' to social goods such as housing, food, education, or development, espoused by some international human rights advocates and expressed in some international agreements, whatever their status in international law and whatever their appeal to jurists and legal scholars in other legal traditions, are simply oxymoronic within the United States rights tradition.[1] The expansive view of human rights as *either* obligating states to take action *or* obligating states to refrain from taking action, held by the international human rights community, is just at odds with the American understanding of rights. Whatever the merits of the aspirational claim that states *ought to* provide whatever social goods are necessary for citizens to achieve some level of dignity in their lives, rights are the wrong vehicle for achieving the goal. Rights limit what states can do to citizens; they don't obligate the state to do anything. It is a misunderstanding of rights to try to spread their reach so widely.

Where did this American view of rights as imposing limits, but not obligations, on states, come from? To a considerable extent, it is a generalization from a more specific claim about the reach of rights expressed in the United States Constitution: the rights contained in the Constitution's Bill of Rights, according to innumerable constitutional lawyers and judges, are essentially 'negative' rights against state action, and not positive rights to state services of any kind whatsoever, particularly where those positive rights might require intervention into the private spheres of market and property.[2] We don't, for example, according to this conventional view, have any constitutional 'right' to a police force, or to any particular body of criminal sanctions such a force might be charged with the task

Further discussion of contemporary American understandings of the rule of law, both by their proponents and their critics, can be found in 'Rethinking the Rule of Law', in *Re-Imagining Justice*, ed. T. Campbell (Aldershot: Ashgate Press, 2003).

1 See generally M. A. Glendon, 'Rights in Twentieth Century Constitutions', (1992) 59 *Chicago Law Review* 519.

2 See, for example, F. Cross, 'The Error of Positive Rights', (2001) 48 *UCLA Law Review* 857.

of enforcing: we might have a constitutional right not to be wrongly arrested by such a force, or wrongly targeted by law, but we don't have a constitutional right to the protection that the police, or the law, or the 'state' might accord against neighbours, or husbands, or parents, or priests, who would neglect, abuse, violate, rape, otherwise harm, or kill us.[3] And obviously, if we don't have a right to a state that will protect us against even the homicidal inclinations of others, we can't possibly have a right to a state that will protect us against the non-lethal but nevertheless destructive inclinations of others to exploit us, through, say, sub-minimal wages or unsafe work conditions. Nor, then, do we have a right to a state that might quite generally protect our welfare. It may well be a good thing to have a state that provides this protection. But we don't have a 'right' to it. Rights limit the reach of states in our lives. They don't mandate the state's presence.

This view, widely held, of the essential negativity of United States constitutional rights is, very likely, fundamentally mistaken, as a substantial body of constitutional scholarship now suggests.[4] It seemingly rests, for example, on a false reading of the text, the plain meaning, and the history of at least the Equal Protection Clause of the Fourteenth Amendment: that Amendment, passed partly in response to waves of lynchings of freed blacks after the civil war, explicitly states that 'No state shall deny the equal protection of the laws', apparently mandating, once the double negative is removed, that states shall provide protection to their citizens, and equally. Contrary to what had become their practice, the states were admonished *to do* something, and the federal Congress empowered in section 5 of the Fourteenth Amendment to take action should the states fail to do so. The conventional view rests as well on a failure to appreciate the substantial rhetorical history of positive constitutional rights in the struggles of marginalized groups in American history to assert their equal status as co-citizens, including not just slaves seeking positive freedom from violent whites, but also women seeking positive rights to vote, and labourers seeking positive rights to unionize and to well-paid, meaningful work. And of course, it ignores the relevance and persuasive authority of the positive rights jurisprudence, in both international human rights law, and the domestic constitutional law of other countries, to the development of constitutional law here.

However, it also seems clear, just from the tenacity of its hold on the American political imagination if nothing else, that the American understanding of rights as essentially negative does not *only* stem from a transparently wrong reading of the United States Constitution. Rather, the American insistence on both the negativity of rights generally, and of United States constitutional rights in particular, also seems to be rooted in an Americanized, neo-Lockean conception of the 'rule of law'. The American conception of the 'rule of law'—indebted

[3] See *DeShaney v Winnebago County Department of Social Services* 489 US 189, 195 (1989).

[4] See, for example, S. Bandes, 'The Negative Constitution: A Critique', (1990) 88 *Michigan Law Review* 2271.

in part, no doubt, to American myths of rugged individualism and overbearing government, as well as to the actual writings of John Locke—holds, in a nutshell, that even a democratic, political state is fundamentally untrustworthy: it is irrational, impassioned, whimsical, envy-driven, meddlesome, unduly paternalistic, and oftentimes dangerous. The 'rule of law'—meaning a commitment to a determinate set of legal rules, rooted in the past, discovered and applied by neutral courts—is a means to contain the danger posed by the state's presence. The rule of law, on this view, does not so much protect individuals against the murderous inclinations of others, but rather, and more fundamentally, it protects individuals and their property against the irrational, redistibutive, envy-driven, and meddlesome inclinations of political states, and state actors. The rule of law constrains, fundamentally, the actions of the political branches of government.

What does this American rule of law have to do with American understandings of rights? Well, rights, even granting that their content is through and through moral, are a part of our fundamental law—meaning, they are a part of that determinate set of legal rules and meta-rules that are discovered (not made) by courts (not legislatures) and then applied against the political branches. As such, rights are a fundamental, constitutive part, not just of our positive law, but of the rule of law. And, as a part of the rule of law, rather than the product of politics, they are poised *against* the political state, constraining it from taking certain sorts of actions at odds with human freedom. Rights then cannot be 'positive': they cannot be spurs to political actors to promote the well-being of the citizenry, for the simple reason that rights are a part of the rule of law, and the rule of law itself is not of that nature. The rule of law, of which rights are a part, is that which constrains political actors, not that which motivates or inspires them.

This chapter presents a different understanding of the rule of law, one which, I believe, is also well within the traditions of liberalism and American constitutionalism, but which is considerably less hostile to the broad understanding of positive rights at the heart of international human rights discourse. In the first part of this chapter I first look to the role of law in Thomas Hobbes's *Leviathan*—widely and correctly regarded as a part of the basic architecture of liberalism. *Leviathan* was also, however, a powerful tract for what may be the most basic positive right a human being can have: a positive human right to the protection of a state against private aggression. If we take this Hobbesian right seriously, it is patently wrong to argue that political liberalism precludes an appreciation of positive rights—the positive right to be protected by the state against violence, for the father of liberalism, was the state's *raison d'être*. The second part of this chapter turns to Thomas Paine's political essays—widely and correctly regarded as instrumental in the country's founding. In *Common Sense and The Rights of Man*, parts I and II, Paine argued for a vision of law and constitutionalism that would enhance, rather than limit, both the democratic underpinning and the reach of political states. He then explicitly tied his conception of law to a large vision of both negative and positive human rights. Whatever the power of our mythic understanding of our own history, I will conclude, neither liberal theory itself, nor the idea of American constitutionalism, at least as articulated by one of the fathers of liberalism and one of the most important American patriots, lend support to the view of the rule of law and of the rights that constitute it, which has so alienated the American community from the expansive conception of rights at the heart of public international law.

The rule of law in Hobbes's *Leviathan*

Did Thomas Hobbes posit a theory of the 'rule of law',[5] much less one that can stand as an alternative to the now dominant American conception?[6] Clearly Hobbes was no early supporter of many of those parts of the Lockean social contract that were eventually transported into American constitutional mythology: Hobbes saw no prima facie reason to prefer democracy to monarchy,[7] and saw no logical space, much less practical need, for negative, individual rights of conscience, property, or liberty against the state.[8] Both are, today, core components of our jurisprudential and constitutional self-understandings. He also quite explicitly rejected the jurisprudential underpinnings of the conventional modern account. Thus, the relentlessly positivistic Hobbes openly derided the Aristotelian ideal, embraced as an article of faith by contemporary rule of law theorists, of a 'government of laws and not of men',[9] as well as Lord Coke's attempt to argue that the 'law' properly consists of principles of right reason, discernible through the long study of judges and commentators on the law.[10] And he was no ally of what might be called the 'full determinacy thesis' at the core of the modern rule of law—the claim that all legal answers must be generated from known, public rules, and applied by judges who passively find, rather than create, pre-existing law. This, Hobbes suggests in arguments that prefigure the late twentieth-century critical legal scholars' claims of indeterminacy, is just not possible, given the ever-present need to interpret law, whether it be common law, legislative, or constitutional.[11] Rather, Hobbes suggested, the judge, as the subordinate representative of the sovereign, who is himself the representative of the commonwealth, must decide cases according to the will and reason

[5] T. Hobbes, *Leviathan* (1651), ed. Richard Tuck, Cambridge Texts in the History of Political Thought (Cambridge: Cambridge University Press, 1999). For ease of reference, citations will be to chapters and page numbers in original edition.

[6] On the Rule of Law's Lockean origins, see S. Kauts, 'Liberty, Justice, and the Rule of Law', (1999) 11 *Yale Journal of Law and the Humanities* 435.

[7] Hobbes, n. 5 above, ch. XIX.

[8] See generally ibid., ch. XXI, pp. 109–10.

[9] Ibid., ch. XLVI, p. 378.

[10] Ibid., ch. XXVI, p. 139.

[11] Ibid., ch. XXVI. For a detailed argument to this effect, see J. Hampton, 'Democracy and the Rule of Law', in I. Shapiro (ed.), *NOMOS XXXVI: The Rule of Law* (New York: New York University Press, 1994), 13, 16–17.

of the sovereign,[12] but at the same time the judge must assume that the sovereign intends results that accord with the demands of equity and justice. The result is that legal decision-making, for Hobbes, will have the elasticity—the indeterminacy—that such an explicit reliance on equity virtually demands.[13]

Most important, however, Hobbes squarely rejected the claim, at the heart of the contemporary conventional conception, that 'law' should be understood as a 'check' on the political state, for the simple reason that law, for Hobbes, is rigorously identified as the *product* of politics, not something standing apart from it, much less superior to it. Law, Hobbes famously held, is nothing but the command of the sovereign—and the sovereign is the representative of the commonwealth.[14] Neither constitutional law, nor common law, nor higher law, nor law in any other sense, can be anything other than the sovereign's will, and none of these sorts or sources of law, therefore, can be invoked as a check on that will.[15] As Professor Jean Hampton has rightly argued, for Hobbes, when the judge interprets law, he speaks as the sovereign or as the sovereign's representative: no matter what the 'law' he is interpreting, he cannot possibly speak as the sovereign's *limit*.[16] Law, thought Hobbes, cannot possibly be a check on the political state. Law is the legislated *product* of the political state.

Does it follow, though, as Hampton argues, that Hobbes was therefore a critic of the rule of law, or a sceptic regarding the possibility of having one?[17] I don't think so; to conclude that it does only begs the question of the meaning of the rule of law. If we assume that the rule of law requires judges who can interpret pre-existing determinate law, and who by so doing can limit the power of political sovereigns, then surely Hobbes was a critic of the rule of law. But there's no reason to define the 'rule of law' in such a question-begging way. If we understand the rule of law, instead, as emblematic of a belief in law's value, then a different picture emerges: understood in such a way, Hobbes was a champion of the rule of law—in fact, a champion like no other. For Hobbes, law and the rule of law, no less than the sovereign that produces it, were social goods with considerable—indeed, nearly absolute—social utility. The difference between Hobbes's understanding of the rule of law, and that of contemporary liberal rule of law theorists is *not* that Hobbes was a rule of law sceptic who derided law's value.

Rather, the difference between them is that, for Hobbes, law derives its value not from its function as a check on the political state but, rather, from its function as a 'check' on the excesses and cruelty of private power. Life under even the near-absolute power of an unchecked state, a Leviathan, Thomas Hobbes urged half a century before the revolutions that Thomas Paine's writings precipitated, is an improvement over the shortness and brutality of life in the state of nature—the very state of war that revolution demands.[18] Without

[12] Hobbes, n. 5 above, ch. XXVI, p. 140.
[13] Ibid., ch. XXVI, p. 144.
[14] Ibid., ch. XXVI, pp. 137–8.
[15] Ibid., ch. XXVI, pp. 138–9.
[16] Hampton, n. 11 above, 13.
[17] Ibid.
[18] Hobbes, n. 5 above, ch. XVII.

'law'—by which Hobbes famously meant the positive edicts of a sovereign authority—those with momentary power in the state of nature terrorize, kill, enslave, or exploit those with less power, and as power is fleeting, all in such a state live either in servitude or in fear of it, virtually all the time. Hobbesian law—facilitated by joint submission of all to an authority—is better than Hobbesian nature—joint terror of the violent propensities of the other.

Because it is better, Hobbes thought, a (quasi-contractual) duty of obedience to law flowed: citizens have a near-absolute interest in consenting to the construction of a near-absolute duty to obey the near-absolute edicts of the commonwealth's sovereign representative, at least so long as the sovereign's rule ensures their relatively greater security in civil as opposed to natural life. A Hobbesian rule of law, then, might be understood in modern terms as expressing a commitment to the relative value of law—understood positivistically as the edicts of a publicly recognized sovereign—over the violent, natural propensities of private parties. It is a preference for *law*—meaning the product of organized political authority—over a state of 'no law', or lawlessness, and it is a preference for 'law' over 'no law' on the grounds that physical insecurity, in the form of vulnerability to private violence, is the greater evil to be avoided through political action. Any form of government that avoids it has earned and deserves its citizens' obedience.

This Hobbesian rule of law contrasts quite sharply with the contemporary view. First, the *source* of law's value is distinctly different in the Hobbesian than in the contemporary conception, as is the nature of the duty to obey it. For Hobbes, law has value, and should be obeyed, not because it operates as a check on politics, but almost for precisely the opposite reason: it has value, and ought to be obeyed, solely by virtue of its thoroughly political role in protecting the security of the citizen from private assault. Secondly, the understanding of what might be called 'law's target'—the evil towards which 'law' is addressed—is not the political or public realm of state action, but rather the private realm of assault, violence, and private subordination. Thus, the private, legally unregulated realm, for Hobbes, is a place of violence, terror, and subordination—in short, of such physical and psychological harm as to render virtually any politically organized monopoly of force preferable. The public realm of political authority, by contrast, at least has the virtue of promoting the security of the people. Thirdly, the activist state the Hobbesian envisions—unencumbered, unlike the Lockean, with natural individual rights that limit its power and authority—obviously contrasts with the minimalist state pictured by the now conventional and generally libertarian account. Fourthly, the 'law' the Hobbesian rule of law endorses is the law that is produced by the legislative sovereign, not the 'law' produced by the restraining hand of a backward-looking court. And, finally, the end, or goal, we seek to accomplish through the project of law is the end of peace and security among private parties, rather than the end, or goal, of a restrained political branch. To summarize, the Hobbesian rule of law is to be valued, and ought to be obeyed, not because it is a *check* on politics, but because it is a product of politics and, as such, is a thoroughly political, positivistic, and preferable alternative to the risks of private violence. The Hobbesian rule of law expresses the basic conviction that law—public authority—is preferable to the terrorizing and subordinating horror of unconstrained private life.

And what is the place of rights in Hobbes's Leviathan? Again, negative rights have no place. But what of positive rights? Hobbes lays the basis not only for an unambiguous *obligation*—a duty—of the state to protect individuals against private violence, but also for a *right*, held by all citizens, to just that. Hobbes was absolutely clear on this point, in a passage which Hampton reminds us caused Hobbes's *Leviathan* to be feared by royalists as a 'rebel's catechism': 'The obligation of Subjects to the Sovereign is understood to last as long, and no longer, than the power lasteth, by which he is able to protect them. Or the right men have by Nature to protect themselves, when none else can protect them, can by no Covenant be relinquished.'[19]

Otherwise, the Hobbesian Leviathan can do what it wishes and the individual citizen must submit: the Hobbesian citizen does indeed lack negative rights of conscience, religion, and speech. Not so, however, with respect to the state's duty to protect the individual against private violence: there, the state is bound, and the individual fully entitled.

Nor was this right to the state's affirmative protection merely a peripheral feature of Hobbes's jurisprudence. Rather, the bargain struck—the individual relinquishes self-help, *in exchange for* the state's obligation to protect him from violence—was, for Hobbes, the *raison d'être* of the state's very existence. The Leviathan's protection of the individual against the private violence of others is the quid pro quo for the individual's relinquishment of his right to self-help available to him in the state of nature.[20] The individual, in other words, is just as contractually entitled to receive that protection as the state is obligated to provide it—in short, the citizen has a right to it. The state's obligation to protect the citizen against private violence, as well as the citizen's continuing right to receive it, in Hobbes's view, was foundational and inalienable. If we take Hobbes seriously, so to speak, the individual clearly has a right to the state's protection against the violence or aggression of other private parties; to borrow a phrase from Steven Heyman's important article on this point, this was, for Hobbes, the 'first duty of government'.[21]

And the right to that Hobbesian protection, in turn, at least as conceived by Hobbes, is clearly both positive and contractual in character: the state is obligated to protect the citizen against private violence by virtue of the citizen's having relinquished his recourse to self-help in exchange for that protection, and the individual has a *right* to receive it. It is a right, in other words, not to state inaction but, rather, to the state's affirmative intervention into what would

[19] Hampton, n. 11 above, 31, quoting from Hobbes, n. 5 above, ch. XXI, p. 272.

[20] Hobbes, n. 5 above, ch. XVII, pp. 85–8.

[21] See S. J. Heyman, 'The First Duty of Government: Protection, Liberty and the Fourteenth Amendment', (1996) 41 *Duke Law Journal* 507.

otherwise be a natural, private, and life-shortening state of war. The state is required to *do* something—to protect the individual—not just refrain from doing something. If Hobbes was right about this, and if this very positive right to protection against violence is central, rather than peripheral, to the metaphoric 'social contract' so central to liberalism, then the distinctively modern and American claim that liberal rights are *essentially* negative—whether insisted by rights proponents, rights critics, or Supreme Court or Fourth Circuit or Seventh Circuit Justices—is mistaken, and even perverse. At least according to Thomas Hobbes, the core, foundational right to which the liberal state owes its existence is indisputably positive in character.

Further, Hobbes's central insight—that freedom from private terror is a necessary part of the good life, and that a sovereign state is necessary to achieve that freedom—is by no means at odds with classically liberal theories of the state, broadly understood, although it may well be at odds with libertarian views.[22] Indeed, if liberalism is understood broadly, it is as central as the conventional account's mandate of judicial constraint. Thus, far from disowning or even distancing himself from a Hobbesian account of the necessity of law, John Rawls, in the same chapter on the rule of law in *A Theory of Justice*, in which he embraces something like the modern conception's understanding of the rule of law as a constraint on judicial whimsy, *also* embraces what he calls 'Hobbes' thesis'.[23] 'Hobbes' thesis', Rawls argues, far from being antithetical to liberalism, constitutes the core rationale of both 'law' and the 'rule of law' in any decent liberal society. The 'rule of law', for Rawls no less than for Hobbes, requires not just fidelity to pre-existing rules but, rather, the necessity of political sovereignty itself, to any measure of individual liberty. 'Hobbes' thesis', as Rawls has dubbed it—that political sovereignty, and the law it produces (rather than the law that constrains it), is necessary to liberty and contentment—is central, not peripheral or antithetical, to liberal understandings of the rule of law.

Finally, how does this Hobbesian alternative fare, as a competitor with the dominant conception, as an interpretation of *American* rule of law ideals? Clearly, if taken unadulterated, the Hobbesian account of the rule of law is unsuitable as an alternative interpretation of the American rule of law: again, there is no pride of place, in Hobbes's jurisprudence, for either democracy or negative rights, and it is not possible to make sense of American understandings of the rule of law without embracing those commitments. Nevertheless, the bedrock Hobbesian understanding of the value of law, the point of law, and hence the rule of law is by no means foreign to American history or practice, or to American understandings of law's value. Hobbes's understanding of the desirability of positive law, and its value as a constraint on private violence,

[22] Locke at no point repudiated the Hobbesian positive right of the citizen to state protection against private violence. In fact he expressly endorsed it; J. Locke, 'Of the Ends of Political Society and Government', in his *Essay Concerning the True Original Extent and End of Civil Government*, §§128–31, in his *Two Treatises of Government* (New York: Cambridge University Press, 1960).

[23] J. Rawls, *A Theory of Justice* (Cambridge, Mass.: Harvard University Press, 1970), 240.

rather than as a constraint on public will, and his insistence on the citizen's positive right to its protection, have been shared by prominent legal movements in our history. Two in particular are noteworthy.

First, much of our constitutional history—and particularly the forward and backward progress of the ideals expressed in the Reconstruction Amendments of the United States Constitution—might be viewed as on a continuum between an increasing appreciation, and then depreciation, of Hobbes's essential insight regarding the desirability of political over natural forms of communal life. Hobbes claimed that all persons in civil societies enter into such states so as to procure the protection of the state against private violence. If so, then the quasi-contractual, positive right of such citizens to such protection is shared, and shared equally, by all who have given up their natural right to assure their own self-protection. Although we still do not perfectly recognize such an equalizing and universally shared right, nevertheless, through the on-again, off-again application of our guarantees of equal protection of the law and due process of law, we have (arguably) repaired our most egregious failures. Most notably, of course, pursuant to the civil war and the Thirteenth Amendment that followed it, we no longer refuse to extend the protection of the law against private violence imposed upon a class of slaves, who, without the state's protections, are thereby subjected to the leviathanic violence of *masters*. This expansion of liberty and freedom was fully dependent, logically and militaristically, on the extension of the *Hobbesian*—not the Lockean—rule of law (in Rawls's language, 'Hobbes' thesis') to freed slaves.[24] The Leviathan must protect the slave against the subordinating violence of the master if the slave is to be free, and for that to occur, the state must assert its power and its authority—not its self-restraint.

Similarly, the entire institutional practice of lynching that followed emancipation was a clear, paradigmatic violation of a Hobbesian—although not a Lockean—rule of law: the state's refusal to protect individual citizens against lethal assault is a quintessential violation of the rule of law, meant in this purely Hobbesian sense.[25] By not policing against lynching, the state failed its one essential duty of protecting the citizen against the lethal savagery of the state of nature. Likewise, the refusal of state authorities to protect wives and children from the violent assaults of domestic patriarchs—justified, in the nineteenth century, by a complex ideological commitment to separate, sexually defined spheres, and the need for an authority within the domestic, and in the twentieth century by an equally complex ideological commitment to 'privacy'—is a stark violation of the rule of law, understood in Hobbes's sense.[26] To generalize from these examples, some of the most praiseworthy 'expansionist' and state-activist

[24] For a general argument that the historical meaning of the Reconstruction Amendments should be understood in this way, see J. TenBroek, *Equal Under Law: The Antislavery Origins of the Fourteenth Amendment* (New York: Collier Books, 1965).

[25] See, generally, Heyman, n. 21 above.

[26] See R. Siegal, 'The Rule of Love? Wife Beating as Prerogative and Privacy', (1996) 105 *Yale Law Journal* 2117.

moments in our legal history—most notably the passage of both the Thirteenth Amendment and the Equal Protection Clause of the Fourteenth Amendment—can be understood as moved by a growing recognition of the central Hobbesian idea that citizenship rests on the expectation that the citizen will be protected against private assault. To that degree, the growing commitment to the Hobbesian (rather than Lockean) rule of law can be regarded as central, rather than peripheral, to America's most transformative and ennobling constitutional moments—and hence to our constitutional history, narrative, and self-identity.

Likewise, Hobbes's understanding of law's value, and his less than cheery conception of private, legally unregulated life on which it rests, and his construction of a positive human right to be free of private aggression through the construction of an artificial state, are at the heart of wide swaths of progressive and radical twentieth-century law reform projects. The labour movement virtually *in toto*, some strands of modern feminism, and a good bit of contemporary critical race theory, for example, share with Hobbes the unhappy, non- or anti-Rousseauian view that private life can be riddled with decidedly non-romantic violence, subordination, irrational subjugation, and terror, and that law can be understood, and ought to be valued, as an antidote to that private domination.[27] Contemporary efforts, based on that Hobbesian world-view, to subject private behaviour to the sanction of law, from unionists attempts to equalize the relations of labour and capital, to feminist efforts to criminalize domestic violence, marital rape, and date rape,[28] to critical race theorists' efforts to impose sanctions on hate speech and to intensify criminal penalties for hate-motivated crimes,[29] can all be viewed as resting on a modern version of the central Hobbesian insight that the presence of law is better than the private hell people impose on each other in law's absence. Some people, when undeterred by law, do create hellish, private states of nature for each other: in the private spheres of intimacy, some people are inclined to rape, and assault, and kill, and in the private spheres of commerce some are inclined to exploit, and subordinate, and oppress. Law, compared to these private hells, according to Hobbes, unionists, radical feminists, left-leaning or Marxist critical-legal scholars, and critical race theorists all, stands as a distinct improvement. A Hobbesian understanding of the rule of law, in short, is more compatible with anti-subordinationist views of justice and of the role of law in eradicating it than is our contemporary equation of the rule of law with limits on political action.

[27] See, for example, C. McKinnon, *Toward a Feminist Theory of the State* (Cambridge, Mass.: Harvard University Press, 1989); R. Colker, 'Anti-Subordination Above All: Sex, Race and Equal Protection', (1986) 61 *New York University Law Review* 1003; K. Crenshaw (ed.), *Critical Race Theory: The Key Writings that Formed the Movement* (New York: New Press, 1995).

[28] See, for example, Siegal, n. 26 above; J. Hasday, 'Contest and Consent: A Legal History of Marital Rape', (2000) 88 *California Law Review* 1373; C. McKinnon, 'Reflections on Sex Equality Under Law', (1991) 100 *Yale Law Journal* 1281.

[29] C. Lawrence III, 'The New First Amendment: If he Hollers, Let him Go. Regulating Racist Speech on Campus', (1990) *Duke Law Journal* 431; M. Matsuda, 'Legal Storytelling: Public Response to Racist Speech. Considering the Victim's Story', (1989) 87 *Michigan Law Review* 2320.

Even more broadly, though, Hobbes's commitment to an activist state, to the value of law produced by such a state, and his concomitant hostility to property or civil rights that might limit such value, render Hobbes's rule of law, in contrast to the Lockean, reflective of a state that is to be desired rather than to be feared, and is so for its activism, rather than for its restraint: the law we purportedly value in a rule of law society, according to Hobbes, is identified with the product of state activity, not with limits upon it. For example, in lengthy passages in *Leviathan* that prefigure contemporary scholarly attempts, by neo-civic republicans and others, to refashion a liberal argument for an activist rather than restrained state,[30] Hobbes argued that a fundamental *duty* (as well as right) of the commonwealth, or the sovereign, whether monarch or assembly, was to distribute property, and to do so in accordance with the common good.[31] Likewise, it is the *sovereign's* judgement, not the individual's, that should guide the distribution of property.[32] While the subject has the right to exclude other subjects from his property, Hobbes thought, prefiguring contemporary arguments put forward by proponents of a constrained reading of the Takings Clause, as well as an expansive conception of the state's 'police powers', the subject does not have the right to exclude the sovereign.[33]

Thus, not just attempts to criminalize private violence, but, likewise, attempts to subject the potentially injurious behaviour of strong private actors of all sorts to politically derived, lawful sanction, can be understood as expressing a Hobbesian, rather than a Lockean, understanding of the value of law, and hence of the rule of law. Examples of such attempts might include New Deal era legislation that requires minimum wage and safe working conditions in labour contracts, contemporary use of tort sanctions and punitive damages awards to sanction the behaviour of corporations otherwise unconcerned with the private injuries it causes, political efforts to limit the reach and impact of globalization and to do so by use of and reference to law, and attempts to force polluting industries and the countries that license them to limit the damage done, somehow, through the operation of law. All of these endorsements of 'law' over 'no-law' might be understood as resting on the fundamentally Hobbesian understanding of the general preferability of law, and a fundamentally Hobbesian distrust of the capacity and will of private actors to achieve the requisite level of regard for others in law's absence. Put differently, they rest on the Hobbesian understanding that the interest of the community is best served through organized political rule, rather than through privatized efforts at self-advancement. The rule of law, for the contemporary proponents of these sorts of constraints, as for Hobbes, is of value, not because law limits politics and the state but, rather, because law is the product of politics, limits private action, and evidences the presence of an active state.

[30] See, for example, C. Sunstein and S. Holmes, *The Cost of Rights: Why Liberty Depends on Taxes* (New York: W. W. Holton, 1999).

[31] Hobbes, n. 5 above, ch. xxiv, p. 128.

[32] Ibid., ch. xxiv, p. 128.

[33] Ibid.

To sum up: Hobbes understood and articulated, as has no other liberal theorist since, the need for and the positive value of states and the laws they produce, particularly as contrasted with the violence and chaos that rule in their absence. Hobbes, more so than Locke (although Locke follows Hobbes on the point) emphasized the root *desirability* of the state, of politics, and of the law that is its product. A Hobbesian understanding of the rule of law, and of the 'value' of law that the 'rule of law' signals, should stand at least as a complement, or counterweight, to the dominant account's now excessive libertarianism, court-centredness, and wilful blindness to the value of politics. Put differently, the Hobbesian rule of law serves as a reminder of the limits of the dominant conception's Lockean heritage, no less than the Lockean conception of liberalism has for 200 years now served as a reminder of the need to limit the reach of Hobbes's Leviathan. Hobbes's insight is precisely what is neglected by the dominant account's insistence that the core purpose of law is to constrain and limit the state, and thereby to maximize rather than limit individual freedom. That law is essential, in the first instance, to secure peace and cooperation, and is for that reason preferable to lawlessness, ought to be regarded as at the core of a full and fully liberal account of the rule of law.

The defects of the Hobbesian rule of law, however, are obvious to modern liberal eyes: as noted above, Hobbes disavows what we now regard as essential negative rights against a state's over-intrusiveness, sees no practical need or logical way to advocate limits on sovereign power, and makes no appeal to democratic accountability as a way to ensure that the interests of the sovereign remain aligned with the interest of the governed who delegated power and authority to the Leviathan in the first instance. To put the problem in terms of Hobbes's own jurisprudence, while Hobbes clearly demonstrated the need for the Leviathan—because of the murderous incompatibility of human inclinations in a state of nature—he provided no reason to think that those human inclinations would be in any way tamed, or civilized, when some, but not all, of the individuals who possess it are elevated to the status of 'sovereign'. The 'public will' he advocated as a solution to the problems posed to security and contentment by the 'private will' seem to be subjected to the same failings, if his general understanding of the nature that requires it is sound. Indeed, Mark Tushnet identifies this problem with Hobbesian thought as *the* central dilemma of classical liberalism, which leads directly to the construction of the conventional account of the rule of law: general legal rules, limiting sovereign authority, according to Locke, Rawls, and most contemporary liberal legalists, are the only way to address, and cabin, the Hobbesian nature of the Leviathan.[34] That solution, in turn, leads to the paradox, or dilemma, on which critical scholars focus: the indeterminacy of rules cannot constrain the judge, who hence becomes, by sheer force of logic, the untamed Leviathan, subjecting the citizenry to the unabated risks of a short and brutal life.

34 M. Tushnet, *Red White and Blue* (Cambridge, Mass.: Harvard University Press, 1988).

It is important to stress (because it is often forgotten) that Hobbes himself recognized the Hobbesian dilemma. Hobbes's Leviathan, according to Hobbes, differs in theory from the powerful individual in the state of nature, by virtue of the fact that the Leviathan 'represents' the commonwealth,[35] is legitimized by its consent to its rule,[36] ideally acts in its interest,[37] and is owed allegiance only so long as it continues to protect it.[38] The Leviathan, in other words, *ought* to act differently from the powerful individual in the state of nature, and apparently, solely by virtue of his public identity, will be inclined to do so: the 'public will' just is superior to the private. The sovereign, to use H. L. A. Hart's helpful phrase, is *not* the gunman situation writ large, even for Hobbes; it is the gunman legitimately empowered by the people, constructed by the people, and with the people's interest as the end of his command. What Hobbes lacked, then, was not so much awareness of the need to differentiate the powerful sovereign from the powerful natural individual but, rather, any explanation of how to hold the Leviathan's feet to the fire: how to ensure the Leviathan's continuing identification with the interests of the commonwealth it represents.

One possible way to do so might be that suggested by Locke, developed by American constitutionalists, advocated by contemporary rule of law theorists, and then criticized by critical-legal scholars: hold the Leviathan to the social contract through constraining rules of law, thus subjecting the political Leviathan to legal constraint. But whether or not that's possible—and again, the bottom-line message of critical scholarship is that it is not—there may be other possible solutions as well. One such possibility may be democratic accountability. It may be—as the Hobbes scholar and political philosopher Jean Hampton suggests—that the best way to complete the logical projectory of Hobbes's thought is not through the idea of constraining the Leviathan through rules enforced by courts but, rather, by ensuring the identity of interest between the embodied Leviathan and the interests of citizens through the various practices of democracy.[39] It is to just that possibility, and its exploration in the American patriot Tom Paine's philosophical and revolutionary tracts, that I turn in the next section.

Thomas Paine's rule of law

Like Thomas Hobbes, Tom Paine never spoke directly of the 'rule of law'. He did, however, like Hobbes, write on the value and meaning of law, constitutions, and courts, and, like Hobbes, he clearly had a passion for law. In America, Paine famously declared, and we today ritualistically repeat, the 'law is king'.[40] But what did he mean by that? Out of context, it is tempting—but mistaken—to read

[35] Hobbes, n. 5 above, ch. XVIII, pp. 88–9. [36] Ibid. [37] Ibid., chs. XII and XIII.
[38] Ibid., ch. XXI, p. 114. [39] Hampton, n. 11 above, 38–42.
[40] T. Paine, 'Common Sense', in his *Collected Writings*, ed. E. Foner (New York: Library of America, 1995), 34.

into Paine's commonsensical claim a quasi-Lockean commitment to constitutionalism. 'Law', on this reading, limits the sovereign, political state in a republican democracy, just as the 'king' limits parliament in a monarchical democracy, the difference, of course, being that 'law' in a democratic republic is discerned by courts, rather than by the less trustworthy king. Read in this way, Paine, like Locke, basically presents constitutionalism—and law—as a unified response to the problem of power implied by, and then left unanswered by, Hobbes: if private will is murderous, as Hobbes feared, why won't that same will, when made public through political ascendancy, be any less so? Again, out of context, Paine's basic declaration—'in America, the law is king'—sounds like tacit support for the Lockean resolution of Hobbes's dilemma: constitutionalism, and the rule of law, is that which limits the sovereign, no less than the sovereign restrains the violence of individual wilfulness.

Read *in* context, however, and against the backdrop of the totality of Paine's writings, Paine's provocative comment regarding the status of law suggests something strikingly different from this Lockean reading. From *Common Sense*[41] itself, but even more so from the later essays *The Rights of Man*, part I,[42] and *The Rights of Man*, part II,[43] it seems clear that the 'law' Paine wanted elevated to kingship was neither the dictate of a powerful, Hobbesian monarch, representative only through a fiction with the well-being and interests of the commonwealth, nor a 'higher law', or 'rule of law', that stands apart from the political state, imposed upon it in the name of reason, and enforced by courts. Rather, what Paine himself seemingly meant by the 'Law that would be King', was the *democratic will of the people*, expressed through representative government, in a functioning, simple democracy. It was not, as in the now conventional, neo-Lockean conception, a common, higher, constitutional, or natural law imposed by courts in a way so as to constrain those democratic workings, and it was not, as in the Hobbesian alternative, the will of just *any* centralized Leviathan that can better protect the people against private power than can those individuals in a natural state. It was the product of a political state, itself democratic, aiming towards the republican end of promoting and protecting the common good.

Paine's political views, and the conception of law that rested on them, can be viewed as resting on two basic principles, one or the other of which, but rarely both, was also shared by his co-patriots. The first was taken, roughly, from the general philosophy of civic republicanism current among some of his political contemporaries. Thus, Paine's 'first principle' of government was that government should serve the interests and well-being of the people, rather than that of an elite or a monarch. Such a government, Paine thought, is properly called 'republican'. Whether or not a government is republican, Paine urged, is entirely

[41] T. Paine, 'Common Sense', in his *Collected Writings*, ed. E. Foner (New York: Library of America, 1995), 5–59.

[42] Ibid. 431.

[43] Ibid. 541.

independent of the form it takes: a democracy, monarchy, or aristocracy all might be, or attempt to be, a republican government. Rather, a republican government is defined by its *purpose*, which is to serve the well-being of the citizens.[44] A government that has at its object the general well-being of the people, thought Paine, is a republic, and a good government. All others, again regardless of form, fail this basic moral test.[45]

Paine goes on to ask: 'What is the best form of government for conducting the RES-PUBLICA, or the PUBLIC BUSINESS of a nation, after it becomes too extensive and populous for the simple democratic form?'[46] The question leads Paine to his second principle: rejecting the elitism, fear of the factionalized mob, and anti-democratic instincts of his fellow civic republicans, he asserts again and again, and throughout his political career, that a *simple democracy*, in which every person participates directly and through equal vote, is the best form, at least in theory. The people, individually and collectively, as a whole, possess the knowledge of their own interest, and the best means to achieve it—neither a monarch nor an aristocracy can better know the interest of a population than the population itself. In practice, however, such a direct democracy is unavailable where the area to be governed is large and the population spread thin. Therefore, Paine concludes, representative government, and only representative government, can best—because most knowledgeably—serve the interests of the people.[47]

Paine was led by his two principles, then, to advocate a simple, straightforward representative democracy, because it was best designed to achieve the republican goal of advancing the interest of the people. He admired America and America's government as much as he did, precisely because in his view it had self-styled itself to achieve just that end, 'a system of representation only',[48] or as he elsewhere put it, 'representation ingrafted upon democracy'.[49] Accordingly, the 'law', implied by Paine's politics, his understanding of human nature, and his conception of the ideal constitution, and that which Paine hoped would replace the status of the monarch, was *the people's will*, expressed through representative democratic politics. It was not a 'law' of either higher principle or past precedent, constraining the expression of political deliberation. The law to be king, in America, was the expression of politics, not a check on it, and the politics that would generate that law would be representative, democratic, and republican, all. It was not a law that limited governmental or state power, applied by courts, through either natural or neutral principles, and as guided by rules of precedent. It was a law, rather, that was constituted by the governmental power of a representative democracy.

Let me try to sharpen Paine's rule of law by drawing some contrasts. How does Paine's Rule of Law—in shorthand, a Rule that asks us both to participate and to respect the outcomes of representative, democratic politics—compare, and

[44] Ibid. 585.
[45] Ibid. 565.
[46] Ibid. 568.
[47] Ibid. 567–8.
[48] Ibid. 566.
[49] Ibid. 568.

contrast, with the conventional Lockean account on the one hand, and the Hobbesian alternative to it, sketched above, on the other? Against Hobbes, the contrast is sharp and twofold: it extends to the place of both rights and democracy in the political theory of each. First, the Hobbesian citizen, as argued above, has a positive right to a state that will protect him against private assault, but has no negative rights, protecting either his property against the state, or his conscience, speech, assembly, or worship against unwarranted state intrusion. For Paine, by contrast, no less than for contemporary liberal thinkers, and as I will elaborate briefly below, the natural rights that survive the transition to civil society consist not only of a right to security against private assault, but also of rights against intrusion by the state.[50]

Secondly, on democracy: there is no account of either the logic or the desirability of democracy—of the basic *identification* of the 'People' as 'sovereign'—in Hobbes's jurisprudence. For Hobbes, the core, justificatory basis for the state was its ability to protect the individual against private assault, and it was an entirely contingent question what form of government would best ensure that end. For Paine, by contrast, the purpose of republican government was much more general: it was to reflect the will and serve the interests of the people. Not just the best but the only way such an end can be ensured is through the mechanism of representative democracy. Law, then, and the rule of law, that should displace the king, for Paine but not for Hobbes, *must be* identified not only with the protection of individual rights, but also with the product of representative democracy. The rule of law that displaces nature, for Hobbes, is the protective arm of the state. The rule of law that displaces the monarch, for Paine, is the voice of the people expressed through the will of their representatives. The rule of law, for Paine, is the rule of democracy.

The distance, though, between Hobbes and Paine should not obscure the ground they shared. Most importantly, they both worked within the parameters of social contract theory: for both, the legitimacy of the 'law' that is the product of a state, which then coerces obedience from citizens, is grounded in a contractual delegation of authority from the governed to the governors. Although he saw no reason ultimately to prefer democracy over monarchy, Hobbes spoke of both the origins of government, and of its justification, in democratic and republican terms that Paine would have found entirely congenial: the 'sovereign', or the 'commonwealth', is the product of a democratic delegation of authority from individuals, the purpose of which is to preserve the security of the people and the peace of the collective.

More important for these purposes, however, Paine clearly shared Hobbes's view that *a* central purpose of the state is to ensure to each citizen protection against the violence and oppression of fellow citizens—and, consequently, shared his general understanding that citizens retain positive rights to state

[50] T. Paine, 'Common Sense', in his *Collected Writings*, ed. E. Foner (New York: Library of America, 1995), 537.

intervention into civil life. Law, and the rule of law, Paine argued, echoing Hobbes, requires a state to whom the enforcement mechanisms for the natural right of self-protection and security have been delegated—thus according to the state a monopoly on the levers of violence. Paine makes this Hobbesian point quite explicit in his discussion of the difference between those natural rights that are retained by individuals after entering into civil society and those, *like the right of self-protection*, that become 'civil rights' when the means for their enforcement are delegated to the state. Thus, in a passage in *The Rights of Man*, noteworthy because it is almost a perfect blend of Lockean and Hobbesian understandings of the rule of law, Paine explains:

> Natural rights are those which appertain to man in right of his existence . . . Civil rights are those which appertain to man in right of his being a member of society. Every civil right has for its foundation some natural right pre-existing in the individual, but to which his individual power is not, in all cases, sufficiently competent. *Of this kind are all those which relate to security and protection . . .*
>
> The natural rights which he retains [after entering into civil society] are all those in which the power to execute is as perfect in the individual as the right itself. Among [them] . . . are all the intellectual rights, or rights of the mind: consequently, religion is one of those rights . . . civil power, properly considered as such, is made up of the aggregate of that class of the natural rights of man, which becomes defective in the individual in point of power, and answers not his purpose; but when collected to a focus, becomes competent to the purpose of every one.[51]

Put in our modern terms, the 'civil rights' to protection, security, and adjudication of private disputes, grounded in a pre-existing natural right to protect oneself, are positive in nature: they impose obligations upon the civil state of enforcement, and rights in the individual to their protection. The 'natural rights' that are retained, in Paine's scheme, are what we today refer to as negative. And they are both clearly a part of the Painean ideal of the operation of law in a constitutional democracy.

Now let me turn to the more striking, certainly more surprising, contrast between Paine's view of the law to be king, in America, and the contemporary conception of the rule of law. Paine obviously held out great hopes for law, and would have had no objection to the bland directive at the core of the modern conception, that courts should find and apply, rather than create, law. But, at the same time, he almost certainly did not share the assumption of contemporary American rule of law theorists that through law and the rule of law, courts should constrain the workings of democratic majorities. Nor did he share the attitudinal assumptions regarding democratic states that typically accompany that claim: that political power is to be distrusted, and towards that end should be divided between warring branches, and that law, or at least 'higher law', by contrast, should be trusted and even revered. Let me take these points sequentially, and in reverse order.

[51] Ibid. 464.

First, and whatever else Paine might have meant by declaring the law to be king, he clearly did not mean that we should replace the habitual love and obedience traditionally accorded to monarchical authority with a love of legal authority—that we should love and obey *law*, and the state that produces it, in the way that monarchists think subjects ought to love the king and obey his edicts. Paine had nothing but contempt for the 'royal brute' and the institution of monarchy he embodied, but he also had nothing but contempt for the infantile, unthinking obedience, born of ignorance, he elicited from his subjects. There is no reason to think that he would have been any more charitable towards unthinking obedience to 'law'. Rather, on the evidence of *Common Sense*, it is safe to say that Paine intended his famous equation of 'law' with the 'king' to mean something very much to the contrary: in America, he was claiming, we have no need to revere authority. We do not wish or need to have a charismatic half-mortal and half-godly creature, ruling by divine right, 'touched by the sun's rays' to use Shakespeare's line, who can do no wrong and is beyond reproach—whose 'authority', in other words, is by definition both moral and political. Rather, we conduct our political business through political institutions, and have no moral or divine or charismatic claim to any sort of blind *allegiance*.

Nor is there any support, in *Common Sense* or elsewhere, for the proposition that Paine shared his co-patriots' fear that man's asocial, selfish, self-serving instincts were so powerful as to require a rule of law that divides government into checking, warring branches, or houses, so as to minimize the influence of particular factions in a popular democracy. In fact, Paine most likely believed quite the reverse. Thus, for Paine, the source of human society is the human impulse towards cooperation and reciprocated sympathy, not fear of the violence of others—as it was for Hobbes—*or* the attempt to secure the greatest individual advantage through limited and self-interested cooperation with others—as it was for most of his contemporaries, including prominently the drafters of the United States Constitution. Consequently, considerably more was to be expected of human society than mutual restraint for reciprocal advantage. Similarly, government acts so as to perfect and underscore human society, and thus is in harmony with human instinct, not the contrary.[52] The government, then, should serve the common interests of the people, whose interests, with or without a state, are intrinsically social and connected.[53]

That common interest, and that common, connected nature, Paine thought, were best ascertained through the deliberations of either direct or representative democracy, not through the deliberations of even a well-meaning monarch, or a wise, even well-intentioned, aristocratic elite: both of these alternatives breed either ignorance or corruption. Paine thus rejected *both* the self-interested case for purely representative democracy—that self-interested representatives

[52] T. Paine, 'Common Sense', in his *Collected Writings*, ed. E. Foner (New York: Library of America, 1995), 551–3.
[53] Ibid. 551.

can and should simply fight for their own or their constituents' self-interests, so as to generate the greatest possible satisfactions—*and* the elitist-republican alternative—that government should seek the common good, but that to do so requires an elite that can perceive the common good, as well as checks that can limit corruption. Rather, government should aim for the common good—not the maximization of individual or factional interest—and should do so through representative democracy—not aristocratic or monarchic elitism.

Now, to return to the meaning of law: there is no support in Paine's writing for the proposition that, by equating law with kingship, Paine meant to suggest that the authority of either a 'higher law', or a 'common law', or even a 'constitutional law' ought constrain the workings of politics in a way analogous to the manner in which, by divine right, a king might constrain the workings of Parliament, or the House of Lords might constrain the House of Commons. As noted, Paine was a harsh critic of the manner in which powerful conquerors claim moral authority, so as to augment their power and the senses of the people. For Paine, no less than for the positivistic Hobbes before him, the basis for governmental legitimacy is purely contractual, nothing 'higher'.[54] And, even more clearly, whatever else Paine might or might not have meant by equating the law with the king, he most assuredly did not mean that courts ought to decide cases by reference to clearly existing prior rules drawn from precedents taken from antiquity: he was a critic, not an advocate, of 'the common law' as a constraint on legislation. Indeed, Paine was as hostile to the authoritarian, mystifying, obfuscating traditions of the 'common law' as to the moralistic pretensions of the 'royal brute'. In contrast to his critical correspondent Edmund Burke, and both echoing Hobbes and also prefiguring Benthamic and Holmesian critiques of judge-made precedent, Paine found the courts' slavish abidance by the 'rule of precedent' both repugnant and somewhat comical. The result of too much respect for the common law, Paine thought, was a superstitious reliance on ancient 'opinion' that defied, rather than embodied, reason.[55] Similarly, he attributed the over-reliance on precedent in England to a *lack* of current law, a condition in turn occasioned by a government overly concerned with foreign affairs and neglectful of domestic issues. Thus the rule of precedent—judge-made common law—far from being the legal paradigm, was, for Paine, the very *antithesis* of the 'law' for which he held out hope.[56] Whatever he did mean, he clearly did *not* mean, then, by equating the 'law' with the 'king', that we ought to enthrone the common law as a constraint on legislation.

Finally, might Paine have meant by the 'law' that is to be king, constitutional law, enforced by courts and constraining the power of representative democracies. To be sure, Paine (unlike Hobbes) was a friend of 'constitutionalism', and particularly of American state constitutions, and ultimately supported the United States federal Constitution as well. He also, in a crucial passage in

[54] Ibid. 467. [55] Ibid. 583–4. [56] Ibid. 584.

The Rights of Man, refers to a well-functioning constitution as 'a law of government' that governs government, just as government governs men.[57] But what Paine meant by a 'constitution' was quite different from what a 'constitution' has come to mean in contemporary United States law and politics. Thus, in Paine's longest sustained discussion of constitutions, appearing in *The Rights of Man*, part II, Paine praised both the American states' constitutions and the French Constitution, precisely because he thought they could be continually revised and redrafted by the people of the generation to be affected.[58] The Pennsylvania Constitution, for example, won his approval because it provided for its own redrafting every seven years, assuring the 'unison of government with the circumstances of the state at all times', and precluding what was to him the absolutely odious possibility that any generation should be ruled by the dead hand of the past.[59] He praised constitutions, and constitutionalism, more generally, because he viewed them as enhancing, rather than constraining, contemporaneous, democratic, political deliberation. Obviously, such an idealized constitution is a very far cry from the constitution, wedded to the rule of law, that constrains politics—precisely by limiting the options of each generation by the presumed intergenerational consensus, enforced by courts and divined some time in the past.

I would sum it up this way: the flexible, democratic 'constitution' that Paine imagined, idealized, and then praised was in many ways the antithesis of the stable, intergenerational document praised by contemporary American rule of law scholars—a document revered for the wisdom of its drafters, respected for its relative antiquity, and that checks and limits the democratic will of the people. Paine consistently favoured a simple and representative form of democracy over any kind of 'mixed' government, which, he thought, could only operate through fraud and corruption, and his faith in constitutionalism was conditioned on that commitment. He favoured, in brief, what the constitutional historian Mark Tushnet has recently and helpfully called a 'thin constitution': the general constitutional guarantees, found in the Document's Preamble, and echoed in the Declaration of Independence, that speak aspirationally of our commitment to justice and equality, and which underscore and strengthen, not undermine, democratic, representative politics.[60] More to the point, nowhere does Paine speak of a 'constitutional law', enforced by courts, against the will of the people. Rather, the constitutions he praises are those that are open to constant revision, and enforced through popular discussion and political self-correction. Notable by its absence is any reference in Paine's writings to judicial review, or any role at all for courts, in the enforcement of constitutional limits on recalcitrant or overreaching political states.

[57] T. Paine, 'Common Sense', in his *Collected Writings*, ed. E. Foner (New York: Library of America, 1995), 468.

[58] Ibid. 594.

[59] Ibid. 573–4.

[60] M. Tushnet, *Taking the Constitution Away from the Courts* (Princeton: Princeton University Press, 1999).

Although surely open to interpretation, it seems to me that on the basis of Paine's collected writings, there is no reason to think that Paine, by declaring the law to be king, intended by 'law' the substantive provisions of an anti-democratic constitution, enforced by unelected judges and written by prior generations, that should constrain the workings of democratic politics by reference to the wisdom of the ages. Rather, both before and after *Common Sense*, Paine was a republican democrat—supportive of broad suffrage, and of giving the vote, rather than the king's edicts, the effect of law. His understanding of, and praise of, constitutionalism was entirely conditional upon his understanding that constitutions would give direct voice to the people—and thus enhance, not constrain, representative politics.

Paine's ambitions, both theoretical and political, when identifying law as king, simply transcended any concern with the workings of courts. Paine wished to sever the states from a monarchic system he hated and to forge a new understanding of the civic relation between citizens, as well as between citizens and their government. His declaration that 'in America, the law is king' was meant to telegraph that new relation. It had nothing to do with the common law, or with the work of courts, or with the interpretation of constitutions by courts so as to check democratic will. It certainly did not dictate a preference for the reasoned, neutral elaboration of a common law, constraining the work of the representative branches. To the degree that courts thwarted the work of legislation, as he thought occurred through the operation of the Rule of Precedent, he stood as a critic, not a supporter, of that usurpation. The contemporary understanding of the rule of law as a Rule of Judicial Reason, directing courts to employ neutral principles so as to constrain state action in order to maximize individual freedom, whatever its merits or demerits, is not even an echo of the revolutionary implications of Paine's commonsensical utterance.

Conclusion

It is surely possible to understand the 'rule of law' in the American legal tradition as expressing a general desire for legal control, or containment, of the political process. It is also possible, however, to understand that tradition as expressing, following Hobbes, a commitment to the positive value of the state, of the politics that produce it, and to its legal fruits, over the condition of natural warfare that obtains in its absence. Likewise, it is surely possible, following our own American patriot Tom Paine, to understand our appreciation of constitutionalism as a commitment to representative government, and the laws that our representatives, acting in our interest and on our behalf, produce, rather than as a commitment to limits on that representation. Putting the two together, we can understand our American commitment to representative democracy as that which produces, rather than as that which is constrained by, our equally American commitment to the rule of law.

It is also possible to situate our own rights tradition within this more expansive understanding of the rule of law. We have, in this country, not only constitutionally guaranteed rights to speech, conscience, religion, and assembly, protected by courts against the legislating, representative branches, but also a host of non-constitutional civil rights guaranteeing non-discrimination in the private sphere, freedom from gendered and race-motivated violence, protection of the aged and disabled against various forms of private exploitation, and some limited protection against the economic pressures of age, poverty, and sickness—all of which originated in legislative, democratic politics, rather than adjudication, and all of which require substantial state action, rather than state inaction, to be made meaningful. These democratically produced positive rights, to the protection of the state against private aggressions and harms, can all be understood in a Hobbesian way as protecting us against the dangers of the state of nature and, following Paine, as a part of the 'Rights of Man' rightly produced by democratic governance. And all of these rights are surely as central to our self-understanding—our highest understanding of our better selves—as the negative rights embodied in constitutional protections. Were we to give these positive and democratic rights their due, the tension we now see, between American understandings of rights on the one hand and international conceptions on the other, might be considerably eased, thereby opening the door to American participation in at least the discourse, if not yet the creation, expansion, or enforcement, of the generous conception of rights at the heart of public international law.

DEMOCRATIC FOUNDATIONS

5

Rights, Rules, and Democracy

RICHARD S. KAY

More and more, the protection of human rights in the world today is a matter of declaring the rights in a written constitution and making that constitution enforceable against the state in some kind of law court. That model has, at least in form, been adopted in the great majority of nation-states. Its propriety, however, has never ceased to be the object of intense political and scholarly criticism. Such criticism is rarely based on serious disagreement with the underlying goal of protecting rights. It is usually agreed that certain human activities should be enabled or allowed to proceed without interference and, as a corollary, that the state—and other actors—should be obliged to undertake or be disabled from certain conduct. Instead, the critics dispute the assumption that this goal is best effectuated through a grant of reviewing power to unelected courts. A society respectful of human rights, they contend, could and should leave its government in the untied hands of elected legislatures.

In this chapter I will deal with these issues generally rather than with respect to one or another particular legal system. The examples of constitutions, institutions, and academic commentary are drawn from several jurisdictions. Necessarily, they bear the special characteristics of the historical experiences in which they were created, and their relevance must be qualified accordingly.[1] I will conclude that views on this question turn critically on one feature: the assumed description of what courts are doing when they engage in constitutional judicial review. When they are understood as making fresh political judgments on the issue before them—when they are seen as legislating—it is hard to defend their authority in competition with the elected legislature. Conversely, the most persuasive case for authoritative constitutional judicial review depends on an understanding that it consists of the application of pre-existing rules of law.

Answers to difficult problems of legal theory start (and sometimes end) with definition. Our terminology, necessarily, is stipulated and, consequently, somewhat arbitrary. When considering the relative roles of courts and legislatures in the protection of human rights, the most obvious definitional issue is the

I received valuable suggestions at a workshop for contributors to this volume held at St Kilda, Australia, Dec. 2001. I am grateful for comments on an earlier draft from Mark Janis, Martin Krygier, Thomas Morawetz, Jeremy Paul, Kenneth Ward, and Carol Weisbrod.

[1] For a useful caution on the need for context in evaluating constitutional designs, see W. Sadurski, 'Judicial Review and the Protection of Constitutional Rights', (2002) 22 *Oxford Journal of Legal Studies* 275.

much-disputed meaning of 'human rights'.[2] For my purposes, it is possible to put forward an understanding 'thin' enough to conform to a broad assortment of approaches. In particular, it will be unnecessary to deal with the complicated issue of what makes a right a 'human' right. That question seems to turn mainly on the scope of application of the right with respect to time, culture, and geography.[3] I will assume that these standards have been settled and that, given this agreement, a basis exists for determining (or contesting) the particular substantive content of these rights. Beyond this, however, it is essential that the rights—once defined—be held against those persons or entities that might actually threaten the activities marked out for protection. In particular, human rights will always be assertable, at least, against the state. Equally critical for my purposes is that a human right—like any right—will suppose some model of appropriate behaviour between the right-holder and some actual or potential right-violator. That is, to say X 'has a right' means that, in some specified set of circumstances, someone must do something for X (positive rights) or refrain from doing something to X (negative rights). Positing a right is thus another way of prescribing desired behaviour in the specified circumstances. I labour this point to emphasize the inevitable conclusion. To say that there is or ought to be a right is necessarily to say that there is or ought to be a *rule* about the conduct or status of the right-holder and some other person or persons.[4]

Once we recognize that the issue under consideration involves the creation, interpretation, and application of rules, it may appear in a somewhat different light. I am concerned here with how the identified human rights may be enforced in a positive law system.[5] In such systems the relative roles of courts and legislators with respect to the rules of the system is a commonplace. Legislatures make rules. Courts apply them in particular disputes. When we are talking about human rights, however, that assumption must be clarified in at least one way. As already stated, the most prominently recognized potential violator of human rights is the state. If we include within the term 'state' all of its makers of decisions and holders of power, then rights must be held against the legislature

[2] T. Campbell, Ch. 1 above; H. Steiner and P. Alston, *International Human Rights in Context: Law, Politics, Morals* (Oxford: Oxford University Press, 1996), 167–80.

[3] C. Powell, 'Symposium in Celebration of the Fiftieth Anniversary of the Universal Declaration of Human Rights. Introduction: Locating Culture, Identity, and Human Rights', (1999) 20 *Columbia Human Rights Law Review* 201; M. Monshipourri, 'Promoting Universal Human Rights: Dilemmas of Integrating Developing Countries', (2001) 4 *Yale Human Rights and Development Law Journal* 25.

[4] F. Schauer, *Playing by the Rules: A Philosophical Examination of Rule-Based Decision-Making in Law and in Life* (Oxford: Oxford University Press, 1991), 64 (a 'rule is explainable in terms of a paired relationship between a behavior within the extension of a rule-formulation and the behavior that takes place'). Although it is not essential to the arguments in this chapter, it seems to me that this is true with respect not only to legal rights but to natural or moral rights as well. The rules in those cases are the rules of nature or of the deity or of any other guide to right behaviour. Thus, human rights may arise in opposition to an established system of positive law rules when it is alleged that those rules violate a superior rule specifying the proper conduct of the challenged state rule-maker. The use of the terminology of rights always assumes some entity (some person), real or postulated, who ought or ought not to do something with respect to the right-holder.

[5] Campbell, Ch. 1 above.

as well as against other potential violators. It is, therefore, implausible to see the legislature as possessing the power to make and unmake the rules that define rights. Indeed, it is something of a contradiction in terms to claim certain rights against the state but to vest in the state the power to say what those rights are. But this does not mean that the ordinary division between legislation and adjudication cannot be employed in this context. The rule-maker in these circumstances must merely be external to the persons and entities subject to the rules. The Western response to this fact has been to resort to a special constituent form of legislation anterior to the state institutions to be governed. This process produces constitutions as a higher level of law. Once such a constitution is in place the ordinary allocation of authority between the (constituent) legislature and the courts may be deployed. The job of the courts is to interpret and apply the rules so created in claims against alleged rights-violators including the ordinary legislature. The result is the familiar system of constitutionalism where courts enforce the constitution against the rest of the government.[6]

The practice of constitutional judicial review of legislation thus appears to be built into the very idea of entrenching human rights in rules of law. It is at this point that a persistent source of discomfort emerges. The judicial enforcement of rights against the legislature is an abridgement of democratic government. Yet the idea of constitutional restraint is most prominent in exactly those societies where political legitimacy is tied to the representative character of the state decision-makers. The consequent tension has been evident from the first assertion of this kind of judicial authority. The classical statement of the resulting concerns for current observers in the United States is Alexander Bickel's. Bickel declared, 'the root difficulty is that judicial review is a counter-majoritarian force in our system' making it a 'deviant institution'.[7] The political actors whose activities are policed by the courts are elected and subject to re-election. The judges (usually) are not. This 'counter-majoritarian difficulty' has famously vexed commentators on constitutional review, especially those in the United States. Barry Friedman does not exaggerate when he refers to this concern as the 'central obsession of modern [American] constitutional scholarship'.[8] A principal project of academic writers has been to reconcile democracy and judicial review. None of these attempts has been entirely successful.

One common democratic defence of judicial review is a simple redefinition of democracy to include the enforcement of human rights norms against the decisions of legislatures. In one of the best-known defences of the practice (written before Bickel's formulation of the problem) Eugene Rostow candidly employed a 'personal definition of the crucial term'. Even in democracies, he noted, some discretionary authority must be granted to unelected officials. Therefore, 'It is

[6] *Marbury v Madison* 5 US (1 Cranch) 137 (1803).

[7] A. Bickel, *The Least Dangerous Branch: The Supreme Court at the Bar of Politics* (Indianapolis: Bobbs-Merrill, 1962), 16, 18.

[8] B. Friedman, 'The History of the Countermajoritarian Difficulty. Part One: The Road to Judicial Supremacy', (1998) 73 *New York University Law Review* 333, 335.

error to insist that no society is democratic unless it has a government of unlimited powers and that no government is democratic unless its legislature has unlimited powers.'[9]

Perhaps unsurprisingly, the redefinition of democratic government to include a reviewing power by the courts seems to be a favourite device of constitutional judges. In a recent lecture Chief Justice MacLachlin of the Supreme Court of Canada put the proposition baldly. With the advent of constitutions 'Democracy was no longer just majority rule. Democracy also required protection of certain fundamental rights.'[10] Judge Abella of the Ontario Court of Appeals was even more forceful in identifying judicial enforcement of rights with democracy: 'since rights and participation define democracies', criticism of judicial review 'come[s] down to the proposition that we have too much democracy and too many institutions to enforce it'.[11]

I have already noted that definitions in these kinds of matters have a necessarily arbitrary element. Without claiming that these definitions are 'wrong', we can note that, by themselves, they are unlikely to assuage democratically motivated critics who are concerned with the character of constitutional decisions and the unelected status of the judges who issue them. But the efforts at redefinition are proof of George Orwell's observation that any attempt to pin down a definition of democracy 'is resisted from all sides. It is almost universally felt that when we call a country democratic we are praising it; consequently the defenders of every kind of regime claim that it is a democracy, and fear that they might have to stop using that word if it were tied down to any one meaning.'[12]

Somewhat more specifically, the attempt to frame judicial constitutional review as consistent with democratic governance is sometimes premissed on the democratic character of the constitution-making process and the possibility of constitutional amendment. Alexander Hamilton, in *The Federalist*, no. 78, insisted that judicial review does not 'suppose a superiority of the judicial to the legislative power. It only supposes the power of the people is superior to both...'.[13] This understanding has continued to appeal to some advocates. Dieter Grimm, a judge of the German Constitutional Court, has argued that 'If the people decides to check government power vis-à-vis the citizens through

[9] E. Rostow, 'The Democratic Character of Judicial Review', (1952) 66 *Harvard Law Review* 193, 199.

[10] B. MacLachlin, 'The Supreme Court and the Public Interest', (2001) 64 *Saskatchewan Law Review* 309, 313.

[11] R. Silberman Abella, 'The Judicial Role in a Democratic State', (2001) 26 *Queen's Law Journal* 573, 574, 577; A. Barak, *Judicial Discretion* (New Haven: Yale University Press, 1989), 195–6; J. Limbach, 'A Concept of the Supremacy of the Constitution', (2001) 64 *Modern Law Review* 1, 3; *Vriend v Alberta* [1998] 1 SCR 493, paras 134, 142 (noting that the adoption of the Charter of Rights and Freedoms effected a 'redefinition of our democracy' and 'judges are not acting undemocratically by intervening when there are indications that a legislative or executive decision was not reached in accordance with democratic principles mandated by the Charter'; Cory J).

[12] G. Orwell, 'Politics and the English Language', in his *Collection of Essays* (New York: Harcourt Brace Jovanovich, 1953), 156.

[13] A. Hamilton, *The Federalist*, ed. C. Rossiter (New York: New American Library, 1961), no. 78, pp. 464, 468.

fundamental rights, enforcement of such rights against a ruling majority can hardly be regarded as anti-democratic.'[14] It may be accurate to characterize an original constitution-making process as democratic, although, in the case of the United States, this is a matter of substantial doubt. But the passage of time corrodes any claim of democratic legitimacy as the human beings represented in the constituent events are replaced by new generations. The continuing force of those constitutional rules cannot really be regarded as self-imposed.[15] References to an old constitution as the mandate 'of the people' are at best rhetorical.[16] Nor, in the ordinary case, does the possibility of popularly initiated or approved amendments change the situation. In most constitutional systems, the specified manner of amending the constitution is designed to frustrate the will of a transient majority, even a substantial majority.[17] It may be that requiring an exceptionally intense expression of democratic preference to make or change a constitution means that the resulting constitutional rights reflect the will of 'the people' in some more authentic sense.[18] But, as was the case with the prior examples, this reconciliation depends on a redefinition of democracy that fails to speak to the disfranchisement of current majorities that concerns the critics of judicial review.[19]

It is true that there is no thorough democracy if that means that every choice and every action taken by the state is reviewed and approved by the majority of the competent population. But recognizing the necessarily mixed character of any practical definition of democracy does not alter the fact there are some forms of public decision-making that are more responsive to the expressed preferences of a majority of the citizenry than others. 'The whole', Bickel observed, 'operates under public scrutiny and criticism' and 'a representative majority has the power to accomplish a reversal'.[20] That is designedly not the case with judges exercising the power of judicial review, and their actions may thus be said to be *less* consonant with democratic decision-making than that of other unelected holders of power.

A last argument for the democratic quality of judicial review is more challenging. It notes the existence of some minimal social and political preconditions for the continuing exercise of democratic authority. There can be no representative democracy without free and fair elections. Such elections cannot be a meaningful gauge of popular sentiment unless it is possible to engage in reasoned discussion

[14] D. Grimm, 'Constitutional Adjudication and Democracy', (1999) 33 *Israel Law Review* 193, 198; see also p. 197; *Vriend v Alberta*, n. 11 above, paras 134–42.

[15] J. Waldron, *Law and Disagreement* (Oxford: Oxford University Press, 1999), 271–4.

[16] M. Klarman, 'Antifidelity', (1997) 70 *Southern California Law Review* 381, 392–3.

[17] S. Levinson (ed.), *Responding to Imperfection: The Theory and Practice of Constitutional Amendment* (Princeton: Princeton University Press, 1995).

[18] B. Ackerman, 'The Storrs Lectures: Discovering the Constitution', (1984) 93 *Yale Law Journal* 1013.

[19] For an interesting variation on this argument, see K. Whittington, *Constitutional Interpretation: Textual Meaning, Original Intent and Judicial Review* (Lawrence: University of Kansas Press, 1999), 132–4.

[20] Bickel, n. 7 above, 17.

of the choices facing the state. Should an elected legislature subvert these conditions, the prospects for the survival of democratic decision-making would be seriously jeopardized. Consequently, it is argued, institutional machinery that guards against interference with these conditions, even by elected representatives, is not inconsistent with respect for democratic decision-making. This is more than a hypothetical concern, as evidenced by the fate of the Weimar democracy in Germany.[21] In a much-remarked argument, John Hart Ely made the case for 'representation-reinforcing' judicial review and attempted to explain many of the constitutional decisions of the United States Supreme Court in terms of that approach.[22] More recently, Ronald Dworkin has made a much broader argument based on the same kind of reasoning. Eschewing a 'statistical' concept of democracy, he insists that 'the defining aim of democracy [is] that collective decisions be made by political institutions whose structure, composition, and practices treat all members of the community, as individuals, with equal concern and respect'. Such government assumes the existence of certain 'democratic conditions' assuring 'the equal status of all citizens'. So legislation excluding members of certain races from public office would be inconsistent with democratic principles. Action by an unelected judiciary that invalidated such a law would 'protect and respect [those principles] better' and would be 'no matter for moral regret'.[23]

Unless we take a moment-to-moment model of democracy, it is hard to resist the argument that constraints in the service of democracy are appropriate even for democratically impeccable decisions. Once we agree to protect a democratic system *over time*, it is hard to object to the intervention of an external guardian to the extent that its actions are limited to maintaining those elements that are genuinely essential to preserve that system. But there are a multiplicity of state institutions and activities that are consistent with genuine representative government.[24] Therefore, the occasions on which legislation will offend on this basis must be extremely rare. This is even clearer when we recall that such legislation will issue from a process that is itself assumed, by hypothesis, to be democratic. In the hands of some of its proponents, however, the reach of constitutional judicial review supposedly required for the maintenance of democracy is far greater. Thus Dworkin finds the judicial invalidation of legislative limitations on abortion, pornography, and euthanasia to be a logical inference from his 'constitutional conception of democracy' (an appropriation which might have astonished even Orwell).[25]

There seems little escape from the proposition that substantive constitutional review by an unelected judiciary is an abridgement of democratic decision-making. Once we have accepted the proposition that there exist human rights

[21] Grimm, n. 14 above, 791–2.
[22] J. Ely, *Democracy and Distrust* (Cambridge, Mass.: Harvard University Press, 1980).
[23] R. Dworkin, *Freedom's Law* (Cambridge, Mass.: Harvard University Press, 1996), 17.
[24] J. Allan, 'Liberalism, Democracy and Hong Kong', (1998) 28 *Hong Kong Law Journal* 156, 160.
[25] Dworkin, n. 23 above, 17, 117–46, 214–26.

that ought to be protected, this should hardly surprise us. The founders of the American Constitution feared first of all legislative interference in personal liberty: 'it is against the enterprising ambition of this [legislative] department', wrote Madison, 'that the people ought to indulge all their jealousy and exhaust all their precautions'.[26] It follows that the United States Constitution 'consciously was structured to confound effectuation of majority will'.[27] The 'counter-majoritarian difficulty' only presents itself as a difficulty if we have made a prior determination that any and every limitation of democratic decision-making is a cause for worry. If, on the other hand, democratic process is seen not as a transcendent value, but as one tool to be employed in the design and operation of a satisfactory social organization, then its compromise with, and limitation by, other institutions designed for the same end is perfectly understandable.[28]

All of this is built into the very idea of human rights as implying rules for conduct, including—and perhaps especially—the conduct of the law-making power. Nonetheless, a respectable body of commentary maintains that it is possible to hold both to a substantive view of human rights and to the idea that the definition, elaboration, and enforcement of those rights may be entrusted to electorally accountable officials including legislators. 'There is no law of nature', Jeffrey Goldsworthy has written, 'that legislatures can never be trusted voluntarily to comply with the deeper principles that confer and limit their moral authority...'.[29] Jeremy Waldron has argued that 'we should not underestimate the extent to which the idea of rights may pervade legislative or electoral politics'.[30] Indeed, it has been suggested that the practice of judicial constitutional review may actually reduce the sensitivity of the elected agents of the state to the importance of respecting rights.[31] Waldron insists that the very idea of human rights presupposes that human beings are competent moral agents with the capacity to make critical choices affecting their own lives and the nature of the society in which they live. It is inconsistent with such a picture to disable the people from making their own decisions about the shape and application of rights. To do so would be to 'consecrate forms of authority which are radically at odds with those entrusted to ordinary rights-bearers in the exercise and contemplation of their rights'.[32] Submitting these matters to legislative judgment may, in

26 Hamilton, n. 13 above, no. 48, pp. 308, 309.

27 R. Bennett, 'Counter-conversationalism and the Sense of Difficulty', (2001) 95 *Northwestern University Law Review* 845, 848.

28 E. Rubin, 'Getting Past Democracy', (2001) 149 *University of Pennsylvania Law Review* 711, 727 ('The tension between democracy and constitutionalism...can be resolved by simply acknowledging that they constitute two separate principles'); J. Kirk, 'Rights, Review and Reasons for Restraint', (2001) 23 *Sydney Law Review* 19, 34–5; Whittington, n. 19 above, 44; M. Perry, *Morality, Politics and Law* (New York: Oxford University Press, 1988), 163–4.

29 J. Goldsworthy, *The Sovereignty of Parliament: History and Philosophy* (Oxford: Oxford University Press, 1999), 257.

30 Waldron, n. 15 above, 307; M. Tushnet, *Taking the Constitution Away from the Courts* (Princeton: Princeton University Press, 1999), 96–124.

31 Goldsworthy, n. 29 above, 262–3; Tushnet, n. 30 above, 66.

32 Waldron, n. 15 above, 254; see also p. 304.

fact, have distinct advantages over entrusting them to an unelected judiciary, especially if we accept the inevitable controvertibility of questions associated with rights and, as a corollary, that these questions cannot have determinate answers.[33] The measures most consonant with human rights will be different in different circumstances. It is unreasonable, on this view, to privilege the resolution preferred at the time of constitution-making. The determination of disputed issues concerning human rights presents difficult and delicate matters of public policy. It has long been understood that legislatures possess certain resources for the investigation of and deliberation on such issues that courts lack.[34]

There is a sense in which this position is simply inconsistent with the notion of rights stipulated at the outset—that they necessarily contemplate rules of conduct for the treatment of individuals that bind—especially bind—the state. If we have further decided to vindicate those rights through law, it is hard to understand how one can insist that the content and applicability of the relevant rules should be committed to the representative agencies of the state. It is in the nature of a rule that it limits the courses of action of those subject to it.[35] It may be, however, that the supporters of this view hold a commitment to rights in a different sense. They may see a society committed to rights as one in which certain broad values are respected without any particular specification of how the application of those values will play out in the conduct of individuals and institutions. They may argue that the general promotion of the preferred values is best left to a democratically responsive legislature. That is to say, such an allocation of responsibility will result in a state of affairs in which those values are best respected.

Such an expectation, of course, is at odds with the modern impulse to reduce the values that ought to inform state conduct to a set of rules—the impulse towards constitutionalism. That idea supposes that some aspects of state behaviour should not be decided action by action, according to the all-things-considered judgment of the actors. Instead they should be governed by abstract standards set out in advance.[36] Two reasons for this approach are particularly relevant in this context. First, reliance on rules can control the tendency of human beings to exaggerate the relative importance of their own interests as compared to those of other people. In law, this presumption underlies the fundamental maxim that no person should be a judge in his or her own cause. Legislators may find it difficult fairly to measure the utility of their own actions against the values associated with human rights. Their very electoral accountability may induce them to give priority to shorter-term political considerations over principles whose pay-off will appear only over time and will, in any event, be hard to recognize and evaluate.[37]

The second advantage of acting according to fixed rules is its relative stability and clarity. The embrace of rights is an embrace of the idea that, in significant

[33] This crucial proposition is considered further below in text at nn. 43–60.
[34] Goldsworthy, n. 29 above, 257, 262–3.
[35] Schauer, n. 4 above, 51–2.
[36] Ibid.
[37] Grimm, n. 14 above, 202.

ways, individuals should be free to make decisions about their own lives. But no such individual autonomy is meaningful if it may be overturned at any time by a fresh state determination. It is no accident that totalitarian governments (in reaction to which much of the modern human rights movement was created) are associated with hidden mandates and surprise intrusions.[38] A common law maxim declared it a miserable slavery to live under unstable or unknown laws.[39] The model whereby human rights are embedded in fixed rules applied by the courts guards against this risk. That of continuing legislative articulation—by definition—cannot. Human rights, that is, go hand in hand with the rule of law.

These two issues have not gone unnoticed by the opponents of judicial enforcement of human rights against legislatures. Among recent commentators, Jeremy Waldron's responses are, perhaps, the most considered. Waldron finds no merit in the charge that the unconstrained legislature becomes its own judge with respect to the conformity of its acts with the relevant human rights norms. He assumes that the model of entrenched constitutional rights is a method by which a 'people' pre-commits itself to the observance of certain standards.[40] It makes no sense to shut out the judgment of the people's representatives when deciding the concrete meaning of those standards: 'the people are authorities—not judges in their own cause, but *authorities*—on what they have pre-committed themselves to'.[41] This response presupposes that the 'people' as represented in the legislature are the same 'people' who have legitimized the constitution. The theory of modern constitutionalism, however, is exactly the opposite. Both kinds of legislation, constitutional and sub-constitutional, derive their authority from popular sanction. But concomitant with the decision to entrench is a decision to commit the making of constitutions to special and irregular procedures designed to establish an expression of the people's will distinct from that which would be consulted in everyday governmental choices.[42] We are dealing with a law made for the legislature by a superior lawmaker—not a self-commitment by an entity with a single continuing will. Looked at this way, the charge of self-judgment is still entirely plausible.

Waldron, however, raises another problem with this 'self-judgment' argument for judicial review. Even if the legislature is an imperfect interpreter of the rights to be safeguarded, it does not follow that the judges are significantly better:

> unless it is seriously imagined that issues of rights should be decided by an outsider—by a Rousseauian 'lawgiver' perhaps, or by some neo-colonial institution that stands in relation

[38] R. Kay, 'American Constitutionalism', in L. Alexander (ed.), *Constitutionalism: Philosophical Foundations* (Cambridge: Cambridge University Press, 1998), 16, 22–3, 27.

[39] 4 *Coke's Institutes* 246. This stability is, in general, one of the primary justifications for the use of rules in the control of human behaviour (see Schauer, n. 4 above, 95–8), and explains the historic association of individual rights and rules of law.

[40] On the idea of constitutional rules as pre-commitments, see J. Elster, *Ulysses and the Sirens: Studies in Rationality and Irrationality* (Cambridge: Cambridge University Press, 1988).

[41] Waldron, n. 15 above, 266; see also p. 298.

[42] G. Wood, *The Creation of the American Republic, 1776–1787* (Chapel Hill: University of North Carolina Press, 1969), 318–43; Ackerman, n. 18 above.

to a given community as (say) the British Privy Council stands in relation to New Zealand—such decisions will inevitably be made by persons whose own rights are affected by the decision. Even a Supreme Court justice gets to have the rights that he determines American citizens to have . . . Facile invocations of *nemo iudex in sua causa* are no excuse for forgetting the elementary logic of authority: people disagree and there is need for a final decision and a final decision-procedure.[43]

This argument presumes that courts and legislature would do effectively the same thing in resolving disagreements about rights. If so, *both* institutions will necessarily be engaged in self-judgment, and the choice between them may reasonably turn on their respective claims to democratic respectability.

This same understanding of the judicial function underlies Waldron's response to the second doubt about legislative authority over human rights questions, the unpredictability of its decisions. He rejects the premiss of the objection. He takes for granted that we will want to change the way we deal with rights issues over time. It follows that 'we must leave the members of the society to work out their differences and change their minds in collective decision-making over time the best way they can'.[44] If the issue is how best to structure the process for 'chang[ing our] minds in collective decision-making over time', the attractiveness of the unelected courts as opposed to the elected, and therefore more popularly responsive, legislature is radically diminished.[45]

Both responses depend on a particular view of constitutional adjudication—one quite different from that traditionally associated with constitutionalism. The conventional view, outlined above, postulated the formulation of a set of fixed constitutional rules and then the application of those rules to contested acts of the state by the constitutional court. In that process the problems of self-judgment and unpredictability are largely absent. This has been thought the most promising way to realize the advantages of government by law expressed by Aristotle in the *Politics*: substitution of the government of 'God and reason' for the 'wild animal' of human appetite and passion that 'warps the rule even of the best man', the law being 'wisdom without desire'.[46] Since this amounts to government by static and, therefore, increasingly mindless rules, it may be seriously criticized as a practical technique of social regulation. But the counter-majoritarian doubts do not seem to have emphasized this defect. That is because, remarkably, they have refused to treat judicial constitutional control as consisting of the application of constitutional rules. It is pictured, instead, as an exercise in political choice.

The counter-majoritarian anxiety, that is, is part and parcel of the American realist critique of adjudication.[47] In his formulation of the problem, Bickel felt he had first to put aside the possibility that the judges could simply apply the rules made by the constitution-makers. He described derisively the idea that the

[43] Waldron, n. 15 above, 297. [44] Ibid. 269–70. [45] Ibid. 306.

[46] Aristotle, *Politics*, trans. H. Rackham (Cambridge, Mass.: Harvard University Press, 1937), 3. 11. 3–5. 265.

[47] K. Ward, 'The Legacy of the Counter-majoritarian Difficulty: Does Law Have a Place in Contemporary Constitutional Theory?', Paper presented at the Annual Meeting of the American Political Science Association, Washington, DC, 2000 (on file with the author), 7.

'Constitution is thought to embody a clear and certain yardstick to measure the actions of the other branches of the government' and invoked the realists for the proposition that legal rules cannot produce determinate results.[48] In particular, he attempted to debunk the idea that what courts did (or were supposed to do) was to consult and apply the meaning of the rules in the constitutional text intended by their creators. With characteristic confidence, he assured the reader that the framers themselves knew that 'nothing but disaster' could result from attempting to adhere to the 'specific intent of the framers of a constitutional provision... history cannot displace judgment [and] it should not if it could'.[49] In the past twenty-five years there has been a vigorous debate on the propriety of reference to historical intentions in constitutional adjudication. It is fair to say, however, that the overwhelming weight of academic opinion has agreed with Bickel that, at least to a significant degree, constitutional courts exercise will as well as judgment.

This vision of judicial decision-making is crucial in understanding criticism based on democratic objections. It assimilates the actions of a court to those of ordinary political actors. Critics are at pains to assert that the courts are not 'mere machines',[50] translating the law to particular cases, but that they, like legislatures, are engaged in making choices. Constitutions, according to Waldron, 'invest a power of decision in [a court] whose job it is to determine *as a matter of judgment* whether conduct' violates the restraints established.[51]

This conception of judicial review seems to have particular force when applied to constitutional rules establishing individual rights. Such provisions, it is contended, are peculiarly resistant to a textual formulation that will minimize the element of judicial choice. In what may be the modern *locus classicus* of American sceptical commentary on the judicial enforcement of constitutional rules against the legislature, Learned Hand singled out the individual rights provisions of the Constitution. In so far as constitutional rules merely divided public power among various agencies, Hand conceded, it was 'hard to escape the necessity' of some monitoring tribunal. But in so far as a constitution goes further so as to 'lay down the general principles to insure the just exercise of these powers', the considerations were different:

> Here history is only a feeble light, for these rubrics were meant to answer future problems unimagined and unimaginable. Nothing, which by the utmost liberality can be called interpretation, describes the process by which they must be applied. Indeed if law be a command for specific conduct, *they are not law at all*... The answers to the questions which they raise demand the appraisal and balancing of human values which there are no scales to weigh...[52]

48 Bickel, n. 7 above, 77, 79–80. 49 Ibid. 106, 108.

50 Wood, n. 42 above, 161 (quoting Thomas Jefferson).

51 Waldron, n. 15 above, 262. Grimm, n. 14 above, 206 (adjudication is a mixture of 'cognitive and voluntary elements').

52 L. Hand, 'The Contribution of an Independent Judiciary to Civilization', in I. Dillard (ed.), *The Spirit of Liberty*, 3rd edn. (New York: Knopf, 1960), 159, 161–2; my emphasis.

This question of whether such provisions can be 'law at all' animates the recent jurisprudential discussion of the coherence of 'soft' or 'inclusive' legal positivism which supposes posited legal rules may incorporate indeterminate moral judgments. For proponents of such an understanding, the practice of constitutional human rights adjudication is exhibit number one.[53] It is interesting that the same conclusion persuaded Hans Kelsen to propose a constitution without a statement of personal rights in Austria in 1920. This constitution was notable for its establishment of a specialized Constitutional Court with the power to hold acts of the legislature unconstitutional—a system that has become the model for modern European constitutional courts. Kelsen believed it would be dangerous to give the court authority to insist that legislation conform to 'the ideals of equity, justice, liberty, equality, morality, etc., without in the least defining [precisely] what are meant by these terms'.[54] The result, he thought, would be the creation of a supreme legislative power in the court, effectively a government of judges. Such power would inevitably stimulate a hostile reaction and subvert the utility of the court in the other areas of its jurisdiction.[55] It is exactly the human rights aspects of constitutions that have aroused the most intense worries among critics of constitutional limitations on legislatures. Jeffrey Goldsworthy summed up these concerns:

> Moreover, those [individual rights] principles must be abstract and flexible, to ensure that government can respond appropriately to all the exigencies of changing circumstances. That is why a judicially-enforceable Bill of Rights consists of abstract and flexible principles of political morality, whose 'interpretation' is indistinguishable from moral and political philosophy.[56]

If, in fact, the enforcement of human rights limitations by courts against legislatures is 'indistinguishable from moral and political philosophy', if it involves not interpretation but 'interpretation', if what it invokes is, as Hand said, 'not law at all', the case for an authoritative judicial power over legislation, based on the application of binding rules, collapses. It can no longer claim to be applying pre-existing rules for the state. Instead it is engaging in an enterprise at bottom indistinguishable from that of the legislature.[57]

[53] W. Waluchow, *Inclusive Legal Positivism* (New York: Oxford University Press, 1994), 142–65. Compare H. L. A. Hart, *The Concept of Law*, 2nd edn. (Oxford: Oxford University Press, 1994), 250–4; A. Marmor, *Positive Law and Objective Values* (Oxford: Oxford University Press, 2001), 67–9 (treating moral concepts embedded in law as creating a limited power to change the law).

[54] A. Stone-Sweet, *Governing with Judges: Constitutional Politics in Europe* (New York: Oxford University Press, 2000), 36.

[55] Ibid.

[56] Goldsworthy, n. 29 above, 278–9; T. Campbell, 'Democracy, Human Rights and Positive Law', (1994) 16 *Sydney Law Review* 195, 200 (judicial enforcement of human rights 'rests on unsupportable ideas about the nature and justification of rights, namely that human rights can be captured in relatively pellucid and simple rules'); J. Hiebert, Ch. 11 below (the interpretation of rights bears 'more resemblance to policy analysis than to the skills or methodology for which judges can reasonably claim to have expertise').

[57] Ward, n. 47 above; Stone-Sweet, n. 54 above, 139. Is there an ideal model of judicial review that does not involve rule-application but still prescribes a non-optional way for courts to decide

The critics of judicial review have taken this understanding to heart. Noting the fact that collegial constitutional courts frequently divide on questions of constitutionality, Jeremy Waldron infers that courts like the United States Supreme Court use

> basically the same decision-rule as the one we use in popular referendums and elections. The only difference lies in the number of people affected by the issue who get to vote: just nine as opposed to millions . . . When people in this community disagree about rights, our rule is not that the right view is to prevail. Our rule is simply that the matter is to be considered and that a bare-majority of five Supreme Court justices over four is to settle the issue.[58]

John Ely summed up this sceptical attitude some time ago: 'We like Rawls, you like Nozick. We win, 6–3. Statute invalidated.'[59]

The constraining effect of law and the special responsibility of courts to be faithful to law have effectively dropped out of this vision. Without them we are presented with two conflicting *legislative* judgments. One emerges from the open deliberations of an electorally accountable legislature. The other issues from the arcane and formalized procedures of a misnamed 'court' composed of life or long-tenured appointees acting, for the most part, in secret and (pretty much) accountable to no one. If these two institutions are really doing more or less the same thing, it is hard to see why, in a community professing a strong commitment to democratic decision-making, the court's determination should prevail over the legislature's.

It might be worth digressing here to note that, even if we accept the idea that courts exercise independent, legislative judgment, rather than apply rules in constitutional adjudication, there might still be a case for it. As a matter of constitutional design, we might prefer a system in which there was a check, even a non-rules-based check, on the effectuation of popular will. That is, we might prefer a complex legislator with both democratic and undemocratic elements. In the long history of government the unchallengeable priority of democratic decision-making is a fairly recent phenomenon. The tempering of democratic representatives with purposefully undemocratic elements has always had an appeal. The idea of 'mixed government' was familiar to the ancients. Canvassing the classical forms of democracy, aristocracy, and monarchy, Cicero was sure that all were 'surpassed by an even and judicious blend of the three simple forms at their best'.[60] At the time of the American founding, the British Constitution was generally agreed to be a model of political wisdom. Its mixture of democratic

constitutional cases? Much of modern constitutional scholarship purports to describe such methods. I believe none of them, at the end, offers a serious restraint on judicial decision. Ely, n. 22 above, 44–72; P. Brest, 'The Fundamental Rights Controversy: The Essential Contradictions of Normative Constitutional Scholarship', (1981) 90 *Yale Law Journal* 1063.

[58] J. Waldron, 'Freeman's Defense of Judicial Review', (1994) 13 *Law and Philosophy* 27, 32, 36.

[59] Ely, n. 22 above, 58. This understanding is also the standard assumption of most of the political science literature on judicial behaviour. For example, J. Brigham, *The Cult of the Court* (Philadelphia: Temple University Press, 1987), 11–12.

[60] Cicero, *The Republic and The Laws*, trans. N. Rudd (Oxford: Oxford University Press, 1998), 32.

and undemocratic institutions was one of the features that attracted the most admiration.[61] The introduction of upper houses in the American legislatures was intended by some of its advocates not only to provide representation to a distinct interest in society, but also to exercise a judgment 'perfectly independent of its electors'.[62] Similarly, the executive veto (in which some proposed the judges have a share) evinced a mistrust of unfettered legislative democracy.[63] Bickel's solution to the counter-majoritarian difficulty was not to eliminate judicial review, but to reserve its exercise for those occasions where courts could contribute to the development and application of enduring principles—a function he conceded to be inconsistent with democratic decision-making.[64] It might be contended that such a complex legislator would better protect the activities favoured by modern conceptions of rights than would a democratically chosen one.

This argument on behalf of mixed government, however, is distinctly different from the explanation of judicial authority I have outlined in this chapter. The latter is entirely dependent on the assumption that courts exist (principally) to vindicate pre-existing rules (and, therefore, rights). Like the idea of a mixed constitution, it denies the automatic priority of democratic government. But more broadly, it prefers the security of defined spheres of protected conduct to the unlimited authority of any institutions—representative or otherwise—to redefine rights on a continuing basis. The arguments against it, however, are unanswerable, even on its own terms, *if the critics' assumptions about the actual operation of constitutional courts are correct.*

Therefore, the defence of the practice of constitutional review I have offered assumes courts can and do enforce rules. But this assumption is notoriously controversial. If it is wrong, the judges will inevitably have to fall back on the same kind of ad hoc and suspect decision-making that we could expect from legislatures. And, at least in the hands of legislators, we would have the satisfactions and safeguards of representative democracy. It follows that our choice as to the structure for the protection of human rights depends crucially on a venerable question: Can we expect courts to follow rules? The answer, here as elsewhere, of course, is—it depends.[65] No one thinks courts are the perfect translators of the rules invoked before them on every occasion. But it is equally clear that rules sometimes decide cases.[66]

I should make clear what I mean by 'following rules'. The mere invocation of a legal text in connection with a decision does not, by itself, signal a case of rule-following. For reasons I have elaborated elsewhere, I believe that to follow a rule means to decide in accordance with a judgment made by the maker of the rule at

[61] Wood, n. 42 above, 197–206.

[62] Ibid. 213 (quoting Thomas Jefferson).

[63] F. McDonald, *Novus Ordo Seclorum: The Intellectual Origins of the Constitution* (Lawrence: University Press of Kansas, 1985), 242, 254.

[64] Bickel, n. 7 above, 24–7; Waldron, n. 15 above, 264 (agreeing that constitutional review results not in an aristocracy but in a 'mixed constitution').

[65] Sadurski, n. 1 above (emphasizing the 'fact-sensitive' nature of such inquiries).

[66] Schauer, n. 4 above, 191–6.

the time of its creation.[67] Rule-application that follows the rule-makers' original design treats the meaning of the rule as fixed. This approach gives a stability to the content of the legal rights that is essential to create the personal security at the heart of the human rights project. Preference for judicial over legislative interpretation of rights, therefore, seems to hang on the question of whether or not judges are capable of subordinating their own judgment to that incorporated in the rules by the constitution-makers. In this chapter I can only mention and respond briefly to some of the arguments that they are not.

First, I have already noted the claim, in a number of critiques of human rights adjudication, that constitutional provisions of this kind are prone to a particularly unconstrained decision procedure. This makes judicial interpretation more or less equivalent to legislative deliberation. This is also matter of degree. Article 1 of Protocol 6 of the European Convention of Human Rights and Fundamental Freedoms says: 'The death penalty shall be abolished. No one shall be condemned to such penalty or executed.' This prohibition, moreover, is declared not subject to abridgement even in cases of 'public emergency threatening the life of the nation'.[68] Such a provision leaves little room for the kind of legislative discretion suggested. At the other extreme, the provisions of the Canadian Charter of Rights and Freedoms are guaranteed by Section One, which declares them to be 'subject only to such reasonable limits prescribed by law as can be demonstrably justified in a free and democratic society'.[69] This text appears to authorize exactly the weighing and balancing of competing interests and values that is characteristic of legislation. And, in this case, the Supreme Court of Canada appears to have accepted the apparent invitation with enthusiasm.[70] There are certainly intermediate cases.

Even constitutional provisions that, on their face, appear to call for the judges' moral evaluation, moreover, might, upon closer examination, turn out to be more bounded. That is, the constitution-makers may have had certain specific factors in mind before a right could be infringed. As I have formulated it, the obligation of judges faithfully to apply pre-existing rules entails the obligation to prohibit or prescribe the category of conduct intended by the rule-maker.[71] It is not impossible that constitution-makers intended to leave the actual definition of the relevant categories to judicial decision.[72] (In the case of the Canadian

[67] Kay, n. 38 above; R. Kay, 'Adherence to the Original Intentions in Constitutional Adjudication: Three Objections and Responses', (1988) 82 *Northwestern University Law Review* 226.

[68] Convention for the Protection of Human Rights and Fundamental Freedoms, 28 Apr. 1983, Council of Europe, Protocol 6, Arts 1, 3. The emergency provision from which the protocol is made immune is in Art 15 of the Convention. Art 2 of the protocol provides an exception for executions under laws applicable only in 'time of war or imminent threat of war'.

[69] Constitution Act, 1982, s 1.

[70] F. Morton, 'The Charter Revolution and the Court Party', (1992) 30 *Osgoode Hall Law Journal* 627.

[71] R. Kay, 'Original Intentions, Standard Meanings and the Legal Character of the Constitution', (1989) 6 *Constitutional Commentary* 39.

[72] Whether or not the exercise of such power results in the application of law engages the debate on the nature of positivism mentioned above. See authorities cited at n. 53.

Constitution Act 1982, there is some fairly persuasive evidence for this view.[73]) But the mere use of broad language in describing rights is certainly not conclusive on this point. That is, there is nothing built into the very idea of protecting rights through an entrenched constitution that entails such judicial authority. In each case the question is contingent on the facts of the constitution-making.

These arguments against describing judicial review as rule-application depend on the character of the particular constitutional text with which judges are entrusted. There is, however, a far broader critique and one less vulnerable to counter-argument. That is the psychological claim that human beings vested with the authority to make conclusive interpretations of the highest law, and immunized from accountability for their decisions, will, inevitably, yield to the temptation to venture beyond the rules they are charged with applying. It would be disingenuous to pretend that there is not much force to this assumption and—more tellingly—that there is not much evidence for it. The 'great cases' of the United States Supreme Court seem to be dominated by decisions that no reasonable person could justify as mere extrapolations from the Constitution of 1787–9 as amended. Other jurisdictions have experienced much the same phenomenon.[74]

Nevertheless, I maintain that, in general, entrenched constitutional rules (and not just constitutional courts) can and do constrain public conduct and protect human rights. More particularly, I think they do so, at least in part, because courts regularly apply, and in any event, it is assumed that they apply, these rules to challenged conduct.[75] The proposition that judges, in general, are incapable of complying with the relevant rules is inconsistent with our everyday knowledge that rules affect human behaviour. Stopping at stop signs, recycling our trash, filing our income tax returns are all common manifestations of our compliance with rules. If rule-following in general is not impossible, it ought not to be impossible for judges to follow the rules of a constitution.

This conclusion is not altered by the fact that, unlike most persons subject to rule, the constitutional court of last resort is neither amenable to correction nor subject to sanction. As a practical matter, that situation is far from unique. We are all familiar with cases where legal rules are largely effective even though the prospect of external enforcement is pretty much non-existent. That is because people in a society governed by law are socialized to respect the law and, at least

[73] P. Hogg, *Constitutional Law of Canada*, 4th edn. (Scarborough, Ont.: Carswell, 1997), ss 57.1(f) and (g). I find the same position with respect to the United States Constitution of 1787–9 to be considerably less persuasive. Kay, n. 67 above, 259–84.

[74] For example, Morton, n. 70 above. No court presents a better example than the Constitutional Court of Germany. For a recent examination of the remarkable breadth and imagination of its judgments, see E. Eberle, *Dignity and Liberty: Constitutional Visions in Germany and the United States* (Westport, Conn.: Praeger, 2001). Even courts administering a statutory bill of rights have been plausibly charged with judicial imperialism; see J. Allan, 'Take Heed Australia: A Statutory Bill of Rights and its Inflationary Effect', (2001) 6 *Deakin Law Review* 322.

[75] I have considered this question at somewhat greater length in Kay, n. 38 above, 39–50; supporting references and citations (such as they are) may be found there.

in a general way, to believe they have a stake in the success of the legal system. There is no reason to think that judges, even constitutional judges, do not share this inclination. Indeed, there is every reason to think that their training, their professional associations, and the evaluations of their peers will make arriving at the 'correct' legal resolution their first objective.[76]

How then can we account for the repeated examples of judicial adventuring that feature so prominently in our constitutional law casebooks? Constitutional courts of last resort necessarily end up with those cases whose resolutions are least clear. Such courts will not be asked whether freedom of expression is violated when the government imprisons dissident newspaper editors. They will be asked instead about the validity of laws prohibiting drive-in theatres from exhibiting movies showing human nudity.[77] Final constitutional adjudication necessarily deals with cases on the outer boundaries of the definitions of rights. The constraints imposed by the constitutional rules, in the circumstances involved in those cases, will be more obscure and, consequently, less confining. To the extent that rule-application is imperfect, those imperfections will appear particularly prominently in these cases.

Even among those cases, human nature and scholarly inclination tend to make us most aware of the ones in which the underlying issues and the contending positions are most controversial. Scholars and critics seek out the complex and novel aspects of any social phenomenon. If hard cases make bad law, these judgments will be especially unreliable examples of the application of constitutional rules. We should no more expect to find ordinary instances of constitutional rule-application in casebooks than we should expect to find healthy people featured in pathology texts.

I do not mean that courts, and the possibility of resort to a final court to resolve difficult and disputed constitutional questions, are peripheral features of constitutionalism. They are essential if the system, as a whole, is to be regarded as obligatory. The knowledge that the rules of the constitution may ultimately be vindicated in a process the society regards as impartial and authoritative lends to those rules the normative force that is reserved for binding law. It thus makes it more likely that less controversial observance and enforcement of the rules by political actors will become unreflective practice. Still, the most prominent cases of a constitutional court will almost certainly fall outside that practice and will not represent the whole, or even the greater part, of the effect of legal entrenchment of constitutional rules.[78]

[76] Compare Goldsworthy, n. 29 above, 271 (judges are especially likely to overstep the rules since 'by virtue of their position, symbols of office, and unchallenged authority [they] are constantly exposed to "the intoxicating notion that they may be wiser, more dispassionate and sure footed than their fellow men"'; quoting Lord McCluskey, *Law, Justice and Democracy* (London: Sweet & Maxwell, 1987), 154).

[77] *Erznonik v Jacksonville* 422 US 205 (1975).

[78] For a valuable discussion of the role of uncontroversial applications of constitutional rules in a legal system, see F. Schauer, 'Easy Cases', (1985) 58 *Southern California Law Review* 399.

None of this is to deny that much of what constitutional courts do is unsupportable as rule-application, nor that their actions may have a profound effect on the society involved. Whether these effects are regarded as the justifiable costs of a system of constitutional protection of rights, or whether they appear as intolerable intrusions in a democratic government, will depend on both empirical and value judgments. The empirical judgments will turn, on the one hand, on how much we expect the courts to deviate from the rules laid down as limits on the state, and, on the other, on how much we fear an unreviewable legislature will invade the areas of human life we have marked off by our definition of human rights.[79] This is a contingent matter—one that will differ in different places and at different times. The value judgments will depend on our estimate of the benefits we derive from the process of representative self-government. Against those benefits we will have to measure the importance we place on being able to live our lives with the security created by a regime of human rights protected by the rule of law.

[79] Tushnet, n. 30 above, 28–9.

6

Rights and Democracy: A Reconciliation of the Institutional Debate

JULIE DEBELJAK

INTRODUCTION

The interdependence of democracy and human rights is accepted within the international law sphere. Human rights guarantee the conditions necessary for the proper functioning of a democracy. Human rights buttress the search for self-rule tempered by political equality. Conversely, democratic institutions and systems of governance allow for the protection and promotion of human rights. Just as many argue that when peace and democracy occur, they tend to occur together; so too, when respect for human rights and democracy occur, they tend to occur together.[1]

However, something is lost in the translation from international law to domestic law. Indeed, within a domestic setting, human rights may be regarded as counter-majoritarian and, in particular, judicially enforceable human rights can be viewed as the antithesis of democracy. Much of the counter-majoritarian view of human rights is attributable to two factors. First, the attitude that democracy can only mean majority rule places different, diverse, unpopular, and minority interests in a precarious position. The majority is free to pay regard to, or to disregard, these interests as it pleases. Human rights, on the other hand, tend to protect and promote these interests. In this chapter concepts and practices of democracy that accommodate rights protection and promotion will be explored.

Secondly, the impact on the power relations between the institutions of government when human rights protection is formally introduced into democratic systems causes tension. Because of the corrupting nature of absolute power, the separation of powers doctrine dictates the dispersal of power between the different arms of government. Separation of powers is tempered by the need

I wish to thank Professor Stephen Parker and Professor Jeff Goldsworthy for their constructive comments on earlier drafts of this chapter.

[1] T. Franck, 'The Emerging Right to Democratic Governance', (1992) 86 *American Journal of International Law* 46; A. Slaughter (Burley), 'Towards an Age of Liberal Nations', (1992) 36 *Harvard International Law Journal* 393; N. Bobbio, *The Future of Democracy: A Defence of the Rules of the Game*, ed. and introd. Richard Bellamy, trans. Roger Griffin (Cambridge: Polity Press, 1987)

for checks and balances, which requires mixed government. The conferral of some aspects of the power of one arm of government upon another arm of government provides vital oversight of the operations of each arm of government. However acceptable the idea of mixed government is in general, the sharing of human rights responsibility between the arms of government is most controversial. Giving an unelected (and thus electorally unaccountable) arm of government the power to review the decisions of the elected (and thus electorally accountable) arms of government for vague human rights purposes is viewed as anti-democratic. An exploration of the actual sharing of power under modern human rights instruments is instructive in allaying this anti-democratic critique. International human rights instruments, as well as the British Human Rights Act and the Canadian Charter of Rights and Freedoms, will be used to ground the theoretical discussion.

Reconciling human rights within a democratic framework

'Democracy'

'The fashionable concentration on democracy as the main value threatened is not without danger. It is largely responsible for the misleading and unfounded belief that so long as the ultimate source of power is the will of the majority, the power cannot be arbitrary.'[2]

There is a multitude of competing models of democracy. The models range from pure majoritarian, statistical market-based democracy, to procedural democracy, to substantive democracy. The basic differences between each model centre on whether or not the rights of the individual and the minority temper the will of the majority; and if so, whether the rights are intended to protect procedural or substantive notions of democracy.[3] Inseparable from the democratic legitimacy of rights issue is the institutional question: Which arm of government should interpret and enforce human rights guarantees? Just as it is argued that human rights guarantees have the capacity to pervert some conceptions of democracy, so too do the institutional arrangements for enforcement.

What is the relationship between human rights and democracy?

Traditionally, democracy has been considered to favour majoritarian decision-making. Thomas Aquinas defined democracy as popular power, through which the ordinary people, by force of numbers, governed the rich. Human rights, in contrast, are traditionally conceived of as recognizing and protecting the

[2] F. Hayek, *The Road to Serfdom* (Sydney: Dymock's Book Arcade, 1945), quoted in C. Kukathas, 'Democracy, Parliament and Responsible Government', *Papers on Parliament*, no. 8, June 1990, issued by the Senate Publishing Unit, Department of the Senate, Parliament House, Canberra, 1.

[3] This can often be reflected in whether the protected rights are considered procedural or substantive in nature.

unpopular or a minority from the power of the majority. Human rights, by declaring minimum standards of behaviour, preclude majorities from acting in certain ways and pursuing certain goals. Civil and political rights, in particular, attempt to guarantee a voice for the unpopular within the popular; a voice for the minority within the majority. Civil and political rights also protect certain human dignities from majority incursion. Thus arises the *supposed* tension between a particular expression of popular opinion, known as majoritarian democracy, and the conditions necessary to guarantee the continuing expression of that opinion, known as civil and political rights.

However, the interrelationship between democracy and human rights need not be viewed as a tension. As Cappelletti suggests:

> far from being inherently antidemocratic and anti-majoritarian, [rights emerge] as a pivotal instrument for shielding the democratic and majoritarian principles from the risk of corruption. Our democratic ideal . . . is not one in which majoritarian will is omnipotent.[4]

Indeed, democracy is dependent on human rights. Democracy could not function without the adoption of some rules regulating political participation and civil freedoms. Moreover, human rights limit democracy. Democracy could not function without some rules limiting the power of those elected to govern.

> . . . rights underpin the institutional structure of constitutional democracy. Basic rights . . . become constitutive of democratic will-formation. Rights provide the basic building blocks of the political structure and give expression to the idea of democracy. Properly understood, rights and democracy do not . . . conflict. Rights and democracy are twin sides of the same coin.[5]

Thus, democracy is an important value, but not *the only* important value.[6] Other values include those embodied in human rights instruments that, aside from promoting and protecting democratic governance, perform other useful tasks. The Preamble to the European Convention on Human Rights (the

[4] In the Hon. Justice R. D. Nicholson, 'Judicial Independence and Accountability: Can They Co-exist?', (1993) 67 *Australian Law Journal* 404, 410–11, quoting Cappelletti. See also D. Davis, M. Chaskalson, and J. de Waal, 'Democracy and Constitutionalism: The Role of Constitutional Interpretation', in D. van Wyk, J. Dugard, B. de Villiers, and D. Davis (eds.), *Rights and Constitutionalism: The New South African Legal Order* (Oxford: Clarendon Press, 1995), 1: 'when "we the people" have formulated a constitutional choice, it binds the more limited authority of the government—the courts have a custodial function of preserving the decisions of "we the people" against the potential undermining thereof by the government. Thus, majoritarianism has no exclusive claim on democracy—there are certain characteristics of democratic enterprise that even the majority cannot deny.'

[5] M. Loughlin, 'Rights, Democracy and the Nature of the Legal Order', in T. Campbell, K. D. Ewing, and A. Tomkins (eds.), *Sceptical Essays on Human Rights* (Oxford: Oxford University Press, 2001), 44. Both Loughlin and Neuborne insist that rights are the necessary linchpin of our institutional structure. See B. Neuborne, 'The Origin of Rights: Constitutionalism, the Stork and the Democratic Dilemma', in S. Shetreet (ed.), *The Role of Courts in Society* (Dordrecht: Martinus Nijhoff, 1988).

[6] '. . . democracy is not a unique fundamental value but rather one that must be understood in the light of a very limited list of other such values', as per M. Darrow and P. Alston, 'Bills of Rights in Comparative Perspective', in P. Alston (ed.), *Promoting Human Rights Through Bills of Rights: Comparative Perspectives* (Oxford: Oxford University Press, 1999), 496.

'European Convention') expressly links the value of human rights protection and the value of democracy:

> those Fundamental Freedoms which are the foundation of justice and peace in the world . . . are best maintained on the one hand by an effective political democracy and on the other by a common understanding and observance of the human rights upon which they depend.

The Preamble emphasizes that *both* an effective political democracy and human rights observance are required for justice and peace. There is no explicit indication as to how the two interact. Yet, there is implicit recognition that an effective political democracy and the observance of human rights are *complementary*, and *together* they maintain the fundamental freedoms necessary for justice and peace. This suggests that, far from the existence of an irresolvable tension, the two ideals can be reconciled. On the basis of the Preamble, it is fair to assume that an effective political democracy protects and promotes human rights, and that human rights reinforce an effective political democracy. As Bobbio suggests:

> The liberal state and the democratic state are doubly interdependent: if liberalism provides those liberties necessary for the proper exercise of democratic power, democracy guarantees the existence and persistence of fundamental liberties . . . [7]

By exploring the notion of an 'effective political democracy', our understanding of the interrelationship between human rights and democracy will be furthered. What are the features of effective political democracy, and which institutions have a role in enforcing human rights as part of it?

An 'effective political democracy'

Difficulties of definition

There are many difficulties associated with attempting to define 'democracy', the first being the diversity of views as to its core. This tends to suggest that there is *no* 'transparent view of the essential meaning of democracy'.[8] Each meaning of democracy is borne of a particular context or a particular historical struggle. If the 'true' definition of democracy is indeterminate (at least without a given context and history), we should limit our enquiry. We should ask what promotes an effective political democracy and, in particular, whether a judicially enforceable instrument for the protection of human rights can be considered part of a true democracy, or at least, not antithetical to democracy.[9]

[7] Bobbio, n. 1 above, 25–6.

[8] M. Koskenniemi, quoted in S. Marks, *The Riddle of All Constitutions: International Law, Democracy, and the Critique of Ideology* (Oxford: Oxford University Press, 2000), 49. See also Bobbio, n. 1 above, 18; T. Campbell, 'Judging in a Democracy', Paper presented at the Australian Judicial Conference, Sydney, Nov. 1997; available from <http://www.jca.asn.au/campbell.html> as at 7 Apr. 2003.

[9] Marks, n. 8 above.

Another difficulty associated with the definition of democracy is that we lose sight of its application. Democracy should not be considered as an end in itself, a final destination or a place we reach.[10] Democracy should be used as a benchmark: a yardstick for criticism and a catalyst for change. It is an ideal political structure that a society aspires to, not a description of existing political institutions and practices.[11] Democracy is not simply a way of legitimizing the institutions and procedures that have served existing democracies to date.[12] Democracy has and will continue to evolve. Grand notions, such as democracy, must be approached in a distinct manner. Society must take a 'provisional approach to their significance, to conceive them "as *ongoing accomplishments*. They are never finished, but have to be constructed, deconstructed and reconstructed in ever-changing circumstances."'[13] In this sense, democracy is an evolving concept.

So too is the notion of human rights an evolving concept. Human rights were first articulated as such during the Enlightenment period in the 1700s, were developed after the Second World War, and continued to expand at the end of the twentieth century. The concept of human rights has been expanded and refined from the libertarian Enlightenment period, to the community-reinforcing ideal after the Second World War, to the mutuality ideals underlying more modern-day documents.[14] That human rights standards are the subject of a continuing and evolving debate bears witness in this expansion and refinement process.

Defining an 'effective political democracy'

What political structure would qualify as an 'effective political democracy'? Democracy must involve notions of self-rule within a community of equals. As Dworkin suggests, democracy is about participation by all as equals and decisions that treat all with equal concern and respect. Statistical conceptions of democracy,

[10] If it were considered an end in itself, Marks argues that this would be a disappointingly undemanding view of democracy. Current democratic theory accepts high levels of citizen passivity. It utilizes existing liberal institutions without addressing the limitations of those institutions. In particular, she queries whether our institutions can function without civil and political rights, and questions the role that should be played by the separation of powers. Further, democratic theory is yet to address the enormous amounts of unaccountable power being exercised over the lives of citizens of the modern state. These shortfalls in current standards of democracy manifest themselves in the contemporary melancholy about democracy and its inability to ensure self-rule and political participation. See Marks, n. 8 above, esp. 146–51.

[11] 'Rather than pursuing questions of whether democracy has a normative component, democracy is often assumed to be the sum of current practices of representative government', as per J. L. Hiebert, *Limiting Rights: The Dilemma of Judicial Review* (Montreal: McGill–Queen's University Press, 1996), 116.

[12] See generally Marks, n. 8 above; Hiebert, n. 11 above.

[13] Marks, n. 8 above, 149.

[14] F. Klug, *Values for a Godless Age: The Story of the United Kingdom's New Bill of Rights* (London: Penguin Books, 2000); F. Klug, K. Starmer, and S. Weir, *The Three Pillars of Liberty: The Democratic Audit of the United Kingdom* (London: Routledge, 1996), 9: 'as the continuing interpretation of the European Convention has shown, human rights evolve as society evolves—in the same way as the common law itself adapts over time.'

which legitimize what an electoral majority favour, are insufficient. Statistical conceptions of democracy do not guarantee participation by all as equals, nor do they necessarily produce decisions that treat all (popular and unpopular, majority and minority) with equal concern and respect. Communal conceptions of democracy, which legitimize the decisions of a majority within a community of equals, should be preferred over statistical conceptions of democracy.[15]

Marks' 'principle of democratic inclusion' best captures this communal conception of democracy. The principle of democratic inclusion is concerned with 'relationships and processes'; it is an 'agenda of enhancing control by citizens of decision-making which affects them and overcoming disparities in the distribution of citizenship rights and opportunities'.[16] The essence of enhanced control by citizens over decisions that affect them is self-rule. The essence of overcoming disparities in rights and opportunities is political equality. Accordingly, the principle of democratic inclusion can be described as identifying and securing those processes and relationships that advance self-rule and political equality. It is much more demanding than merely securing episodic elections (with the concomitant episodic accountability), formalities, and securing certain institutional arrangements. This view is supported by a report of the Secretary-General of the United Nations:

> Elections themselves do not constitute democracy. They are not an end but a step, albeit an important and often essential one, on the path towards the democratisation of societies and the realisation of the right to take part in the government of one's own country... democracy implies far more than the mere act of periodically casting a vote, but covers the entire process of participation by citizens in the political life of their country.[17]

The principle of democratic inclusion addresses the two difficulties identified earlier. First, the recognition of democracy as a matter of processes and relations confirms that there is no absolute core meaning of democracy. Our task is not about definitive meanings, but about symbiotic relationships: it is to decide whether judicial review of executive and legislative action based on human rights standards is antithetical to a definition of democracy. Secondly, the principle of democratic inclusion appreciates that democratic theory is incomplete; it is still under construction. Democracy is 'an open-ended and continually recontextualized'[18] discussion about the aims of governing structures, their roles, their limits, and the most appropriate dispersal or mixing of power between the structures.

Theories expounding on the principle of democratic inclusion

Two additional theories operationalize the principle of democratic inclusion. The 'deliberative theory of democracy' embraces the ongoing nature of democratic definition, the need for self-rule via continual dialogue within a polity, and the

15 See R. Dworkin, *Freedom's Law* (Oxford: Oxford University Press, 1996).
16 Marks, n. 8 above, 116.
17 See *Report of the Secretary-General of the United Nations*, UN Doc. (1991), A/46/609.
18 Marks, n. 8 above, 110.

necessity of political equality. According to the deliberative theory of democracy, democracy is a process of developing preferences through dialogue which, in the absence of unanimity, will be interrupted by a majority decision.[19] This majority decision is provisional; it is the practical compromise citizens live with until further agreement can be reached. Although the aim is to reach a rational consensus in order for the polity to move forward, it by no means considers this to be, or expects there ever to be, an ideal consensus. The theory of 'incompletely theorized agreements' is also useful, in terms of encouraging the exchange of ideas and keeping the channels of debate and change open.[20]

Let us begin with the dialogue aspects. The deliberative theory of democracy is concerned with 'open and uncoerced deliberation aimed at reaching a rational consensus concerning the common good or the public interest'.[21] The deliberative theory recognizes the capacity for impersonal reflection and the ability of each individual to engage in reasoned deliberations. The deliberative theory is civic and communitarian in nature. It is concerned with the rights *and* responsibilities of its electorate. It requires choice between rival concepts of the common good, not the making of individual demands or mutually beneficial agreements.[22] Real alternatives must be presented and choice between these alternatives must be uncoerced.

The deliberative theory of democracy is especially important in a plural society where diversity, disagreement, and uncertainty abound. Pluralism demonstrates that the basic trait of modern democracy is dissent: 'the fundamental feature of modern democracy is based on the principle that dissent . . . does not undermine a society but underpins it.'[23] People will disagree about the common settlement of an issue, say, the enactment of a certain law. Although there may be disagreement about the common settlement of the content of the law, people will agree that there should be a common settlement, in preference to each group trying to implement its own view. Free and vigorous debate under fair procedures that allow *all* to participate *equally* in determining the specifics of the particular law is a necessary precursor to the enactment of that law. Indeed,

[19] Campbell, n. 8 above, 45.

[20] C. Sunstein, *Legal Reasoning and Political Conflict* (Oxford: Oxford University Press, 1996).

[21] David Couzens Hoy and Thomas McCarthy, *Critical Theory* (1994), 7, quoted in Campbell, n. 8 above, 44.

[22] As per Bobbio, n. 1 above, 48: 'In most representative democracies the answer to "who" the representative is, is that he is a fiduciary and not a delegate, and "what" he represents are general rather than particular interests. (Moreover, it is precisely because general and not particular interests are represented that there is a principle in force in democracies forbidding the use of binding mandates.) . . . a representative means a person with two very specific attributes: someone who (a) enjoys the trust of the electorate by virtue of election, and (b) who is not directly answerable to the electorate precisely because he is called upon to safeguard the general interests of civil society and not the particular interests of any one group.'

[23] See Bobbio, n. 1 above, 60. Also see ibid. 58–9: 'That our societies, in contrast to the classical *polis*, have several centres of power is an undeniable fact . . . There is pluralism at an economic level . . . There is political pluralism . . . Ideological pluralism obtains from the moment there is not just one doctrine of the state but various currents of thought . . . which have free rein and are reflected in a public opinion which is far from homogenous or uniform.'

Waldron argues that disagreement is the normal background to law-formation: do 'not be fooled into thinking that calmness and solemnity are necessarily the mark of a good polity, and noise and conflict a symptom of political pathology'.[24] In other words, noise and conflict are signs of a healthy polity.

Similarly, noise and conflict resulting from a diversity of views about democracy, its institutions of governance, and the powers and limits of its institutions are signs of a system of healthy democracy. Given that the definition of democracy is indeterminate, noise and conflict over democracy is the natural state of affairs. It is through noisy and discordant deliberation that the search for improved meanings of democracy is advanced, thereby advancing the conditions for self-rule. This is particularly vital when the debate is about the functioning of democracy and the direction of society.

Noise and conflict also promote the notion of political equality. Political equality is aimed at a more inclusionary political community that treats all with equal concern and respect. Deliberative democracy promotes such inclusion through the expression, discussion, and exploration of differing perspectives. The broader the range of perspectives that are included in the deliberation, the less likely exclusionary decisions will be made—at the very least, any exclusionary decisions that are made will not be monopolized by the dominant group.[25]

Furthermore, the exploration of differing perspectives also promotes a critical analysis of the current provisional consensus about the best form of governance and the current provisional consensus about the direction of society. The ongoing debate ensures that nothing is permanent. Given that democracy is not a status to be reached or a given set of institutions and procedures to adopt, the ongoing nature of the debate allows existing democratic standards to act as a benchmark for critical analysis and as a catalyst for change.

The constitution of a society embodies the provisional agreement reached about democracy via the deliberative process and embeds the political structure which best reflects the provisional agreement. Constitutional arrangements are provisional and should be viewed as incompletely theorized agreements that reflect the provisional agreement reached about democracy, but which are open to review and revision. Accordingly, constitutional interpretation should focus on the incompleteness of the standards so adopted.

Sunstein developed this notion of incompletely theorized agreements.[26] It is suited to a society that contains a plurality of views, which is a common characteristic of modern societies. If there is dissension on a large-scale issue, people may converge on particular outcomes and low-level principles without having to agree on the general principle. Conversely, there may be agreement on the general principle, which allows us to leave open the range of outcomes in particular cases. Indeed, society may disagree on the general principle and the particular application, but find agreement on mid-level principles.

[24] J. Waldron, 'Legislation by Assembly', in T. Campbell and J. Goldsworthy (eds.), *Judicial Power, Democracy, and Legal Positivism* (Aldershot: Dartmouth, 1999), 26.

[25] As per Linklater, as quoted by Marks, n. 8 above, 110.

[26] Sunstein, n. 20 above.

At whichever level the consensus is reached, the point is that a consensus is reached. There is a common settlement of the disagreement, which promotes stability, mutual respect, and reciprocity. By reaching an incompletely theorized agreement, the deepest and most defining beliefs and commitments of some people are not rejected by or subordinated to another's. Moreover, by not once and for all committing society to overarching general principles or particular outcomes, the morals and values of society can evolve and respond to changing circumstances. Finally, society can move ahead on the basis of the provisional settlement. In the words of Bobbio: 'Political life proceeds through a series of conflicts which are never definitely resolved, and whose temporary resolution comes about through provisional agreements, truces, and those more durable peace treaties called constitutions.'[27]

Incompletely theorized agreements are part of Sunstein's theory of just institutions.[28] In particular, incompletely theorized agreements are part of the theory of deliberative democracy. Power can only be legitimately exerted by just institutions, and just institutions must be founded on democratic considerations. However, Sunstein insists that some interests are immune from democratic intrusions (as does the principle of democratic inclusion). Constitutions are used to define what is and is not immune from democratic intrusion. Constitutions establish democracy, its just institutions, and the limits of the powers of its just institutions.

Constitutions tend to contain a particular type of incompletely theorized agreement: that is, agreement at a high level of abstraction, because people can agree at the abstract level about how to live, but cannot agree about its specification. For instance, we can agree to live by the rule of law, but we cannot agree what this means. In the context of rights, most people would agree that cruel, unusual, and inhuman treatment is inappropriate, but will disagree about what constitutes cruel, unusual, and inhuman treatment. To approach constitutions as incompletely theorized agreements ensures that disagreements are provisionally settled, but in a manner that promotes stability, mutual respect, and reciprocity.

Overall, the principle of democratic inclusion will secure an effective political democracy. The principle of democratic inclusion emphasizes the need for self-rule and political equality. The deliberative theory of democracy, coupled with the incompletely theorized agreement theory, is best suited to improving self-rule and political equality. The principle of democratic inclusion does have human rights implications. In particular, both the deliberative theory of democracy and incompletely theorized constitutional agreements envisage human rights guarantees enforced by (at least) the judiciary. Before turning to the human rights and institutional implications of the principle of democratic inclusion, a consideration of the ramifications of substantive theories of democracy is necessary.

Substantive or procedural democracy?

There is an ongoing debate over whether democracy is concerned solely with procedures and has no (or little) quality control over the outcomes of the process,

[27] Bobbio, n. 1 above, 120.

[28] Sunstein, n. 19 above, 53–61.

or is concerned also with substantive outcomes without respect for which the procedures are considered illegitimate. There are many reasons to favour a substantive theory of democracy over a purely procedural (or electoral) theory. Substantive notions of democracy are better able to meet the demands of internationally recognized human rights obligations than are procedural notions. Procedural democracy has no greater commitment to human rights guarantees than the majority allows. Procedural notions can easily degenerate into non-democratic, or even anti-democratic, formalism. The core values of democracy can be subordinated to majority pressure.[29] Moreover, procedural mechanisms designed to implement democracy are themselves based on substantive values, and their application involves the evaluation of substantive questions of political morality. A theory that acknowledges these questions of substantive political morality is to be preferred.[30]

The ascendancy of substantive over procedural theories is demonstrated by Dworkin's theory of communal democracy, which is concerned with legitimizing what a majority, within a community of equals, prefers. This type of self-rule requires a community with moral membership. Moral membership of a community contains two relational conditions:[31] every person must be able to take part in collective decisions, and participation must be under conditions that do not make assumptions about the individual's worth, talent, or the credibility of their convictions. Also, equal concern and respect must be extended to all members of the community: '. . . political decisions that affect the distribution of wealth, benefits, and burdens must be consistent with equal concern for all.'[32] The procedural and substantive elements of communal democracy require the guarantee of fundamental civil and political rights.

The principle of democratic inclusion is consistent with communal democracy. The principle of democratic inclusion is a substantive theory. First, citizens need *better* control over the decisions that affect them. There is a qualitative aspect to self-rule. It is not just minimum participation, such as casting a vote in a periodic election. *Better* self-rule requires a fully informed citizenry, an open public space for debate, and scope for participation for all in the decision-making processes of the community. For rule to be truly self-rule, it must be exercised in a community with moral membership. Without moral membership, different weight can be given to different individuals (and their ideas) within a community, undermining

[29] See, generally, J. Donnelly, 'Human Rights, Democracy, and Development', (1999) 21 *Human Rights Quarterly* 608–32.

[30] See, generally, P. Monahan, *Politics and the Constitution: The Charter, Federalism and the Supreme Court of Canada* (Toronto: Carswell, 1987).

[31] In addition to the relational conditions, a community with moral membership also requires: (*a*) structural conditions, such as membership of a genuine political community which shares culture, territorial boundaries, a political history, common language, and values; and (*b*) the condition of moral independence, which means that people in a community must consider themselves partners in a joint venture, and they must freely accept the types of decision the joint venture is considered competent to make. See Dworkin, n. 15 above, esp. 24–6.

[32] Dworkin, n. 15 above, 25.

self-rule. Secondly, greater parity in the distribution of the rights and opportunities of citizens is required. Substantive notions of political equality are to be preferred to formal notions of political equality. To treat all citizens formally in the same manner does not address existing imbalances in rights and opportunities. The extension of equal concern and respect for *all* members of a community is vital. Improved self-rule is illegitimate without substantive political equality.

Self-rule and political equality cannot be furthered without guaranteeing human rights. Let us focus on civil and political rights. Civil and political rights not only ensure the freedom to stand for public office and establish the procedural voting mechanisms that are a necessary precursor to self-rule and formal political equality. Civil and political rights are also concerned with the quality of the self-rule and improving substantive political equality.

More particularly, freedoms of thought, conscience, and religion, freedom of expression, and freedoms of assembly and association improve the quality of self-rule. They also promote political equality. Guaranteeing rights to the holding of, and expression of, diverse thoughts and religious beliefs, and the freedom to live by personal sensibilities of conscience, promotes self rule and substantive political equality. The state must remain neutral among these diverse views, convictions, and talents. Moreover, without rights to liberty, physical integrity, security of the person, due process, and privacy, self-rule and political equality would be threatened. Such civil rights ensure individuals control over their personal lives, and allow individuals the luxury to participate in public life without fear, thereby furthering self-rule. These civil rights also promote equality of opportunity between citizens. Furthermore, non-discrimination rights and minority rights promote political equality. Voting rights are explicitly guaranteed to be without distinction. Non-discrimination rights and minority rights also encourage tolerance, broad-mindedness, and understanding within a diverse population. All views, aspirations, and perspectives are protected and thus legitimized. Decisions produced from a plurality of perspectives are more likely to dissipate disparities in the availability of opportunities.

The ramifications of a substantive theory of democracy

What are the ramifications of a substantive theory of democracy, such as the principle of democratic inclusion? Many critics argue that a substantive theory erroneously insists that democracy must produce 'right answers'. Distinctions are drawn between human rights safeguards that are necessary to produce a form of self-rule, such as the right to vote, and human rights safeguards that are designed to ensure that democracy produces the 'right' outcomes. The former are said to be acceptable constraints on democracy, but the latter are not.[33]

[33] A. Hutchinson and P. Monahan, 'Democracy and the Rule of Law', in A. Hutchinson and P. Monahan (eds.), *The Rule of Law: Ideal or Ideology* (Toronto: Carswell, 1987), 122: 'A commitment to democracy does not mean that constraints on popular decision-making must always and everywhere be condemned . . . But there is a distinction between constitutional safeguards which constrain democratic activity in the name of democracy [i.e. rights to vote, non-discrimination] and

Waldron details such difficulties associated with substantive theories of democracy. According to Waldron, substantive theories wrongly focus on the *outcomes* of democratic procedures, rather than on the democratic *procedures* alone. Waldron rejects theories that focus on decisions *about* democracy (right answers), rather than theories that focus on decisions *made by* democratic means (democratic procedures):

> There *is* something lost, from a democratic point of view, when an unelected and unaccountable individual or institution makes a binding decision about what democracy requires... Process may not be all that there is to democratic decision making; but we should not say that, since the decision is *about* democracy, process is therefore irrelevant.[34]

These concerns are misplaced. The principle of democratic inclusion does not focus on 'right answers'. The principle of democratic inclusion recognizes that democracy is an indeterminate concept. It recognizes that democracy may be incapable of producing *a* single right answer or outcome. Indeed, in a pluralistic society right answers are unlikely and indeed undesirable. Even Dworkin admits that reasonable citizens may disagree about what democracy requires and what rights it presupposes.[35] The principle of democratic inclusion is premissed on the fact that democratic deliberation is an ongoing process of trial and error, aimed at securing and enhancing self-rule and political equality.

At best, we may have to settle for provisional truces that enable us to get on with life, leaving the portals open for debate and change. The elected arms of government will strike provisional truces after public debate and participation. The unelected arm will be empowered to assess the truce and alter it where the deliberative democratic process breaks down or is unreliable. This occurs where self-rule is vulnerable and where majority interests are liable to threaten minority interests, thereby undermining political equality. Thus, civil and political rights will protect against such violations of self-rule and political equality. The capacity for judicial intervention improves the quality of self-rule within the context of political equality.

those which constrain democratic activity in the name of "right answers". The latter type of constraints seek to substitute the judgments of philosophy for those of the people simply because the popular judgments are regarded as tainted.' Consider also Ely's focus on a representation-reinforcing rights theory, which sanctions only rights that are procedurally constitutive of democracy: J. H. Ely, *Democracy and Distrust: A Theory of Judicial Review* (Cambridge, Mass.: Harvard University Press, 1980); J. H. Ely, 'Democracy and Judicial Review', in his *On Constitutional Ground* (Princeton: Princeton University Press, 1996), 6; J. H. Ely, 'Another Such Victory: Constitutional Theory and Practice in a World Where Courts are No Different from Legislatures', in his *On Constitutional Ground*, 340.

[34] J. Waldron, 'Judicial Review and the Conditions of Democracy', (1999) 7 *Journal of Political Philosophy* 346. Compare with M. S. Moore, 'Natural Rights, Judicial Review, and Constitutional Interpretation', in J. Goldsworthy and T. Campbell (eds.), *Legal Interpretation in Democratic States* (Dartmouth: Ashgate, 2002), 221: 'Those who value participatory democracy highly, such as Waldron, can still retort that court-enforced constitutional rights cost us something we should value, namely, the right to determine by majority vote what rights there are. We thus must balance this loss in democratic determinations of foundational issues against the gain in the protection of rights promised by judicial review. For what it is worth, I find the balance easy [in favour of judicial review].'

[35] Dworkin, n. 15 above.

Moreover, if we accept that democracy and rights reflect incompletely theorized agreements based on incompletely theorized standards, all provisional truces are open to challenge, debate, and change. No majority preference, no judicial ruling, no arm of government, no single voice has a monopoly on power. Such decisions cannot be characterized as providing the 'right answer'.

In response to Waldron, process is not irrelevant to the principle of democratic inclusion. Admittedly, the principle does focus on decisions *about* democracy. It insists that democracy be concerned about improving self-rule and promoting political equality. Some decisions *about* democracy will be illegitimate because of their tendency to undermine self-rule and their political inequality. However, it does not follow that process is therefore irrelevant. All provisional decisions that are made *about* democracy are made after deliberation and debate. The deliberation occurs between the citizens, the executive, the legislature, and the judiciary. No one participant can trump the outcome of the deliberations, and any decisions made *about* democracy are open to change. The process of consultation and debate is very much a cornerstone of the provisional decisions made *about* democracy.

What are the outcomes of substantive democratic theory?

The outcomes of the substantive principle of democratic inclusion, based on debate and dialogue, are more appropriately described as producing *better answers*. In the elected arms of government, rights-based debate 'will generate a *better, and more principled, answer* to complex and contested issues than a policy process where rights-based assessments are absent'.[36] If rights-based considerations are not mandatory, policy choices need only be defended in terms of reconciling conflicting interests within society. If democracy means nothing more than statistical democracy, such conflicts will more often than not be resolved in favour of the majority.

In contrast, if rights-based considerations play a role during the drafting, debate, and adoption of legislative schemes, the impact of policies on protected rights would be better exposed. To be forced to defend a policy that infringes or limits protected rights 'would better expose the discriminating effects of policies or possible unintended consequences that impair or undermine protected rights'.[37] At the end of the day, 'It is more difficult to justify the reasons for pursuing policies that require limiting protected rights than it is to pursue competing interests.'[38] Placing burdens of justification on the legislature does protect significant values, without wholly depriving our democratic institutions the power to act.[39] There is a democratic difference between telling the

[36] Hiebert, n. 11 above, 119; my emphasis. [37] Ibid. 120. [38] Ibid.

[39] See Neuborne, n. 5 above. He argues that rights are a product of democratic governmental institutions. The institutional view of the origins of rights generates less tension with democracy. Rights are the real-life consequences of the interplay of our institutions and have no independent existence from our institutions. When protecting rights, judges do 'not enforce a tangible phenomenon with some substantive meaning, but rather [the judge] applies error-deflection rules to assure a given

legislature that it cannot do something and requiring it to be sure of its premisses before acting.

Further, it mischaracterizes the role of the judiciary to say that, when it joins the debate and dialogue within the principle of democratic inclusion, it seeks the 'right answers'. When enforcing protected rights within the principle of democratic inclusion, the judiciary is neither producing (nor precluding for that matter) the discovery of the 'right answer'. There may be no single right answer. Rather, in enforcing protected rights, the judiciary precludes provisional truces that were *not* reached in compliance with the goals of self-rule and political equality. In other words, the judiciary precludes provisional truces that violate protected rights in an unjustified manner. Stated in the positive, only provisional truces that are the product of self-rule and political equality, as guaranteed by rights, are justified.[40] A debate that produced policies or legislation that does not respect self-rule and substantive political equality is precluded.

> The decision to uphold the legislative response to a complex policy problem, which does not compromise a core right and which has been the product of rigorous and sincere debate about its justification and the merits of alternative means, would be consistent with the democratic ideal of governing through discussion and debate.[41]

Thus, the principle of democratic inclusion is substantive in nature. It precludes some provisional outcomes that are unjustifiably made in violation of the principles of self-rule and political equality. It is the preclusion of majority outcomes that violate self-rule and political equality, as opposed to the search for a right answer, that is the essence of the principle of democratic inclusion. The principle of democratic inclusion 'does not accept that these exceptions [to majority decision-making] are a cause of moral regret'[42] or democratically illegitimate.

level of certainty about the choices made by the legislature concerning its textual authority and factual justification' (p. 200). The permissive error-deflection standard is the reasonable decision-maker: could a reasonable decision-maker have believed this choice was correct in terms of constitutional authority and factual justification? Thus, rights are the result of error-deflection rules imposed by the judiciary on the legislature. Error-deflection may not be totally democratic: who chooses the 'values in favor of which error should be deflected'; who chooses the 'precise degree of error deflection' (p. 201)? If the answer is the judiciary, the problem of democratic illegitimacy arises. Yet, there is a democratic 'difference between telling the legislature that they cannot do something at all and telling the legislature that it must be sure of its . . . premises before it acts in derogation of certain values. Placing . . . burdens of justification on legislatures . . . has the effect of shielding significant values from unnecessary derogation without wholly depriving the popular institutions of the power to act' (p. 201).

[40] 'The Court's contribution is not to scrutinize the merits of the particular legislative scheme but to evaluate the quality of how that legislative decision was made and to ensure that the core rights have not been unduly compromised', as per Hiebert, n. 11 above, 155.

[41] Ibid. 124.

[42] Dworkin, n. 15 above, 17. I have used Dworkin's words and sentiment here because I agree with most of his principles. However, the conclusions that Dworkin draws are not always relevant as his analysis proceeds in the context of a fully enforceable bill of rights in the United States; whereas my analysis proceeds in the context of the Canadian Charter and the British Human Rights Act, both of which do not give the judiciary the final word.

The human rights implications of the principle of democratic inclusion

The protection of civil and political rights

The principle of democratic inclusion, with its aim to improve self-rule and political equality, has human rights implications: 'securing respect for all categories of human rights must assume priority.'[43] Human rights norms recognize, protect, and promote many values including, but not limited to, democracy.

Focusing on the International Covenant on Civil and Political Rights (the International Covenant) highlights, first, the *dependency* of democracy on human rights.[44] The right to self-determination is the essence of democracy. Among other things, self-determination is the right of a people to determine its political status collectively. This includes the right to free, fair, and open participation in the democratic processes of government.[45] Additional rights are needed to provide the framework for exercising the democratic power guaranteed by the right to self-determination. These include the right to vote and the right to run for public office.[46] Freedom of expression and of assembly and association create the conditions for debate that are necessary to a democratic order.[47] Individuals could not participate effectively in a democracy without the right to liberty, physical integrity, and due process.[48] Indeed, even economic, social, and cultural rights promote effective democracy. For instance, without education, housing, food, and shelter, individuals cannot exercise their civil and political rights effectively.[49]

Secondly, the International Covenant illustrates the *limits* human rights impose on democratic power. Democratic power is not self-limiting, yet it requires limitation. Hence, the limiting aspects of civil and political rights are internal to the democratic order. The guarantee of regular, free, and genuine

[43] Marks, n. 8 above, 116. See also Hiebert, n. 11 above, 118: 'But public debate is not the only goal of a democratic polity. Policy choices should respect fundamental rights, those contained explicitly in the *Charter* and others related to its core values.'

[44] The regional conventions also demonstrate the dependency of democracy on human rights. See the European Convention on Human Rights (ECHR), the American Convention on Human Rights (ACHR), and the African Charter on Human and Peoples' Rights (African Charter).

[45] Franck, n. 1 above.

[46] See Art 25 of the International Covenant on Civil and Political Rights (ICCPR), as well as Art 3 of Protocol 1 to the ECHR, Art 5 of the Charter of the Organisation of American States, and Art 13 of the African Charter.

[47] For freedom of expression, see Art 19 of the ICCPR, as well as Art 19 of the Universal Declaration of Human Rights (UDHR), Art 10 of the ECHR, Art 13 of the ACHR, and Art 9 of the African Charter. For freedom of assembly and association, see Art 22 of the ICCPR, as well as Art 20 of the UDHR, Art 11 of the ECHR, Arts 15 and 16 of the ACHR, and Arts 10 to 12 of the African Charter.

[48] See Arts 6 to 10 and 14 of the ICCPR, as well as Arts 5 to 7 of the ECHR, Arts 4 to 9 of the ACHR, and Arts 6 and 7 of the African Charter.

[49] See, generally, the International Covenant on Economic, Social and Cultural Rights. Given the length of this chapter, in-depth consideration of economic, social, and cultural rights cannot be undertaken. See Ewing, Ch. 16 below, and Otto, Ch. 14 below, for more complete coverage of these issues.

elections ensures the periodic accountability of the representative arms of government. Freedom of expression and freedom of assembly and association create the conditions for debate and accountability that are essential to controlling and limiting power within a democracy.[50] Freedom of conscience, religious belief, and thought, rights of non-discrimination, and rights of minorities ensure that all views can be aired and debated without fear, which serves to increase the accountability of the majority.[51]

Thirdly, the improvement of the conditions of *self-rule* by enhancing control by citizens of decisions that affect them requires human rights protection. Not only do human rights guarantee the participation in the public decision-making process through voting rights and representation rights. They also, particularly in the form of constitutional rights, require the 'state authority . . . to justify itself to the citizenry on a continuing basis'.[52] Constitutional rights ensure a continuing justification to the citizenry that political power has been exercised in a rational and reasonable manner.[53] Judicial review of legislative action would not 'scrutinize the merits of the particular legislative scheme but . . . evaluate the quality of how the legislative decisions was made and . . . ensure that core rights have not been unduly compromised'.[54] The more transparent and open the processes and reasoning of the elected arms of government, the more fully informed is the citizenry about the direction the government is taking society. This augments genuine self-rule.

Moreover, self-rule requires an authentic opportunity for all to participate in the decision-making process. The deliberative theory of democracy has participation at its core. The quality of participation improves with the protection of human rights. According to Campbell, the exemplary model of democracy includes a pre-enacted instrument protecting human rights and fundamental freedoms to be used by the judiciary to review legislation.[55] Any conflicts between the guaranteed rights and the legislation found by the judiciary should be referred back to the legislature. Thus, the deliberative theory not only insists on a genuine dialogue between the represented and those representing them. It also insists on the establishment of a dialogue between the unelected and the

[50] See Arts 19 to 22 of the ICCPR, as well as Arts 10 and 11 of the ECHR, Arts 13, 15, and 16 of the ACHR, and Arts 9 to 12 of the African Charter.

[51] See Arts 2, 3, 18, 26, and 27 of the ICCPR, as well as Arts 9 and 14 of the ECHR, Arts 12 and 24 of the ACHR, and Arts 2, 3, 8, 19, and 28 of the African Charter.

[52] Marks, n. 8 above, 59.

[53] If governments are required to justify laws as per constitutional rights, 'Any law that burdened or withheld a benefit from an individual or group' would need to 'meet the standards of justice which the principles of rationality and proportionality imply', as per D. Beatty, 'Human Rights and the Rule of Law', in Beatty (ed.), *Human Rights and Judicial Review: A Comparative Perspective* (Dordrecht: Martinus Nijhoff, 1994), 23.

[54] As per Hiebert, n. 11 above, 155.

[55] Campbell insists that the conditions for free and open debate should be determined by parliament, with the courts upholding these. Judges may be given the task of *protecting* fundamental rights, but they should not be given the additional task of *defining* fundamental rights. The definition of rights is preferably to be the product of consensus. See Campbell, n. 8 above.

elected arm of government, over which neither has the final word. This form of dialogue is precisely what the British and Canadian human rights instruments attempt to achieve.[56]

Finally, human rights have an imperative role to play in attaining *political equality*. Political equality seeks to overcome disparities in rights and opportunities. Human rights inhere in all human beings in a non-discriminatory manner. Guarantees of non-discrimination contained in human rights instruments have the potential to break down existing disparities. The protection of minority rights, interests, and views also promotes political equality. Moreover, the remaining civil and political rights ensure that minority voices are heard and accounted for in decisions concerning the direction of society. All views are protected and thus legitimized, such that decisions should treat all individuals with equal concern and respect. Such decisions should lead to the elimination of disparities in the availability of opportunities and the protection of rights.

The judicial review task

Focusing briefly on the role of the judiciary under a rights instrument, we should recall the interpretation theory of incompletely theorized agreements. Within this theory, there is a general presumption against *high-level* judicial theorizing. There is also a presumption in favour of judges reaching *incompletely* theorized agreements when adjudicating disputes.[57] Such agreements ensure concrete outcomes to disputes in the short term, promote stability in the midst of pluralism,[58] and allow for the civic evolution of shared values and morals. This does *not* mean that judgments should not incorporate abstractions or have moral or legal foundations, but it does mean that society's commitments are *not* finally defined within the courtroom. Rather, judicial opinion is one voice among many in the ongoing discussion and debate.

In the context of human rights instruments, judicial interpretation of the human rights instrument should focus on the incompleteness of the specified standards, and judges, thereby, should be reluctant to completely theorize a decision. More importantly, the presumption against judicial decisions based on high-level theories does not apply, *inter alia*, where human rights instruments permit the judiciary to use relatively large-scale principles. Thus, the judiciary

[56] A. Bayefsky, 'Mechanisms for Entrenchment and Protection of a Bill of Rights: The Canadian Experience', [1997] 5 *European Human Rights Law Review* 496; S. M. Zifcak, 'The Charter as a Dialogue: An Analysis of Canada's Experience with the Constitutional Charter of Rights and Freedoms', (1988) 6 *Law in Context* 62; C. Collins and B. Wells, Lord Chancellor's Department, interview, 4 Dec. 2000.

[57] Sunstein gives many reasons for settling on incompletely theorized agreements: judges may not be able to think of a good theory, or agree upon a theory; to pursue unnecessary contestations about rights divulges a lack of respect for the deepest and most defining commitments of others; it avoids the democratic pedigree of the judiciary debate; and the judiciary cannot achieve the large-scale reform that may be needed in certain circumstances. See Sunstein, n. 20 above.

[58] In the sense that a judgment that is not reliant on a general theory does not undermine one's deepest ideals and commitments in favour of another's.

should resolve disputes under human rights instruments according to incompletely theorized agreements, which may need to be specified at a high level of theory, although lesser levels are preferable, especially when multiple theories can justify the agreement.[59]

Modern bills of rights and the 'effective political democracy'

Modern bills of rights (whether constitutional or not) incorporate the provisional nature of democracy and human rights, and have the capacity to accommodate the diverse views, disagreements, and uncertainties that exist within pluralistic societies.[60] The potential for dissension about the direction of society and the need for evolution are recognized within modern bills of rights, both explicitly and implicitly. Both notions are evident in the amending provisions of rights instruments, the breadth of the articulation of human rights guarantees, the non-absoluteness of rights, and the ability for legislatures and executives to react to judicial assessments of their actions. Each will be considered in turn.

Amendment of protected rights

Most rights-protective instruments, whether constitutional or not, allow for change. If rights are protected only by ordinary statute, any later inconsistent legislation can override the rights, subject to manner and form provisions. A capacity to accommodate diverse views, future disagreements, and uncertainties is retained.[61] In constitutional rights instruments, the inclusion of provisions allowing for constitutional amendment to bills of rights explicitly

[59] Sunstein reviews the interpretative methods under the United States Constitution. His preferred interpretative method, based partly on the need to constrain judges when interpreting constitutions for democratic reasons, has three components. First, there is a strong preference for soft originalism. Secondly, case-by-case judgments and analogical reasoning should be used to limit judicial discretion. Thirdly, judges may need to engage in a certain level of theoretical decision-making when the democratic process breaks down or is less reliable (p. 179). Deliberative democracy means more than majority rule. Deliberative democratic norms include the protection of political rights and the protection of minorities. Where the majoritarian process ignores or threatens deliberative democratic norms, 'the case for judicial control becomes stronger' (p. 180). Judges should adopt a 'presumption in favor of democratic outcomes', but the presumption weakens 'when democratic rights are at stake or when politically vulnerable groups are at risk' (p. 180). Sunstein's view of constitutional interpretation is very close to that of J. H. Ely, *Democracy and Distrust*, n. 33 above. See generally Sunstein, n. 20 above, 167–90. The United States example serves to highlight the application of the interpretative theory in the constitutional law context. However, this precise constitutional interpretative method will not apply to modern human rights instruments because of the differing context and role of the interpreters. In particular, modern human rights instruments contain much greater ambiguity than the more traditional United States Constitution, the rights are subject to various qualifications and limitations, the adjudicative powers of the judiciary are curtailed, and the elected arms of government can respond to judicial assessments of constitutional rights.

[60] For example, although Prime Minister Trudeau fought for the adoption of the Charter to unify Canada, the Charter essentially protects everyone's right to stay diverse.

[61] This is the case under the Human Rights Act; see s 3.

acknowledges that disagreements may arise and unforeseen circumstances may require change. Express constitutional amending provisions may contain extraordinary requirements for amendments to be carried, but this does not detract from the capacity of such instruments to accommodate unforeseen disagreements or changed circumstances.[62]

Constitutional ambiguity

The provisional and flexible nature of rights is further illustrated in their vagueness. Constitutional ambiguity is deliberately used in situations of diversity, disagreement, and uncertainty. Things that cannot be known and agreed upon in any verifiable manner are 'left undefined and allowed to remain "sufficiently obscure to allow them to retain an approximate appearance of internal coherence and clarity, while at the same time accommodating several potentially conflicting and quite unresolved points of issue"'.[63] In the words of Tushnet, 'the language of rights is so open and indeterminate that opposing parties can use the same language to express their positions'.[64] Tushnet considers this to be a downfall, as 'rights talk can provide only momentary advantages in ongoing political struggles'.[65] However, the principle of democratic inclusion—along with the deliberative theory of democracy and incompletely theorized agreements that expound it—views this as a strength, democracy being defined by its ongoing political struggles.

Rights are not 'trumps'

The fact that most rights are not absolute highlights the fact that diverse views and disagreement will exist. Many rights are internally qualified. For example, under the European Convention—which the Human Rights Act incorporates—every person has the right to liberty and security of the person, but this may be displaced in specified circumstances, such as lawful detention after conviction by a competent court or the detention of a minor for the lawful purpose of educational supervision.[66] Even the right to life is internally qualified.[67]

Rights can also be internally limited. Under the European Convention the rights contained in Articles 8 to 11 are guaranteed, subject to interference in specified circumstances, such as the protection of public health, public order, morals, the national interest, or the rights and freedoms of others.[68] The precise

[62] This is the case under the Charter. See the general amending provision under Part V of the Constitution Act 1982, particularly s 38.

[63] Darrow and Alston, n. 6 above, 497.

[64] M. Tushnet, 'An Essay on Rights', (1984) 62 *Texas Law Review* 1363, 1371.

[65] Ibid.

[66] See Art 5 of the ECHR, as well as Arts 9 and 14 of the ICCPR, and ss 7 to 14 of the Charter.

[67] See Art 2 of the ECHR.

[68] For example, Art 9(2) states that 'Freedom to manifest one's religion or beliefs shall be subject only to such limitations as are prescribed by law and are necessary in a democratic society in the

terms and justifications for the internal limits of each article differ, but the European Court has adopted the same test when considering the validity of the limitations. Once the prima facie right is engaged, the validity of any limitation on the right must be assessed. Limitations are only valid if they are prescribed by law, intended to achieve a legitimate objective, and are necessary in a democratic society (that is, proportionate to the end to be achieved). Moreover, the limitation must not be discriminatory, in the sense that any distinction must have an objective and reasonable justification, and must be proportional.[69]

In addition, rights can be externally limited. The Charter is a good example of this. Section 1 of the Charter guarantees all the rights contained in the Charter, that is, the rights in sections 2 to 23.[70] However, under section 1 the rights and freedoms so guaranteed are subject to any reasonable limits prescribed by law and that can be demonstrably justified in a free and democratic society. The difference between the external and internal limits should be noted. First, the external limit applies to all of the rights guaranteed, compared to the internal limit which is more selective. Secondly, in the external limit context, the legitimate objectives that may justify interference with the right are left completely undefined. The test under section 1 is not that dissimilar to that under the European Convention.

The salient point is that the non-absoluteness of rights accommodates diversity and difference of opinion. The limiting or balancing of rights may be required as the result of the conflict of two protected rights. It may be required because of a clash of individual vis-à-vis group rights. It may also be required when a guaranteed right conflicts with other democratic values that were not guaranteed but that emerge as important in a particular situation, or when a guaranteed right conflicts with the broader common good or public interest. The point is that rights are flexible, indeterminate, and provisional, just as democracy is. Rights do not necessarily trump other values and, in fact, are designed to be able to accommodate competing democratic values where circumstance requires. Rights are capable of being 'constructed, deconstructed and reconstructed in ever-changing circumstances'.[71] Rights establish a formalized rights-based dialogue within a deliberative democratic system.

Institutionalized dialogue: legislative and executive responses

Many modern bills of rights allow for legislative and/or executive reaction after judicial review. Let us consider the scope for institutional reaction under the Human Rights Act. Rather than empowering the judiciary to invalidate laws

interests of public safety, for the protection of public order, health or morals, or for the protection of the rights and freedoms of others.'

[69] Art 14 of the ECHR.

[70] The Charter guarantees various categories of rights and freedoms: fundamental freedoms, democratic rights, mobility rights, legal rights, equality rights, official language rights, and minority language educational rights.

[71] T. McCarthy, as quoted by Marks, n. 8 above, 149.

that are incompatible with the now protected Convention rights, the judiciary is only empowered to make declarations of incompatibility. A declaration of incompatibility does not affect the validity, continuing operation, or enforcement of the provision to which the declaration applies, nor is the declaration binding on the parties to the proceeding in which it is made.[72] In other words, the judge must apply the incompatible law in the case at hand.

The elected arms of government have a number of responses to a declaration of incompatibility. The legislature may decide to do nothing. This would indicate that the legislature has not altered its view of the legislation in light of the institutional perspective of the judiciary. In this situation, the particular individual can still seek redress in the European Court of Human Rights, and the public in general can express their (dis)satisfaction with the legislature's response at the next general election. Alternatively, the legislature may decide to pass ordinary legislation in response to the judicial reaction to the impugned legislation. In addition, the relevant minister is empowered to take remedial action, empowering the minister to rectify an incompatibility by executive action.[73]

Both the declaration of incompatibility and the response mechanisms are consistent with the principle of democratic inclusion. The declaration of incompatibility ensures self-rule subject to an institutional debate based on rational and reasoned judicial input. Judicial review of legislative and executive action demonstrates a commitment to human rights that promote political equality. However, the legislative and executive response mechanisms under the Human Rights Act keep the channels of change open, such that society's deepest commitments are not set in stone.

The Convention rights themselves are likened to a 'living tree', evolving and flexible. Moreover, the declaration of incompatibility structure ensures a continuing debate between the elected and unelected arms of government. The executive and legislature can expect there to be intense public interest in response to a declaration of incompatibility and strong public pressure to change the law. A declaration of incompatibility will prompt debate between the represented and the elected and unelected arms of government. If the elected arms of government disregard the judicial view of human rights as expressed in a declaration of incompatibility, the citizenry will express their views at election time. Further, the remedial action procedure gives the executive a defined and important role in demarcating the requirements of self-rule and political equality. This further justifies the notion that it is only with the input of all perspectives that democracy can be truly inclusive. Overall, the elements of self-rule and political equality imperative to the principle of democratic inclusion are open to change as differing perspectives are brought to bear.

[72] S 4(6) of the Human Rights Act.

[73] See s 10 and Sch 2. If the minister considers that there are 'compelling reasons' for proceeding, the minister *may* by order make such amendments to the legislation *as are considered necessary to remove the incompatibility*. All remedial orders must be by statutory instrument. Remedial orders must ultimately receive the approval by resolution of both Houses of Parliament.

Under the Charter there are many responses available to the elected arms of government in the face of a judicial decision invalidating legislation as an unjustified limitation of a *Charter* right. First, the legislature may not respond at all; the legislature may be happy to hand over certain issues to the judiciary because of an absence of political will or an absence of clear political preference. Secondly, the legislature may enact similar legislation which takes account of the reasons for the initial invalidation. Thirdly, the legislature may re-enact the impugned legislation *notwithstanding* the Charter under section 33. With section 33 there is no foreclosure on what the fundamental commitments of society should be. However, before acting under section 33, the legislature will have to assess the rational and reasoned judicial decision on its own merits, gauge the public mood, and decide whether it truly believes the judges misunderstood a core value.

The essence of the principle of democratic inclusion is that no arm of government should have exclusive power to interpret the limits of liberal constitutional rights. The protection of fundamental rights and freedoms enhance self-rule and political equality by distributing power between the various arms of government. *Both* the legislature and the judiciary have a legitimate role to play. There are brakes on both the excessive or unreasonable exercise of power of the judiciary (s 33) and the legislature (s 1). While the guarantees in the Charter act as a check on the legislature, section 1 gives the legislature a chance to justify its rights limiting choices, and section 33 acts as a check on judicial power. Section 33 provides 'a structural check on judicial power that better balances "the principle of constitutionalism with active popular sovereignty"'.[74]

Conclusion

Hence, if we accept that the principle of democratic inclusion provides an 'effective political democracy', we have a theory that reconciles the basics of democracy and human rights. The principle stresses that democracy is about self-rule, but not self-rule alone. It requires self-rule within a community of political equals. Deliberative democracy and the notion of incompletely theorized constitutional agreements best implement the principle of democratic inclusion. Deliberative democracy, aimed at achieving rational consensus on the common good after open and uncoerced deliberation, achieves self-rule under the condition of political equality via human rights guarantees. Deliberative democracy itself, combined with the notion of incompletely theorized human rights standards, allows the debate about the deep beliefs and commitments of society to continue and evolve. Thus, human rights and democracy can coexist, and the

[74] C. P. Manfredi, *Judicial Power and the Charter: Canada and the Paradox of Liberal Constitutionalism*, 2nd edn. (Oxford: Oxford University Press, 2001), 195.

limitations human rights guarantees place on the scope of majoritarian decision-making are not necessarily anti-democratic.[75]

There is great scope within democracy to respect the value of all human beings and to listen to the voice of all human beings. It is only when all voices are heard, and given equal respect, that society can begin to grapple with our defining commitments and human rights.

[75] T. R. S. Allan, 'The Politics of the British Constitution: A Response to Professor Ewing's Paper', Autumn [2000] *Public Law* 374, 374: 'It is not "undemocratic", except in the most superficial understanding of that term, to insist that politics should be constrained by legal safeguards for individuals and minorities.'

7

Representation-Reinforcing Review: Comparing Experiences in the United States and Australia

DAVID TUCKER

'Representation-reinforcing review' describes a justification for judicial review. It offers judges the opportunity to defend human rights in the name of democracy and has been influential in both Australia and the United States. A problem arises, however, about the suitability of courts in securing human rights when developing constitutional law in an innovative way. Thus, this chapter raises questions about the competence of the judiciary in offering this kind of leadership. To evaluate the institutional competence of courts, the chapter considers some policy choices that judges have made in supervising electoral arrangements in Australia and the United States.

The representation-reinforcing approach developed from a remark made in 1938 by Justice Harlan F. Stone in *United States v Carolene Products Company.*[1] In a famous footnote to his opinion in this case (no. 4) he states: 'It is unnecessary to consider now whether legislation which restricts those political processes which can ordinarily be expected to bring about repeal of undesirable legislation is to be subjected to more exacting judicial scrutiny under the general prohibitions of the Fourteenth Amendment than are most other types of legislation.'

Justice Stone's idea, suggested in footnote 4, is that conventions and institutions that facilitate democracy may need to be protected against politicians who wish to entrench themselves in power. The problem we face, which makes Justice Stone think judicial reticence is inappropriate when laws relating to the electoral processes are under review, is that unscrupulous individuals may be able to muster a legislative majority that will enable them to pass laws that give them an advantage in electoral competition, making it difficult for challengers to succeed. Elected representatives, it is speculated, may not be trustworthy when their own special interest in gaining re-election is likely to be affected.

Even conceding this assumption, it does not follow that judges should be allocated the task of policing electoral processes. We first need to be sure that judges are likely to perform well when undertaking this kind of supervision.

1 304 US 144 (1938).

How do we know that they will be neutral? What evidence is there that judges are well equipped to undertake the supervisory tasks?

In this chapter I make a start in providing an answer to these questions by discussing three problems that can give rise to the entrenchment that bothers Justice Stone. I look at judicial policy-making with regard to electoral districting, campaign finance reform, and the 'Australian ballot'. A question I ask is whether judges should perform the role that Justice Stone's reasoning assigns, and I argue that judges may lack the necessary relevant experience to make wise choices. The three case-studies I have chosen provide some evidence for claims I make about the institutional competence of the judiciary. They also enable me to compare developments in Australia and the United States. As I show, there have been times when courts in both jurisdictions have been prepared to secure abstract democratic ideals, but the supervision of electoral arrangements by judges has not been very consistent, and it is not usually informed by a coherent theory of democracy.

Although my exploration reviews a very small part of the relevant evidence, it suggests that judges in both jurisdictions have been inconsistent and that the result of their work is not always helpful. In Australia, as we shall see, there has been a pattern of advance and retreat. The High Court discovered implied representational rights when it recognized freedom of speech in *Nationwide News v Wills*[2] and in *Australian Capital Television v Commonwealth* (*ACTV*).[3] However, after noting the significance of the representation-reinforcing rationale, the Court has recently retreated from the abstract theorizing this approach requires, adopting more traditional interpretative techniques.[4] In the United States the work of the Supreme Court is also largely incoherent, and seems to reflect nothing more substantial than the political instincts of the presiding judges in any case.

Campaign finance

In the United States a potential source of judicial subjectivity has been demonstrated by controversy over the meaning of the First and Fourteenth Amendments to the United States Constitution, which insist, among other things, that 'Congress shall make no law... abridging freedom of speech' and that 'No State shall make or enforce any law which shall abridge the privileges and immunities of citizens... or deny to any person the equal protection of the laws.' Given the abstract nature of these commitments, it is not surprising that commentators and judges in that country have engaged in a perennial debate about how these entrenched phrases should be read. In Australia the High Court has had to rely on the representation-reinforcing rationale to claim that, taken as a whole, the

2 (1992) 177 CLR 1.

3 (1992) 177 CLR 106.

4 *Lange v Australian Broadcasting Corporation* (1997) 189 CLR 520.

constitutional arrangements can be said to have put into place a system of representative government. Disagreements arise in both systems precisely because it is not clear how much freedom or equality is needed to ensure that any political system is fully representative. There is little agreement about this because the concept 'representative government' is itself contested, as are related ideals such as 'equal protection' and 'freedom of speech'.

Certainly the United States Supreme Court decision in the landmark case *Buckley v Valeo*,[5] in which it held that Congress could not impose compulsory expenditure limits on candidates standing for office, has been subjected to sustained criticism. The justices had to decide whether and to what extent rich groups and individuals should be able to use their wealth to gain political influence. More specifically, whether laws that attempt to impose limits on spending for political purposes are acceptable in a 'free and democratic society'. As it turned out, the Court saw its duty as requiring a very assertive defence of property rights. It did not think that rich citizens should enjoy fewer rights than others, and it was happy to afford them every opportunity to use their wealth to gain political influence. Thus, the Court attempted to protect the representative system by allowing wealthy citizens to communicate their ideas using whatever resources they chose to commit to the task.

Despite the criticism that it has faced because of this decision, the Supreme Court has recently reaffirmed the distinction it articulated in *Buckley* between donations to a candidate (that may be regulated because they may be potentially corrupting) and expenditures for political and communicative purposes (that may not be regulated).[6] The problem with this framework is that a wealthy donor is easily able to please a candidate by offering to help him or her indirectly, providing services or entering into the public arena by purchasing advertisements that convey messages with which the candidate is associated. Most significantly, if donors have already reached the maximum that they are allowed to give a candidate, they have sometimes provided additional sums of money to the candidate's political party. This agency can then use the money to offer very significant help to him or her and can run advertisements of its own supporting the party's policies. It can even run independent negative advertisements against rival candidates. Of course, there is usually collusion between candidates and their political parties. Giving money to a party is virtually the same thing as giving it to the candidate because the money is used to achieve the same objective—enhancing the power and influence of the candidate. Yet, in a recent case, *Colorado Republican Federal Campaign Committee v FEC* (*CRFCC*),[7] the Supreme Court has signalled that it is inclined to allow political parties a great deal of leeway in raising and spending funds, provided they do this independently of the candidates. This ruling has had the result of encouraging very large amounts of money to flow to the political parties, known as 'soft money' donations.[8]

[5] 424 US 1 (1976). [6] Ibid. 38–9 (*per curiam*). [7] 518 US 604 (1996).

[8] The importance of 'soft money' is described in R. K. Goidel, D. A. Gross, and T. G. Shields, *Money Matters: Consequences of Campaign Finance Reform in US House Elections* (Totowa, NJ:

It remains to be seen whether the Supreme Court will continue to protect this practice. In *CRFCC* the circumstances were unusual, in that the contested expenditures were made at a time when the Republican Party had not yet nominated a candidate. Thus, the party's spending could not be construed as a 'coordinated expenditure'. Even so, four members of the Court (Justices Kennedy, Scalia, and Thomas, and Chief Justice Rehnquist) signalled that they believed that all campaign spending constraints on political parties was unconstitutional.[9] If there are eventually five votes for this point of view, effective campaign finance reform will be impossible to achieve in the United States.

In Australia there are provisions in the Constitution that could potentially be used to protect rights, but these have usually been interpreted in a very narrow way.[10] This is consistent with assumptions held by the founding generation in 1901. The framers were unwilling to bind themselves or future generations by making pre-commitments and had a deep scepticism about American constitutionalism, which, in their view, secures the 'dead hand' of the past in a very unhelpful manner. They preferred to place their trust in parliaments to make good laws, leaving each generation free to determine their own destiny working through the system of representation that had been inherited from the British colonial period.[11] Nevertheless, the Australian High Court has now made it clear that the powers enjoyed by the Commonwealth (and by the states[12]) are qualified by the fact that the framers intended Australia to be a free society governed in accordance with the principles of representative parliamentary democracy. This conception, the justices tell us, is deduced from the commitment made to hold direct elections and by other arrangements set out in the constitutional document when read as a whole. However, judges and commentators have found it difficult to agree about what 'representative government/democracy' requires. Thus, Australian judges must face many of the dilemmas that the United States Supreme Court confronts in interpreting the citizenship provisions in the Bill of Rights.

It is controversial in Australia whether the Commonwealth can limit political advertising to secure greater fairness. In the landmark case *Australian Capital Television v Commonwealth* (*ACTV*) the High Court refused to allow the Commonwealth Parliament to impose substantial limits on political advertising that severely restricted the access to broadcast media that candidates could secure to communicate their ideas. Yet, in a dissenting opinion, Justice Brennan tells us,

Rowman & Littlefield, 1999), ch. 8. The authors show the enormous increases that occurred in 1996; see fig. 8.1, p. 147. These changes are described in the text on the same page.

[9] *CRFCC*, n. 7 above, 628–9 (Kennedy J).

[10] See G. Williams, *Human Rights Under the Australian Constitution* (Melbourne: Oxford University Press, 1999), 129–55.

[11] Chief Justice Mason made this point in *ACTV*, n. 3 above, 135–6, citing Sir Owen Dixon in *Jesting Pilate* (Melbourne: Law Book Co., 1965), 102.

[12] *Stephens v West Australian Newspapers Ltd* (1994) 182 CLR 211.

It was open to Parliament to make a low assessment of the contribution made by electronic advertising to the formation of political judgments. It was open to the Parliament to conclude, as the experience of the majority of liberal democracies has demonstrated, that representative government can survive and flourish without paid political advertising on the electronic media during election periods.[13]

The disagreement between Justice Brennan and the majority of the justices in *ACTV* is partly about 'democracy', in that he did not think the attempt to forbid broadcasting was seriously threatening. But it is also about process—in that he claims that the High Court should not frustrate the Commonwealth Parliament when it is making a policy choice after reaching a considered and reasonable conclusion about the requirements of 'representative democracy'. Thus, even if he had disagreed with the legislators about the role of the electronic media in a modern democracy, he would have been prepared to allow the Commonwealth to regulate political campaigns so long as its actions were not arbitrary or manifestly self-serving. In reaching this conclusion he was not persuaded by Justice Stone's footnote 4, which suggests that judges may need to exempt the representative system itself from parliamentary control by imposing a strict scrutiny. In contrast, the majority in *ACTV* agreed that the Commonwealth's scheme to apportion access to the electronic media was an attempt to restrict effective opposition. They supposed that the Labor Government was seeking to gain an advantage at the expense of independent candidates and smaller parties.

Since *ACTV* Justice Brennan's view that the 'representation-reinforcing' rationale needs to be used with great caution has come to prevail on the High Court. We find that most of the Australian justices have felt uncomfortable about relying on abstract general principles and have looked for ways to ground their decisions historically, using an originalist methodology.[14] While it would be going too far to suggest that *ACTV* has been effectively overruled, it is true to say that many of those who saw the 1992 decision as an occasion 'for dancing in the streets' have been disappointed. In any event, if the Commonwealth Parliament was to readdress the problem of campaign finance, it could probably draft amendments to the Broadcast Act that would accommodate the difficulties that troubled the justices in *ACTV*, and it is likely that the more conservative group of justices who now preside would be sympathetic to the view that they should allow the Commonwealth to impose reasonable restraints in regulating election campaigns.

Disagreements about what 'a free and democratic society' requires are inevitable, and, of course, the debate about the influence of money and the role of advertising in elections goes on in every democracy. People have strong views, but there is no consensus. One problem is that it is not easy to say, for example, whether or not advertising soundbites are a worthy form of speech that offer citizens an essential forum in contemporary political systems. Of course, people

13 *ACTV*, n. 3 above, 161 (Brennan J).

14 J. Goldsworthy, 'Originalism in Constitutional Interpretation', (1997) 25 *Federal Law Review* 1.

have very strong views about this. But these are held on both sides of the debate. And whatever choice we make may well be contingent; we are likely to change our minds dramatically as circumstances change. For example, advertising may become a less potent weapon as cable television and the Internet come to erode the mass audiences that have previously been enjoyed by broadcasters. Indeed, our answer to the question about the importance of soundbites within democratic deliberation may well depend on whether the elections under consideration are to be candidate-centred, as in the United States, or whether the profile of the various contesting political parties is largely what matters (as in Australia). In a system in which the name recognition of the incumbent is a very great advantage, those who challenge may need to use a very large amount of paid political advertising to have any chance at all. This is why some argue that the Supreme Court acted wisely in *Buckley v Valeo*.[15] According to this view, candidates who are challenging an incumbent will need to use soundbites to get the recognition that will be needed to launch a competitive campaign. On the other hand, when a candidate's prospects depend mostly on his or her party affiliation (as they do in Australia), name-recognition may not matter (except for the minor parties, who do not usually have the resources to advertise very much at all). In this circumstance, it may not be important for major-party candidates to advertise in the electronic media. They will be able to ride on the coat-tails of the party with which they are affiliated.

Speculations of this kind are relevant in considering electoral arrangements. But this is a good reason for questioning whether judges have the necessary experience to make good choices. Lack of relevant expertise in a policy area is a good reason why judges should be reticent about interfering.

The 'Australian Ballot' and fusion

In Australia citizens are able to vote for a small party such as the Greens or One Nation without losing the opportunity to influence the outcome of the election. This is achieved by allowing their second preference to count. When the candidate of the small party is eliminated, his or her ballots are re-counted so that the electors' second preferences can be taken into account. This is an enormously useful arrangement because a weakness of the single-member district system that Australians and Americans have both taken from the United Kingdom is that candidates standing on small-party tickets are almost always eliminated. This makes it very difficult for small or single-issue parties to participate effectively because they are usually unable to secure a majority in any district, even though a considerable number of citizens may support them.

In the United States there are also single-member districts used for the election to the House of Representatives. But the Australian system of preferences has not

[15] B. A. Smith, *Unfree Speech: The Folly of Campaign Finance Reform* (Princeton: Princeton University Press, 2001), 66–70.

been adopted, so many citizens are seriously frustrated. This is because they cannot find any parties on the ballot that reflect their point of view on matters of deepest concern to them. This is one reason why the turnout in congressional elections in the United States is so low.

Australia avoids this difficulty. By allowing second preferences to count, those with strong views on issues that have been ignored by the major parties can often find a smaller party to represent them. These small parties are still able to secure some influence because they can bargain with the major parties by promising to direct second preferences to them. Often a major party in Australia will do a deal with the Greens or Democrats, making policy commitments that might not otherwise be made. But even if deals are not entered into, the Australian ballot enables citizens to send a message to the major parties without losing their vote.

Given the representation-reinforcing benefits of the system of counting second preferences in Australia, it is not surprising that small parties in the United States should seek ways of securing the same result. One way this is done is by the practice known as 'fusion'. A small party will choose as its candidate a person who is also standing as the endorsed candidate for one of the major parties. Of course, the candidate will have to agree to be nominated by different parties in this way. But he or she is likely to agree if there is a good chance that this strategy will increase the total number of votes he or she can expect to achieve. This device enables those who vote for the candidate to choose which party they wish to be associated with. Thus, those who favour the policies advocated by a small party can make this manifest without having to waste their vote. Moreover, the advantages associated with two-party competition remain largely intact.

Fusion is an important practice because, unless the smaller parties are in a position to choose a candidate that has a chance of winning, they confront electors with the dilemma of a wasted vote. Fusion is representation-reinforcing in ensuring that candidates have a clearer idea where their support is coming from, and it allows the general electorate to see his or her political affiliations. Instead of allowing candidates to hide behind the amorphous label of a major party that is usually a very broad church, the fusion with smaller parties discloses the more specific ideological leanings of the candidates. For example, if a Democrat is also listed as a Green, people will perceive that he or she will want to protect the environment.

Fusion is not complicated or confusing, and it has been practised for a long time without serious problems. It was very popular in the United States during the eighteenth century. Nevertheless, the major parties usually prefer to have a duopoly system in which small parties are unable to secure much influence or leverage. Certainly, if fusion is helping one or other of the major parties, the other major party will seek to have the practice banned.[16] Not surprisingly, most state governments in the United States have legislated to forbid the practice,

[16] D. J. Amy, 'The Supreme Court's Fusion Decision', in D. K. Ryden (ed.), *The Supreme Court and the Electoral Process* (Washington: Georgetown University Press, 2000), 144–6.

arguing that it is confusing or can lead to ballot-manipulation if frivolous parties seek places on the ballot.

In *Timmons v Twin Cities Area New Party*[17] the United States Supreme Court considered whether Minnesota should be allowed to ban fusion. The Twin Cities Area New Party claimed that it had a constitutional right to choose its own candidate. It said this claim was based on the liberty to associate and equality of citizenship, both of which are protected under the First and Fourteenth Amendments. The New Party argued that it needed to select the candidate that it thought could represent its view most effectively and who best provided it with a leader who could engage the electorate and secure the broadest possible support. But the Supreme Court was not persuaded. Chief Justice Rehnquist, writing for a majority, argued that Minnesota had justified its ban on fusion by showing that it had set in place reasonable election regulations to prevent voter confusion. He tells us,

> the States' interest permits them to enact reasonable election regulations that may, in practice, favor the traditional two party system . . . and that temper the destabilizing effects of party-splintering and excessive factionalism. The Constitution permits the Minnesota Legislature to decide that political stability is best served through a healthy two party system.[18]

Chief Justice Rehnquist and the justices who support his view are saying, in effect, that Minnesota may reinforce a duopoly of the two major parties!

According to this view, the strict scrutiny requirement in the footnote 4 rationale simply does not apply because Minnesota was not preventing any potential minor party from choosing an alternative candidate or from participating in elections. Although the regulation restricted the choices available to minor parties, to this degree favouring the traditional two-party system, Chief Justice Rehnquist claimed that this did not constitute a serious burden because all the parties were still free to compete on the same terms.

It is worth noting that this reticence about protecting fusion, shown by the justices in *Timmons*, is very different from the strict scrutiny (inspired by *Carolene Products*, footnote 4) that they applied in dealing with campaign finance regulations in *Buckley* and in *CRFCC*. The Supreme Court has been prepared to apply strict scrutiny when frustrating well-considered efforts to deal with the adverse consequences that money and the resort to soundbite advertising is having on campaigns. Yet a less burdensome 'rationality' standard is applied when state governments are manifestly entrenching a duopoly, even when the concerns that are said to motivate the bans (about potential ballot overcrowding and confusion) are speculative and could easily have been addressed without restricting association rights. This difference in treatment may be explained by the fact that many of the justices seem to distinguish between major and minor parties. But a major-party duopoly is not constitutionally protected in the United States, so it is difficult to justify this discrimination.

[17] 520 US 351 (1997).

[18] Ibid. 367.

Districting

With regard to the House of Representatives, a distribution of seats that is proportional to the population size of the various states is required in both the United States and Australia. But both Constitutions are silent about how the electoral divisions are to be allocated. In Australia section 29 tells us that:

Until the Parliament of the Commonwealth otherwise provides, the Parliament of any State may make laws for determining the divisions in each State for which members of the House of Representatives may be chosen, and the number of members to be chosen for each division.

As for the United States Constitution, it also allows each state legislature to make its own arrangements about how its representatives are to be elected. Historically, however, most state constitutions require that its representatives be elected from single-member districts of equal, or nearly equal, populations. But, until the early 1960s, when the Warren Court took over supervision, these provisions were often ignored in the United States, and many states stubbornly refused to adjust the district boundaries to take population changes into account. Incumbent office-holders, who enjoyed enormous power and influence, simply resisted having the boundaries redrawn. In Australia, where a small population is often dispersed over vast areas, there has been a tradition (until very recently) of deliberately allowing rural districts to have a smaller number of people. Thus, a malapportionment between urban and rural districts has often been tolerated.

Both the High Court of Australia and the United States Supreme Court have addressed the problem of whether electoral districts should be drawn so that each member represents roughly the same number of people—the 'one vote, one value' principle. But they have reached very different answers.

In the landmark United States case *Wesberry v Sanders* Justice Hugo Black states the basic principle that has guided the Supreme Court's work in this area, declaring:

We hold that, construed in its historical context, the command of Art. I, s. 2 that Representatives be chosen 'by the People of the several States' means that, as nearly as is practicable, one man's vote in a congressional election is to be worth as much as another's... To say that a vote is worth more in one district than in another would not only run counter to our fundamental ideas of democratic government, it would cast aside the principle of a House of Representatives elected 'by the People,' a principle tenaciously fought for and established at the Constitutional Convention.[19]

Although Justice Black was usually inclined to stick closely to 'plain meaning' when engaging in constitutional interpretation, in finding the 'one vote, one value' principle in Article 1 he needed to make an inference from an abstract conception of 'fundamental ideas of democratic government'. In any event, the 'one vote, one value' principle articulated by Justice Black has guided the

[19] *Wesberry v Sanders* 376 US 1 (1964), 8.

Supreme Court, and, using the Fourteenth Amendment, the justices have also applied it to strike down malapportionment within various states.

In dissenting opinions Justices Frankfurter and Harlan showed that Justice Black's reading of Article 1 was in conflict with the historical record.[20] They go into great detail to show that the founding generation never shared the ideals of 'democratic government' that Justice Black attributes to them.

This dissenting view very much influenced the Australian High Court when Justice Black's opinion for the majority in *Wesberry v Sanders* was called to its attention. Although Chief Justice Barwick was strongly attracted to the kind of textualism that Justice Black is associated with, he expressed serious doubts about the way that the latter interpreted the phrase 'directly chosen by the people'. According to Chief Justice Barwick:

> Examination of the reasons for judgment in *Wesberry v. Sanders* clearly demonstrates that the meaning attributed to the expression 'directly chosen by the people'... depended heavily, if not almost entirely, upon the view taken by the majority of American history and of statements made in the constitutional conventions preceding the adoption of that Constitution. It is evident on reading the views of the minority in that case that there is, to say the least, great doubt as to the validity of the view of that history and of those statements taken by the majority.[21]

Despite having similar materials to work with, the two constitutional courts reached quite different conclusions. According to Chief Justice Barwick, the historical record in Australia in 1901 makes it impossible to argue that the 'one vote, one value' principle can be inferred. Justice Mason makes the point even more strongly, arguing:

> The interpretation adopted in *Wesberry v. Sanders* is again a modern development that altered the inequality in electoral divisions which prevailed in the United States from early times. This inequality was understood to involve no contravention of Art. 1, s. 2 until *Wesberry v. Sanders* was decided. When our Constitution was enacted it had not been decided that Art. 1, s. 2 insisted upon an equality in the value of a vote. The American provision was not thought to carry that message. And it is simply not correct to say that provisions in our Constitution should receive the same construction as that given to similarly worded provisions in the United States Constitution which have a different context and a different history, more particularly when the suggested construction is of recent origin, reversing an interpretation previously accepted.[22]

This seems a compelling argument for anyone who thinks the legal interpretation of a constitutional phrase ought to be guided by what we know of the intentions of its framers.[23]

[20] Frankfurter J (joined by Harlan J) dissenting, in *Baker v Carr* 389 US 186 (1962), 301–9; Harlan J dissenting, *Wesberry v Sanders*, n. 20 above.

[21] *Attorney-General (Cth); Ex rel McKinlay v Commonwealth*, (1975) 135 CLR 1, 22–3 (Barwick CJ).

[22] Ibid. 62–3 (Mason J).

[23] This view was upheld in *McGinty v Western Australia* (1996) 186 CLR 140. One reason why the High Court may have been reluctant to reverse itself is that in the referendum held in September 1988

The 'one vote, one value' principle is ambiguous because it includes two quite different ideas:

(1) There is the purely statistical notion of worth—that each district must include approximately the same number of people. This is an easy rule to work with and allows a clear message to be sent about what will be tolerated. It allows for an almost mechanical application. The clarity of this sense of 'equal worth' is the key to the success of the Supreme Court's work in this area.

(2) There is also a more elusive sense of 'equal worth' that has been more difficult for judges to work with. This arises because of the many different ways that electoral districts can be drawn. District boundaries can easily disadvantage a particular community if there are conflicting interests between groups in a single district. For example, if country people are included in districts that also include large numbers of suburban voters, the distinct interests of regional and farming communities may be ignored as representatives seek to please the city-voters.

Chief Justice Barwick noticed this problem, telling us:

> Again, to ignore community of interest in the creation of electoral divisions and to insist on mere equality of numbers will be likely, in my opinion, to produce inequality rather than equality of voting value. It is probably impossible to devise a formula for electoral distribution which will necessarily produce equality in voting value, which will ensure that each vote is of equal weight in an election as a whole or even as between electoral divisions.[24]

What Chief Justice Barwick noticed is that district lines can be deliberately drawn to alter 'equal worth' in this second sense of its meaning. This is because the simple rule that districts include the same number of persons fails to ensure that there is no discrimination. For example, to help one party in the electoral competition gain more worth from its votes, a state merely needs to ensure that most of its rival party's supporters are in one or two districts. By conceding a few districts to the opposition, the dominant party can virtually assure itself of capturing the remaining districts. Even more effective is the choice to make use of an at-large election district by amalgamating a number of districts. This allows electors to vote for three or four candidates in a winner-takes-all contest. In this case the largest party easily captures all the allocated seats (as happened in the 2000 United States presidential contest when all the Florida Electoral College votes went to George W. Bush even though the election in Florida was a virtual tie).

The only way that the second sense of 'one vote, one worth' can be fully realized is by a system of proportional representation in which every party that competes is entitled to the number of seats that reflects its overall proportion of

the Australian people refused to endorse the proposal that the Constitution be amended 'to provide fair and democratic parliamentary elections throughout Australia'.

24 *Attorney-General (Cth); Ex rel McKinlay v Commonwealth*, 25 (Barwick CJ).

the vote. Any arrangement that uses district boundaries with a first-past-the-post rule is sure to fall short of the fair value requirement—unless second preferences are counted. Another difficulty is that whenever a district is drawn to ensure that one section of the community is not disadvantaged (for example, constructing a minority–majority district to ensure fairness to African American voters), others are likely to have their vote diluted (for example, Hasidic Jews). However, it is clear that the founding generation in both Australia and the United States deliberately designed the electoral system so that community interests could be taken into account even though everyone knew that this was inherently unfair. This follows the British practice in which Members of Parliament are always referred to as 'the Member from . . . '. The identification of the region signals the communitarian alignment—a matter that has nothing to do with population size.

We can conclude that the founding generation in both the United States and Australia contemplated vote dilution because their communitarian concerns necessarily undermine the individualist 'one vote, one value' principle.

Leaving aside the poor fit between Justice Black's principle and the republican–communitarian concerns that motivated the eighteenth-century founding generation in the United States, a serious problem with the ruling in *Wesberry v Sanders* is that it brings the Supreme Court deeply into the political process in an unhelpful way. There simply is no way that the 'one vote, one value' principle can be applied in a non-arbitrary manner. Not surprisingly, the Court's rulings relating to districting seem to be guided by little more than the political instincts of the justices who happen to be on the Court at the time a case is heard. Let me consider some of the problems briefly.

In 1973 the Supreme Court was asked to review a complaint made on behalf of African American voters that had suffered vote dilution. Justice White, writing for the Court, articulated a rule that has served as a guide. He tells us that relief will be granted for unequal worth of the vote if it is shown that the political processes are effectively closed to a racial group so that its members 'had less opportunity than did other residents in the district to participate in the political processes and to elect legislators of their choice'.[25] The usual remedy for this kind of discrimination is that the districts be redrawn so that the group suffering the discrimination can be represented by someone that they had effectively chosen. Where multi-member districts are the cause of the problem, these have had to be dismantled into single-member districts. The regulative idea is the communitarian notion that each ethnic group (where the voting is polarized on ethnic lines as it almost always is in the United States) should be entitled to representation in proportion to its numbers in the community.

This formula was ultimately embodied in a 1982 amendment to the Voting Rights Act 1965 (VRA) that was itself read by the Supreme Court to require dismantling of all at-large districts whenever it could be shown that there was

[25] *White v Register* 412 US 755 (1973), 766.

'racially polarised voting'.[26] Within a few years, American politics was transformed as more than 200 cities were forced to abandon at-large systems. Nor was the process of redrawing districts to ensure the fair worth of the votes of racial groups confined to the state level or to the at-large districts. The Federal Electoral Commission was authorized to secure effective representation for minorities whenever racially polarized politics effectively undermined the worth of their votes.

One would have thought that the Republican Party would be very angry about the creation of majority–minority districts. After all, most minority voters are Democrats. In fact, the establishment of these kinds of districts often enables the Republicans to succeed because it involves packing Democratic voters into a district—in effect securing a gerrymander favourable to the Republicans. Moreover, the majority–minority districts tend to produce candidates that associate the Democrats with leaders who have positioned themselves far to the left on the political spectrum or who articulate ethnic concerns that are not broadly shared, leaving the Republicans an easy passage to the middle ground. Some even argue that the 1994 Newt Gingrich-led victory in the House of Representatives was heavily influenced by racial politics that allowed majority–minority districts to be drawn.

Of course, racial districting has also encouraged the Republicans to abandon any hope of achieving gains by appealing to African Americans. The best strategy for the Republican candidates in many situations is to ignore the African American voters, who have often been packed into safe seats that a Republican cannot possibly win.

Despite the advantage that Republicans seem to be securing because of minority–majority districting, the Supreme Court has had second thoughts about the practice. Its problem is that at least five of the justices dislike racially motivated affirmative action plans. Although they do not want to prevent states from taking a broad range of factors into account when drawing district boundaries, even including the political affiliation of the communities involved, the justices regard race as a suspect category that, for most purposes, may only be resorted to for remedial purposes when there is clear evidence of past discrimination.[27] As districting decisions are not always remedial, in this sense, the Supreme Court has recently shown some reluctance to allow racial factors to be the primary determining factor. It has now ruled that although the race of electors may be taken into account when a district's boundaries are drawn, to ensure that the votes of minority communities are not diluted, race must not be the 'predominant factor'.[28] However, it has experienced difficulty distinguishing districts in which race is the key to the way that the boundaries have been drawn from districts that reflect legitimate communitarian concerns (that may also

[26] In *Thornburg v Gingles* 478 US 30 (1986).
[27] *Adarand Constructors, Inc v Pena* 515 US 200 (1995).
[28] *Bush v Vera* 517 US 952 (1996).

include race as a factor). Unfortunately, however, there is no principled way of doing this because race, class, and political affiliation are hopelessly intertwined in American politics today. Indeed, as we have seen, the establishment of a minority–majority district is often a gerrymander for the Republican Party because nearly all African Americans and most Hispanic voters are Democrats. Had these districts been drawn for political reasons or to protect incumbents—and not with the motive of advancing African Americans or Hispanic candidates—the justices might have tolerated them. But when securing racial representation is the primary motivation in constructing districts, the justices have felt obliged to interfere.

To distinguish what the Court considers to be legitimate districting from what it regards as illegitimate, the justices have looked at the shape of districts. Because many poor people from minority communities live along highways, close to railway lines, or are dispersed in pockets around housing estates in suburbs, cartographers have often drawn minority–majority districts with very strange boundaries. When this is the case, the Supreme Court has scrutinized the motivation to see whether 'the predominant factor' in constructing the district is race. They have ruled that districts that have an unexpected shape at variance with traditional districting principles (that require compactness, contiguity, and respect for political subdivisions) will be treated suspiciously to see whether they have been designed specifically to advantage a racial group. Although totally subjective, this rule of thumb—that the shape of a district must not be 'bizarre'[29]—has offered the justices a serviceable solution. But the Supreme Court is apparently prepared to tolerate racially motivated districting if race is not the predominant factor and the shape of the districts is not 'bizarre'.[30]

Conclusion

There is no doubt that judges have had a significant influence over the electoral processes in Australia and the United States. Even though the United States Constitution makes no mention of money and the eighteenth-century founders could never have contemplated the problems we face today because of political advertising and the use of census data in districting, the Supreme Court in the United States has made it very difficult for legislators to do anything effective about the problems associated with these developments. In Australia the High Court has been more restrained. But even it has frustrated a well-considered reform of the campaign finance system.

In this connection a crucial difference between the United States and Australia needs to be kept in mind. In the former there is often good authority for judicial

[29] *Shaw v Reno* 509 US 630 (1993).

[30] See N. Maveety, 'Representation Rights and the Rehnquist Years: The Viability of the "Communities of Interest" Approach', in D. K. Ryden (ed.), *The US Supreme Court and the Electoral Process* (Washington: Georgetown University Press, 2000), 28–9.

intervention to secure open and fair representation because citizenship and freedom of speech are protected in the Bill of Rights. Because of this, judges are authorized to take on the representative-reinforcing role that footnote 4 envisages. But in Australia judges have had to argue that freedom of speech is an implication of the constitutional arrangements viewed in their totality. Review is more controversial when judges who cannot cite well-recognized legal principles or texts are forced to use the representation-reinforcing rationale to explain why they are justified in supplementing more traditional sources of legal authority. And this is especially the case when they must rely on speculative assessment about the consequences of proposed policy changes.

This difference is one reason why the Australian High Court has been more reticent. But the United States Supreme Court could have elected to follow a similar path, as Justices Harlan and Frankfurter both recommended. Instead, it has chosen an interventionist path in dealing with the quagmires of campaign finance and affirmative action in districting, both issues over which judges are unlikely to be able to offer useful guidance. Yet the American justices have also chosen to be reticent in allowing states to forbid a practice that would have enhanced the system of representation by allowing small parties to compete more effectively, even though this could have been achieved without drawing the Court into the political processes. This contradictory jurisprudence seems to be arbitrary and unwise.

Of course it can be argued that the United States Supreme Court's intervention in districting was extremely successful. As I have noted, the formula that Justice White made use of in challenging at-large elections was incorporated into the Voting Rights Act in 1982 and federal courts did assist in the very dramatic and successful changes that followed, empowering African Americans. This was a significant victory for the Civil Rights Movement. Whether these changes would have occurred without the intervention of the Court is not easy to say.

Taken as a whole, the record I have reviewed shows that a constitutional court may sometimes need to reinforce representative government, acting in the name of abstract ideals. But it also shows that we must face the fact that courts may not be very well suited to this task. It often requires them to move very far beyond the traditional skills of reasoning and analysis for which most members of the judiciary have been trained. For this reason some judges may prefer not to exercise representation-reinforcing review even when it is clear that some legislators are trying to entrench themselves in power by one strategy or another (for example, the Supreme Court in dealing with fusion).

We also need to recognize the peculiar nature of courts, as distinct institutions for conflict resolution, may be compromised if they are frequently interfering in political life. More importantly, judges have a duty to confine their power because they are unelected. If they fail to develop a collective sense of the kinds of arguments that can count as 'legal', they leave themselves vulnerable to claims that they are overreaching.

In *Carolene Products* itself Justice Stone faced this issue (of the limitations of judicial competence and the special nature of judicial reasoning) when he argued that judges should not overturn economic regulations unless there is evidence that they are wholly arbitrary and irrational. He calls for judges to restrain themselves so as to allow legislators to take responsibility for economic management. Yet he is not compelled to advocate this reticence for any good legal reason. After all, the Supreme Court had traditionally exercised review over economic decisions. *Carolene Products* is one of a number of cases that overturned settled understandings. Its rationale is pragmatic, based on Justice Stone's sense that courts had been overreaching in trying to second-guess economic managers. This is why he articulates the resolve of the Court to exercise its power of review more deferentially in the future. Of course, he realizes that judicial restraint and deference in the economic area will allow legislators to act unfairly, taking from some more than they were willing to take from others. But this kind of resource allocation is not a matter that courts can easily address, and Justice Stone is on strong ground when he advocates restraint.

Similarly, in many cases, although representative review may be warranted, it will be foolhardy for judges to trespass on the role that other decision-makers may be playing. Achieving a good solution when making rulings about matters such as campaign finance, or the drawing of district boundaries, or the role of political parties in the political system is not something that judges can be sure about. Indeed, those judges who try to secure good results may well find that they unintentionally discredit the judicial role. This is not to say that judges should never challenge legislators when the latter act in self-interested ways to entrench themselves in office. However, it is not always easy to identify the circumstances when interference will produce good results or even when it is necessary.

8

A Defence of the Status Quo

JAMES ALLAN

> That what we have we prize not to the worth
> Whiles we enjoy it, but being lack'd and lost,
> Why, then we rack the value, then we find
> The virtue that possession would not show us
> Whiles it was ours.
>
> (*Much Ado About Nothing*, IV. i. 218–22)

In this chapter I defend the current constitutional status quo in Australia, arguing particularly against the need for (or desirability of) any sort of bill of rights, whether constitutionally entrenched or simply statutory. My perspective is that of the majoritarian democrat who prefers important social disputes—including disputes about rights—to be decided on the widest practical basis, one in which each has some sort of say and everyone's say counts about the same. From that standpoint, I attempt to convince the reader that Australia today is fully capable of protecting basic human interests—the very stuff of rights—without any sort of bill of rights.

In making this argument I begin with a brief survey of the notable features of the present Australian system. In any assessment of the need for, or desirability of, a bill of rights, context certainly cannot be ignored, and so these features of the existing set-up in Australia have first to be mentioned. This comprises the first section of this chapter.

To modern eyes, however, one glaring feature of the Australian constitutional structure relates to what is not there, rather than what is. It is the absence of any sort of bill of rights. As far as I am aware, Australia is now the only country in the Western world without some kind of bill of rights—be it a constitutionalized or statutory model, the incorporation (in justiciable form) of the European Convention on Human Rights into domestic law, or simply a series of Basic Laws which amount to more or less the same thing. Australia, alone, has none of these things. So this absence is a notable feature of Australia's constitutional structure. The second section of this chapter will note the singularity of lacking a bill of rights and then comment upon the judiciary's related efforts to 'discover' implied

I wish to thank Mirko Bagaric, Tom Campbell, Richard Cullen, Andrew Geddis, Jeff Goldsworthy, Grant Huscroft, Janet McLean, John Smillie, and all the participants at the Human Rights Workshop in Melbourne, Dec. 2001, for their helpful comments on and criticisms of earlier versions of this chapter.

rights (or, less kindly, to give themselves the tools that no one else seemed prepared to grant them).

The next section begins with something of a digression, albeit a necessary one. Here I turn to look briefly at rights themselves: what they are, their colonizing power, and their capacity to overwhelm all disagreement not itself framed in terms of rights. This complete, I turn back to bills of rights and note a main effect of such instruments, including whether non-entrenched, statutory models or override clauses alleviate such an effect.

The last section of all in this chapter brings together the earlier strands and asks whether the desire to protect certain human interests, of the sort that fall under the aegis of 'human rights', requires some sort of bill of rights. I answer no. In a state such as Australia these important human interests are at least as well protected, on an ongoing basis, by elected representatives of the people as by unelected judges. Australia today has one of the most democratic systems in the world, one fully capable of protecting basic human interests—or rights if you prefer—without any participation-sapping bill of rights.

The gist of this chapter, then, is a defence of Australia's lack of any overt constitutional or quasi-constitutional protection of rights. In that sense, what follows is a defence of the status quo by a non-Australian outsider.

Notable features of the status quo

The decision whether it is desirable or not to opt for any sort of constitutional or quasi-constitutional protection of rights cannot sensibly be made in the abstract. Context matters. A jurisdiction such as Hong Kong, for instance, might have good reason to reach for any possible protections going. There, after all, democratic government is a recent innovation and the current version of that democracy most charitably described as enervated. In such a situation, with a unique 'one country, two systems' arrangement more or less thrust upon them, and with good grounds existing to fear abuse of sovereign power and the infringement of important rights, the danger of over-mighty judges may seem of lesser importance. 'Grab whatever potential protections you can, their likely costs and bad effects notwithstanding', may appear a wise counsel of action.

On the other hand, a developed country with a strong, long-standing democratic tradition and record, where people's basic interests have fared no worse—often better—than in other developed countries, might reach a different answer. There, perhaps, the various costs of entrenching an overriding bill of rights or of enacting a statutory, quasi-constitutional bill of rights will outweigh any benefits, be the calculation done in terms of rights themselves or in a more hard-nosed utilitarian currency.

The point is, to repeat myself, that context matters. When we turn to look at whether Australia's current lack of a bill of rights (of any special powers, one might be tempted to put it, having been handed over to unelected judges so that *they* can protect certain enunciated rights) is a good thing or a bad thing, we need first some detail about the existing system of government beyond the widely known facts that it is a bicameral, federal, constitutional monarchy system with a written Constitution in parts on the general lines of the American model.

Let us start then with voting and electoral matters, the sort of things that have some relation to John Ely's views about when the judiciary is a legitimate guardian of constitutional rights.[1] Here we can examine how an Australian democracy, one unencumbered with constitutionalized individual rights and their judicial guardians, has done in terms of letting its citizens take part in the decision-making process on more or less equal terms.

There is a variety of voting systems in effect in Australia at the state and Commonwealth (or federal) levels. Here, I will discuss only the latter. The Lower House of Parliament, the House of Representatives, is the more important of the two Houses in so far as it initiates and controls money bills, is the home of the prime minister, and has about the same number of electors per seat, or rough voter equality. As nearly as is practicable it has twice the number of representatives as does the Upper House, the Senate.[2]

Until 1918 the House of Representatives was elected by a 'first-past-the-post' voting system of the sort used today in the United Kingdom, Canada, and the United States. The essence of such a system is that whoever gets the most votes wins that race; hence the reason first-past-the-post is often described as a 'winner-takes-all' system. All the winner needs is a plurality of votes, more than any other single candidate, however low his or her overall percentage of the votes may be.

Since 1918, however, a preferential voting system operating in single-member constituencies has been employed for elections to the House of Representatives. Such a system requires voters to mark preferences other than simply their first preference. The winner must obtain more than 50 per cent of the votes cast, though often no one will win a majority of first preferences.[3] But the point, for our purposes, is that every elected representative will have received the support of an absolute majority of voters in his or her constituency.

In my opinion this voting system compares favourably to first-past-the-post systems *and* even more so to proportional systems. On the one hand, it avoids the closed lists of some versions of the latter, the undue influence of small parties,

[1] See J. Ely, *Democracy and Distrust: A Theory of Judicial Review* (Cambridge, Mass.: Harvard University Press, 1980), esp. ch. 4.

[2] See s 24 of the Australian Constitution. The Senate currently has seventy-six seats and the House 150 seats.

[3] In simplified terms what happens is that the lowest-polling candidates are serially eliminated and the second preferences of their supporters (or if a second preference happens already to have been eliminated then a third—and similarly fourth, etc.—preference) are redistributed until some candidate gets to the 50 per cent plus 1 threshold and is the winner. This is sometimes called the ATV or AV system. As of 1997 only two countries elected parliamentarians using preferential voting: Australia and (in somewhat different form) Nauru.

the increased power of party hierarchies, the making of much policy *post*-election during coalition negotiations, and Karl Popper's concern about the inability of voters in proportional systems clearly to be able to reject parties and policies they dislike.[4] On the other hand, preferential voting avoids wasted votes, allows a few independents to win occasionally, and yet delivers the majority governments (and their easy removal) of first-past-the-post systems, but without the often claimed unfairness of winners having received only, say, 35 or 40 per cent of the cast votes.

Preferential voting also measures, to some extent, whom the voter does *not* want to win, not just whom she favours. Dislikes play a role, not just likes. In some ways this seems to me to reflect an element of human nature, and to be very much in line with what many people are seeking to accomplish when they vote.[5]

So Australian elected representatives, without any judicial promptings or commands, have opted for a voting system for the country's most important legislative chamber that requires each constituency winner to get the support of an absolute majority of electors, that measures to some extent what voters do *not* want, and that avoids many of the disadvantages of proportional and first-past-the-post systems. So far, John Ely could hardly complain.

As for the voting system used to elect Australian Senators, this is a single transferable vote (STV) system—a proportional representation system with an element of preferential voting—which has no mandated closed lists and so somewhat avoids the shift of power such closed lists transfer to party hierarchies and away from voters. Of course, the Senate voting system is certainly complicated, and has the effect of making it most unlikely the government will obtain a majority here. But if a main goal of an upper chamber be to give the opportunity for a second, calm look before passing legislation—truth be told, to make passage more difficult and so strengthen the hand of the legislature against the executive—then a voting system that makes one-party control of that chamber more unlikely does nothing to help the case of those who say we need unelected judges overseeing a bill of rights in order to protect us from our elected representatives (and indeed ourselves) in those imagined moments of moral and political weakness or akrasia.[6] (Certainly it is true that in terms of its democratic

[4] See, for example, Karl Popper's invited article 'Popper on Democracy', *The Economist*, 23 Apr. 1988, 19–22, esp. 21–2. 'Proportional representation . . . may therefore have a detrimental effect on the decisive issue of how to get rid of a government by voting it out of office . . . As a result, on election day none of the parties is dismissed, none is convicted' (ibid. 22). Popper there gives various arguments for rejecting proportional representation.

[5] Consider someone who lives in Pauline Hanson's constituency. This person may not care much who wins, provided Hanson does not. Preferential voting measures this desire better than other systems. And this matters. According to the web site <http://www.aceproject.org/main/english/es/esy_au.htm> the results of the 1961, 1969, and 1990 Australian House of Representatives elections would all have been reversed under a first-past-the-post system (if we assume people's first preferences equated to whom they would tick under first-past-the-post). '. . . the impact of preference voting has been higher during the 1990s than at any time in the past' (ibid. 1).

[6] This is sometimes described as the Sirens argument on the assumption that it is somehow analogous to asking to be tied to the mast now because you cannot trust yourself not to jump in the

legitimacy and its performance, the Australian Senate—unlike, say, Canada's—is a genuine House of Review, a point to bear in mind on the larger question of the non-judicial protection of rights.)

My point is that on any such criteria as 'preventing the exclusion of some group from the political process' or 'allowing citizens to take part in the decision-making process on more or less equal terms',[7] the voting systems used in Australia score very highly. Indeed, if equality of input is one's most cherished goal, Australia's compulsory voting regime will presumably greatly appeal and further enhance that score. And even if not, Australia, without any bill-of-rights-based judicial oversight, seems to have nothing to learn on the matter of voting from such places as the United States or Canada, where unelected judges do have a rights-based constitutional role, including over the electoral system (though, admittedly, these judges have never claimed oversight of the method of voting itself).

On other electoral matters the same question can be asked: Where is the need for any sort of bill of rights and supervising judiciary? A statutory authority, the Australian Electoral Commission, has been made responsible for the administration of such Commonwealth electoral matters as the conduct of elections, maintaining the electoral rolls, and the redistribution (i.e. number of electors per division) of House of Representatives constituencies.[8] Likewise, the allocation of boundaries is undertaken by redistribution committees appointed for each state. These mean Commonwealth parliamentarians have foreclosed gerrymandering as some sort of perk of majority government, and have done so on their own without 'judicializing' such issues.

In the same vein, the Lower House has a three-year maximum term, and so more frequent appeals to the electorate are required than in the United Kingdom or Canada, where the limit is five years. In addition, Australia was first to introduce Saturday polling. Then there are the campaign finance rules governing Commonwealth elections. In essence, Australia has a system of public funding of election campaigns joined to an enforced system of disclosure of election financing, but without regulation of expenditure.[9]

Leaving electoral matters, what about the method laid down for amending the Australian Constitution?[10] Section 128 of the Australian Constitution requires

water later. For a short but excellent analysis of why the analogy is misplaced and why this argument fails as a defence of strong judicial review, see J. Waldron, 'Freeman's Defense of Judicial Review', (1994) 13 *Law and Philosophy* 27, 36; and J. Waldron, 'A Right-Based Critique of Constitutional Rights', (1993) 13 *Oxford Journal of Legal Studies* 18, 46. See too Waldron's *Law and Disagreement* (Oxford: Clarendon Press, 1999), ch. 12.

[7] I do not ignore the historical exclusion of Aborigines; rather, I leave that point for specific comment below.

[8] See Commonwealth Electoral Act 1918.

[9] For more detail on all of this, see D. Cass and S. Burrows, 'Commonwealth Regulation of Campaign Finance—Public Funding, Disclosure and Expenditure Limits', (2000) 22 *Sydney Law Review* 477. See too E. Charles, 'Public Funding of Elections in Australia', in H. Alexander (ed.), *Comparative Political Finance in the 1980s* (Cambridge: Cambridge University Press, 1989).

[10] Australia's Constitution—like Canada's was until 1982—is an Act of the UK Parliament.

proposed constitutional amendments first to pass through Parliament[11] and then to win approval in a referendum. The approval needed in this referendum is both (1) a majority of electors in a majority of states and (2) a majority of all electors.

Notice straight off that comparable English-speaking jurisdictions, such as Canada or the United States, do *not* make constitutional change subject to the direct say of the people voting in a referendum. In Australia, by contrast, the elected representatives, all part of the political elite, cannot bring about change on their own. Of course, the fact that the preponderance of constitutional amendment proposals have failed to win the support of half the voters does *not* mean this, or even the majority of states requirement, is onerous procedurally. In Australia it means simply that the majority is not in favour,[12] frequently to the chagrin of the political elite. Had the rule for constitutional amendment been the American or Canadian one, where the final say lay solely with elected representatives, it is quite possible that Australia today would be a republic rather than a constitutional monarchy. Whatever one's views of the merits of that or any other first-order referendum outcome, one can—as I do—certainly endorse the Australian second-order rule for constitutional change requiring, as it does, approval in a referendum.

Indeed, one reason this book on rights and bills of rights is being written is that the Australian political elite is unable to impose its preferences in the face of the opposition of a majority of voters. Were it otherwise, there is a fair chance that Australia would already have such an instrument[13] (and next to no chance a book would be written mooting its removal).

So the method in which constitutional amendments need to be made in Australia, the direct appeal to the people, is a central feature of the status quo. Allowing citizens to take part in this ultimate decision-making process on more or less equal terms lies at its heart.

In putting the debate about a bill of rights for Australia into context, more specifics could be given—about how the American legislative model was grafted on to a Westminster constitutional monarchy; about the division of Commonwealth and state powers; about double dissolutions; about the inherited British freedoms of association, religion, and basic civil liberties; and more. Clearly no set of political arrangements will be widely seen as perfect, and virtually every-

[11] Both the House and Senate if possible, but the Governor-General may put the amendment to a referendum where only one of the two Houses passes it.

[12] Since Federation there have been twenty-one referenda in which forty-six questions were put to electors, forty-four of which sought to alter the Constitution. Of the forty-four, eight have been successful. (The overwhelming majority of these failed referenda, including two (of four) 1988 proposals specifically seeking to insert such relatively weak rights guarantees as religious freedom and the right to vote, have foundered on the inability to obtain a simple majority of electors overall, *not* on the usually harder need to obtain a majority of states. In fact, in only four referenda has a proposal received a majority of electors but failed to win in a majority of states.)

[13] Each of the four proposals (see n. 12 above) in the 1988 referendum failed to carry in any state, let alone nationally. The proposals were part of a larger number of changes to the Constitution mooted by a Constitutional Commission. These four were meant to test the waters. In the light of the response, no other proposals were put to a referendum.

one will have his or her own suggested improvements to offer in Australia, or anywhere else. But we need only set the stage for assessing the desirability of a bill of rights, not touch on everything, and so all that is essential before concluding this first section of the chapter is to comment on the historical exclusion of Aborigines from the political process.

On any set of criteria the record looking back is pretty awful. But the question we need to ask is whether some sort of bill of rights, some allocation of rights-based powers to unelected judges, would have improved that record. Provided we refrain from cheating by comparing, say, Canada or the United States *today* with Australia *thirty, fifty, or 100 years ago*, there appears to be no grounds for thinking a bill of rights would have improved things. Looking back, the treatment of native Americans (and indeed black Americans) in the United States thirty, fifty, or 100 years ago was no better than the Australian treatment of Aborigines. By our standards, both were awful. The relevant point, though, is that the American judges overseeing the vague, amorphous rights in the Bill of Rights did not stand out against the prevailing majority sentiments as some sort of specially endowed moral guardians. Indeed, to find (by the standards of the time) enlightened treatment of the indigenous population one has to turn to New Zealand, where Maori men were granted the vote in 1867 and four seats out of seventy-six were reserved for Maori. Yes, New Zealand, which not only lacked a bill of rights but also operated (and still does) without a written constitution and with a sovereign Parliament.

I mention New Zealand, Canada, and the United States simply to refute, pre-emptively, the fuzzy, rarely fully articulated feeling that perhaps the historical exclusion of Aborigines from the political process, even their poor treatment generally, somehow *proves* the case for a bill of rights. The evidence, such as it is, shows nothing of the sort.

Enough has been said, I hope, to allow the reader to put the debate about a bill of rights for Australia into rough context. Space demands we now move on.

No bill of rights, only implied rights

As I noted above, Australia is unique among developed Western nations in lacking any sort of bill of rights—constitutionalized, statutory, incorporated convention, or series of Basic Laws. This absence was not due to oversight. It was a deliberate decision of the Founding Fathers of the Australian Constitution, fully alive to the American Bill of Rights and the Fourteenth Amendment.[14]

[14] See, for example, Australia's former chief justice Sir Gerard Brennan, 'The Impact of a Bill of Rights on the Role of the Judiciary: An Australian Perspective', in P. Alston (ed.), *Promoting Human Rights Through Bills of Rights* (Oxford: Oxford University Press, 1999), 454, 455, and G. Craven, 'The High Court of Australia: A Study in the Abuse of Power', 31st Alfred Deakin Lecture (Melbourne: Alfred Deakin Lecture Trust, Oct. 1997), in particular 6. See too J. Goldsworthy, 'Interpreting the *Constitution* in its Second Century', (2000) 24 *Melbourne University Law Review* 677, *inter alia* at 685.

However, let us be clear about what is missing; it is *not* the legal protection of rights (even human rights if you prefer). In the past quarter-century the various parliaments in Australia have passed numerous pieces of legislation covering such rights-based issues as equal opportunity and discrimination. Clearly, there is plenty of specific legislation aimed at protecting rights. No, what is missing in Australia is something else. It is the constitutional, or quasi-constitutional, instrument (or series of instruments) that sets out very general standards about the place and entitlements of the individual in society—an emotionally attractive statement of individual rights in broad, somewhat amorphous terms. That is what Australia so unusually lacks. The United States, Canada, France, the Netherlands, Germany, New Zealand, now the United Kingdom, and even Israel have a version. But not Australia.

Were it otherwise, were Australia part of the now near-universal international trend, it is uncontroversial to state that the Australian judiciary would play a significantly greater role in social policy-making. It is the absence of this enhanced, more powerful, overseeing role for unelected judges, then, that distinguishes Australia. Yet while, to some Australian judges, 'the heady powers conferred by a Bill of Rights would present a welcome challenge and an opportunity to sweep aside legislative and Executive action which impedes the doing of justice in the instant case',[15] the fact remains that the Australian electorate has not yet shown any desire for a bill of rights and its judicial overlords.

> We could introduce a Bill of Rights and have it administered by our existing Courts, but would Australians wish that to be done? The voting at the 1988 referendum suggests that the answer is resoundingly negative.[16]

Perhaps in frustration at how this lack of faith left them without any sort of bill of rights, and so beyond what they see as the international Pale, or perhaps for any number of other possible reasons,[17] the fact is that some ninety years after the Australian Constitution came into force, the High Court held a limited freedom of communication concerning political matters to be an implication of the text and structure of that Constitution.

What can be said of this judicial construct, implied rights? A cynical observer might find he cannot refrain from pointing out that, as most of the cases in which the plaintiffs succeeded concerned defamation laws and fighting attempts to limit political advertising, the main beneficiaries of these implied rights cases have been the media barons. Nor was it a necessary outcome that once the right was 'discovered', the law of defamation had to be reformed in this way, as is clear from the fact that in Canada, with its Charter of Rights, the judges declined to amend the law of defamation.[18] But be those as they may, let me focus

[15] Brennan, n. 14 above, 463.

[16] Ibid. 455.

[17] For a fairly caustic analysis of why he thinks the Australian High Court 'discovered' implied rights, see Craven, n. 14 above, 18–24.

[18] See *Hill v Church of Scientology of Toronto* (1995) 126 DLR (4th) 129. I have intentionally left for others more versed than I in Australian High Court jurisprudence any detailed analysis of the 'implied rights' cases.

elsewhere, on a comparison between implied rights and explicit rights. The former are somehow found to be (or teased out as) an implication of a text that nowhere specifically sets out, refers to, or in anyway mentions them. The latter, by contrast, are explicitly proclaimed, and in open-textured, highly emotive, appealing, and often absolutist-sounding language to boot. How then do the two, implied and explicit, compare?

In response I want to make two related claims that bear on the thesis of this chapter. First, it is difficult to use the text of the Australian Constitution to 'find' implied rights.[19] So much is working against any judge who travels down this route. There is the detailed history of that Constitution in which the Founding Fathers specifically rejected any American-style bill of rights. There is the concomitant implausibility of relying on implications where implication is understood as a function of intention—some sort of actually held but never expressed intention. The difficulty here is to say exactly who implied these rights or freedoms. And if one attempts to escape from that dilemma by severing the process of implication from any actually held intention, the difficulty then becomes trying not to look as though you are making it up as you go along, of simply reading in your own political and moral preferences.[20] In short, the ground available for implying very many rights into the Australian Constitution does not appear to this non-Australian observer to be very fertile.

Of course, one should never underestimate the judiciary in matters affecting its own jurisdiction. A more pessimistic view (for the majoritarian democrat, that is) is certainly available:

> I have little doubt that, like a train delayed in station, implied rights eventually will move off once more. The important point to recall here is that, once the Court has accepted the legitimacy of one vague, bogus implied right (in this case, the freedom of political communication), then most of the constitutional damage has been done. It will be relatively easy in the future for an even more adventurous Court to take up the cudgels again, and to stretch the reasoning that has been used to support the existence of this right to found further constitutional guarantees.[21]

I am inclined to be more hopeful. More to the point though, and this is my second claim, whatever the Australian judiciary might do using the vehicle of implied rights, they could—and certainly would—do much, much more with a set of explicit rights laid down in some sort of constitutional or quasi-constitutional form. Explicitly proclaimed individual rights simply give the unelected judiciary much more scope to get its own way against the elected branches of government, be it by regularly striking down legislation or by

[19] It is not, however, by any means impossible. For example, consider the history of s 92 of the Constitution. For detail, see P. Hanks, *Constitutional Law in Australia*, 2nd edn. (Sydney: Butterworths, 1996), 516–30. See too R. Cullen, 'Section 92: Quo Vadis?', (1989) 19 *University of Western Australia Law Review* 90.

[20] For the extent to which one senior Australian judge endorses theories of interpretation that seem to amount to just this, see Goldsworthy, n. 14 above.

[21] Craven, n. 14 above, 24.

deliberately interpreting other legislation in a new, 'human rights way' so that it is made to be consistent with what *the judges* take the bill of rights to demand.[22]

In the absence of an explicit bill of rights, constitutional or statutory, there is only so much the public will swallow as a legitimate, and only just now discovered, implication flowing from a century-old Constitution. With a bill of rights in place, by contrast, there sometimes seems no limit to what the public will swallow when judges give these expansive, indeterminate rights 'a content specific to the case in hand'.[23]

For those leery of over-mighty judges presiding over a rights-based jurisprudence, it is this relatively much greater danger of explicit as opposed to implied rights that must be kept in mind.

Rights and bills of rights: a digression

It is tempting now to press on to the matter of weighing up the desirability of some sort of bill of rights for Australia. Questions of constitutionalism, of the importance to be afforded democratic self-government, of the power to be accorded judges, and more await consideration. But the temptation is worth resisting for just a little longer. Paying some prior heed to rights and bills of rights themselves looks likely to benefit those other inquiries. What we need in this section is to gain a basic grasp of the power of rights, the provenances that can be claimed for them, and an indisputable effect they have when enumerated in the form of a bill of rights.

Let us start, therefore, with rights themselves.

I take to be uncontroversial the claim that most moral and political debate is these days conducted in the language of rights. Nearly two decades ago H. L. A. Hart was already of the view that 'the doctrine of human rights has at least temporarily replaced the doctrine of maximising utilitarianism as the prime philosophical inspiration of political and social reform'.[24] The language of rights, with its connotations of entitlements and at times stark absolutism, is to most people immensely emotionally attractive and seems often to carry with it a capacity to overwhelm all disagreement not itself framed in terms of rights.

However, conceding the observably verifiable colonizing power of rights is one thing; finding a satisfactory ontological basis for them—either a solid foundation on which they can be supported or grounds for accepting them as *starting points* of political morality in and of themselves—is another. And a very difficult other at that.

[22] In addition, and this point should not be overlooked, once explicit rights are in place, the judges can use them to imply further rights in a ratcheting-up exercise. This is precisely what happened in New Zealand. See n. 40 below.

[23] Brennan, n. 14 above, 458.

[24] H. L. A. Hart, *Essays in Jurisprudence and Philosophy* (Oxford: Clarendon Press, 1983), 196–7.

Not unrelatedly nor unsurprisingly, then, we find that vast amounts have been written about rights—and clearly I refer here specifically to *moral, non-legal rights* lacking the obvious Benthamite correlation to positive legal rules and duties (and so to a final set of standards to which ultimate appeal is constrained, thereby massively narrowing what is contestable)—that leave the question of foundations untouched. There are all the analyses of the concept of a right in the Hohfeldian tradition. There is the debate between the will theory of rights (rights as opportunities or powers to make choices) and the interest theory of rights (rights as protections of certain non-trivial interests). There is the matter of how rights-based theories differ from duty-based and goal-based theories. There are the various claims that rights should be understood as trumps or immunities, as constraints on the kinds of reasons government can act upon,[25] as defining the boundaries of allowable deliberation, or as preventing the corruption of welfare calculations by foreclosing external preferences.[26] There are disputes about how to rank competing rights, about which human interests are important enough to warrant the protection of rights, and about whether what began as a protective device for individuals can, without contradiction or inconsistency, be extended to groups. There is contention over what right to think of as pre-eminent—be it the one to autonomy, to equal concern and respect, to choose progressively how one should live, to dignity, to property, to justice, to participate in political decision-making, or to some other option. There is even the old argument about whether it is wise to accept socio-economic rights into the club.

However, none of these debates, claims, contentions, or analyses deals with providing a precise foundation for accepting the claimed conclusiveness of rights in political argument. Outside the positive law, what is the basis of rights? Why should we think rights actually exist?

Some are tempted to look for that basis in certain aspects or qualities of human nature. But this is to infringe Hume's Law, to succumb to the naturalistic fallacy, by moving unwarrantedly from the copula 'is' (namely, from certain features all or most humans happen to share) to the copula 'ought' (namely, to certain protections or entitlements or rights that humans should be accorded). Others simply ignore the vexed issue of foundations. Others still rely on shared, perhaps widely shared, intuitions to tell us where rights come from.

In this chapter I intend simply to state my own view, which is that there are only three plausible groundings for non-legal, moral rights. At the end of the day, such rights must rest either on utilitarian (or more broadly, consequentialist) grounds *or* they must rest on what Jeremy Bentham described as the principle of

[25] Richard Pildes calls this a structural conception of rights. See R. Pildes, 'Why Rights Are Not Trumps: Social Meanings, Expressive Harms, and Constitutionalism', (1998) 27 *Journal of Legal Studies* 725, and R. Pildes, 'Dworkin's Two Conceptions of Rights', (2000) 29 *Journal of Legal Studies* 309.

[26] For a short, but powerful, critique to the effect that the distinction between internal and external preferences is unintelligible for evaluating public policies and tends anyway to be used in ambiguous and contradictory ways, see Pildes, 'Dworkin's Two Conceptions of Rights', n. 25 above, n. 12. See too Hart, n. 24 above, 210–21, for this and other criticisms of the supposed distinction.

sympathy and antipathy[27] (where 'the party whose interest is in question [merely happens to] find himself disposed to approve or disapprove of [it]'[28]) *or* they are a function of an evolved system of intersubjective sentiments and evaluations, on something like the Hume or Mackie model. The last of these, however, provides no ultimate justification (as opposed to explanation) other than the way things happen to be. And one supports the way things are—or one does not—on the basis of one of the first two, either good consequences or a subjective sympathy and antipathy evaluation.

This latter basis, though, amounts to nothing more than a personal, subjective evaluation of 'I like it' or 'I don't like it'. Rights, or indeed *any* evaluative or normative claim whatsoever, can certainly be grounded in a particular person's subjective sentiments and such a grounding is clearly not consequentialist.[29]

Of course, many of those who place great weight on rights will not like the sceptical implications of my view about their only plausible foundations. Here I note only that my view is not an idiosyncratic one. Jeremy Waldron, back in 1984, observed that 'Non-utilitarian theories [of rights]...often contain little more than a bare assertion that certain rights are intuitively evident or are at any rate to be taken as first principles.'[30] I have read nothing in his subsequent works to make me think he has changed his mind. And even a renowned anti-consequentialist like Ronald Dworkin, in attempting to defend moral objectivism generally, conceded that the moral objectivist 'may not be able to say very much to the utilitarian in defense of [her] moral attitude; perhaps [she] cannot say even as much to him as he can to [her]'.[31] The same is presumably true when it comes to moral rights. Which seems to take us back to an old H. L. A. Hart assertion, still true in my opinion, that 'it cannot be said that we have had...a sufficiently detailed or adequately articulated theory showing the foundation for...[moral, non-legal] rights and how they are related to other values... Indeed the revived doctrines of basic rights are...in spite of much brilliance still unconvincing.'[32]

At this point, those who agree with me so far might want to ask why rights should be entrusted to unelected judges to be given specific content as cases arise. Why should *their views* of moral rights count more than anyone else's? Why

[27] See J. Bentham, *An Introduction to the Principles of Morals and Legislation* (first pub. 1789, printed 1780), ch. 2, paras XI–XVII, incl. footnotes.

[28] Ibid., para XI.

[29] Bentham, however, is scathing in his attacks on sympathy and antipathy, calling it really 'the negation of all principle' (ch. 2, para XII). Interestingly, though, Bentham was of the view that *all* non-consequentialist justifications ultimately collapse into sympathy and antipathy. I agree.

[30] J. Waldron, 'Introduction', in Waldron (ed.), *Theories of Rights* (Oxford: Oxford University Press, 1984), 19.

[31] R. Dworkin, 'Objectivity and Truth: You'd Better Believe It', (1996) 25 *Philosophy and Public Affairs* 87, 135.

[32] Hart, n. 24 above, 195. Going back much further still we have John Stuart Mill's comment that 'to have a right is to have something society ought to defend...if [asked why]...I can give no other reason than general utility'. See his 'Utilitarianism', in Mill, *Utilitarianism*, ed. M. Warnock (1861; Glasgow: Fontana Press, 1981), 309.

should we accept the judiciary's opinions about rights as somehow amounting to what rights 'really' require, thereby handing hefty amounts of social policy-making over to judges?

These questions seem obvious enough if rights rest ultimately either on the good consequences they generally produce or on the sentiments in their favour that some people happen to feel. As it happens, they can also be fairly obvious questions for the person who believes rights *can* be given some sort of firmer grounding. This person too will ask these officious questions of judges *provided he has a modicum of modesty about his own moral discernment*. After all, it is one thing for you to believe there are objectively right moral propositions or that some set of rights rests on a higher, non-subjective, objective basis; it is quite another for you to believe that *you know* what those objective rights are, or what the objectively right way is for them to play out in specific situations.[33]

We can summarize quite concisely the argument thus far in this section: the nature of rights themselves, the provenance that can plausibly be claimed for them, may itself lead us to doubt the wisdom of placing a set of these rights at (or near) the apex of the legal and constitutional system, where of necessity unelected judges would have to give them specific content. At any rate, anyone who values widespread participation in the political process, and more so anyone who thinks democracy (in the sense of self-government by the people) is as likely to lead to morally acceptable outcomes as any elitist, judicially driven alternative, will entertain this doubt.

And that is just the philosophical doubts. There are practical issues here too. The emphasis on rights can be argued to lead to an excessive politicization of the judiciary, to promote an individualistic, entitlement culture, or to encourage excessive litigiousness. Likewise, there is the danger that rights challenges through the courts might end up being largely captured by one political perspective. There is even the chance that ordinary citizens' participation in political life, of necessity already downgraded once unelected judges are allowed to pass a privileged judgment on legislation's compatibility with articulated rights, might be redirected from the political arena to the legal, judicial arena as the latter becomes seen as more likely to bring favourable results.

Whatever the force of these practical concerns, enough has been said about rights themselves for the purposes of this chapter. We can end this section with a few paragraphs about bills of rights, about an indisputable effect of these instruments which enumerate, and turn from moral into legal, a set of comparatively vague, amorphous—but emotionally attractive—rights.

The main effect of entrenching a bill of rights in a Western democracy is to transfer a significant degree of social policy-making power to unelected judges (and, less directly, to the legal profession). It is the judges, and no one else

33 This point is made superbly well by Jeremy Waldron in 'The Irrelevance of Moral Objectivity', in R. George (ed.), *Natural Law Theory: Contemporary Essays* (Oxford: Clarendon Press, 1992). See too my 'Positively Fabulous: Why it Is Good to Be a Legal Positivist', (1997) 10 *Canadian Journal of Law and Jurisprudence* 231, 245–7.

(though lawyers help them in this), who will take these open-textured rights guarantees—the broad and imprecise standards embodied in the language of rights—and apply them to specific situations where legislation passed by the democratically elected legislature has been argued to infringe or conflict with the rights guarantees. It is the judges who will decide: how long those accused of serious criminal offences can be kept waiting for trial before judges order their release;[34] what the permissibility and extent of abortions should be;[35] when free speech protection should trump health and safety concerns[36] or worries about pornography;[37] when police misconduct triggers an exclusion of evidence thereby obtained;[38] and much else.[39]

Those who are attracted to bills of rights, but find disconcerting this undeniable effect of a rather massive transfer of social policy-making power to the judiciary, often find refuge in two alternatives to the fully entrenched, wholly justiciable model. Some opt for a non-entrenched, statutory model. Others advocate including an override clause in the entrenched bill of rights. All I need say about these two alternatives here is that there is little, if any, evidence that either does all that much to reduce or alleviate the power of judges. Take New Zealand, which embraced the statutory alternative. In fact, New Zealand opted for one of the most enervated bills of rights imaginable, removing any provision allowing for legal remedies for breach and inserting an operative provision which basically stated that in the event of inconsistency with *any* other statute, future *or* past, the other statute prevails. But in the course of fewer than a dozen years the New Zealand judges have transformed what was patently—in terms of a plain-meaning reading or the enactors' intentions—an enervated bill of rights statute into an instrument that allows them to do remarkably more than most would ever have anticipated. Let loose on this statutory alternative, the judges have 'read in' powers for themselves to issue declarations of inconsistency, to undertake potentially sweeping abridging inquiries (with the Brandeis Brief-type reliance on contestable social science which they necessitate), and to grant remedies for an ad hoc Bill of Rights Act cause of action subjecting the Crown to potentially unlimited liability for its breach.[40]

[34] See *R v Askov* (1990) 74 DLR (4th) 355, then an extra-judicial rationalization and apology for that decision in the 26 July 1991 *Lawyers Weekly* (vol. 11, no. 13) followed by the recanting of *Askov* in *R v Morin* (1992) 72 CCC (3d) 11 (SCC).

[35] See *Roe v Wade* 410 US 113 (1973).

[36] See *R J R MacDonald Inc v Canada* (1995) 127 DLR (4th) 1.

[37] See *R v Butler* (1992) 89 DLR (4th) 449.

[38] See *R v Grayson and Taylor* [1997] 1 NZLR 399.

[39] Even to the point of rewriting a province's human rights legislation to add a new ground; see *Vriend v Alberta* (1998) 156 DLR (4th) 385.

[40] For my full views on the New Zealand Bill of Rights Act 1990, see 'Turning Clark Kent into Superman: The New Zealand Bill of Rights Act 1990', (2000) 9 *Otago Law Review* 613; 'The Effect of a Statutory Bill of Rights Act Where Parliament Is Sovereign: The Lesson from New Zealand', in T. Campbell, K. D. Ewing, and A. Tomkins (eds.), *Sceptical Essays on the Human Rights Act 1998* (Oxford: Oxford University Press, 2001); and 'Take Heed Australia—A Statutory Bill of Rights and Its Inflationary Effect', (2001) 6 *Deakin Law Review* 322.

As for override clauses, the lesson from Canada (with its section 33 'notwithstanding' clause) is clear: they have next to no practical effect in terms of limiting judicial power. They may even have the perverse effect of freeing judges to be even more activist and unconstrained than they would be without the 'cover' of such an override. But I leave discussion of that topic to Jeffrey Goldsworthy's chapter in this book.

The point for us is that neither alternative appears to do much in the way of reducing the power of judges once a bill of rights is adopted. With that concession, we can press on with a weighing up.

A BILL OF RIGHTS FOR AUSTRALIA?

There *is* something lost, from a democratic point of view, when an unelected and unaccountable individual or institution makes a binding decision about what democracy requires.[41]

It is time to bring together the earlier strands in this chapter and consider whether, in Australia, the protection of the sort of important human interests that fall under the aegis of rights (or of human rights) calls for some sort of bill of rights. I have said already that my answer is no. In fact, I have already given some of my grounds for gainsaying the current fashion in favour of such instruments. In this final section I want to support that answer further, and defend the status quo, in two distinct ways. One will consider the issue in the specific context of constitutionalism, of a country with a written constitution. The other will ignore that fact, and make several points that would apply even if Australia were like the United Kingdom and New Zealand and had no written constitution. As the latter is the less focused, let us start there.

First off, the adoption of a bill of rights comes at the expense of widespread participation in decision-making. Once one is in place, the overwhelming majority of the population will be disenfranchised (in favour of a few select judges) on a significant number of major social policy questions, and indeed on basic rights questions. For those who support rights on 'strong', non-utilitarian (and non-sympathy and antipathy) bases,[42] it is hard to see why the right to participate should be discounted this way. Indeed, most such non-utilitarian groundings of rights seek to give great weight to the notion of humans as autonomous, self-governing beings. Certainly any ultimate appeal by such 'strong rights' supporters to a utilitarian justification (namely, the unelected judges get the 'right' answer more frequently than the elected legislature) is at least ironic and can be enjoyed for the squirming it does—or should—cause.

[41] Waldron, *Law and Disagreement*, n. 6 above, 293.

[42] For this argument in full, see my 'Bills of Rights and Judicial Power—A Liberal's Quandary', (1996) 16 *Oxford Journal of Legal Studies* 337. Notice here that any sort of pathological distrust of elected politicians, and of the democratic process, is almost certainly grounded on a utilitarian or consequentialist basis.

Secondly, few, if any, rights adherents today believe that how rights should play out—including how they should rank against one another, who is to possess them, and whether and when they should lose out to broader social interests—is self-evident. Put in place a bill of rights with its broad and imprecise standards embodied in the language of rights and no one should expect consensus, or even widespread agreement, when they have to be applied in specific situations. The point is that *if* Australia opts for a bill of rights, then the judges will end up deciding controversial questions of social policy over which sincere, intelligent, well-meaning people disagree—questions about where to draw the line when it comes to abortion, privacy, free speech, police powers, religious practices, how refugee claimants are to be treated, who can marry, and much else. The apocalyptic scenario of judges stopping the rest of us from indulging in obviously wicked acts seems to me to be a myth. In any imaginable scenario in which elected legislators would contemplate the sort of things most of us today (when times are good and there is no external threat) would consider wicked, the judges too would contemplate the same measures. So bills of rights end up delivering from elected politicians to unelected judges power to decide highly contestable social policy issues (even if they are sold under the guise of upholding and protecting universally desired and uncontentious rights).

Thirdly, in thinking about a bill of rights it is worth taking any claims about Australia being an international outcast or pariah, because it lacks one, with more than a pinch of salt. The United Nations itself recently scored Australia the second-best place in the world to live behind only Norway. (Or more accurately, the 2001 UN Human Development Report built an index based on life expectancy, literacy, educational attainment, and gross domestic product per capita, and when the numbers went in, Australia came out number two in the world, for what that is worth.)

Fourthly, there is little doubt that once a bill of rights is in place, it is highly unlikely (to put it mildly) that any political party will ever expend the political capital needed to get rid of it. In other words, there will be no going back in the foreseeable future. This is an asymmetrical decision. Consequently, I would argue that an extra burden lies on proponents—knowing we can never go back—to convince us that adopting a bill of rights is a good idea.

Fifthly, I can think of no plausible grounds for believing that the unelected judges who would operate a bill of rights have a more highly developed sense of moral perspicacity than elected politicians. Nor do I find the institutional arguments convincing, the sort that refer approvingly to such factors as the life tenure of judges, the need for judges to give reasons for their decisions, and their separation from the political maelstrom.

These points, together with those made earlier in this chapter, all seem to me to buttress my claim that the status quo in Australia is fully capable of protecting—and in relative international terms when like is compared with like, largely has protected—the important, but contestable, human interests meant to be covered by a bill of rights. I, for one, looking from the outside in at one of the most democratic systems in the world, put no stock in the all too modish suspicion of majoritarian democracy, tinged as it is with contempt for elected politicians and an apotheosis of the judiciary.

However, we are not quite home yet. Before we can conclude that a bill of rights is unneeded, and undesirable, in Australia, we must finally consider the issue in the context of constitutionalism. After all, Australia long ago opted for a written constitution. It has entrenched federalism, bicameralism, constitutional monarchy, and other structural matters against repeal by a simple majority of elected representatives in one or both Houses. Having travelled that route, having embraced constitutionalism, is it now somehow harder or inconsistent to rest one's objections to a bill of rights on what amounts to a liking for majoritarian democracy—to support for the fuzzy old notion that each generation can be trusted to decide for itself (through its elected representatives) about preferred social policies, whether they be framed and understood in terms of rights or not? Does Australia's century-old embrace of constitutionalism undermine, in whole or in part, my arguments against adopting a bill of rights? This chapter will finish with my attempts to answer those questions in the negative.

Larry Alexander, in his introduction to *Constitutionalism: Philosophical Foundations*,[43] tells us he agrees with the claim, in Richard Kay's chapter of that same book, that 'the purpose of a constitution is to lay down fixed rules that can affect human conduct and thereby keep government in good order... Constitutionalism... sides with risking rigidity rather than risking security'.[44] A constitution, in other words, is about locking things in, and one justifies that sort of entrenchment 'by reference to distrust of our future politics'.[45]

> We may believe that we have the best rules we can ever have, and that there is far more danger of loss of political wisdom and morality or of political akrasia than there is danger that wide agreement on better rules will be thwarted.[46]

So constitutions are valuable, in the Alexander scheme of things, because they lock in—and make hard to change—a better set-up than we would be likely to get under the 'vicissitudes of democratic politics'.[47]

Two things are clear on this view of constitutionalism. First, democratic decision-making will on some occasions have to lose out to the locked-in rules and values. 'It should be stated immediately that the preference for a constitutional regime depends on an implicit or explicit judgment that self-government, immediate or long-term, is *not* a pre-emptive value.'[48]

[43] L. Alexander (ed.), *Constitutionalism: Philosophical Foundations* (Cambridge: Cambridge University Press, 1998).

[44] Ibid. 4. [45] Ibid. 6. [46] Ibid. 2. [47] Ibid. 8.

[48] R. Kay, 'American Constitutionalism', in Alexander (ed.), n. 43 above, 25; my emphasis. See too pp. 4 and 11 of Alexander's introduction in that same book.

Secondly, there is at least an element of paternalism to any distrust of future politics or future generations or to fears of looming political akrasia. From the point of view of those adopting a new constitution, a main belief behind such fears is that *they themselves* know better than future generations what is best *for those future generations.* (Relatedly, for those looking back and endorsing an old constitution because, *inter alia*, it is better than any set of rules current democratic politics would be likely to produce, then a main belief is that the Founding Fathers knew best.)

Alexander is a supporter of both constitutionalism and a bill of rights. The task for us, however, is to offer a defence of the former that abjures the latter. Let us approach that task by taking his three points in order.

We begin with the claim that constitutionalism is about locking things in and making change difficult, certainly more difficult than what is required, say, to enact a statute. In my opinion, this claim is indubitably correct. Indeed, I can think of no other point to a written constitution save one that few are prepared to voice honestly, namely, as a means to transfer power, surreptitiously, to the point-of-application interpreter of that constitution. Proponents of methods of constitutional interpretation that completely reject any constraining links to the intentions or understandings of those living when the constitution was adopted do manage to sever constitutionalism from the rationale of 'locking in rules and values'. But the cost is immense because it is only the point-of-application interpreters, the judges, who are thereby freed from the constitution's constraints. Proponents of such a 'living tree', 'contemporary needs' type of interpretation of constitutions trade what they see as ancestor worship for what seems to me to be the worship of unelected judges.[49]

At any rate, suffice it here to say that I agree with Alexander that constitutionalism can only be justified in terms of wanting to lock things in. Where I disagree is with his only suggested motive, 'the distrust of future politics' and 'fear of political akrasia'. One can be free of all fear of political akrasia, even bubblingly optimistic about future politics, and yet wish to lock in a catalogue of division of powers between regional and central governments. In fact, in any federal structure this is a necessity; it may be the price of nationhood. We can all see the difference between locking in a set of vague, amorphous individual rights and locking in the division of powers underpinning a federal structure. The latter in no way mandates or presupposes the former.

Of course in making that point I have merely begged the question at the heart of Alexander's second assertion. To what extent is constitutionalism incompatible with attempts to make self-government a pre-emptive value? Here one must concede immediately that majoritarian self-government is *not* the ultimate

[49] For a thorough skewering of one Australian High Court judge who rejects originalism as a basis for interpreting the Constitution, see Goldsworthy, n. 14 above, 684: 'Taken to the extreme, this [judge's] non-originalism argument entails that "this Constitution" is a meaningless text, a mere assemblage of marks on paper, which can be given any meaning at all by those entrusted with its "interpretation".'

currency in Australia today. It is ancillary to the requirements of federalism as well as being bracketed by a strong version of bicameralism. Judges clearly have the role of division of powers arbiters so that no single parliament can be said to be supreme or sovereign. On the other hand, save for the limited freedom of communication mentioned above and a few matters related to federalism,[50] it is also true that one of the legislatures—the particular state legislature or the Commonwealth Parliament—has the judicially unrestrained power to do whatever is attempting to be done. Majoritarian self-government may not be accorded pre-emptive value in Australia today, but it is accorded much greater weight than it would be were a bill of rights adopted.

My point is that one can be prepared to make some bargains at the expense of self-government but still say other bargains come at too high a cost. Moreover, the actual cost or limit on self-government in Australia today is manifestly a small one. Constitutionalism and democracy overwhelmingly coexist.

That just leaves for brief discussion the danger of undue paternalism, which I have suggested seems to be implicit in Alexander's view of constitutionalism. Must the adoption of (or support for) a written constitution entail the belief that the adopters know what is best for later generations better than those later generations—at least to the extent that those later generations will have higher than normal hurdles to jump if they wish to make changes?

The easiest reply to this involves simply noting that the Australian Constitution is remarkably lacking in such paternalistic assumptions. The people, including future generations of the Australian people, are entrusted with their own destiny. Even the section 128 amendment process, with its direct appeal by referendum to the people, does no more than federalist bargains require. Larry Alexander's 'distrust of future politics' seems to me almost wholly absent in the Australian Constitution. It is a strikingly anti-paternalistic work,[51] and none the worse for it in my view.

Perhaps, now, we are home at last. We have seen that one need not be against constitutionalism per se to be against the sort that imposes a bill of rights and judicial overseers. We have seen that nothing in the current constitutional status

[50] See n. 19 above. It follows from federalism that if the federal distribution of powers is to be secure, judicial power must be separated from legislative power. So whereas the UK Parliament can (but does not) exercise judicial power, the Australian Commonwealth Parliament (and likewise state parliaments with respect to the national Constitution) cannot. This is a procedural rather than substantive limit. Thanks to Jeff Goldsworthy for this point.

[51] I should note that Alexander himself, presumably writing about more paternalistic constitutions than Australia's, attempts to overcome the problem of paternalism—'Why... the majority [ought] *now* to feel bound by what a majority—even a supermajority—said then' (Alexander (ed.), n. 43 above, 8)—by appealing to contemporary consent today: 'we believe... the old constitution [is] a better moral bet than the vicissitudes of democratic politics' (ibid.). The problem with this response, in my view, is that in fact we (the present people) are never really asked if we believe majoritarianism is a worse moral bet. The actual option is the status quo or revolution and potential anarchy, which makes almost any status quo look good. This sort of defence against the charge of paternalism reminds me of the remark about social contract theories attributed to David Hume: 'They aren't worth the paper they weren't written on.'

quo in Australia prevents any change being made piecemeal fashion by legislation,[52] provided the change is done within federalist parameters and has the support of the elected representatives, and very occasionally also of the people voting in a referendum. We have seen that that status quo is remarkably anti-paternalistic and that its faith in each generation to decide for itself—certainly about electoral matters and letting citizens take part in decision-making on more or less equal terms—has not been misplaced. Nor do we really need to be reminded that a bill of rights does not somehow become a democratic decision-making device *even if* it be itself established democratically.[53] We have also observed that neither statutory bills of rights nor override clauses do nearly enough to reduce the social policy-making power of the unelected judiciary. In this context, however egregious implied rights may be, they seem almost trifling next to the latitude afforded judges by an explicitly adopted bill of rights.

So this chapter may also serve as a plea for Australia to stand outside the worldwide trend, to forswear any sort of bill of rights. Were that route to be travelled, there would be no going back. The status quo is worth prizing now, not left until it is lacked and lost and too late.

If I am lucky, there may be readers, perhaps even some more optimistic than I about the effects of a bill of rights in a democracy, who nevertheless read this chapter and think, 'Well, we don't need one in Australia.'

[52] And even interstitially by common law.

[53] Larry Alexander makes the point bluntly: 'a democratic delegation to the courts of the power to invalidate legislation in the name of rights does not make such judicial invalidations democratic' (Alexander (ed.), n. 43 above, 10–11).

9

Aspiring to the Rule of Law

DAVID DYZENHAUS

> ...a recognition that the internal morality of law may support and give efficacy to a wide variety of substantive aims should not mislead us into believing that *any* substantive aim may be adopted without any compromise of legality.
>
> (Lon L. Fuller[1])

INTRODUCTION

In the last fifty or so years the topic of the rule of law has received surprisingly little attention from legal theorists writing in English. Much more attention has come from lawyers concerned with quite practical issues about the failure of societies to live up to the values of the rule of law, assumed to be the values of liberal democratic societies, or with the problems that attend implementing the rule of law in societies that lack the legal institutions of Western democracies. The reports of commissions of jurists on the state of the rule of law in apartheid South Africa or more recently in Zimbabwe are examples.

In that same fifty-year period more or less that same group of lawyers found a focus for their concerns emerging in the idea of human rights. Organizations such as Amnesty International argued that the main standard for evaluating the moral record of a country is respect for human rights. The failure of the law of the land to give effective expression to human rights is these days often very closely associated, even equated, with a failure of the rule of law.

Philosophers of law have not bothered much with analysis of the rule of law because their focus has been the question 'What is law?' and, more particularly, whether the answer to that question shows that there is a necessary connection between law and morality. Their thought has been that once one has worked out the answer to that question, one will know what the law is that rules when one has the rule of law. The lawyers concerned with the practical questions seem, therefore, to assume precisely what is at stake in the philosophical debate—the rule of law is for them the rule of morality or of liberal democratic values, taken to include, or even to be defined by, a suitable list of human rights.

I thank Jim Allan, Cheryl Misak, and Mike Taggart for comments on a draft of this chapter.

1 L. Fuller, *The Morality of Law*, rev. edn. (New Haven: Yale University Press, 1969), 153.

These practical lawyers might well think that the philosophical debate is particularly rarefied, even irrelevant, taking place as it does for the most part in countries which, with the exception of Australia, have joined the family of legal orders which give explicit statutory recognition to human rights. The changed world of legal practice seems to have left legal theory behind.

I hope to show that this bleak conclusion is not inevitable. The next section sets out the general area of agreement within legal theory that leads to lack of interest in the rule of law. Fortunately, the recent entry of a position I call democratic legal positivism into the debate opens up the possibility for the fruitful engagement of legal theory with the rule of law, despite the fact that that position is also a party to the general agreement. But, as I will suggest in the last section, that engagement is not likely to be on democratic positivist terms, since it invites a renewed interest in a position that is not party to the agreement—Lon L. Fuller's account of the rule of law.

Legal theory and the rule of law

The central point of agreement in legal theory today is that law-making procedures are neutral with respect to substance: in the absence of specific constitutional constraints, those with authority to make law can make any law they please. This point is most closely associated with the tradition of legal positivism. Legal positivists argue that the rule of law is simply the rule of the law made by those who wield legal power. If the powerful are liberal democrats or enthusiasts of human rights, the law will reflect their values. These values might even be incorporated by a constitution into the law, so that the values become a test for the validity of the law. Here, substantive moral values, for example the right to freedom of expression, are incorporated into the positive law as general criteria for the validity of other positive laws. But the rule of law is as compatible with the rule of illiberal or anti-democratic values as it is with liberal democratic values. To make the same point, the law can, and has often, been used to violate human rights.

If positivists are to recognize any intrinsic virtue to the rule of law, as Joseph Raz has argued, it will be the virtue of instrumentality—the virtue of making it possible for rulers effectively to guide the actions of those subject to the law. A legal order which lives up to the rule of law will be more effective. But efficacy is not equivalent to goodness. Goodness turns on the values of which the law is the instrument.[2]

Since positivists are generally liberal democrats and human rights enthusiasts, they agree that societies are legitimate when values such as human rights are respected by the law of the land. But for positivists, the argument about what

[2] J. Raz, 'The Rule of Law and Its Virtue', in Raz (ed.), *The Authority of Law: Essays on Law and Morality* (Oxford: Clarendon Press, 1979).

makes a society legitimate, as well as issues about institutional design in the service of legitimacy, find their proper place in political, not legal, philosophy.

Ronald Dworkin's main challenge to legal positivism is to the distinction between political and legal philosophy. That challenge is posed through his account of adjudication, in which he seeks to show that how judges decide hard cases—cases in which the law is contested—is determined by their different conceptions of the political point of law. Judges who take their duty seriously in adjudicating hard cases will find that they are compelled to present an answer to the legal question posed which shows the law relevant to the case in its best political light. That light is shed by extracting principles from the law which both fit the law and supply the best possible justification for it. Dworkin also claims that the justification of these principles will reveal them to be moral, so that his account of adjudication establishes the connection between law and moral values denied by legal positivism.

Positivists argue that the presence of such values in the law is contingent on the political history of the particular country. To them, Dworkin is vulnerable to a version of the same problem as the practice-oriented lawyers. He operates with the assumption that the law already includes certain values, and so it follows for him that the rule of law is the rule of such law. It is more fruitful, they think, to respect the distinction between legal and political philosophy and to see that the equation of the law and of the rule of law with liberal democratic values, or with a respect for human rights, is a disguised wish or aspiration that the law respect these values and rights.

This disagreement between Dworkin and the positivists is premissed on a large measure of agreement. Both agree that the question of the connection between law and morality is settled by determining whether the law of particular jurisdictions, necessarily contains certain moral values. They also agree that the rule of law is the rule of the law of a particular jurisdiction, and in that sense they both hold what I will call substantive theories of the rule of law. Their theories are substantive in that any viable case for a connection between law and morality, and thus for the legitimacy of the rule of law, is one that shows a necessary connection between the substantive content of the law and morality.

This area of agreement has squeezed out of the philosophical debate another position, one which H. L. A. Hart, in his 1958 manifesto for legal positivism, saw as a distinct challenge to the positivist tradition.[3] While Hart was mainly concerned to deal with claims about the connection between law and morality that turn on the content of the law, he also thought it important to respond to the argument that inherent in the kind of order imposed by a choice to govern through law are moral principles that constrain government. Here the emphasis is not on the substance of the law, but on the process of governing through law. Put differently, the kind of theory of the rule of law that arises out of this second

[3] H. L. A. Hart, 'Positivism and the Separation of Law and Morals', in his *Essays in Jurisprudence and Philosophy* (Oxford: Clarendon Press, 1983), 49.

challenge seems procedural rather than substantive since it emphasizes the 'rule' component of the rule of law rather than the substantive content of the 'law'.

Notice that this procedural emphasis seems more in tune with the phrase 'the rule of law' than its substantive counterpart, which insists on turning the phrase into the cumbersome 'the rule of the law'. Moreover, in insisting that what is at issue is the rule of 'law' rather than the rule of 'the law', this emphasis might seem to meet the positivists on their own ground—answering questions about law in general rather than about the law of a particular jurisdiction.

I do not want to make too much of linguistic intuitions, though I do want to note that Hart's own innovation in the 1958 manifesto could, at points, be interpreted as aligning positivism with the family of procedural theories.[4] For Hart departed from his positivist predecessors by arguing that there is no such thing as an uncommanded legal commander—the ultimate legal authority unconstrained by law. Rather, there is a fundamental, constitutional rule in all legal orders that constrains the exercise of legal power. Hart developed this idea in *The Concept of Law* as the rule of recognition, a rule that sets out the criteria which particular laws must meet if they are to be recognized as valid.[5]

Hart, however, was anxious to stress in the manifesto that the constraint of this fundamental rule did not in any way endanger the Separation Thesis—the positivist claim that there is no necessary connection between law and morality. And his elaboration of the rule of recognition was carefully designed to preserve that thesis. Even though a rule of recognition account of law is procedural, one about the procedures one has to follow to make valid law, the procedures are neutral with respect to substance. As long as they are followed, any content at all can be injected into law.

Exactly this point seems to be the burden of Raz's response to Fuller, the most important proponent of the proceduralist challenge to legal positivism. Fuller argues that inherent in legal order are by and large procedural principles of morality—generality, publicity, non-retroactivity, clarity or intelligibility, non-contradiction, possibility of compliance, constancy through time, and congruence between declared rule and official action.[6] Raz responds, following Hart, that Fuller is right that there are principles intrinsic to the idea of government under the rule of law. But Raz tries to show that these principles are not moral principles: they merely make the law into a more effective instrument.[7]

It is worth recalling that Dworkin, in one of his earliest publications, joined in this kind of positivist critique of Fuller.[8] Moreover, in his later work Dworkin seems to equate fairness or process with the democratic reasons that require

[4] Robert Alexy claims that positivism is generally more concerned with procedures than with substantive outcomes; see D. Dyzenhaus, 'A Defence of Radbruch's Formula', in Dyzenhaus (ed.), *Recrafting the Rule of Law: The Limits of Legal Order* (Oxford: Hart, 1999), 15, 23.

[5] H. L. A. Hart, *The Concept of Law* (Oxford: Clarendon Press, 1961).

[6] Fuller, n. 1 above, esp. the section replying to critics, 187–253.

[7] Raz, n. 2 above.

[8] R. Dworkin, 'Philosophy, Morality, and Law: Observations Prompted by Professor Fuller's Novel Claim', (1965) 113 *University of Pennsylvania Law Review* 672.

judicial deference to legislative intent.[9] So we find here another point of agreement between Dworkin and the positivists. The process of making law is neutral with respect to substance. Hence, if a connection between law and morality is to be established, one should look elsewhere than the law-making process, and the natural candidate is the content of the law.

That legal positivists today seem rather obsessed with the role of moral values in adjudication is curious from the perspective of their own tradition. One of the two main contemporary options—exclusive legal positivism—insists that adjudication on the basis of such values amounts to a quasi-legislative exercise of discretion. On this option, the reach of the authority of law diminishes as the role of values in the law increases, though at the moment that the judges declare their judgment, law comes into being. This option is exclusive not because it excludes values from being incorporated into a rule of recognition's criteria of validity, but because it denies that judgments based on the interpretation of such values are determined by the law. The other option—incorporationist or inclusive legal positivism—differs only in that it accepts that such judgments are fully determined by law. It maintains its positivist credentials through insisting that the presence of such values is contingent.[10]

The positivist tradition is, however, best interpreted as a kind of exclusive legal positivism, but one where the exclusionary moves happen not for the conceptual kind of reasons offered by most contemporary positivists, but for political reasons to do with views about the best way to construct legal order. In this tradition, legislation or statutes are regarded as the primary form of law because it is statutes that are the best means of communicating determinate sovereign judgment to legal subjects. Judicial interpretation is inevitable because even the clearest statutes can neither anticipate every situation nor communicate altogether clearly. But the more that can be settled in advance by statute, the better. And so judicial interpretation should be kept to its proper place—at the margins of legal order. In other words, interpretation is excluded for political reasons from taking more than a marginal role in legal order.

The other exclusionary move is that the recognition of the inevitability of interpretation is mitigated by denying legal authority to it. The first move depicts interpretation as the realm of subjective value judgment, not part of the communication of the authoritative, determinate content of the positive law. The second move follows through by arguing that such interpretation should not be given legal force beyond the dispute between the particular individuals, because to grant more force is to give to judges a legislative authority that should be reserved to the sovereign lawmaker.

Put differently, this gift to judges puts in place a competitor for sovereign authority. If the subjective value judgments of judges are dignified with legal

[9] R. Dworkin, *Law's Empire* (London: Fontana, 1986).

[10] Joseph Raz is the foremost proponent of the exclusive version, while Jules Coleman and Wil Waluchow have pioneered the development of the inclusive version.

status by being recognized as a source of law, judges will be tempted to elevate their role in the legal order, imposing their views on statutes while claiming that all they are doing is interpreting the law. In sum, the second exclusionary move follows through on the first, because it is necessary in order to accomplish the political task of maintaining the integrity of positivistically conceived legal order.

In the 1958 manifesto Hart indicated at times his allegiance to these aspects of the positivist tradition. The manifesto was delivered as a lecture at Harvard Law School, and Hart warned American law students about the dangers of thinking that law could be understood entirely through the lens of the value-laden process of judicial interpretation, which settles problems in the 'penumbra' of uncertainty in the law. Not only did this lens neglect the bulk of the law—its 'core' of certainty—but it distorted the object of its study, since the authority of law lies not in the penumbra; rather, authority is in the core with its determinate content.

But while this warning makes the first exclusionary move, Hart did not make the second follow-through move. While he claimed that value-based judicial interpretation happens outside the core where true legal authority is to be found, he refrained from denying legal authority to judges' interpretations of the law. The very claim that judicial interpretation is quasi-legislative grants legal authority to judicial interpretation. But that grant undermines the political point of the first move and thus its bid to maintain the integrity of a particular vision of legal order.

Now Hart found himself in this position because, in contrast to his tradition, he conceived of the enterprise of legal theory as descriptive rather than (politically) prescriptive. His readiness to recognize judicial interpretation as a source of law is of a piece with his readiness to recognize legal constraints on ultimate sovereign authority. The idea that there might be such constraints is anathema to a positivist only if he regards it as politically important to have the ultimate legal authority completely unconstrained—or unconstrained as far as possible—in order to avoid the problems that are thought to ensue when law-making authority is divided between different institutions.

However, the political anxiety of the positivist tradition about undermining the authority of law by letting values in persists in Hart's description both of judicial interpretation and of the rule of recognition. Interpretation happens in the penumbra, and so not in the law properly so called, and the fundamental constraint of legality is not a moral constraint. The same anxiety is also manifested in the debate between exclusive and inclusive legal positivists. In terms of the above discussion, it can be recast as a debate about whether the logic of recognizing the authoritative status of judicial interpretations should extend to dropping the insistence that such interpretations are quasi-legislative or discretionary.

The inclusive legal positivists are less anxious in this regard, and it is no accident that they are mostly North Americans, politically more comfortable than their British colleagues with constitutional judicial review. But even for them anxiety persists in the very language they and the exclusive positivists adopt to describe value in law. Value is something external or foreign, which has to be expressly included or incorporated through appropriate law-making procedures—much the same idea as animates the view that it is illegitimate for judges to take account of international human rights instruments in the absence of express legislative incorporation.

Recently, however, there has been a revival of the positivist tradition that promises to move the theoretical debate onto different terrain. James Allan, Tom Campbell, Jeffrey Goldsworthy, and Jeremy Waldron have argued for a fully political version of legal positivism in which there is no free-floating anxiety about the role of value in law, but rather a democratically anchored determination to reserve final moral judgment to 'the people'. In this version of legal positivism—democratic legal positivism—there is a rule of recognition constraining ultimate legal authority. But the constraints should be limited to the constraints of manner and form that make it possible for the legislature to communicate its judgments authoritatively.[11]

This new terrain is one where democratic legal positivists meet Dworkin's challenge to legal positivism, though not by providing a rival account of adjudication. Rather, judicial interpretation is argued to be illegitimate when it is the kind of judicial interpretation that either imposes judges' sense of morality on statute law or, even worse, strikes down statutes as invalid when these conflict with the judges' moral sensibilities. Conversely, this version of legal positivism argues for the legitimacy of the law produced when law-making procedures are confined to manner and form criteria. Procedural neutrality with respect to substance is a normative requirement, based in the democratic right of the people to use the law to enforce their moral judgment. Values are to be kept out of the determination of the law as far as possible in order to permit the law to be used as a conduit for the values of the people.

While democratic legal positivism does not disturb the philosophical agreement about procedural neutrality with respect to substance, it is important that its reason for subscribing to this agreement is deeply political. It is not only, as I have just noted, that the terrain of argument about law between at least some positivists and Dworkin becomes political and thus recalls the vibrancy of the tradition established by Thomas Hobbes and Jeremy Bentham. Democratic legal positivism also resurrects for legal philosophy the contention that the rule of law—and not of the law—is the appropriate focus of debate about the connection between law and morality.

However, with that resurrection comes vulnerability, something to be welcomed in light of the unsatisfactory nature of a debate where the positivist side

[11] See Allan, Ch. 8 above; J. Goldsworthy, *The Sovereignty of Parliament: History and Philosophy* (Oxford: Clarendon Press, 1999); J. Waldron, *The Dignity of Legislation* (Cambridge: Cambridge University Press, 1999) and *Law and Disagreement* (Oxford: Clarendon Press, 1999); and T. D. Campbell, *The Legal Theory of Ethical Positivism* (Aldershot: Dartmouth, 1996).

made political points against rivals while claiming for itself a conceptual high ground unreachable by political argument.[12]

This vulnerability is frankly acknowledged by Jeffrey Goldsworthy in his contribution to this volume[13] and the next section tests it.

Constructing the new terrain

Goldsworthy has recently become interested in the Canadian Charter of Rights and Freedoms because it presents a structure of constitutional adjudication that appears rather different from the usual target of legal positivists opposed to judicial review for democratic reasons. The usual target is a constitution that purports to regard its values as absolute, so that the Supreme Court's decision that there has been a legislative infringement of the values is fatal to the particular statute.[14] Dworkin's claim that important liberal constitutional rights are to be understood as 'trumps' over majoritarian decision-making and the whole American starting point for discussion about the 'counter-majoritarian difficulty' assume that this kind of constitution is in place. And so the constitutional options were, for a long time, seen as either such a constitution or a more or less legally unlimited legislature.[15]

The Canadian Charter of Rights and Freedoms is a prominent example of more recent experiments with a different kind of constitutional option. Section 1 of the Charter gives government the opportunity to argue that statutes that are found to limit Charter-protected values are still constitutionally valid as long as the limits are shown to be 'reasonable limits prescribed by law as can be demonstrably justified in a free and democratic society'. In addition, section 33 permits a legislature to override judicial determinations of unconstitutionality in terms of certain sections of the Charter, although the override has to be renewed after five years. One can thus argue that the Charter is an attractive compromise between the either/or options of an absolutist constitution and a supreme parliament. It ensures that statutes will be tested for compliance with rights. It also removes—through section 33—the ultimate say over validity from the courts. Indeed, section 1 permits the democratic process a further point of intervention in that it gives government an opportunity to defend statutory limits on rights on the basis of democratic considerations.

[12] For discussion of relevant issues, see J. Coleman (ed.), *Hart's Postscript: Essays on the Postscript to The Concept of Law* (Oxford: Clarendon Press, 2001), esp. S. R. Perry, 'Hart's Methodological Positivism', 311; L. Murphy, 'The Political Question of the Concept of Law', 371; J. Waldron, 'Normative (or Ethical) Positivism', 410.

[13] Goldsworthy, Ch. 13 below.

[14] As Goldsworthy notes, courts working with such a constitution will often find subtle ways of avoiding this all-or-nothing approach to the validity of statutes.

[15] For an exploration of the legitimacy of judicial review that accepts the boundaries set by these options, see Kay, Ch. 5 above. Kay proposes a positivistic solution to the problem of legitimacy through an account of adjudication on Dworkin's substantive terrain—judicial review is legitimate when the constitutional values judges enforce are expressed in rules with a determinate content.

Goldsworthy considers the Canadian model a sufficient response to the rights-based critique of constitutional rights put by democratic positivists, most notably, Jeremy Waldron. The premiss is that the people, or rather their representatives, must have the right of rights—the people's right to the last word—and section 33 preserves this right. However, Canadian legislatures have hardly ever used the override, so Goldsworthy considers a different objection, one akin to the argument that the democratic decision to put in place an absolutist constitution does not make such a constitution democratic any more than a democratic decision to establish a dictatorship makes a dictatorship democratic. The different objection is that if reluctance to use the override is routine, we have in effect a democratic abdication of democracy. But the right of democracy is, he argues, compatible with delegations of power subject to the right to override the exercise of power, something shown, he thinks, by the fact that much 'modern law-making consists of regulations made by executive governments, which elected legislatures can scrutinize before they come into operation, and disallow as they see fit. Even if it were the case that legislatures seldom disallow such regulations, that would not in itself demonstrate a diminution of democracy.... It follows that we regard democracy as based on a *right* to participate *indirectly*, rather than a *duty* to participate *directly*, in public decision-making.'

Goldsworthy still thinks there is a consequentialist case for objecting to entrenched rights, especially the problem he calls (following Mark Tushnet) 'democratic debilitation'. Debilitation can manifest itself in legislatures delegating to the courts issues about the compatibility of statutes with rights, even passing the buck when the required decision will be unpopular; in letting lawyers' jargon dominate the electorate's understanding of rights; in sustaining the thought that a court's finding that a statute is constitutional settles the issue of its legitimacy; in, finally, the diversion of energy, time, and money away from politics to litigation. Another prominent consequentialist objection is represented in this volume by James Allan's chapter, 'A Defence of the Status Quo' (Chapter 8). This objection states that countries such as Australia have done at least as good a job of protecting human rights as countries that entrench rights, without the costs associated with democratic debilitation to participation in politics.

This last objection does not propose that it is a mistake to think about important issues in terms of human rights. The mistake is in supposing that the courts should be trusted with the job of guarding rights. And this same point is presupposed in several of the strands of the debilitation objection—the complaint is not about the appropriateness of rights talk in politics, but about letting the judiciary hijack politics, including the meaning of rights. The impression is that it is considered a sign of the health of society if among people's political concerns is a concern for human rights, so that the people participate in securing their human rights.

This impression—the sense that the debate is not so much about the debilitating effects of the rhetoric of rights, but about who is the best guardian of rights—is significant. The objection to judicial review looks very different when it is that rights talk is nonsense, that judges use rights talk, and so we should get down to real politics—the hard-headed politics of human interests where the majority's perceptions of its interests is always right.[16]

It is difficult to know, however, whether Allan is assuming only for the sake of argument that rights talk is not per se the problem. For example, in his discussion of the status of rights he seems to argue that rights-based judicial review should be shunned either because rights have no uncontroversial basis or because, even if one assumes an uncontroversial basis, no uncontroversial conclusions can be drawn from it.

Allan's argumentative dilemma is between condemning rights talk altogether and accepting its appropriateness, even if just for the sake of argument. Something akin to this dilemma manifests itself in the countries whose parliamentary systems the democratic legal positivists wish to defend against the imperialism of rights-talking judges. Such countries adopt the classic dualist position, closely associated with democratic legal positivism, that international treaties and conventions have no domestic force unless explicitly incorporated by parliament. Ratification by itself does not suffice to create legal obligations internally, within the domestic order. And this is so despite the fact that executive ratification happens after a government audit of the domestic legal order for compliance, because ratification is seen as a signal to the outside world alone, especially to the other high contracting parties, and so the remedies for failure to comply are purely external.

When the treaties or conventions in issue are human rights instruments, dualism looks anomalous as countries ratify the treaties in order to signal their membership in the international community of civilized nations, but dualism requires that the signal should not be heard with any internal legal effect. So what we have is democratic legal positivism for domestic purposes and human rights talk for the international audience. The problem here is only akin to Allan's dilemma, since ratification stipulates acceptance of the legitimacy of the human rights instrument and internal compliance, subject to express reservation. What we have is not then a dilemma, but contradictory messages. And that is why the majority of the High Court of Australia could argue, in a case concerning the Convention on the Rights of the Child, as follows:

> ratification by Australia of an international convention is not to be dismissed as a merely platitudinous or ineffectual act... particularly when the instrument evidences internationally accepted standards to be applied by courts and administrative authorities in dealing with basic human rights... Rather, ratification of a convention is a positive statement by

[16] In Allan's picture, commitment to democracy is the product of consequentialist argument. Such wholesale commitment to consequentialism might make his argument as circular as any rights talk. Why, for example, should one commit to consequentialism? The answer cannot be because that commitment produces the best results, for that answer merely restates the issue. But if the answer is that consequentialism is the most appropriate decision method for a democracy, one is back with the right of rights as basic.

the executive government of this country to the world and to the Australian people that the executive government and its agencies will act in accordance with the Convention.[17]

The majority thus concluded that the applicant in this case had a legitimate expectation that the rights of his children would be considered, as the Convention said, a 'primary factor' in the administrative decision to deport him.[18]

This argument was strongly contested by McHugh J in his dissent, mostly on the basis that the majority had sought to achieve what they themselves denied—'back-door' incorporation of the Convention. And it is worth recalling that in the wake of this decision the federal government sought by public statements to contradict the impression that people should have expectations about the domestic effect of ratification, and has initiated at least two bills to legislate this contradiction.

However, that the bills have not yet made it into statute might point to a feature of many proponents of dualism today that is also to be found in McHugh J's judgment, an unwillingness to go the whole hog of resigning from the human rights community. For McHugh J, after pouring scorn on the majority's reasoning, argued that in any case the rights of the applicant's children had been taken into account in exactly the way the Convention demanded.[19]

This feature of the contemporary dualist position makes it look as platitudinous as that of governments that rely on dualism to save them from domestic follow-through on their voluntarily incurred international obligations. It is made even more unattractive by the fact that it gives credence to the claim that doctrines of human rights were thought of by Western democracies as an export commodity to the uncivilized world, there to protect decolonizing colonial peoples from themselves, and not needed for internal consumption since, of course, Western democracies already subscribed to human rights. Judges who have attempted to give legal effect to unincorporated human rights instruments might then be said to have called the bluff of their own countries or, put more positively, to take seriously the moral commitments announced by their countries to the world. It only adds more irony to the picture to note that many of the cases that arise on these matters are about the Western democracies' desire to be able to send uncivilized trespassers back to their home countries in as efficient a manner as possible, that is, without the obstacles created by treating them as human beings with rights.

17 *Minister for Immigration and Ethnic Affairs v Teoh* (1995) 183 CLR 273, 291 (Mason CJ and Brennan J). The text of the first elisions in the quoted text contains a footnote reference to President Cooke's assertion in the New Zealand Court of Appeal, in respect of the same convention, that the dualist argument was 'unattractive, apparently implying that New Zealand's adherence to the international instruments has been partly window dressing'; *Tavita v Minister of Immigration* [1994] 2 NZLR 257, 266. For detailed discussion, on which I rely in the argument that follows in the text, see D. Dyzenhaus, M. Hunt, and M. Taggart, 'The Principle of Legality in Administrative Law: Internationalisation as Constitutionalisation', (2001) 1 *Oxford University Commonwealth Law Journal* 5.

18 The majority, however, confined the effect of this expectation, so that the decision-maker who wanted not to take the children's interests into account had merely to inform the applicant and afford him a hearing at which the applicant could argue against this view.

19 *Minister for Immigration and Ethnic Affairs v Teoh*, n. 18 above, 320–1.

I have associated dualism with democratic legal positivism, which is not unfair in that dualism is no more than the expression of the idea that the only legitimate source of legal obligations is the legislation of a democratically elected parliament. The association is, however, not altogether tight when dualists say that human rights have a legitimate role in the domestic legal order as long as they are explicitly incorporated. As suggested in the last section, this position is rather similar to that of inclusive legal positivism, even to that of exclusive legal positivism, with the caveat that exclusive legal positivists deny that values, once incorporated, determine the law. The readiness of all these positions to make this concession is, as I also suggested, traceable to their abandonment of legal positivism's political anchor, a loss which also seems to create problems for contemporary dualists.

The abandonment is not, however, total. It is more in the nature of a repression of the political determination of the original democratic legal positivists—the Benthamites—to keep values from infiltrating legal order. The only legitimate entry for values is through their capture in a wholly determinate fashion in statutes, a capture that is legitimate because these values have been determined to be in the interests of the majority by the majority. That repression has various manifestations: an apparently free-floating anxiety about values; the sense that values should not be permitted entry to the legal order unless explicitly incorporated by positive law; and the claim of exclusive legal positivists that even when values are expressly incorporated, it is a mistake to regard the results the judges reach as fully determined by law, unless the values are incorporated in such a way that they have a determinate content that can be merely applied.

I want to suggest that contemporary democratic legal positivists find themselves caught in the same set of unhelpful anxieties as soon as they begin to let go of the anchor. It is surely no accident that some positivists rediscovered that anchor at a time when the countries they came from became deeply involved in debates about the wisdom of adopting bills of rights and about the relationship between international human rights instruments and the domestic legal order. But the anchor holds only if it has as one of its hooks the claim that rights talk per se is bad because there is no such thing as a right, only democratically determined and legally captured expressions of interest.

On the basis of that hook, one can argue that values have a role in legal order only when they are determinately expressed, so they need no further value-laden interpretation. Only then are the occasions for judges' imposition of their own subjective perceptions excluded, or at least minimized. Put differently, once the intersubjective, democratic process of value determination has come up with a result from the slew of individual subjective preferences, that result becomes objective through its determinate expression in a statute, and the institutions of legal order must preserve that expression in its determinate form.[20]

[20] Like all positivists, Bentham had to acknowledge the need for interpretation. Indeed, he went further and allowed judges to determine individual cases in accordance with the utilities of the situation rather than in accordance with the determinate statutory expression of utility, though

But once rights talk is considered to be not merely talk, but the expression of important aspirations for any civilized society, democratic legal positivists have to join a debate about how rights are best realized, a debate that includes questions about how best to give expression to rights through legal institutions. They are committed to joining that debate just because they agree with Dworkin that the terrain is political, rather than conceptual or descriptive, so that they too work out the issue of what law is at the same time as they work out their aspirations for law. But, as I will now argue, their engagement in that debate will not be on their terms or Dworkin's. Their procedural focus invites a renewed interest in a position that is not party to the agreement about neutrality of procedures, Fuller's account of the rule of law.

Process and Substance in the Rule of Law

I will focus in this section on Fuller's claim made in the epigraph to this chapter, though I want to shift emphasis from his first 'any' to the second: 'a recognition that the internal morality of law may support and give efficacy to a wide variety of substantive aims should not mislead us into believing that any substantive aim may be adopted without *any* compromise of legality.'

With this thought, Fuller recognizes that his account of the inner morality of law is more procedural in nature than substantive. That does not mean, however, that process is neutral with respect to substance, because some substantive aims will be inconsistent with the principles of the inner morality. However, that a substantive aim is so inconsistent does not necessarily lead to the invalidation of the legal instrument in which the aim is expressed. All that matters—hence the shift in emphasis—is that one sees that legality is compromised. Put differently, the test for substantive inconsistency is not the positivist one, apparently accepted by Dworkin, that requires that some institution have the authority to invalidate a law inconsistent with the morality of the law, but only that one sees that the inner morality of law is compromised or put under stress.

Two other points are important here. First, the claim that there is an inner morality is itself based on a conception of the substantive point of law, a point Fuller expressed variously as aspiring to open up the channels of public communication, or as establishing a relationship of reciprocity between ruler and ruled. One might say with little, if any, distortion that the point of law is to give expression to the democratic, intersubjective determination of interests—to the democratic right of the people. Secondly, beyond the values expressed by the principles of the inner morality of law—which are more or less values to do with accountability of those with legal authority to law and participation

there would be no precedential effect to such an individualized judicial determination, for the same reason as judges were generally stripped of law-making authority. See G. Postema, *Bentham and the Common Law Tradition* (Oxford: Clarendon Press, 1986).

by those subject to law in the determination of the law—there is no fixed list of values that either can or have to enter into law.

However, because the point of law is to serve the interests of the individual, particular laws that seem to violate any intelligible conception of what it is to serve such interests, or that violate a particular legal order's public articulation of a conception of such service, will put law under stress. Judicial review has then a twofold function: to attempt to offer an interpretation of the law that is consistent with it serving the interests of the individuals subject to it, and, if an interpretation of this sort is not possible, to bring to the surface—to the attention of the public—the inconsistency. Values then play a legitimate role in interpretation but do not necessarily or even desirably determine outcomes. The triumph of the rule of law, on the procedural conception, does not reside in assured judicial victory over politicians, but in politicians being forced in the last resort to make absolutely explicit what their intentions are.

The methodology of the rule of law is nothing new; it is little more than a rearticulation of the common law tradition, as Fuller himself acknowledged in his analysis of Coke's famous claim in *Dr Bonham's Case* that: 'the common law will control Acts of Parliament, and sometimes adjudge them to be utterly void: for when an Act of Parliament is against common right and reason, or repugnant, or impossible to be performed, the common law will control it, and adjudge such act to be void.'[21]

As Fuller points out, the reference to substantive rightness in the idea of common right might seem odd in a case where the issue was the independence of a disciplinary body which collected half of the penalties levied on the physicians it regulated. But it is not so odd if by common right Coke meant rights acquired through law and then taken away by law and if the legislative indecency he detected was a matter of a statute contradicting 'essential purposive efforts moving in an opposite direction'.[22] In other words, the requirement that adjudication be impartial and independent was an aspiration of the legal order at the time, one undermined by the royal grant of authority to the physicians. The willingness of the monarch to respond positively to the judgment would indicate his seriousness about governing by law—in accordance with legality—rather than by some other means.

Goldsworthy seems to accept this methodology wholesale when, as we saw, he responds to the issue of abdication of the democratic right of rights by saying that the right is compatible with delegations of power subject to the right to override the exercise of power. What this tells us is that in Goldsworthy's view the common law basis of judicial review is legitimate, as long as judges are subject to legislative override. He might add that it is not the values on the basis of which judges review that make review legitimate, but the ability of the legislature to override the judges, so that the decision by the legislature not to override is a kind of tacit consent. But it is worth recalling that in the 1958

[21] Fuller, n. 1 above, 99–101.

[22] Ibid.

manifesto Hart rejected just this device of the tacit consent of the legislature, one that dates back at least as far as Hobbes, as the key to understanding constraints on ultimate legal authority.

In this respect, Hart was right. Once one understands ultimate legal authority as constrained, the constraints cannot be regarded as the property of the very body that is supposed to be constrained, otherwise the constraints prove illusory. The site of articulation of the constraints must lie elsewhere, even if the legislature can override them. Hart's mistake is to suppose that that articulation can happen without a conception of the values that are served by the constraints.[23]

Moreover, that the site for articulation must lie elsewhere does not amount to saying that judges are in exclusive occupation of the site. Other officials—including those who staff the agencies of government—have a legitimate role in giving expression to such values, and the legislature itself is presumed to be in the same business, which is why judges should operate with a principle of charity in interpretation, lest they insult the ultimate legal authority. In short, all the institutions of legal order are to be understood as involved in a common project, one that seeks to justify exercise of public power by explicit references to the values that make it an authority rather than the 'gunman writ large'.

This understanding makes a lot more sense of the idea put forward by the democratic legal positivists of the 'dignity' of legislation than their own Rosseauian thought that the dignity is the product of some alchemy in voting.[24] It invites the attention of legal theory to such important issues as the democratic deficit involved in the control of parliament by the executive, a fact of life in parliamentary democracies which might be far more debilitating to democracy that the often exaggerated effects of giving judges explicit review authority. Moreover, it raises directly issues about the acceptability of limits on even the most fundamental values, as long as the limits are appropriately justified. As Janet Hiebert suggests in Chapter 11 in this volume, we need to turn our attention from Dworkin's suggestion that we should take rights seriously, to taking limits on rights seriously. But that thought presupposes that we take rights seriously and construct an account of the rule of law that accommodates both rights and their justified limits.

[23] Hart himself wavered on this point, both in his account of the point of the rule of recognition and in his account of the minimum content of natural law. See Fuller, n. 1 above, 142–4 and 184–6.

[24] For valuable suggestions about how these values should be articulated by other official actors, see Hiebert, Ch. 11 below, and Tushnet, Ch. 10 below. Hiebert is sceptical of the idea that this common project amounts to a 'dialogue'. That idea is defended by George Williams, Ch. 12 below.

INSTITUTIONAL DESIGNS

10

Non-judicial Review

MARK TUSHNET

If nothing else, familiarity leads us to assume that constitutional review must occur in courts and that non-judicial actors—politicians, said in a disparaging tone of voice—could not do a decent job of constitutional review were they given the chance. Courts are said to be distinctively the forum of principle, the legislature and executive the forum of politics. And, while politics is good enough in its place, constitutionalism requires constraints on politics that politics itself cannot supply. On a different level, courts are said to perform a function of constitutional settlement that would be less effective were non-judicial actors to engage in constitutional review.[1]

In this chapter I examine three practices of non-judicial constitutional review, which involve constitutional review conducted by elected officials (or their direct subordinates). The contrasts with judicial behaviour are largely implicit, and so I briefly identify here the incentives and structures for judges and quasi-judicial bureaucrats who interpret constitutional norms. A judge has a disinterested desire to interpret the constitution correctly according to some normative theory she or he holds, an interest in advancing public policy goals—ensuring that the government performs well—to the extent compatible with the judge's normative interpretative theory, an interest in developing a reputation as a good judge among some real or imagined reference group, an interest in being an important player in the nation's constitutional order, an interest in getting the job done while leaving adequate time for leisure, and perhaps some additional interests. Some non-judicial officials may have the first of these interests, which I sometimes refer to as a professional and bureaucratic interest in providing disinterested constitutional interpretation. What the judge does *not* have is an interest in satisfying the demands of some constituency in a position to affect the judge's tenure in the job.[2]

A substantially longer version of this chapter appears in the *Harvard Journal on Legislation*, where I acknowledge assistance from and comments by a large number of readers of the chapter's earlier versions. The previously published material is reproduced here by kind permission of the *Harvard Journal on Legislation*.

[1] L. Alexander and F. Schauer, 'On Extrajudicial Constitutional Interpretation', (1997) 110 *Harvard Law Review* 1359–87.

[2] Elected judges do have electoral interests of this sort, and a judge who desires promotion to some other position—whether elevation to a different judicial post or appointment to a non-judicial one—can be responsive indirectly to the electoral interests of the appointing official.

In examining constitutional review by non-judicial officials, I try to bring out the effects that different institutional structures and, in particular, different incentives have on the officials' performance, with an eye to comparing the effectiveness of non-judicial constitutional review with that of judicial constitutional review. Why would electoral actors and their subordinates take the task of constitutional review seriously? In particular, why would elected officials resist pressures from their constituencies to pursue some policies arguably inconsistent with constitutional requirements? The answer lies in incentives and structures that, taken together, make the practices I examine not dramatically different from judicial review. I end by identifying what might be truly distinctive about judicial constitutional review, and suggest that the necessary comparative judgment about the relative ability of courts and non-judicial actors to perform constitutional review well is harder than our familiar understandings would have it.

The Constitutional Point of Order in the United States Senate

A US senator may raise a point of order regarding any bill under consideration, to the effect that the bill if adopted would violate the Constitution. Ordinarily the Senate's presiding officer initially rules on points of order, with the possibility of appeal to the Senate as a whole. Senate precedent establishes, however, that points of order based on constitutionality are automatically referred to the Senate for disposition by a roll-call vote recording the votes of each senator.

Formal constitutional points of order are rare. I have been able to identify fewer than ten constitutional points of order raised since 1970. Plainly, many bills and enacted statutes raise constitutional questions that are never subject to a constitutional point of order. Senators have no obligation to use the procedure. This points to an important and obvious difference between senatorial and judicial consideration of constitutional questions: subject only to justiciability questions, courts *must* address constitutional questions litigants present to them, while senators have no obligation to raise a constitutional point of order. Conceding, then, that the constitutional point of order is not a substitute for judicial review, I turn to examining the quality of the senators' discussions when they do deal with constitutional points of order.

Debates on constitutional points of order contain several elements, the proportions varying with the subject matter and the political context. First, senators discuss whether a proposal is constitutional by referring to relevant judicial decisions. Secondly, senators supplement their use of court decisions by invoking the constitutional principles they believe underlie those decisions. Thirdly, senators rely directly on the Constitution and basic principle, without drawing in any significant way on court decisions. Senators refer to 'the simple language of the U.S. Constitution',[3] and invoke general separation-of-powers principles.[4]

Finally, senators discuss whether they should even make their own independent judgments about the constitutionality of the proposals. In a sense, these debates are about whether a constitutional point of order is itself out of order. A supporter of a proposal to allow the president to veto particular appropriations in a larger bill, for example, said, 'I want to pass this amendment, send it to the House, have them pass it, have the President sign it, and let the Supreme Court decide whether it is constitutional to do this.'[5] More often, and not surprisingly, senators assert their constitutional responsibility to interpret the Constitution on their own, sometimes referring to the oath of office they take to uphold the Constitution.

The constitutional arguments made in these debates are usually quite truncated. They contain few quotations from cases or even the Constitution, and, of course, no citations. They are, after all, debates and not judicial opinions. In some ways, too, the debates are telegraphic, with senators making shorthand allusions to more elaborate arguments they do not develop fully. Taking these considerations into account, it seems to me that nearly all the debates contain the skeletons of decent constitutional arguments, and sometimes there is a bit of flesh on the bones. We do not have transcripts of the discussions at the closed conferences of Supreme Court justices, but the evidence we have from notes the justices take suggests that the Senate discussions of constitutional questions are not that different from the actual face-to-face discussions the justices have.[6] If conference discussions set the standard (rather than, for example, published Supreme Court opinions), the senators seem to do a decent job of constitutional interpretation.

But, a sceptic might suggest, these debates on constitutional points of order are no more than sideshows to the main stage, the Senate's consideration of the policy wisdom of the proposals before it. The correspondence between votes on constitutional points of order and votes on the merits is extremely close. This correspondence suggests that the constitutional point of order does not in fact narrow the range of matters senators think about before they vote. It seems as if the constitutional analysis senators engage in actually does no independent work. Senators take the position on the constitutional point of order that matches their position on the merits, and they do so because of their views on the merits.

The suggestion, then, is that senators' votes on constitutional points of order simply reflect, without change, their views on the policy questions raised by the

[3] See, for example, 130 *Congressional Record* 10857 (statement of Senator Pete Domenici).

[4] See, for example, ibid. 10858 (statement of Senator John Stennis).

[5] Ibid. 10861 (statement of Senator Alan Dixon).

[6] For a compilation of the notes, see D. Dickson (ed.), *The Supreme Court in Conference (1940–1985): The Private Discussions Behind Nearly 300 Supreme Court Decisions* (New York: Oxford University Press, 2001).

underlying proposals. This suggestion might be bolstered by two related observations. Senators rarely raise constitutional points of order even though many proposals could certainly be the subject of such points. Senators also advert to constitutional questions in ordinary debate without raising a constitutional point of order.

Why, then, use the constitutional point of order? The answer might be something like this: the appearance of identity between policy views and constitutional ones is misleading. Actually, some senators believe that the proposal is *unwise* as a matter of public policy. They also believe that their constituents mistakenly believe that the proposal is a good one. The senators therefore fear adverse electoral consequences from voting according to their policy views. But, the senators believe as well that their constituents will *not* punish them electorally for voting against a proposal that the senators believe to be unconstitutional.

Why might senators think that voting to uphold a constitutional point of order will insulate them from electoral harm? Consider two possibilities: *timing* and *responsibility*.

Nelson Lund's brief discussion of Congress's adoption of a statute that would have made it a crime to burn an American flag in the context of a political protest illustrates the timing explanation.[7] Congress had before it two proposals, a statute (largely supported by Democrats) that sought to conform a prohibition of flag-burning to the Supreme Court's invalidation of a Texas flag-burning statute, and a constitutional amendment (largely supported by Republicans) that would have specifically authorized legislatures to adopt flag-burning legislation. By adopting the statute, senators deferred consideration of the constitutional amendment. The deferral would have been permanent had the Supreme Court upheld the new federal statute, but even a temporary deferral might be valuable for senators opposed to anti-flag-burning legislation but facing a public demand that something be done. Deferral would be 'a delaying tactic meant to divert attention away from a constitutional amendment until after popular interest in the matter subsided'.[8] Lund finds support for this explanation from the votes of senators who 'voted against the constitutional amendment that would have authorized the statute they purported to support even after the Supreme Court struck that statute down'.[9]

The reason that timing might matter in this way needs elaboration. Electoral retaliation is always delayed until the next election. On Lund's account, the risk of electoral retaliation evaporates because senators believe that voters' preferences will change: voters who wanted an enforceable flag-burning statute in 1989 would care more about other things by 1990 or 1992, when they would consider whether to re-elect a senator who voted for the statute but against the constitutional amendment.

[7] N. Lund, 'Rational Choice at the Office of Legal Counsel', (1993) 15 *Cardozo Law Review* 471–2.
[8] Ibid. 471. [9] Ibid.

There are several difficulties with the timing explanation. References to the desirability of letting things cool off pervade the arguments favouring the adoption of an anti-flag-burning statute over amending the Constitution. Senators who voted for the statute simply to defer consideration of the constitutional amendment, it might be said, voted in a way that assured the implementation of their constituents' *long-term* preferences rather than of their passing preferences.

There is another reason to discount the timing explanation for the Senate votes in the flag-burning controversy. Notably, the timing explanation does not by itself explain why a senator would vote to *reject* the constitutional point of order and adopt a statute the senator believes will be held unconstitutional. The length of time between the vote on the constitutional point of order and the next election is the same no matter how the senator votes. What seems to matter is that the senator might be able to say to constituents, 'I tried to get you a flag-burning statute, but the Supreme Court wouldn't let me'. The possibility that the senator will also have to explain a vote against a constitutional amendment that would have authorized a flag-burning statute complicates the picture. The senator's response actually assumes that the constituents continue to desire the adoption of an enforceable flag-burning statute. The senator's challenger can point out that by voting against the constitutional amendment, the senator did not try as hard as he or she could have to get the constituents the flag-burning statute they still want.

Perhaps that complication actually explains how the timing explanation works. The senator may not be able to explain to constituents why the existing Constitution—the one invoked in the constitutional point of order—makes it impossible to enact an enforceable flag-burning statute. But, the senator *might* be able to explain to constituents why it would be a bad thing to amend the Constitution to authorize such a statute.

A senator who sincerely wanted a flag-burning statute might think that obtaining one by means of amending the Constitution would leave the nation worse off than it would be without a flag-burning statute. The senator's concern might be twofold. An apparently narrow constitutional amendment directed solely at authorizing flag-burning statutes might be taken by future Congresses and Supreme Courts as expressing a broader policy about the basic principles of free expression, thereby authorizing larger incursions on free expression than the senator believes appropriate. Or, the senator might be concerned about setting a precedent not about free expression but about amending the Constitution itself. The senator might believe that proponents of unwise constitutional amendments (as the senator sees the proposals) would be emboldened were the Constitution amended to authorize flag-burning statutes. The cost of forgoing an enforceable flag-burning statute might be lower than the costs associated with amending the Constitution. Making sense of the timing explanation requires that we add to the constitutional point of order itself the possibility that a proposal will be made to amend the Constitution.

The *responsibility* explanation for invoking the Constitution rather than policy is that the constitutional point of order allows senators to shift responsibility for the proposal's defeat from themselves to the Constitution. Senator David Boren's statements in the line-item veto debate illustrate how the responsibility explanation might work. The debate concerned a proposal that would have allowed the president to strike specific appropriations from a comprehensive budget bill. Many opponents of the line-item veto statute thought it was bad policy. Senator Boren, a former governor who had exercised a line-item veto over his state's budget, clearly did not. He expressed his willingness to co-sponsor a constitutional amendment creating a line-item veto power. But, he said, 'as much as I favor the line-item veto, I feel I have no choice but to vote that it does not comply with the Constitution of the United States'.[10] This sense of compulsion makes the Constitution and not the senator responsible for the proposal's defeat.

Why might senators take the Constitution seriously? To answer that question we must know more generally why senators take the positions they do. Political scientists' studies of legislative behaviour suggest that legislators seek to develop what they personally believe to be good public policy within the constraints imposed by their constituents' desires.[11] That is, legislators want to do good as they see it, but they also want to be re-elected.

A senator might hold a personal belief that good public policy includes compliance with the Constitution. That is, she might think that no policy is a good one that violates what the senator believes to be constitutional requirements. Senators with such a belief take the Constitution seriously just because they take their role in making good public policy seriously, and the problems they may have with their constituents over their personal constitutional views are no different from the problems they may have over ordinary policy questions.

In addition, a legislator may gain some freedom to act on his personal constitutional views by delivering the pork to his constituency, building up a reservoir of goodwill that leads constituents to accept the legislator's rejection on constitutional grounds of a policy the constituents favour.

Finally, constituents themselves may think that complying with the Constitution is a component of good public policy. Such constituents may agree with the senator's constitutional views, or may defer to the senator's judgment about what the Constitution requires. In either case, these constituents provide electoral support for the senator.

These considerations suggest why senators' electoral incentives do not necessarily lead them to ignore their own considered constitutional views when voting on a constitutional point of order. Possibility is not necessity, of course, and the coincidence between constitutional positions and policy positions might be suspicious. But, it may be wrong to see votes on constitutional points of order

[10] 130 *Congressional Record* 10863 (3 May 1984).

[11] See R. F. Fenno, Jr., *Congressmen in Committees* (Boston: Little, Brown, 1973).

as politically expedient reflections of underlying policy views. We might instead see the votes on the constitutional points of order as reflecting considered *constitutional* judgments, influenced but not dictated by policy views.

Consider the following theory of constitutional interpretation. The Constitution should be interpreted in light of text, original understanding, accumulated precedent, and fundamental principle. Often, and particularly in the most contentious cases, those sources will not conclusively establish that a proposal (or enacted statute) is constitutional or unconstitutional. If they do not, one can properly resolve the constitutional question by taking into account whether the proposal or statute would improve the functioning of the government as an ongoing operation. Sometimes senators holding this theory of constitutional interpretation will find themselves in precisely this situation of interpretative openness. When they do, the coincidence between their policy views and their votes on a constitutional point of order indicates a fully responsible exercise of the senators' duty to vote on the constitutional point of order solely with reference to their theoretically informed view of the proposal's constitutionality.

Finally, it seems worth emphasizing that the constitutional theory I have described is a perfectly respectable one that judges could hold as well. In a sense, then, the Senate's practice on constitutional points of order *might* support the proposition that non-judicial constitutional review can be little different from judicial constitutional review—if judicial review is understood in a specific way and if senators in fact adopt the theory of constitutional interpretation that could justify the apparent congruence between policy views and votes on constitutional points of order.

Senators' incentives may be less mysterious than judges'. Still, to the extent that practice on constitutional points of order can inform our judgment, senators stack up reasonably well in the comparison with judges, in part because we can understand how senators' incentives might actually lead them to take the Constitution seriously.

Bill clearances at the Office of Legal Counsel

The Office of Legal Counsel (OLC) in the US Department of Justice, acting by delegation from the attorney-general as the executive branch's legal adviser, reviews legislative proposals introduced in Congress for constitutionality. OLC is headed by an assistant attorney-general nominated by the president and confirmed by the Senate. The office staff includes several deputies, one of whom has primary responsibility for bill comments. All the deputies are political appointees. The staff lawyers are a combination of young attorneys, drawn to serving a particular administration but sometimes staying with the office for at least a few years after the administration they joined has departed, and career civil servants, who provide a long-term institutional memory. The bill clearance process, which is only one part of OLC's role as chief constitutional adviser to the executive branch, involves an attempt to screen *all* legislative proposals for constitutionality.

OLC's constitutional analysis occurs within an executive department, by subordinate officials in an administration with its own political agenda. That OLC is part of a specific administration means that OLC's constitutional comments might be affected by the administration's interest in moving its agenda through Congress. That it is part of the executive branch means that OLC typically defends the president's prerogatives against what its attorneys see as threats to the presidency as an institution. Observers suggest that the latter effect is more substantial than the former.

Staff attorneys will of course usually know the administration's position on major proposals important to the administration, where OLC will interact with the White House in developing the proposals to avoid constitutional difficulties. But sometimes the staff attorneys drafting comments on a particular bill offered by a member of Congress might not be aware that the administration has a position on the proposal. Even more, the attorneys will rarely know whether a proposal comes from an ally of the administration or is being pushed by someone whose vote the administration needs on other issues. Finally, as a matter of interpretative method, the courts have often said a great deal about substantive constitutional questions raised by legislative proposals. Judicial decisions as a source for constitutional interpretation thus may weigh against the incumbent administration's policy positions. OLC's bill comments may therefore be reasonably disinterested relative to the specific legislative agenda of the administration in office.

OLC has good strategic reasons for being reasonably disinterested. As Randolph Moss observes, 'Congress is less likely to take seriously a constitutional objection to proposed legislation if that objection, or the general approach of the Office, is seen as policy—as opposed to legally—driven.'[12] An administration that seeks political cover by obtaining a statement from OLC that some proposal is unconstitutional will hardly be helped if the perception becomes widespread that OLC's comments simply use constitutional terminology as a way of advancing the administration's policy agenda. Yet, as I argued in connection with the congruence between senators' constitutional and policy positions, principled constitutional analysis often leaves ample room for policy considerations. Where it does, OLC's comments will be consistent with both existing doctrine and the administration's policy agenda.

The flag-burning episode illustrates how OLC's legal analysis might conflict with an administration's legislative agenda. OLC's position was that Supreme Court doctrine clearly indicated that no anti-flag-burning statute would be held constitutional. The Bush Administration therefore supported adopting a constitutional amendment. The OLC view may actually have weakened the Adminis-

[12] R. D. Moss, 'Executive Branch Legal Interpretation: A Perspective from the Office of Legal Counsel', (2000) 52 *Administrative Law Review* 1311.

tration's position, because it allowed opponents to make the argument that it was unwise to amend the Constitution.

The line-item veto controversy provides another example of how OLC legal analyses might conflict with an administration's agenda. The Reagan Administration believed that it could gain greater control over fiscal policy if the president had the power to veto specific items in larger appropriations bills. The Constitution provides that the president shall have the opportunity to sign or veto 'Every Bill which shall have passed' both houses of Congress. Conservatives had argued that the practice of packaging a large number of unrelated appropriations in a single statute transformed that statute from a single constitutional 'Bill'. Instead, they argued, each sub-unit within these larger packages was a 'Bill' within the meaning of the Constitution, and therefore could be vetoed individually. Charles Cooper, the OLC head, concluded, however, that the Constitution could not be read in this way.[13] Here too OLC's legal analysis appeared to conflict with the administration's policy agenda, supporting the proposition that OLC *can* offer legal advice in a reasonably disinterested way.

Administration proposals are likely to be vetted by OLC for constitutionality before they emerge in the public eye, and OLC's participation in drafting legislation allows it to trim away the most constitutionally problematic features, modifying legislative proposals—and thereby altering the administration's initial (politically driven) agenda—in the service of a more disinterested view of the Constitution's requirements. When embodied in concrete proposals, that is, an administration's agenda may raise few constitutional red flags within OLC. In addition, many legislative proposals do no more than pose a 'litigation risk', in OLC's terms, and disinterested advice to that effect is likely to do little to impede the progress of an administration proposal.

But modifying proposals to take account of OLC's constitutional concerns almost inevitably reduces the degree to which the proposal, if enacted, will advance the administration's policy goals. Students of the Canadian Charter of Rights have criticized the process of what they call Charter-proofing, in which the executive branch modifies its proposals in response to constitutional concerns expressed by the civil servants who vet legislation for compatibility with the Charter, but offers modifications that are more extensive than are strictly required by the Charter. Charter-proofing can be a problem when legally oriented civil servants advise policy-oriented Cabinet members, because the civil servants may be less attentive than they should be to the administration's policy goals and the Cabinet member may not be in a good position to observe that the civil servants may be overestimating the risk that the legislation would be held unconstitutional.[14] The organization of OLC reduces the chance that excessive risk will distort the administration's policy agenda through its

[13] (1988) 12 *Opinions of the Office of Legal Counsel* 159.

[14] For some examples, see Ewing, Ch. 16 below; and for a general discussion and defence of Charter-proofing, see K. Roach, 'The Attorney General and the Charter Revisited', (2000) 50 *University of Toronto Law Journal* 1.

combination of civil servants with legally trained political appointees, but some degree of risk aversion probably remains and may adversely affect the shape of an administration's legislative proposals.

Proposals adversely affecting the prerogatives of the presidency as an institution are different from the general run of legislation. With respect to such proposals, OLC takes as its charge protecting the presidency, not the incumbent president. Sometimes protecting the presidency means *opposing* the incumbent,[15] who might have a view of the Constitution different from that taken by OLC, or who might have political reasons for accepting, in exchange for what the president regards as more important immediate policy goals, what OLC regards as incursions on the office. In short, OLC provides advice that is more interested than disinterested when the presidency's prerogatives are in question.

Judicial guidance on questions regarding the institutional presidency is less available than it is with respect to other constitutional questions. When courts have addressed such questions, 'OLC regularly gives cases unfavorable to executive branch prerogatives *vis-à-vis* Congress a far more limited reading than cases in other areas and, conversely, gives favorable cases a very broad reading.'[16] Because judicial interpretations provide less guidance here than in other areas, historic practice plays a more important role in interpretation. The president may wish to give up some aspect of the presidency's prerogatives for reasons of policy or principle. Yet, because in this area constitutional precedent is often set by the executive's course of conduct, relinquishing a constitutional position to gain some other policy advantage undermines the office of the presidency in two ways. It directly sets a precedent about what counts as a permissible incursion on that office, and it demonstrates that the office can survive and continue to function after a particular prerogative has been limited. Thus, OLC's position as defender of the institution of the presidency may bring it into conflict with the policy objectives of the president it serves.

Precise and systematic information of OLC's bill clearance practice is obviously thin. Several conclusions seem justified, however. First, OLC probably presents constitutional analyses as disinterested as those of the courts when it assesses proposals that OLC staff attorneys and deputies do not believe to be part of incumbent administration's legislative programme. That class may be larger than one might initially think, because those accustomed to thinking about legislative politics may assimilate proposals by administration allies to administration proposals, while OLC attorneys and even deputies may not. The fact that OLC staff attorneys are civil service bureaucrats, that is, weighs against the fact that they also serve particular administrations. At the same time, however, the disinterestedness of OLC analyses arises in part because OLC attorneys assess constitutionality with existing court decisions in mind.

[15] Obviously, *opposing* here means something like 'forcefully advocating an alternative position within the administration'.

[16] J. O. McGinnis, 'Models of the Opinion Function of the Attorney General: A Normative, Descriptive, and Historical Prolegomenon', (1993) 15 *Cardozo Law Review* 431.

Secondly, OLC analyses of core administration proposals will certainly be slanted to favour the administration's position. OLC may help shape the proposals to avoid severe litigation risks, but the aim will be to ensure that the legislation, if enacted, would survive constitutional attack, not to ensure that the legislation actually is constitutional according to a disinterested approach to constitutional interpretation.

Thirdly, OLC analyses of proposals that OLC attorneys believe would undermine the presidency's prerogatives will take quite aggressive positions in support of the presidency, again because of OLC's self-identified bureaucratic mission to defend the presidency's prerogatives. As indicated earlier, the relevant constitutional law in this area is made, in large part, by practice and, in much smaller part, by judicial decision. This, in turn, has two implications. We will rarely have independent criteria by which we could assess whether OLC's position is 'correct' in some ultimate sense. Yet, the near-absence of judicial intervention means that we cannot really compare OLC's performance as an interpreter of the Constitution with the courts' performance. All we can say is that in this particular area OLC has incentives that push it away from disinterestedness.

Ministerial statements of compatibility under the Human Rights Act 1998

The Human Rights Act 1998 makes many provisions of the European Convention on Human Rights enforceable in the British courts. The creation of a form of judicial review in Great Britain has attracted by far the largest share of the attention lavished on the Act, because of the tension between judicial review and traditions of parliamentary supremacy. Section 19 of the Act requires that a minister in charge of a legislative proposal: 'make a statement to the effect that in his view the provisions of the Bill are compatible with the Convention rights . . . or . . . make a statement to the effect that although he is unable to make a statement of compatibility the government nevertheless wishes the House to proceed with the Bill.'[17] I will call the latter type of statement an *inability* statement.

The point of these provisions is clear. Just as judges are supposed to become comfortable with interpreting statutes to make them consistent with the Convention, so ministers are supposed to become comfortable with submitting to Parliament only bills that are in their view consistent with the Convention. But, as one supporter of the Human Rights Act puts it, 'governments are rarely, if ever, prepared to own up to violating fundamental rights'.[18] How are the

[17] Human Rights Act 1998, s 19(1). These statements of compatibility or inability to make such a statement 'must be in writing and be published in such manner as the Minister making it considers appropriate'; s 19(2).

[18] F. Klug, *Values for a Godless Age: The Story of the UK's New Bill of Rights* (London: Penguin Books, 2000), 166.

statements of compatibility supposed to make governments more likely to do that?

The answer combines political and bureaucratic elements. The ministerial statement of compatibility itself can be brief, but Members of Parliament might use the statement as a predicate for questions about the reasons the minister has for believing the legislative proposal to be compatible with the European Convention. And, obviously, a minister who introduces a proposal accompanied by an inability statement might be embarrassed at having to face charges of violating fundamental rights (where the proposal is thought to be incompatible with Convention rights) or of incompetence for being unable to do part of the job, that is, to determine compatibility.

Ministers will rely on their departments' civil servants, or on some general 'Human Rights Act Compliance Unit', to provide the detailed justifications that they can expect other Members of Parliament to demand. The civil servants charged with determining whether a minister can make a statement of compatibility will be committed to ensuring adherence to the European Convention because that is their job.

Francesca Klug suggests, however, that the requirement of statements of compatibility 'has a farcical element', because ministerial statements will become as routine 'as a cry of "order, order", from the Speaker, making its value appear somewhat dubious'.[19] The problem goes deeper than that. Accurate and sincere statements of compatibility and inability statements may both be so easy to issue that they may not place much constraint on a government's ability to advance whatever legislative agenda it has.

The reason that inability statements may be easy to make is that a statement that a minister is *unable* to make a statement of a proposal's compatibility with the Convention is not a statement that the proposal *is* incompatible with the Convention. Actual incompatibility is, of course, one reason a minister might have to make an inability statement, but it is not the only reason. As Geoffrey Marshall points out, a minister can make an inability statement for a variety of other reasons; for example, because, in the minister's view, there is insufficient time to determine whether it is possible to make a statement of compatibility but there is a pressing need for the legislation.[20] Or, a minister might say, in effect, that the question of the proposal's compatibility with the Convention is a quite difficult one, which the minister has been unable to resolve in the time available. Or, finally, the minister might refrain from making a statement of compatibility on the ground that the complex issues are better explored in debate in the House of Commons. Marshall suggests the possibility of ministers taking a position similar to that taken by some senators. The minister might defend an inability statement

[19] F. Klug, *Values for a Godless Age: The Story of the UK's New Bill of Rights* (London: Penguin Books, 2000), 170.

[20] G. Marshall, 'The United Kingdom Human Rights Act, 1998', in V. C. Jackson and M. Tushnet (eds.), *Comparative Constitutional Law: Defining the Field* (Westport, Conn.: Greenwood Press, 2002).

by referring to the possibility of judicial consideration of compatibility after the proposal is adopted: 'I am unable to state that the proposal is compatible with Convention rights, but there's no need to worry about my inability, because if the proposal is in fact incompatible with those rights, the courts will say so later.'

Inability statements, then, might not have the political effects hoped for, because they need not be public statements of the government's willingness to violate Convention rights. Further, with the stick of political discipline taken away, civil servants may have less power, and therefore less bureaucratic reason, to insist that legislation move forward only if they can draft statements of compatibility.

Statements of compatibility may be easy to make, too. First, as with bill clearance at the OLC, the largest portion of proposed legislation will raise no substantial questions under the Convention. Secondly, and more importantly, the Home Office has announced the sensible policy that the mere existence of arguments supporting the conclusion that a proposal is compatible with Convention rights is insufficient to justify issuing a statement of compatibility, but also that such a statement will be issued when 'the balance of argument supports the view that the provisions are compatible' with Convention rights.[21] The Convention simultaneously defines rights at a relatively high level of abstraction and incorporates in the definition of particular rights qualifications to the effect that the right is not violated when a government pursues valuable social objectives. Under such provisions it will not be difficult for a minister to conclude that the 'balance of arguments' supports a statement of compatibility.

Thirdly, and probably most importantly, the Human Rights Act directs that Convention rights are to be interpreted by referring to decisions by the European Court of Human Rights.[22] That Court, in turn, has developed a doctrine of deference that gives nations a 'margin of appreciation' in their actions alleged to violate the Convention.[23] The 'margin of appreciation' doctrine gives civil servants even more space within which to find proposals compatible with Convention rights.

The 'margin of appreciation' doctrine has two components. The first is ordinary deference to administrative or executive judgment. Civil servants attempting to determine compatibility should not invoke this component of the 'margin of appreciation' doctrine. It is simply incoherent for such a civil servant to invoke a doctrine of deference to administrative discretion. The question for the civil servant, after all, is precisely whether to exercise discretion in a way that violates the Convention as the civil servant sees things.

The 'margin of appreciation' doctrine's second component, however, can play a large role in the civil servant's deliberations. The European Court developed the doctrine because it recognized that it was an international court with

[21] *Hansard* 83540 (statement of Home Secretary Jack Straw, 5 May 1999).
[22] Human Rights Act 1998, s 2(1)(a).
[23] See *Handyside v United Kingdom*, 24 Eur Ct HR (ser A), 1 EHRR 737 (1976).

authority to review legislation adopted by numerous states facing widely varying problems and with distinctive cultures, some of whose elements should rationally be taken into account in determining whether a particular statute violates Convention rights. The civil servant whose task is to determine whether a proposal is compatible with Convention rights can sensibly ask 'Does this proposal lie within that portion of the margin of appreciation arising from distinctive national problems and characteristics?' Ministers and their governments always have good reasons, from their own point of view, for proposing new legislation. A good lawyer will find it relatively easy to find in those reasons some distinctive national characteristics or problems that place the proposal within the margin of appreciation.

Two sceptics about the utility of statements of compatibility point to the rapid enactment of the Criminal Justice (Terrorism and Conspiracy) Act in 1998 to show how politicians can 'brush aside concerns about patent breaches' of Convention rights.[24] The Act was the Government's response to a terrorist bombing in Omagh, Northern Ireland, in August 1998. The provisions the critics questioned modify rules of evidence in terrorism cases. For example, a defendant's guilt can be inferred from his or her failure to mention any material facts to a police officer after the defendant had been given the opportunity to consult a lawyer.

The European Court of Human Rights has held that legislation affecting an accused person's right to remain silent may violate the Convention's provisions guaranteeing a fair trial and a presumption of innocence.[25] The Court assesses the impact of inferences from silence on the particular trial: 'The Court must... concentrate its attention on the role played by the inferences in the proceedings against the applicant and especially in his conviction.'[26] Under this sort of balancing test, sometimes applying the provisions of the Criminal Justice (Terrorism and Conspiracy) Act will violate the Convention.

Does that mean that the legislation contemplates 'patent breaches' of the Convention and that a statement of compatibility necessarily must 'brush aside' such concerns? I doubt it. Drawing on concepts familiar in US constitutional law, we can say that we are considering a proposal that, as applied, might be unconstitutional. The statement of compatibility, however, refers to the proposal's facial validity. Distinguishing between facial validity and 'as applied' unconstitutionality helps us understand why a minister might find it easy to make a statement of compatibility. It seems unreasonable to deny ministers the opportunity to make such statements merely because one can identify some circumstances under which applying the proposal would violate Convention rights. Then, however, it becomes easier to issue a statement of compatibility

[24] C. Walker and R. L. Weaver, 'The United Kingdom Bill of Rights 1998: The Modernisation of Rights in the Old World', (2000) 33 *University of Michigan Journal of Law Reform* 557. The Government had indicated its intention to comply with the Human Rights Act 1998 before its effective date.

[25] *(John) Murray v United Kingdom*, 22 EHRR 29 (1996).

[26] Ibid. 50.

in the face of well-founded arguments that the proposal might be applied in a way that violates Convention rights. The minister can assert, reasonably, that the balance of arguments favours facial validity even though critics are unquestionably right in spinning out scenarios where the proposal would violate Convention rights.

The statement of compatibility issued in connection with another statute illustrates the way in which interaction between facial validity and the statement of compatibility might work to reduce the constraint imposed by requiring such a statement. The Immigration and Asylum Act 1999 gives ministers broad authority to transmit or receive personal information about asylum-seekers and other immigrants to or from other nations. Article 8 of the European Convention creates a 'right to respect for... private... life', which has been interpreted to cover informational privacy.[27] The authority given ministers might be exercised in a way that violated Article 8. The minister in charge of the legislation made a statement of compatibility, asserting that 'those using the Act would not use or disclose information in a way which was incompatible with... Article 8 of the Convention'.[28] Here the minister avoided possible facial invalidity by making a commitment to principles of implementation. But, it would seem easy enough for a minister to assert, with respect to *any* proposed statute, that it would not be implemented in a manner that violated Convention rights.

A ministerial practice allowing a statement of compatibility to be made despite a serious possibility that the statute would authorize many violations of Convention rights, when the statement is supplemented by representations about enforcement, cannot be a serious constraint on ministers. Civil servants will be asked to draft statements of compatibility *and* the enforcement representations, rather than drafting statutes that avoid the underlying questions about rights violations. Just as the statutes would be written with an eye to substantive Convention rights, so the enforcement representations would be written with an eye to avoiding the equivalent of a vagueness challenge—in this context, a challenge that the statute and representations do not satisfy the Convention requirement that limitations on Convention rights be prescribed by law.

Having argued that ministers will have little difficulty in making, and civil servants little difficulty in drafting, inability statements and statements of compatibility, I nonetheless resist the conclusion that the Human Rights Act strategy for securing non-judicial enforcement of fundamental rights must fail. The reason is simple. The statements of compatibility are just that: statements that the proposal is in fact compatible with Convention rights. The arguments about how easy it might be to make such statements are not arguments that the statements are inaccurate. Ministers will in fact be complying with fundamental

[27] See, for example, *Z v Finland*, 25 EHRR 371 (1998) (involving the disclosure of personal medical records in a criminal trial).

[28] H. Mansfield, 'The Concept of a Lawful Interference with Fundamental Rights', in J. Jowell and J. Cooper (eds.), *Understanding Human Rights Principles* (Oxford: Hart, 2001), 23.

rights when they conclude that the balance of arguments supports a statement of compatibility. The problem is not that ministers and civil servants will disingenuously evade their obligation to determine whether a proposal violates Convention rights. The problem, if there is one, is that the European Convention defines fundamental rights in a way that may be insufficient.

Conclusion

Examining non-judicial constitutional review shows that non-judicial institutions have incentives that provide some 'insulation from political winds'.[29] Because courts are not fully insulated from those winds, and have other institutional characteristics that reduce the value of the settlements they impose, this chapter suggests that the empirical case against non-judicial constitutional review remains to be established.

The activities I have examined do suggest that non-judicial constitutional review may have different characteristics from judicial constitutional review. The experience with the Senate's constitutional point of order brings out the fact that, unlike non-judicial institutions, courts have a general obligation to address questions litigants present to them, subject only to the relatively minor restrictions imposed by justiciability requirements. The Office of Legal Counsel's bill-clearance practice brings out the fact that courts are likely to be marginally more disinterested in assessing the constitutional implications of the sitting administration's legislative programme, and that courts may be substantially more disinterested in assessing the constitutionality of legislation affecting the president's prerogatives. The likely shape of statements of compatibility suggests that courts will do a better job in assessing constitutionality facial validity, that is, its validity without regard to its application in any particular case, unless (as is often the case) the most reasonable approach to constitutionality calls for balancing the competing interests implicated in the range of cases to which the statute applies.

How well, then, does non-judicial constitutional review stack up against judicial constitutional review? Reasonably well, I believe. Non-judicial institutions can balance competing constitutional interests, and, as we have seen, they do so, because they have incentives guiding them towards balancing. Non-judicial institutions may do a reasonable job in assessing legislation that is not central to an administration's policy agenda. Judicial constitutional review may be distinctively valuable when courts make only as-applied rulings invoking rules that the Constitution itself dictates, rather than balancing competing interests. As-applied rulings might be quite common, but the situations in which the Constitution generates rules rather than balancing tests seem far less so.

[29] Alexander and Schauer, n. 1 above, 476.

In the end, I suspect that deeper commitments drive scholars' views on the extent to which they think a constitutional democracy could persist with far more non-judicial constitutional review and far less judicial review. Knowing what happens when non-judicial institutions actually engage in constitutional review might, however, inform the discussion. And so I end with the lame but always accurate observation that this is an area where we need more empirical investigation.

11

Parliament and Rights

JANET L. HIEBERT

Canada adopted the Canadian Charter of Rights and Freedoms in 1982 and, in so doing, fundamentally changed its governing principles. The Charter sets out the rights of the members of the polity in a constitutional bill of rights, empowers individuals to ask courts to review state actions to determine whether protected rights are violated, and authorizes judges to grant remedies where rights have been unjustifiably infringed, which can include nullifying legislation. The decision to adopt the Charter is viewed by many as abandoning reliance on Parliament's judgment in a rights-protecting capacity. But this perspective underestimates the continued importance and potential influence of Parliament's judgment on issues of rights, even under a constitutional bill of rights.

The idea that Parliament continues to have a valid role to resolve social conflicts that involve rights claims might seem odd, particularly to those who equate the salutary benefits of the Charter with judicial review and the power given to judges to nullify legislation that violates rights. But this response reflects the strong influence of American debates about rights, and a corresponding lack of awareness for the range of rights-protecting procedures that exist and which entail different ways of allowing political participation in judgment about rights. This chapter will explore the following three questions: does a political community's decision to utilize a bill of rights, as an instrument for evaluating the merits of legislative decisions, necessarily require that judicial opinions always prevail over political judgment? Should Parliament focus on rights when exercising legislative judgment? And has Parliament the capacity to evaluate legislation from a rights perspective? The context for my discussion will be Parliament's role under the Canadian Charter of Rights and Freedoms. But the argument has broader applicability and is relevant to other political communities that adopt a bill of rights, particularly if the bill of rights includes textual provisions that anticipate and recognize the legitimacy of judicial and political disagreements.

Challenging judicial-centric interpretations of rights

The adoption of the Charter is viewed by many as requiring the primacy of legal judgment about how to reconcile legislative objectives with rights. Many

The material presented in this chapter builds upon the arguments presented in my *Charter Conflicts: What is Parliament's Role?* (Montreal: McGill–Queen's University Press, 2002). The kind permission of McGill–Queen's University Press, is gratefully acknowledged.

Canadian commentators, particularly from the legal community, have been influenced by the calls of some scholars of American constitutionalism to conceive of rights as trumps over political decisions, and to consider judicial determination as final and superior to political judgment.[1] Judicial review of rights, it is argued, places a higher priority on principled decision-making than would otherwise be accorded by the bureaucracy or by Parliament. The office judges hold requires them to resolve conflicts by working 'objectively from the most basic principles and values which underlie the Charter'.[2] Moreover, many are confident that legal judgment is superior to political judgment with respect to ascertaining the meaning of rights and assessing the merits of state actions where rights are implicated. Not only are judges insulated from public and partisan pressures, but many believe that legal rules and constitutional principles, used to review political disagreements involving rights, allow for resolutions that reflect the correct or obviously superior answer. The only qualm some commentators express about the judicial capacity to protect rights is whether judges will have the necessary fortitude to resist pressures for deference towards legislative decisions.

The legislative role, in contrast, is thought of as having little to do with uncovering the meaning of constitutional values or making principled decisions where rights are at stake. Legislative objectives gain their inspiration not from rights but from majoritarian preferences or utilitarian considerations that are informed by costs and convenience. Thus, Parliament's relationship to rights is not that of defender and interpreter. Its decisions, when contrary to judicial interpretations, are said to ignore, restrict, or override rights.

This confidence in the relative merits of legal rulings as distinct from political judgments is well represented in Lorraine Weinrib's work. Weinrib suggests that Canada has undergone a transformation from a legislative to a constitutional state. She characterizes the latter as an advanced evolutionary stage of political development because it subjects majority rule to restrictions that are necessary to respect rights. Weinrib considers judicial review and the power to invalidate legislation essential because legislative decisions, if left unchecked against an external standard of rights, would imperil rights by promoting other (non-rights) goals or by utilizing legislative means that infringe upon rights. Weinrib sees Canada's transformation to a constitutional democracy as nothing short of a revolution, because it has corrected what she considers to be a defective form of governance by removing Parliament's supremacy over the features of liberal democracy.[3]

[1] R. Dworkin, 'Liberalism', in S. Hampshire (ed.), *Public and Private Morality* (New York: Cambridge University Press, 1978); R. Dworkin, *Law's Empire* (Cambridge, Mass.: Harvard University Press, 1986); R. Dworkin, *A Matter of Principle* (Cambridge, Mass.: Harvard University Press, 1985).

[2] D. Beatty, *Talking Heads and the Supremes: The Canadian Production of Constitutional Review* (Toronto: Carswell, 1990), 36.

[3] L. E. Weinrib, 'Canada's Constitutional Revolution', (1999) 33 *Israel Law Review* 13.

Yet the discretion inherent in the task of determining how abstract rights principles should be interpreted and applied to specific legislative circumstances challenges the claim that judicial resolutions of these conflicts deserve primacy over political judgments. Judgment about how rights principles should guide or constrain social policy will be influenced by philosophical assumptions about the role of the state and societal obligations to its more vulnerable members. For example, what are the government's responsibilities to respond to imbalances that accrue because of unequal distributions of resources or power? How active should the government be when trying to anticipate and redress societal harms or social prejudices? In addition to these philosophical and political judgments, the merits of particular legislation can rarely be determined without value-added assumptions about the nature of social problems or the desirability or feasibility of specific legislative responses. Should the state restrict obscenity because many women feel exploited and degraded by obscene images of them? Is mandatory retirement valid, if the decision to provide job opportunities for younger individuals restricts the choices of older people? Can the amount of money that candidates and parties spend in elections be regulated if this restriction on their expression serves to enhance the fairness and equity of opportunities to engage in political debate?

The discretionary nature of judicial review is not confined to philosophical differences about the meaning and scope of rights or the role of the state in redressing social problems. It also arises when evaluating legislative objectives in terms of how they comply with judicial concerns for proportionality. The Canadian Charter differs from the United States Bill of Rights, which does not specifically address the need to reconcile rights with compelling societal objectives. The Charter acknowledges this necessity in its very first clause, which states that rights are subject to limitations where these are reasonable, prescribed by law, and consistent with a free and democratic society. The inclusion of this clause may affect how broadly or narrowly the judiciary interprets rights or conceives of valid state purposes.[4] But whether a bill of rights recognizes explicitly that legislation might justifiably restrict rights, or this fact is implicit in judicial review and revealed by varying the degree of scrutiny that is afforded to particular constitutional provisions, the consequences in terms of the nature of the judicial task are similar. Judges engage in some form of proportionality analysis to evaluate the constitutional justification of legislation when rights are implicated. But the criteria employed necessarily constitute highly discretionary evaluations of the fit between a legislative objective and the means used to achieve it. No matter how the judiciary may attempt to portray proportionality criteria as comprised of objective rules, these judicial assessments entail subjective judgments about how a social policy objective was conceptualized and

[4] S 1 of the Canadian Charter of Rights and Freedoms provides: '*The Canadian Charter of Rights and Freedoms* guarantees the rights and freedoms set out in it subject only to such reasonable limits prescribed by law as can be demonstrably justified in a free and democratic society.'

drafted, and the utility and prudence of alternative and often hypothetical scenarios.

In Canada, the judiciary asks the following questions: is there a rational connection between the legislative objective and means chosen; did the legislation impair rights as little as practically possible; and are the salutary effects of the legislation sufficient to justify its deleterious effects? These inquiries bear more resemblance to policy analysis than to the skills or methodology for which judges can reasonably claim to have expertise. All three questions inevitably lead judges to query whether a better way existed to pursue the legislative objective. Yet judges will generally lack the specialized policy background that is relevant for the analysis undertaken. Judges are also poorly placed to differentiate between conflicting scientific and other scholarly opinions about the merits of conflicting perspectives, and thus may be influenced by the partisan or self-interested interpretations of this evidence that others may offer when trying to argue the merits of their case.[5]

Both the normative and policy elements of resolving rights conflicts give rise to the following question: why should the fact that a political community has decided in favour of rights, as critical standards for evaluating the merits of legislation, necessarily commit itself to accepting only judicial perspectives on how to resolve rights conflicts?

Should Parliament be engaged in rights-based assessments?

The adoption of a bill of rights does not negate a parliamentary role to make careful decisions about whether legislation is consistent with protected rights and values. The idea that only courts can interpret rights represents a cynical and narrow view of a society's commitment to rights. It is cynical because it denies any moral value to Parliament's political judgment about how to resolve rights conflicts and is narrow because it confines the meaning and protection of rights exclusively to what evolves from legal rulings. Moreover, a judicial-centric approach for interpreting rights and resolving conflicts offers only partial protection. Those who view a bill of rights almost entirely as an after-the-fact corrective give insufficient attention to the likelihood that only a fraction of legislative decisions will ever be subject to judicial review. Since legislation often represents a final and authoritative decision about how to reconcile social conflicts where rights claims arise, those who worry about restrictions on rights should be particularly troubled if the protection of rights is dependent entirely upon litigation. The assumption that the Charter will be effective only when courts correct unreasonable legislation provides little security if Parliament does not view itself, or is expected by others, as having an obligation to satisfy

[5] J. L. Hiebert, *Limiting Rights: The Dilemma of Judicial Review* (Montreal: McGill–Queen's University Press, 1996).

itself that its judgment is justified and reasonable in light of the values in the Charter.

The structure of the Charter allows for political judgment about how best to reconcile conflicting values when rights claims arise. It includes a general limitation clause (s 1), which allows Parliament to express its reasons for concluding that legislation is justifiable despite its implications for rights. It is trite to suggest that rights are not absolute. Nevertheless, the prestige associated with the language of rights obscures the fact that not all activities that are claimed as rights, even if so recognized by a court, necessarily warrant uniformly strict protection. Often rights claims will be made that bear little resemblance to a political community's reasons for protecting human actions from the state's coercive powers. Elsewhere I have argued that the importance and significance of the general limitation clause extend beyond the symbolic recognition that rights are not absolute and will be subject to limitations. What this clause allows is broad debate on what kinds of social values and policy objectives are worthwhile, despite their implications for protected rights.[6]

The Charter also contains a legislative override, or notwithstanding clause (s 33), that enables Parliament to give temporary effect to its judgment, even when the judiciary declares legislation inconsistent with the rights in the Charter. The legislative override was included in the Charter as a fundamental concession for provincial government support for this significant constitutional change.[7] But the clause has become unpopular, and the substantial controversy associated with it has meant that most governments are extremely reluctant to invoke this power. Nevertheless, the clause remains an important part of the Charter because it preserves Parliament's ability to disagree with a judicial ruling and give primacy to its judgment, at least temporarily. This prevents institutional stalemates from occurring where the judiciary and Parliament reach profoundly different conclusions about the resolution of conflicting values. Both of these provisions allow for political judgment about how the rights in the Charter should guide or constrain legislative decisions.

Some who share my scepticism about the benefits of a court-centred approach for resolving rights conflicts may not be any more enthusiastic about the merits of a bill of rights even if it can be structured to allow some measure of parliamentary participation in judgment about rights. One concern is the potential of a bill of rights to transform social and political disagreements into technical legal questions. The worry is that citizens will too often abdicate 'responsibility for working out reasonable and mutually acceptable resolutions of the issues which divide them' and will too often look to courts for answers.[8] A related concern is

[6] Ibid.

[7] The legislative override in s 33(1) provides that 'Parliament or the legislature of a province may expressly declare in an Act of Parliament or of the legislature, as the case may be, that the Act or a provision thereof shall operate notwithstanding a provision included in section 2 or sections 7 to 15 of this Charter'.

[8] P. H. Russell, 'The Political Purposes of the Canadian Charter of Rights and Freedoms', (1983) 61 *Canadian Bar Review* 52, 30–54.

whether parliamentarians will view a bill of rights as a convenient refuge to avoid or delay difficult political and moral decisions. Elected representatives can insulate themselves from criticism, and political parties can avoid risking party cohesion, by ignoring controversial issues and claiming that fundamental issues of rights should first be resolved by courts before political decisions are taken.[9]

In addition to these fundamental concerns about the desirability of a bill of rights, some might question the prudence of encouraging Parliament to engage consciously in rights-based judgments. I can anticipate at least four criticisms of the suggestion that Parliament should focus on the rights dimension of a social policy conflict. The first is that this would reify rights, by treating rights claims as separate or distinct considerations in the policy process. If political judgment about the validity of legislative objectives were contingent upon rights not being infringed, this would introduce a rigid framework for determining the scope of allowable state actions and the means for accomplishing these. This is particularly worrisome since the inflationary character of the language of rights often produces claims that bear little resemblance to the philosophical reasons a polity wishes to protect human action from the coercive powers of the state.

Secondly, Parliament is neither suited to, nor serves the public interest by, trying to resolve political disagreements on the basis of rights-based principles. Governments have a policy agenda to implement legislation to promote the public interest, however the governing party determines this, and to broker and mediate among disparate opinions, assumptions, and expectations. Once a particular governmental objective has been crystallized in the form of a legislative bill, Parliament's task is to assess and vote on this. In so doing, members express their judgment based on a combination of factors: the position of the political party to which they are associated, their interpretation of local or community perspectives, and, occasionally, the dictates of their conscience.

Parliament functions in an adversarial manner under the Westminster tradition. Although Parliament provides the necessary authority and authorizes the resources for governing the country, its principal roles are to check the government and provide an alternative choice to the existing governing party by enabling the opposition to present publicly why it is a credible choice to replace the political party in power. Parliamentary deliberations are structured as a contest and debate between the government and opposition parties.[10] Yet if Parliament were viewed as a forum in which members were to take different cues—for example, whether legislation is consistent with rights—this adversarial format, and its emphasis on representing contrary and divergent perspectives, could take on an entirely different, and perhaps contrary, focus. This revised perspective might emphasize working towards a consensus to ascertain the correct, rights-based answer to a social conflict. But this reorientation overlooks

[9] M. Mandel, *The Charter of Rights and the Legalization of Politics in Canada* (Toronto: Wall & Thompson, 1989).

[10] C. E. S. Franks, *The Parliament of Canada* (Toronto: University of Toronto Press, 1987), 4–5.

the importance of political disagreement, the relevance of competing ideologies, and the necessary venting of contrary opinions about what problems trouble a political community and what forms of state actions are appropriate. Parliamentary deliberation and voting are intended not to reach a compromise or consensus, but to express differences and to fight for the articulation and recognition of these in the competitive political process in which government responds to pressures placed by the Opposition. Persistent disagreement should be regarded 'as one of the elementary conditions of modern politics'.[11] Thus, some believe that the resolution of political differences should not be driven by efforts to differentiate legislative choices on the basis of their consistency with rights. Instead, political disagreements should be resolved by reliance on the majority principle to give effect to the views of one side or one coalition of supporters over those with contrary views. Jeremy Waldron characterizes the virtue of the majority principle in politics as accepting the need to live with disagreement. In this sense, Parliament's judgment is distinct from that of political philosophers or judges, who do not have to accommodate alternative normative conceptions of a well-ordered society within their theories or judgments.[12]

Thirdly, a rights framework for evaluating social policy disagreements would distort legislative decision-making by encouraging parliamentarians to adopt legal perspectives to resolve social and political conflicts. These perspectives could influence legislative agendas by discouraging the pursuit of options where it cannot be demonstrated that the relationship between the legislative objective and means is rational, or where it cannot be proven that the means used will actually achieve the intended goal. Mark Tushnet warns that if legal views of constitutional norms have too much influence on the law-making process, legal perspectives will replace legislative considerations that may be more relevant.[13] Similarly, Robert Nagel suggests that a legal orientation for political decision-making is inappropriate because legislative decisions depend on 'trusting and honouring the reactions of the public to the experience of being governed'. The dignity and importance of political involvement is not measured by the formulation of neat intellectual solutions but consists of trying, failing, and learning.[14] Thus, while the legislative process 'works imperfectly and looks worse', attempts to evaluate its integrity and the quality of its outcomes in terms of 'unconstrained standards of constitutional rationalism undermine much of the usefulness of legislatures in a democracy'.[15]

Fourthly, if Parliament were to focus on the rights dimension of a legislative conflict, those defending its legislation from legal challenges would then attempt

[11] J. Waldron, *The Dignity of Legislation* (Cambridge: Cambridge University Press, 1999), 153.

[12] Ibid. 90–1.

[13] M. Tushnet, 'Policy Distortion and Democratic Debilitation: Comparative Illumination of the Countermajoritarian Difficulty', (1995) 94 *Michigan Law Review* 245, 245–301.

[14] R. E. Nagel, *Constitutional Cultures: The Mentality and Consequences of Judicial Review* (Berkeley: University of California Press, 1993), 116.

[15] Ibid. 120.

to describe and characterize Parliament's intent with respect to how rights and social policy objectives should be reconciled. But this would neglect the importance of diversity and disagreement within Parliament's judgment. Waldron is critical of attempts to elicit from Parliament an overarching legislative intent on specific issues of social policy. He argues that to do so misunderstands the nature of legislative activity. To reduce the motivations and reasons for any legislative decision to a singular intent ignores the realization that hundreds of members make up this assembly and have radically diverse opinions and ideological perspectives that influence their decisions.[16]

It is difficult to deny the merits of most of these concerns. Nevertheless, I don't accept that parliamentary judgment about rights will necessarily result in the reification of rights or will distort political decision-making with legal preoccupations of rationality and proportionality. Parliament may have to fight the inclination of some government legal advisers to pursue non-ambitious, risk-averse measures. Nevertheless, it is important to recognize legitimate differences between political and legal perspectives about whether legislation is justified under the Charter. Moreover, I'm not convinced that Parliament's role or responsibilities will be compromised by a more conscious focus on whether legislative choices are justified from a rights perspective. A political community's decision to adopt a bill of rights represents its acceptance that rights will, and should, serve as constraints on state actions. As for the fourth concern, I suspect that Waldron and I will have to agree to disagree. The ability of Parliament to express intent(s) about how the Charter should or should not constrain legislative intentions may contribute to the success in defending legislation against a Charter legal challenge. This is important because of the inevitability of different opinions about whether legislative decisions are appropriate under the Charter. The authority of the judiciary to invalidate legislation that it considers inconsistent with the Charter reinforces the need for Parliament to satisfy itself that legislation is reasonable and justified in light of constitutional principles. If Parliament does not make a concerted effort to grapple with how Charter principles should influence legislative objectives at the time legislation is being evaluated and passed, it will have forfeited the opportunity to influence how the judiciary views and assesses these conflicts in subsequent litigation. Furthermore, if Parliament appears indifferent about these issues, the judiciary will have little incentive to be sensitive to its perspective. Consequently, legislation may be more vulnerable to judicial invalidation.

I conceive of the significance of the Charter's adoption in Canada, and its effects on political responsibilities, in very different terms than most other commentators. Rather than broach the Charter as an instrument under which the judiciary strives to identify the 'correct' answer for impugned legislation that gives rise to a rights claim, I envisage it as facilitating both political and judicial reflection on whether legislation is justified and reasonable in light of the

[16] Waldron, n. 11 above, 25–35.

Charter's normative values. But these are, and should remain, distinct inquiries that neither mimic each other, nor assume that one approach is inherently superior. The two institutions share responsibility for evaluating the merits of legislative choices and bring to their respective judgments different perspectives that reflect their distinctive roles and the fact that they are situated differently, relative to the Charter conflict. The Charter's virtue lies in its capacity to 'ratchet up' the quality of scrutiny that is brought to bear on the validity of governmental action, not in its promise for judicial resolution of legislative conflicts involving rights.[17]

What I mean by parliamentary judgment with respect to how the Charter should guide or constrain legislative decisions is that Parliament should satisfy itself that legislation is justified. This political judgment should reflect upon whether the legislative objective is important enough to be given primacy in a political conflict, in light of the importance of that objective and given the severity and nature of the rights infringement. When reviewing legislative choices, Parliament might benefit from a well-reasoned judicial decision that sheds light on the meaning and scope of rights and the possible ways legislation may have discriminated against individuals or groups, whether intentionally or not. But legal opinion should not replace political judgment. Parliamentarians should not approach the Charter as if it were a rigid template that casts approval only on those legislative goals that conform to how lawyers have defined its boundaries. The stature of legal judgment should not blind Parliament to the philosophical nature of resolving rights disputes and the possibility that a range of reasonable answers may exist. Legislation will often give rise to claims of rights and yet represent compelling and justifiable social purposes. The normative criterion for evaluating the merits of legislative decisions is whether these are consistent with a free and democratic society. Since this, in essence, is a philosophical and political standard rather than a legal one, Parliament should be a prominent force when identifying and defending policy objectives that are both important and consistent with the norms of a free and democratic society.

The Charter has had a significant effect on how policy is developed and conceived. The capacity of courts to nullify legislation has increased incentives within the government to anticipate judicial concerns before bills are introduced to Parliament. Legal advisers have become more important players in policy development. They analyse relevant jurisprudence to anticipate reasons that the judiciary might deem legislation inconsistent with the Charter, and offer advice to relevant departments about how to minimize the chances that legislation will be declared invalid. This legal advisory role is often conceived of in terms of 'rights-proofing' or 'Charter-proofing' legislation. What is implied by this notion is that all potentially serious judicial Charter concerns with legislation

[17] The idea that interpreting the Charter is a shared responsibility is developed more fully in J. L. Hiebert, *Charter Conflicts: What Is Parliament's Role?* (Montreal: McGill–Queen's University Press, 2002), ch. 3.

be anticipated and redressed before legislation is passed. Many applaud this form of policy development as a welcome sign that the Charter is improving the quality of political decision-making. But the implication of this approach is that policy development may be characterized by risk management, encouraging less ambitious legislative goals and means to minimize the likelihood that the judiciary will set aside legislation, in whole or in part.

I don't accept that basing legislative choices on risk aversion represents responsible political judgment. It is one thing for Parliament to reflect on judicial concerns when evaluating whether policy goals and the choices of means are appropriate and justified. It is quite another, however, to reject legislative objectives out of hand, or to forgo effective means to pursue these, whenever a governmental legal adviser or some legal commentator claims that this choice runs the risk of being invalidated under the Charter. Judicial rulings present important perspectives rather than final answers. Not only does the judiciary enter a policy dispute at a later stage, without the responsibility of identifying social problems or considering factors that may interfere with the effective pursuit of a legislative goal, but it is not well situated to offer sage advice on how best to pursue complex legislative initiatives. The idea of confining legislative goals and means to those for which the government's legal advisers can confidently predict success in future litigation does not recognize that it is Parliament, and not the judiciary, that is best situated to decide how complex legislative goals are best achieved. Policy development is necessarily a discretionary exercise. Those responsible must address multiple objectives, make distinctions about who will benefit or be affected by the policy decision, and anticipate circumstances that may undermine or influence the realization of the objectives. Policy decisions are based upon specialized expertise, relevant information and data, previous trials and failures, comparative experience, and informed best estimates. The discretionary qualities inherent in this process are incongruent with what are presented as objective rules for after-the-fact judicial decisions about whether the means chosen were rational or significantly more restrictive than some other hypothetical possibility. To even contemplate that exact or scientific policy means exist to redress identified social problems suggests false confidence that a political community has the requisite knowledge, or the appropriate methodology, to identify how to remedy problems or to anticipate circumstances that may compromise the objective.

If Parliament adopts risk-averse measures, which may be suggested by the government's legal advisers (whose professional background may be inclined to prefer legal to political perspectives) the scope of legislative goals will be constrained by parameters established by a form of scrutiny that is not particularly conducive to effective or prudent policy. Legal consideration for rationality and proportionality are distinctly different queries from legislative interest in accommodation and mediation or concern for effectiveness, comprehensiveness, and practicality. As a result, the different focal points between developing effective policy and external assessments of its fit with proportionality criteria may themselves enhance the appearance and extent of the conflict. Even though judicial rulings might provide obviously useful guidelines, anticipating how the judiciary will rule on a particular legislative challenge is extremely difficult, despite the best attempts of legal advisers. Jurisprudence evolves, and judges may not have addressed the relevant issues in a conclusive or consistent manner. When judges retire, new members who are appointed to a court may have a different view of how rights should be interpreted and applied. To adopt a risk-averse position by focusing heavily on what a court would possibly say might simply guess wrong.

Has Parliament the capacity to reach judgments about rights?

A serious tension arises between the executive-based process for evaluating legislation and Parliament's ability to scrutinize whether legislation is justified in light of Charter values. At the federal level in Canada, the minister of justice has a statutory responsibility to advise Parliament when legislation is being introduced that is inconsistent with the Charter.[18] No report has been made or is likely to be made. This is explained not by a disregard for the Charter but rather by the development of a bureaucratic and political culture within the executive that frowns upon introducing legislation that would require such a report. Rather than report to Parliament that the government is proceeding with a bill that is in conflict with the Charter, the office of the minister of justice has established the norm that all proposed legislation must be considered as justifiable under the Charter before a proposal can proceed through Cabinet and be introduced as a legislative bill. The criterion for this is whether a credible argument can be made that the legislation is likely to survive Charter litigation. If a proposal fails this, it must either be amended to satisfy this criterion or it must be withdrawn.[19]

The secrecy and confidentiality that characterize this executive vetting process make it extremely difficult for Parliament to ascertain what considerations influenced the scope of a legislative goal or the means chosen to pursue it. Did the government eschew more effective measures because of fear of Charter risks? Or did it choose goals and means that may stand a good chance of being invalidated? Parliament should not be placed in the untenable position of having to determine whether to support a bill that may be unduly cautious or overly risky, despite insufficient information to make an informed judgment. My argument is not that Parliament should ignore concerns that rights might be unduly jeopardized or automatically reject legislative goals that stand a reasonable chance of

[18] S 4.1 of the Department of Justice Act represents a similar obligation to the reporting requirement still in force in s 3 of the 1960 Canadian Bill of Rights.

[19] This process of executive scrutiny, and how it has evolved, is discussed in J. L. Hiebert, 'Wrestling with Rights: Judges, Parliament and the Making of Social Policy', (July 1999) 5 *Choices* 1.

being nullified. Rather, it is that Parliament satisfies itself that its judgment is reasonable. But this requires appreciation for the significance of and severity of the potential rights conflict.

Government bills that raise potential Charter issues will generally be assessed by a parliamentary standing committee in each chamber that focuses on their consistency with the Charter. These two committees are the House of Commons Standing Committee on Justice and Legal Affairs (formerly known as Justice and Human Rights) and the Standing Senate Committee on Legal and Constitutional Affairs. These committees often hear from witnesses who present a range of opinions on Charter and other relevant issues. Yet committee members have expressed concern that they often lack adequate time and information to make informed judgments about the extent and nature of Charter concerns. Moreover, the fact that the government has not reported to Parliament that a bill is inconsistent with the Charter may be troubling if committee testimony by individuals or groups allege a serious Charter breach.

The federal government has encountered an interesting dilemma when passing legislation that is susceptible to a Charter challenge. When the government pursues legislation that is likely to result in litigation, it has an incentive to demonstrate to the judiciary that the legislation was influenced by careful and responsible judgment. Yet the secrecy of the internal process of evaluation makes it difficult to argue that Parliament actually has grappled with the issue of whether the legislation is justified under the Charter. Moreover, Parliament's inherent weakness in a political system where the executive dominates may be a liability in terms of defending legislation that raises a potentially serious Charter conflict. Judges may be reluctant to accept the assurances of governmental lawyers that Charter concerns were fully considered, particularly in the absence of a fulsome parliamentary record. Yet if the government were to encourage more robust parliamentary scrutiny, this would conflict with its natural inclination to dominate the parliamentary process. Parliamentary hearings with broader public participation could result in criticism of the government for failing to respect rights. Witnesses may contribute to a record that is not supportive of a government's claim that legislation is justified.

Although the government rarely advises Parliament about the degree of Charter risk that is associated with a particular bill, there have been occasional exceptions of broaching Parliament as a forum for debate on alternative views of how the Charter should guide legislative actions. The government has recognized the importance of more transparent parliamentary judgment in anticipation of having to defend legislation in Charter litigation. An example was the government's decision to pass legislation to reverse the Supreme Court's new common law rule, which introduced a defence of extreme intoxication for sexual assault charges.[20] The government consciously focused on parliamentary debate to express policy and philosophical differences with the court and recorded this

[20] *R v Daviault* [1994] 3 SCR 63.

political disagreement with the court in a legislative preamble. This preamble was consciously constructed to support arguments about why the legislation should be considered a valid judgment about how to reconcile conflicting values under the Charter, despite the fact that it contradicted the judiciary's judgment. Parliament played a significant role evaluating legislative proposals, proposing changes that were accepted, and hearing from witnesses who provided testimony that may be useful if the legislation was subsequently challenged.[21]

Parliamentary scrutiny could be strengthened if the government were to alert Parliament more regularly about the reasons it wishes to proceed with a bill that incurs a *substantial* Charter risk, *even if the minister of justice believes that the bill has a credible chance of surviving litigation*. This is a different standard from the existing interpretation of the statutory obligation, which is to advise Parliament only where no credible Charter argument can be made. The purpose of encouraging this different interpretation is to focus parliamentary deliberation on the justification of legislation that the government anticipates will likely culminate in litigation under the Charter. This report should be introduced at the second reading stage so it will become a central focus for committee deliberation. Some might worry that preoccupation with technical, jurisprudential issues could distort policy choices. But this is not how I envisage parliamentary judgment about whether legislative decisions are justified in light of the normative values in the Charter. The report should avoid overly technical or 'lawyerly' analysis of judicial precedents and, instead, should provide information relevant for debate about the merits and justification of the legislative objective, such as the harm or social concern that the legislation seeks to address, the severity of the rights infringement, and the degree of anticipated Charter risk. The purpose of parliamentary Charter scrutiny is not to focus on the correct 'rights' answer to a political conflict, but to provide parliamentarians with sufficient information to reach careful judgment about whether they believe that legislation is reasonable and justified.

Many will be understandably sceptical about whether Parliament's weakness is too deeply entrenched to exercise meaningful political scrutiny. Parliament is an institution whose structure of power ensures that members, disciplined along party lines, assume a subordinate role. An examination of political power in Ottawa reveals extreme concentration and centralization of power in the office of the prime minister, which has increased since the Trudeau era.[22] This suggests that Parliament's power, in relative terms, is almost certainly weaker, and its capacity to compel substantive changes to a legislative agenda may be frustrated when the prime minister considers a particular bill a vital part of his or her legislative agenda. Other political systems may have more internal checks that

21 For more discussion, see Hiebert, n. 17 above.

22 Exceptions are the minister of finance and the president of the Treasury Board, who lead their own central agencies; D. J. Savoie, *Governing from the Centre: The Concentration of Power in Canadian Politics* (Toronto: University of Toronto Press, 1999), 338.

increase Parliament's power. But Canada lacks an effective or elected Upper House, which attenuates the government's power.

Yet this acknowledgement of Parliament's weakness does not mean that its influence is inconsequential. Those who are sceptical about the benefits of parliamentary deliberation give insufficient consideration to the significance of parliamentary disagreement or to the independent judgment of interest groups and individuals who appear before parliamentary committees. The very real possibility in Canada of judicial nullification of legislation enhances the influence Parliament might otherwise exert over government legislation. Parliamentary deliberation provides a useful public record that can be utilized both by those arguing that legislative judgment is reasonable, as well as by those claiming that no sound reasons exist for violating rights in the manner proposed. These opinions may make it difficult for the government to orchestrate or control Charter deliberations in Parliament. The failure of the government to address serious Charter concerns, whether raised by parliamentarians or by independent groups and commentators, may increase the risk that legislation will be nullified if courts begin to take a closer look at the reasons and background for legislative judgments.

Even if parliamentary judgment is more robust and transparent, judges may still conclude that rights have been unduly infringed. But this does not mean that Parliament must abandon its legislative goals. Those who have been strongly influenced by American constitutionalism, to expect that judicial rulings will put an end to conflicts about rights, might be discomforted by the idea that judicial interpretations may not bring finality. But institutional disagreements need not result in political stalemates. When parliamentary judgment differs from judicial opinion with respect to how to reconcile Charter conflicts, these differences can be expressed in several ways depending on the nature of the disagreement. Parliament can object to a judicial change to a common law rule and pass legislation that assigns a different priority to the conflicting values involved. A different form of disagreement may arise after legislation has been declared inconsistent with the Charter. Parliament may decide to pass new legislation that differs from the Supreme Court's approach, in which government lawyers will have to try to convince the Court that Parliament's perspective is reasonable and justified. In this case, the government lawyers will likely focus on section 1 arguments in defending Parliament's decision about the appropriate resolution of conflicting values. The most extreme form of disagreement will be use of the legislative override to temporarily allow the impugned legislation to prevail over the Court's judgment.

Despite the often polarized positions taken on the override, this power should not be viewed in mutually exclusive terms: either it is antithetical to the purposes of a bill of rights or it embodies a non-problematic way to give effect to political judgment. If used to insulate political judgment from judicial review, without regard for the rights of minorities or others who are vulnerable, its use would reinforce critics' fears that it conflicts with a fundamental purpose of a bill of rights: to protect minority rights from contrary political judgments.[23] Yet, the override could be invoked to protect a political judgment about rights that is reasonable, particularly when the source of judicial difficulty was not whether the legislative goal is important enough but the reasonableness of the means used. What is required in Canada is a reasoned debate about the conditions under which the override should or should not be used and the procedures that are likely to facilitate thoughtful reflection on its justification in a particular circumstance.[24]

Conclusion

Not all who are sceptical about the merits of a bill of rights will likely be persuaded to change their opinion simply because a bill of rights can be structured in a manner that allows Parliament the opportunity to express its judgment on the appropriate resolution of rights conflicts. Yet I believe that a political community can benefit from the emphasis a bill of rights places on questioning whether political decisions that restrict rights are justified. This is particularly important in Canada, which suffers from extremely concentrated power in the executive, an electoral system that produces majority governments easily, extreme party discipline that provides few checks on government power, and an ineffective Upper House. Judicial review of a bill of rights provides important insights into whether rights have been unduly infringed, not so much because of the superior reasoning skills and methods for resolving conflicts involving rights, but because of the liberty judges have from political and partisan pressures that influence political judgment. The political consequences that arise from the threat that legislation could be nullified ensure that political leaders take the responsibility that legislative judgment is reasonable more seriously than if these decisions were not subject to judicial review or if judicial rulings were merely advisory. Yet, these incentives for thinking about whether legislation is consistent with the normative values in the Constitution do not require political judgment always to yield to judicial perspectives.

Parliament may have a different conclusion than the judiciary about how to resolve a rights conflict. But the mere fact of difference does not mean that Parliament's judgment is not reasonable. This is not to suggest, in any way, that all legislative decisions that differ from judicial interpretations should be considered as responsible judgments about rights. Rather, it is to point out that it

[23] The override has majoritarian qualities, arising from both the initial decision itself (where a simple majority in Parliament is all that is required to support its use) and the fact that subsequent decisions to renew it appeal to majority will (because temporal restrictions will ensure that an election has occurred, affording voters an opportunity to contribute to judgment about its use).

[24] Arguably, any decision to use the override should be subject to a more difficult standard than normal majority approval in Parliament. The decision to use the override should be subject to a free parliamentary vote and supported by larger than normal parliamentary majority. The focal point of deliberation should be the consequences of using the override and not consensus for the decision.

is only when we uncritically equate judicial interpretation of a bill of rights with the meaning of the bill of rights that we will assume that contrary political judgment is inherently inconsistent with rights.

To a considerable extent, Parliament is likely to get the kinds of judicial rulings it deserves. If it passes non-ambitious legislation that utilizes risk-averse measures, rather than try to convince the court about the merits of more effective legislative strategies, we can hardly blame the judiciary. Moreover, if serious questions arise about the merits of legislative choices, and these uncertainties haven't been persuasively addressed in any public or transparent fashion, or convincingly argued in litigation, judges will be understandably reluctant to accept Parliament's judgment.

A government can facilitate a far richer parliamentary contribution to Charter judgment than the restrictive option of simply reacting to negative judicial rulings. The federal government's conscious use of parliamentary hearings when disagreeing with the Supreme Court's creation of an intoxication defence for sexual assault suggests expectations of a linkage between parliamentary deliberation and success in litigation. But there is little reason why the government should be so selective in viewing Parliament's contributory role. The government has a vested interest that its legislation will survive Charter litigation. But this may coincide with necessary respect for Parliament's role to scrutinize bills for consistency with Charter values, and to establish a public record of the reasons why legislation diverges from judicial interpretation of the Charter. Otherwise, legislative responses that reflect political disagreements with judicial rulings may be more vulnerable to judicial nullification. Moreover, the lack of any publicly available record indicating there has been careful political judgment about how Charter values should guide, and be reflected in, legislation will reinforce the assumption, already prevalent in Canada, that the judiciary is the only capable and credible body to respect rights.

12

Constructing a Community-Based Bill of Rights

GEORGE WILLIAMS

Introduction

By themselves, bills of rights are unlikely to achieve much in the way of protecting fundamental human rights. There are many nations in which a bill of rights has proved to be little more than a symbol of the powerlessness of law, and hence nothing more than words on a page. History and experience suggest that, to be effective, a bill of rights must be embedded in a culture of democratic constitutionalism, which entails, among other things, community and political respect for the rule of law and for public institutions such as parliament and the courts. Hence, the failure of a bill of rights to protect citizens against abrogation of their liberty may often be traced to a deeper problem, a failure of constitutionalism.

The need of a supportive framework to underpin a bill of rights is borne out by the problems faced by some post-communist and post-colonial societies. In such nations a bill of rights may wither without an appropriate political, legal, and community culture. Fiji is a good example. It achieved independence from the United Kingdom in 1970, and with its 1997 Constitution gained what might be seen as a world-class bill of rights. The Fiji Bill of Rights (contained in the Fiji Constitution, Chapter 4) is comprehensive and drafted in clear language. However, it has been little used. Moreover, Fiji has seen serious abrogation of basic human rights, including a failed attempt by those with economic and military power to overturn basic democratic institutions by a *coup d'état*.[1] Despite possessing a bill of rights, Fiji has possessed a 'weak' legal culture[2] and hence lacks the culture of democratic constitutionalism that might have enabled its Bill of Rights to operate with more success. Fortunately, there are signs in Fiji of a strengthening of the rule of law, and its bill of rights may yet prove to be effective.

Such examples demonstrate no more than what is obvious: a necessary condition for an effective bill of rights is a supportive political, legal, and cultural framework. However, a bill of rights is important not only for its ability to protect human rights within such a context, but also for its capacity to deepen and

[1] See G. Williams, 'The Case that Stopped a Coup? The Rule of Law and Constitutionalism in Fiji', (2001) 1 *Oxford University Commonwealth Law Journal* 73.

[2] R. Hughes and C. Laksman, 'Fiji Islands: Failure of Constitutionalism?', (2001) 32 *Victoria University of Wellington Law Review* 915, 942.

strengthen the supportive framework within which it operates. It may, for example, reinforce community and political commitment to concepts such as the rule of law. The capacity of a bill of rights to strengthen an existing culture of democratic constitutionalism may be the most important contribution made by such an instrument. This contribution may be more significant in the longer term than the contribution made to protect rights as they come before the courts.

Australia presents a particularly interesting context within which to examine the bill of rights debate. Australia possesses a strong culture of democratic constitutionalism characterized by a commitment to concepts such as the rule of law, representative and responsible government, and the separation of powers. However, it does not have a bill of rights despite several attempts and frequent public debate about the merits or otherwise of such an instrument. In fact, since the Human Rights Act 1998 (UK) came fully into force on 2 October 2000, Australia is now the only Western common law nation without a bill of rights. Australia, then, is in a unique position to design and implement a bill of rights taking into account the strengths and weaknesses of comparative models, as well as what I have argued is the most significant contribution of a bill of rights: its capacity to deepen existing respect for human rights within political institutions and the community.[3]

In this chapter I focus on the ways in which a bill of rights could be designed to achieve such outcomes. The role of the community in the rights-protection process is often neglected in favour of a court-based analysis of how particular rights have been interpreted and applied by the judicial sphere of government. However, a bill of rights divorced from the community will not achieve its broader aims, including community education and the promotion of respect for difference and tolerance of diversity. One important way of engaging the community is to ensure that a bill of rights explicitly provides a role for the community in the rights-protection process. This might be in the form of a dialogue about the protection of rights between courts, parliaments, and the people.

The idea of dialogue

Bills of rights are frequently seen as creating tension or exacerbating opposition between the judiciary and other institutions of government. This characterization is understandable given the traditional place of a bill of rights within a framework of checks and balances. In Australia this view has played an important role in the rejection of a range of bill of rights proposals at the federal level and in different states and territories. Governments and parliaments have, understandably, been sceptical about establishing a bill of rights when the apparent result will be to create a fresh area of conflict with the judiciary as a

[3] G. Williams, *A Bill of Rights for Australia* (Sydney: University of New South Wales Press, 2000).

consequence of the judiciary gaining increased powers at the expense of Parliament.[4]

I recognize that bills of rights will have implications for parliamentary sovereignty and may change the relationship between courts and parliaments so as to produce a more adversarial relationship. However, it is possible to construct a bill of rights model that will also leave important decisions regarding social, economic, and public policy where they belong, that is, with parliaments and communities. One way of achieving this, as well as the broader aspirations for a bill of rights, is to construct the instrument around the idea of dialogue. This model has two advantages. First, as a purely pragmatic concern, it is more likely to be acceptable to the powers that be, most notably the governments that determine whether to introduce a bill of rights. Secondly, it may be more likely to achieve some of the functional aims of a bill of rights model. By functional aims I do not refer to the argument that dialogue is a means of countering the majoritarian difficulties of courts exercising judicial review,[5] but mean, rather, that dialogue, particularly where it involves the communities that the bill of rights is designed to serve, may actually promote a more effective scheme of rights-protection.

My aim then is to construct a bill of rights model based upon a concept of dialogue. By this I mean an instrument that recognizes and expressly provides for shared roles and responsibilities for parliaments, courts, and communities in constructing legal and cultural understandings of rights, including the process of balancing rights against each other and in determining whether governmental action actually breaches a listed right. My focus in developing a concept of dialogue is different from other writers in this field in that I am particularly concerned about the role of the community in the rights-protection process. I see dialogue as being necessary for an effective rights regime because, without community support and constructive community interaction—both of which must be underpinned by education—the regime is not likely to achieve sufficient symbolic, political, or legal force to achieve its aims, the most important of which is a vibrant rights culture.

My dialogue model is based upon indirect forms of community participation such as through elected representatives or by community interaction with parliamentary committees. I adopt this model in preference to more direct forms of community participation such as citizens' initiated referenda. As I have written elsewhere,[6] the benefits of citizens' initiated referenda are illusory in that they can undermine the strengths of an existing parliamentary system based on responsible and representative democracy without granting citizens an effective

[4] See, for example, Standing Committee on Law and Justice, *A NSW Bill of Rights*, Report no. 17 (Oct. 2001).

[5] See, for example, P. W. Hogg and A. A. Bushell, 'The *Charter* Dialogue between Courts and Legislatures', (1997) 35 *Osgoode Hall Law Journal* 75, 105.

[6] G. Williams and G. Chin, 'Australian Experiments with Community Initiated Referendum: CIR for the ACT?', (1998) 7 *Griffith Law Review* 274.

voice in public debate or in determining important policy choices. Direct forms of community participation are also inconsistent with the need for a bill of rights, which must be able to protect minority interests and be resistant to majoritarian pressures. Not all forms of enhanced community participation are acceptable—only those that are compatible with the functional aims of a bill of rights.[7]

While my argument is focused upon the Australian position, dialogue models of bills of rights are equally applicable in the assessment of existing bills of rights. Hence, this chapter suggests and promotes general patterns of interaction between parliaments, courts, and communities as well as paths of future legislative and judicial development and institutional reform. Indeed, the concept of dialogue is derived in part from observation of the features of other comparative jurisdictions, especially Canada, the United Kingdom, and New Zealand. My arguments also draw upon and owe an obvious debt to the work of other scholars who have written in this area, particularly Janet Hiebert[8] and David Kinley.[9]

The Canadian experience is instructive. Much has been written about the capacity for the Canadian Charter of Rights and Freedoms to promote dialogue between courts and legislatures. This theme has even been expressed explicitly by members of the Supreme Court of Canada, who have adopted the view of dialogue developed by Hogg and Bushell.[10] As Iacobucci J stated in *Vriend v Alberta*:[11]

> To my mind, a great value of judicial review and this dialogue among the branches is that each of the branches is made somewhat accountable to the other. The work of the legislature is reviewed by the courts and the work of the court in its decisions can be reacted to by the legislature in the passing of new legislation (or even overarching laws under s 33 of the *Charter*). This dialogue between and accountability of each of the branches have the effect of enhancing the democratic process, not denying it.

[7] There are many ways that indirect community involvement can be enhanced. See G. Williams and G. Chin, 'The Failure of Citizens' Initiated Referenda Proposals in Australia: New Directions for Popular Participation?', (2000) 35 *Australian Journal of Political Science* 27.

[8] See J. L. Hiebert, 'A Hybrid-Approach to Protect Rights? An Argument in Favour of Supplementing Canadian Judicial Review with Australia's Model of Parliamentary Scrutiny', (1998) 26 *Federal Law Review* 115; J. L. Hiebert, 'Why Must a Bill of Rights Be a Contest of Political and Judicial Wills? The Canadian Alternative', (1999) 10 *Public Law Review* 22; J. L. Hiebert, 'Wrestling with Rights: Judges, Parliament and the Making of Social Policy', in *Choices: Courts and Legislatures* (Montreal: Institute for Research on Public Policy, June 1999), vol. 5 no. 3.

[9] See D. Kinley, *The European Convention on Human Rights: Compliance Without Incorporation* (Aldershot: Dartmouth, 1993); D. Kinley, 'Human Rights Scrutiny in Parliament: Westminster Set to Leap Ahead', (1999) 10 *Public Law Review* 252.

[10] P. W. Hogg and A. A. Bushell, 'The *Charter* Dialogue between Courts and Legislatures', (1997) 35 *Osgoode Hall Law Journal* 75. See the response by C. P. Manfredi and J. B. Kelly, 'Six Degrees of Dialogue: A Response to Hogg and Bushell', (1999) 37 *Osgoode Hall Law Journal* 513, and the further response by P. W. Hogg and A. A. Thornton, 'Reply to "Six Degrees of Dialogue"', (1999) 37 *Osgoode Hall Law Journal* 529.

[11] [1998] 1 SCR 493, 566. See also ibid. 562–7, per Iacobucci J; *M v H* [1999] 2 SCR 3, 59–60, per Iacobucci J; *R v Mills* [1999] 3 SCR 668, para 57, per McLachlin and Iacobucci JJ.

This model of dialogue as applied in Canada can be developed further by acknowledging a role for the community as part of such a process.

THE AUSTRALIAN BILL OF RIGHTS DEBATE: A RECORD OF FAILURE

In many countries with a written constitution, constitutional development in the second half of the twentieth century was dominated by concepts of human rights. For example, Canada and South Africa gained bills of rights,[12] while the United States saw an existing bill of rights expanded through judicial interpretation. In other nations international norms and the proliferation of treaties and conventions acted as a catalyst for the examination of domestic human rights concerns, including in the process of constitutional interpretation.[13] In countries without a written constitution, such as New Zealand and the United Kingdom, international human rights standards were incorporated into domestic law through statutory bills of rights.[14]

Australia stands apart from these developments. While federal and state parliaments have enacted important human rights legislation, particularly in the form of anti-discrimination statutes,[15] they have not brought about a constitutional or statutory bill of rights. Australia is alone among comparable nations in not having a domestic bill of rights in some form. This is not due to a lack of attempts to bring about bills of rights. In fact, many attempts have been made, but none have thus far been successful.[16] Several states and territories have made faltering steps towards enacting a bill of rights. Despite reports advocating a bill of rights,[17] and even the introduction of such bills into state parliaments,[18] the necessary state or territory legislation has yet to be passed.

At the federal level, amendment of the Australian Constitution is provided for by means of a referendum under section 128. A referendum proposal under

[12] Canadian Bill of Rights 1960 (Canada); Canadian Charter of Rights and Freedoms 1982; Constitution of the Republic of South Africa, ch. 2.

[13] See A. Simpson and G. Williams, 'International Law and Constitutional Interpretation', (2000) 11 *Public Law Review* 205.

[14] New Zealand Bill of Rights Act 1990 (NZ); Human Rights Act 1998 (UK).

[15] At the federal level, see Racial Discrimination Act 1975 (Cth); Sex Discrimination Act 1984 (Cth); Disability Discrimination Act 1992 (Cth).

[16] See, generally, G. Williams, *Human Rights Under the Australian Constitution* (Melbourne: Oxford University Press, 1999), 250–7.

[17] Australian Capital Territory Attorney General's Department, *A Bill of Rights for the ACT?* (1993); Constitutional Committee of the Victorian Parliament, *Report on the Desirability or Otherwise of Legislation Defining and Protecting Human Rights* (1987); Electoral and Administrative Review Commission, *Report on Review of the Preservation and Enhancement of Individuals' Rights and Freedoms* (Aug. 1993); Sessional Committee on Constitutional Development, *Final Draft Constitution for the Northern Territory* (Aug. 1996); Standing Committee on Law and Justice, *A NSW Bill of Rights*, Report no. 17 (Oct. 2001); ACT Bill of Rights Consultative Committee, *Towards an ACT Human Rights Act* (May 2003).

[18] Constitution (Declaration of Rights) Bill 1959 (Qld); Constitution (Declaration of Rights and Freedoms) Bill 1988 (Vic).

section 128 must be passed by an absolute majority of both Houses of the federal Parliament, or by one House twice, and then by a majority of the people and by a majority of the people in a majority of the states (that is, in at least four of the six states). Forty-four proposals have been put to the Australian people under section 128. Only eight have navigated section 128 successfully.[19]

Two attempts have been made to bring about greater rights protection by constitutional amendment, although neither would have brought about a bill of rights. In a referendum held on 19 August 1944 a proposal was put to the people that the Constitution be amended to grant the Commonwealth fourteen new heads of power over post-war reconstruction. The proposal also sought to insert guarantees of speech and expression as well as extend the guarantee of religious freedom in section 116 to the states.[20] These powers and guarantees would only have operated for a period of five years. The referendum was lost with a 45.39 per cent 'yes' vote to a 53.30 per cent 'no' vote.

Another referendum was held on 3 September 1988, when the Australian people were asked to vote on four proposals. The second proposal sought to guarantee 'one vote, one value' by requiring that the population count in each electorate not deviate by more than 10 per cent. This proposal would also have inserted a right to vote into the Constitution.[21] The fourth proposal also sought to guarantee basic freedoms, but only by extending the operation of existing guarantees in the Constitution, including trial by jury and freedom of religion.[22] All four proposals were defeated. The fourth proposal received the smallest vote of any of the proposals. Nationally, 30.33 per cent of voters registered a 'yes' vote, while 68.19 per cent voted 'no'. This remains the lowest 'yes' vote ever recorded.

Two attempts have also been made to bring about a bill of rights at the federal level in a statutory form. In 1973 Lionel Murphy, as Attorney-General in the Whitlam Labor Government, introduced the Human Rights Bill 1973 (Cth) into the federal Parliament. The bill sought to implement the International Covenant on Civil and Political Rights 1966 in Australia and would have protected a range of rights such as freedom of expression, freedom of movement, the right to marry and found a family, and individual privacy.[23] The Human Rights Bill met strong opposition and was never enacted, lapsing with the prorogation of Parliament in early 1974.

In the early 1980s Senator Gareth Evans, as Attorney-General in the Hawke Labor Government, sought to take up where Murphy had left off in promoting a statutory bill of rights. In 1983 he oversaw the drafting of a bill of rights bill, which, like its 1973 predecessor, would have implemented international rights

[19] T. Blackshield and G. Williams, *Australian Constitutional Law and Theory*, 3rd edn. (Sydney: Federation Press, 2002), 1303–8.

[20] Constitutional Alteration (Post-War Reconstruction and Democratic Rights) Bill 1944 (Cth).

[21] Constitution Alteration (Fair Elections) Bill 1988.

[22] Constitution Alteration (Rights and Freedoms) Bill 1988.

[23] Human Rights Bill 1973 (Cth), ss 11, 16, 18, 19.

instruments. Although the Evans bill was given Cabinet support, it was not introduced into Parliament. Lionel Bowen replaced Evans as Attorney-General after the December 1984 federal election. After being redrafted, the bill was introduced into the federal Parliament in November 1985 as the Australian Human Rights Bill 1985 (Cth). It was passed by the Lower House, the House of Representatives, but failed to gain majority support in the Senate. Encountering strong opposition, the bill was finally withdrawn in November 1986.

The need for new models and approaches

The failure to achieve a bill of rights in Australia at any level of government may indicate that Australia, unlike other nations, has never had its 'constitutional moment' in which a bill of rights has become politically achievable; that is, one of those 'fleeting junctures of opportunity for radical re-design of a polity'.[24] However, in addition to the absence of the right 'moment', the record of failure also demonstrates the need for new approaches that harness the respective responsibilities and interests of parliaments and the courts, as well as the community. The community, whose support will be vital for the successful implementation of any bill of rights, must be engaged.

Significantly, none of these constitutional or statutory proposals for a bill of rights explicitly recognized a role for the community in the rights-protection process. Each was essentially a bill of rights model in the traditional form in which the focus would have been on the judicial interpretation and application of rights. The failure of each model can in part be attributed to a lack of support from the Australian people, whether directly at a referendum or indirectly through the actions of their political representatives. Nevertheless, at least one opinion survey has indicated strong underlying community support for the concept of a bill of rights; in that case 72 per cent of those surveyed favoured some form of bill of rights for Australia.[25] This suggests problems with the models relating to their design and to the political leadership backing them.

The role of the community is also important because a necessary condition of an effective rights regime is popular support and understanding. In Australia direct and indirect forms of community engagement may be particularly necessary given low community awareness of the system of government. A 1987 survey conducted for the Constitutional Commission found that 47 per cent of Australians were unaware that Australia has a written Constitution.[26] Similarly, the 1994 report of the Civics Expert Group found that only 18 per cent of Australians have some understanding of what their Constitution contains,

[24] N. MacCormick, 'Democracy, Subsidiarity, and Citizenship in the "European Commonwealth"', (1997) 16 *Law and Philosophy* 331, 333.

[25] B. Galligan and I. McAllister, 'Citizen and Elite Attitudes Towards an Australian Bill of Rights', in B. Galligan and C. Sampford (eds.), *Rethinking Human Rights* (Sydney: Federation Press, 1997), 149.

[26] Constitutional Commission, *Bulletin*, no. 5 (Sept. 1987).

while more than a quarter of those surveyed nominated the Supreme Court, rather than the High Court, as the 'top' court in Australia. Significantly, only one in three people felt reasonably well informed about their rights and responsibilities as Australian citizens.[27]

The failure of the several attempts to bring about statutory or constitutional change to better protect human rights demonstrates that a rights regime cannot be imposed upon the Australian people. Neither should it be. An imposed regime would not achieve the aims of an Australian bill of rights. Rights are meaningless unless they are respected within an appropriate legal and cultural environment. What is necessary is change that engenders a culture of rights protection, including a tolerance and respect for rights, built upon the fundamental values held by the Australian people. Accordingly, any scheme that is designed to better protect civil liberties by way of constitutional or statutory change must be judged according to its scope not only to change the text of the law but to also enhance the culture of rights-protection.

Republican theory views 'freedom as non-domination',[28] that is, that individual liberty exists where a person is independent from the dominion of another. One precondition of non-domination is that rights are known by the person entitled to the right and are a matter of common knowledge in the rest of the community.[29] In essence, rights are only effective, and individuals are only free from domination, within a community permeated by a culture of rights-protection. Rights that exist as a matter of shared knowledge can be located within a social and political context, and not merely as legal phenomena. Otherwise, rights are merely text on a page, and suffer from many of the criticisms that have been levelled as part of the critique of rights debate.[30]

This also exposes the inadequacies of any system of rights-protection based upon the High Court of Australia implying a bill of rights from the Constitution. A former Chief Justice of the High Court, Sir Gerard Brennan, has argued that 'It is clear that the Australian judiciary could not perform a role under a Bill of Rights unless the Australian people consciously casts that role upon them.'[31] His comments raise questions about both the capacity and the legitimacy of a court engaging in the rights-protection process without a popular and political

[27] Civics Expert Group, *Whereas the People: Civics and Citizenship Education* (Canberra: Australian Government Publishing Service, 1994).

[28] P. Pettit, *Republicanism: A Theory of Freedom and Government* (Oxford: Oxford University Press, 1997), 51.

[29] J. Braithwaite and P. Pettit, *Not Just Deserts: A Republican Theory of Criminal Justice* (Oxford: Oxford University Press, 1990), 64–5.

[30] See, for example, J. Morgan, 'Equality Rights in the Australian Context: A Feminist Assessment', in P. Alston (ed.), *Towards an Australian Bill of Rights* (Canberra: Centre for International and Public Law, Australian National University, 1994), 123 ('"Rights" are indeterminate, abstract and decontexualized, alienating, obfuscate political claims, can be constantly set off against one another, and Bills of Rights pass power from the political arena to the judicial').

[31] G. Brennan, 'The Impact of a Bill of Rights on the Role of the Judiciary: An Australian Response', in Alston (ed.), n. 30 above, 183–4.

mandate to do so. Conversely, a scheme of rights-protection that has been forged through a community or parliamentary-based process is more likely to be given judicial support. This also suggests a weakness of the rights already implied by the High Court from the separation of judicial power and the system of representative government created by the Constitution.[32] Implied rights are unlikely to become matters of common knowledge and invocation if they are created by the High Court, even if they are soundly based in the text of the Constitution. They lack the community participation involved in the process of bringing about either a statutory or constitutional bill of rights. While judicial leadership on rights is better than no leadership at all, it is a poor substitute for political and popular leadership. It will be extremely difficult to bring about a rights culture in Australia except where rights are founded upon the commitment of the Australian people or their elected representatives.

A COMMUNITY-BASED BILL OF RIGHTS

The Australian setting provides a new opportunity to construct a bill of rights based on the notion of dialogue between parliaments, courts, and the community. I set out below some of the features and design issues that should be considered in constructing such a model.

Bringing about a bill of rights

The drafting process for a bill of rights should engage the community from the early stage of considering the options for models as well as their substantive content. Such a debate might focus on the work of a parliamentary committee, or a specially convened inquiry consisting of both parliamentarians and members of the community. Parliamentary committees, at least where their membership has not been dominated by the government of the day and where they are committed to a genuine process of review, have often proved effective in capturing popular interest and involvement. For example, the Senate Legal and Constitutional Legislation Committee received 12,577 submissions, and convened public hearings in its 1997 inquiry into the federal proposal to override voluntary euthanasia laws operating in the Northern Territory.[33] Similarly, the recent inquiry by that committee into proposed anti-terrorism laws attracted 431 submissions and considerable media coverage.[34]

[32] See Williams, n. 16 above, 155–226.

[33] See Senate Legal and Constitutional Legislation Committee, *Consideration of Legislation Referred to the Committee: Euthanasia Laws Bill 1996* (Mar. 1997).

[34] See Senate Legal and Constitutional Legislation Committee, *Consideration of Legislation Referred to the Committee* (May 2002).

Popular involvement through a parliamentary committee process was a notable success in the drafting of the Canadian Charter of Rights and Freedoms, which has been praised for its 'success in enhancing the "culture of liberty" in Canada'.[35] The Charter was forged in what has been called a 'democratic crucible'[36] in which the concept of a Charter guaranteeing the rights of citizenship was embraced by the Canadian people. A draft of the Charter prepared by the Trudeau Government was scrutinized by a joint parliamentary committee, the proceedings of which were nationally televised. The committee received submissions from over 1,000 individuals and 300 groups petitioning for change. After sixty days of hearings, the committee successfully proposed sixty-five substantial amendments. The Charter came into effect in 1982, and has been the subject of extensive coverage in the written and electronic media. In a large-scale opinion survey taken some six years later Peter Russell found that 90 per cent of English Canadians and 70 per cent of French Canadians had heard of the Charter, with a substantive majority agreeing that it 'is a good thing for Canada'.[37]

A statutory instrument

A community-based bill of rights model does not mean that it must be created via a popular referendum. A ballot in which the people are simply given a 'yes' or 'no' vote to a specified bill of rights is likely to be counter-productive, particularly where there has been little civics education on human rights issues and where the community has had no prior exposure to the operation of a bill of rights. The Australian referendum experience in this respect is certainly salutary. A more effective means of developing a bill of rights would be first to develop a statutory instrument enacted by Parliament with appropriate involvement and engagement of the Australian people.

The experience of the New Zealand Bill of Rights Act 1990 demonstrates the potential effectiveness of a statutory bill of rights and the value, at least initially, of protecting rights via this means. Indeed, if the goal is to bring about an effective scheme of rights-protection in Australia, there should not be any immediate move to insert a bill of rights in the Constitution. The concept of dialogue suggests that a bill of rights should be susceptible to ongoing development in light of judicial interpretation, changing parliamentary practices, and community input. A constitutional bill of rights with an appropriate override clause can achieve a measure of dialogue. However, a statutory instrument is more appropriate as it would place a higher degree of emphasis upon parliamentary outcomes and upon dialogue within Parliament itself.

[35] R. Penner, 'The Canadian Experience with the Charter of Rights: Are There Lessons for the United Kingdom?', [1996] *Public Law* 104, 123.

[36] Ibid. 107.

[37] P. H. Russell, 'Canada's Charter of Rights and Freedoms: A Political Report', [1988] *Public Law* 385. By comparison, the drafting of the Canadian Bill of Rights 1960 (Canada) did not involve such a process and never achieved the same level of recognition or support in the Canadian community.

An override clause

A statutory bill of rights ought to provide that Parliament can, through expressly stating a legislative intention, override any particular judicial enforcement of a bill of rights. Such a clause would only be necessary if the statutory instrument gave the judicial arm of government the express power to declare legislation to be invalid owing to its inconsistency with the rights listed in the bill of rights. In any event, an override clause would merely make explicit the existing position that Parliament can always amend its own Acts, including a statutory bill of rights, and is incapable of preventing future parliaments from legislating on a topic. Section 33(1) of the Canadian Charter of Rights and Freedoms provides: 'Parliament or the legislature of a province may expressly declare in an Act of Parliament or of the legislature, as the case may be, that the Act or a provision thereof shall operate notwithstanding a provision included in section 2 or sections 7 to 15 of this Charter.'

A declaration made under section 33(1) has, under section 33(3), an operation of five years, after which time the declaration may be re-enacted. It is important to note that the notwithstanding clause requirement in section 33(1) does not apply to all of the rights listed in the Charter, just to the rights lists in sections 2 and 7–15. This means that a legislature can abrogate rights such as 'the right not to be arbitrarily detained or imprisoned' in section 8 or even the right to equality under the law and freedom from discrimination on the basis of race in section 15. On the other hand, other rights such as the right to vote in federal elections in section 3 are beyond the reach of a notwithstanding clause.

Quebec did not give its approval to the Canadian Charter of Rights and Freedoms. It argued that a federal charter was unnecessary in Quebec given the Quebec Charter of Human Rights and Freedoms 1975. Much of Quebec's early use of section 33(1) came as a protest against the imposition of the Charter of Rights and Freedoms. Soon after the Charter came into effect the Quebec Parliament passed An Act Respecting the Constitution Act 1982 (Quebec), which added a standard-form notwithstanding clause to every statute then in force in Quebec.[38] Each new piece of legislation was also drafted to include the notwithstanding clause. This latter practice stopped with a change of government in Quebec in December 1985. The new government also refrained from re-enacting the 'blanket override' in the 1982 Act when, under section 33(3) of the Charter, the Act ceased to operate after five years in 1987.[39] This government did, however, apply the notwithstanding clause in five pieces of legislation, including in An Act to Amend the Charter of the French Language 1988 (Quebec), which prohibited the use of the English language on outside commercial signs. Quebec's willingness to take advantage of section 33(1) of the Charter has not been repeated in other parts of Canada. The only other provinces to take advantage of section 33(1) have been Alberta, in defining

[38] This legislation was upheld in *Ford v Quebec (Attorney-General)* [1988] 2 SCR 712.
[39] P. Hogg, *Constitutional Law of Canada*, 4th edn. (Scarborough, Ont.: Carswell, 1997), 909.

marriage as being between 'a man and a woman' in its Marriage Act 2000 (Alberta), and Saskatchewan, whose use of section 33(1) ultimately proved unnecessary when the Supreme Court of Canada held that its law did not breach the Charter.[40] No other province, nor the federal legislature, has passed legislation applying section 33(1). The political price to be paid in invoking section 33(1) has been too high. A government desiring, for example, to override the 'right not to be subjected to any cruel and unusual treatment or punishment' in section 13 of the Charter must be prepared to meet strong and organized resistance from many sections of the community.[41] It is also arguable that the section 33 process has been stigmatized by its frequent use by Quebec.

Thirty-two years before the Canadian Charter of Rights and Freedoms was enacted, the Canadian Parliament passed the Canadian Bill of Rights 1960. This Act continues to guarantee a wide range of rights, such as 'freedom of religion' and 'freedom of speech' (s 1), and rights such as 'freedom from cruel and unusual treatment or punishment' (s 2). Section 2 also provides that laws passed by the federal legislature should, 'unless it is expressly declared by an Act of the Parliament of Canada that it shall operate notwithstanding the Canadian Bill of Rights', be construed and applied so as not to abrogate any of the rights listed in the Canadian Bill of Rights. In *R v Drybones*[42] the Supreme Court of Canada considered the effect of section 2. It was held that section 2 was effective in rendering 'inoperative' federal legislation inconsistent with any of the rights listed in the Canadian Bill of Rights.[43] This can be explained by viewing section 2 as a manner and form limitation upon the law-making process by the Canadian Parliament.[44] *R v Drybones* suggests that, at least in the field of human rights, a notwithstanding clause has the potential to bind the legislature. The decision of the House of Lords in the litigation in *R v Secretary of State for Transport; Ex parte Factortame Ltd*[45] suggests that this is not limited to the field of human rights but applies more generally.

In a statutory bill of rights constructed around the idea of dialogue, a notwithstanding clause would force Parliament to state explicitly an intention to override a listed right should it wish to do so. This would have the effect of raising the override as a political issue and could thereby force a dialogue within the Parliament and at the community level on the appropriateness of using the override in a particular case.[46] This would avoid the situation that arose in Australia in regard to the Racial Discrimination Act 1975 (Cth), which was effectively overridden by amendments to the Native Title Act 1993 (Cth). Those

[40] *RWDSU v Saskatchewan* [1987] 1 SCR 460.
[41] Hogg, n. 39 above, 914.
[42] [1970] SCR 282.
[43] Ibid. 294.
[44] n. 41 above, 794.
[45] [1990] 2 AC 85; [1991] 1 AC 603.
[46] Compare Standing Committee on Law and Justice, *A NSW Bill of Rights*, Report no. 17 (Oct. 2001), 111 ('Rather than facilitating a "dialogue" between Parliament and the Judiciary, the existence of an override sets up a potential conflict between these two arms of government. A possible scenario is one in which legislation is judged by a court to be in breach of human rights as set out in a Bill of Rights, and subsequently Parliament indicates its intention to let the incompatibility stand, and exercise its power of override. This process highlights the conflict when it arises').

amendments 'clarified' the relationship between the two pieces of legislation, but in a way that meant, in the event of an inconsistency, that the Native Title Act would override the protection from discrimination on the basis of race provided for in the Racial Discrimination Act. Hence, while subsection 7(1) of the Native Title Act now states 'this Act is intended to be read and construed subject to the provisions of the Racial Discrimination Act', subsection (2) provides that the Racial Discrimination Act has no operation if the intention to override native title is unambiguous.

Judicial review or a declaration of incompatibility

A central concern of the drafters of the United Kingdom Human Rights Act was that it should not enable courts to strike down or set aside legislation. In other words, the Act was not to confer a power of judicial review.[47] Section 3 of the Human Rights Act establishes an interpretative obligation on a court to read and give effect to legislation in a way that is consistent with the protected rights in so as far as it is possible to do so. If a court is unable to read and give effect to legislation in this way, it then may issue a declaration of incompatibility under section 4. In response to a declaration of incompatibility, section 10 empowers a minister to take remedial action to amend the offending legislation.

The discretionary power provided by section 4 is a novel and effective means of enabling a court to establish that an Act breaches a right, while at the same time preserving the responsibility of Parliament to make or unmake legislation. In *R v A*[48] Lord Steyn referred to the declaration of incompatibility as a 'measure of last resort',[49] and that 'It must be avoided unless it is plainly impossible to do so.'[50] Even though a declaration of incompatibility establishes that a litigant has had their rights infringed, the infringement of such rights does not impact upon the offending legislation. There is also no remedy unless the minister decides to issue a remedial order under section 10. As this remedial power is itself discretionary, it further emphasizes the limits of judicial power. The declaration of incompatibility mechanism plays a key role in informing Parliament of inconsistencies between its legislation and rights. Any constraint upon Parliament is political rather than legal.

One difficultly with the declaration of incompatibility mechanism is that it may provide litigants with 'a form of booby prize since the Act clearly states that incompatible legislation remains effective and valid'.[51] It means that a court may find that legislation is inconsistent with a right, and yet if there is no response

[47] The Human Rights Act does, however, enable a court to strike down subordinate legislation in a limited set of circumstances. See Human Rights Act, s 3(2)(c).

[48] [2001] 3 All ER 1. See also *R v North and East London Region Mental Health Review Tribunal (Secretary of State for Health intervening)* [2001] 3 WLR 512.

[49] *R v A*, n. 48 above, 17.

[50] Ibid.

[51] I. Leigh, 'The UK's Human Rights Act 1998: An Early Assessment', in G. Huscroft and P. Rishworth (eds.), *Litigating Rights: Perspectives from Domestic and International Law* (Oxford: Hart, 2002), 324.

from Parliament or the relevant minister (or merely a response such as a further inquiry that delays remedial action indefinitely), no remedial action will result. This is a serous limitation. A better approach is to empower courts to strike down legislation that breaches listed rights, while also enabling Parliament to then, under an override clause, re-enact that same legislation, perhaps in a modified form, or if it desires in exactly the same form. This is preferable because it means that a judicial decision finding a breach of a right will bring about an immediate remedy and also places the responsibility back on Parliament to respond. This is likely to provoke parliamentary and community debate on the merits of any attempt to overcome a judicial decision, a preferable alternative to the possibility that a court decision may simply be forgotten. The better course then is to confer a power of judicial review upon courts in respect of a bill of rights, but to make such a power subject to parliamentary override.

A power of judicial review should be subject to two further limitations. First, judicial review should be subject to a generic limitation clause that demonstrates that the rights must be weighed up against other important societal interests. A good example is section 1 of the Canadian Charter of Rights and Freedoms, which provides: 'The Canadian Charter of Rights and Freedoms guarantees the rights and freedoms set out in it subject only to such reasonable limits prescribed by law as can be demonstrably justified in a free and democratic society.' Secondly, a court should be required, before exercising any power to strike down legislation, to attempt to interpret the legislation in conformity with the listed rights. This interpretative power should be established as the primary means by which a court seeks to protect rights. The power should be broadly worded, like section 3(1) of the Human Rights Act, which states, 'So far as it is possible to do so, primary legislation and subordinate legislation must be read and given effect in a way which is compatible with the [protected rights].'

A power of judicial review made subject to such limitations, and, more significantly, to the possibility of parliamentary override, would achieve the same result as a declaration of incompatibility in ensuring that Parliament would have the final say. However, it would also foster a greater degree of dialogue and community participation. It would also recognize that, where there has been a breach of a fundamental right, the onus should be placed upon Parliament to re-enact its legislation and in doing so publicly justify why the right should be breached. It is not appropriate that a fundamental right could be abrogated with no remedy or even a requirement for consequential action or debate.

Effective parliamentary committees

A statutory bill of rights should be supported by the establishment of a parliamentary standing committee charged with examining legislation for the purpose of ascertaining compliance with the listed rights. Each of the Canadian Bill of Rights, the New Zealand Bill of Rights Act, and the United Kingdom Human Rights Act contains a like non-judicial means of securing compliance.

Under section 3 of the Canadian Bill of Rights, section 7 of the New Zealand Bill of Rights Act, and section 19 of the Human Rights Act, the minister in charge of a bill is required to state whether the bill is compatible with the protected rights. The weakness in such an approach, by itself, is that it entrusts the responsibility for detecting breaches of fundamental rights to the government that has proposed the legislation and which may suffer political damage if the legislation it has sponsored is found to breach civil liberties. As a Canadian commentator has suggested: 'To put real teeth into such a provision, a standing committee of the House of Commons would have to be established.'[52] This has been recognized in the United Kingdom, where a committee of the United Kingdom Parliament, the Joint Committee on Human Rights, has been created to consider human rights issues in the United Kingdom and remedial orders made under the Human Rights Act.[53] The committee may also scrutinize proposed legislation.[54]

The creation of a parliamentary committee as part of the implementation of an Australian bill of rights would serve two purposes. It would allow the vetting of legislation before enactment so as to reduce the likelihood of Commonwealth legislation being found invalid. It would also build parliamentarians into the rights-protection process.[55] This latter aspect should contribute to a greater understanding of rights issues by representatives and, through media coverage of committee deliberations, by the community. Through the power to make submissions, it would also give people and interest groups a means of contributing to the deliberation process.

Conclusion

In this chapter I have sought to set out the core elements of a community-based bill of rights model incorporating the notion of dialogue between courts,

[52] P. H. Russell, 'A Democratic Approach to Civil Liberties', (1969) 19 *University of Toronto Law Journal* 109, 126.

[53] The terms of reference of the committee are:

To consider:

(a) matters relating to human rights in the United Kingdom (but excluding consideration of individual cases);
(b) proposals for remedial orders, draft remedial orders and remedial orders made under section 10 of and laid under Schedule 2 to the Human Rights Act 1998; and
(c) in respect of draft remedial orders and remedial orders, whether the special attention of the House should be drawn to them on any of the grounds specified in Standing Order 73 (Joint Committee on Statutory Instruments).

[54] See Joint Committee on Human Rights, *Press Notice*, no. 1 of 2001–2002 (20 July 2001), found at http://www.parliament.uk/commons/selcom/hrpnt01.htm>, last visited 31 Mar. 2003).

[55] This already occurs in Australia to a limited extent through the work of the Senate Standing Committee for the Scrutiny of Bills. Under Senate Standing Order 24 the committee is charged with reporting whether bills and Acts, among other things, 'trespass unduly on personal rights and liberties'. However, the committee does not hold public hearings or invite submissions from the community on such questions.

parliaments, and communities. In Australia such a model is appropriate because a bill of rights is likely neither to be implemented nor to be effective unless it occurs within a culture of rights-protection that promotes such interaction and fosters community education about rights issues. In being directed at such outcomes, the model would be designed to deepen and strengthen Australia's existing culture of democratic constitutionalism.

A rights culture and dialogue cannot be created overnight in Australia. The history of constitutional reform demonstrates the need for a gradual approach involving popular participation as well as political leadership. In any event, Australia needs more than just a change to the text of the Constitution. It needs to reinforce its culture of liberty. The dialogue approach maximizes the chances of enabling the judiciary to foster the rights of Australians without vesting misplaced faith in the High Court to solve Australia's pressing social, moral, and political problems.

13

Judicial Review, Legislative Override, and Democracy

JEFFREY GOLDSWORTHY

THE 'NOTWITHSTANDING CLAUSE'

Section 33 of the Canadian Charter of Rights famously provides that Canadian legislation 'may expressly declare . . . that the Act or a provision therefore shall operate notwithstanding a provision included in section 2 or sections 7 to 15 of this Charter'. This 'notwithstanding' or 'override' clause enables legislatures to override those specified sections of the Charter, and the rights they protect, although only for renewable five-year periods.[1]

Section 33 has been strongly criticized by many supporters of the Charter, on the predictable ground that it is incompatible with the main purpose of constitutionally entrenching rights.[2] As they see it, that purpose is to protect rights from being overridden by legislation—in other words, to prevent precisely what section 33 expressly permits. On their view, what the Charter purports to grant with one hand, it takes away with the other. While posing as a constraint on the power of the majority to override the rights of individuals and minorities, it explicitly authorizes the majority to do just that (in relation to the rights specified).

Section 33 has been eloquently defended by other supporters of the Charter, who reject this criticism as too simplistic. There are basically two ways of defending the clause. One is to argue that a legislature might sometimes be justified in overriding Charter rights in order to protect some competing right or interest, of greater weight in the circumstances, which is not mentioned in the Charter. But the Charter itself already provides for this possibility: section 1 explicitly states that Charter rights are 'subject . . . to such reasonable limits prescribed by law as can be demonstrably justified in a free and democratic society'. In this regard, those who drafted the Charter wisely avoided the impression conveyed by the American Bill of Rights (but seldom taken seriously by the courts) that the rights it protects are absolute and indefeasible. It follows that section 33 was not needed to permit legislatures to subordinate protected

[1] It does not apply to other sections that protect democratic rights, mobility rights, and language rights.

[2] See criticisms quoted in M. Mandel, *The Charter of Rights and the Legalization of Politics in Canada*, 2nd edn. (Toronto: Thompson Educational Publishing., 1994), 88–9 and 96.

rights to other rights or interests.[3] The real problem that section 33 was designed to overcome has to do with judicial interpretations of Charter provisions, including section 1. This leads to the second way of defending the section, which is to argue that its real purpose is to enable legislatures to override judicial interpretations or applications of Charter rights with which they reasonably disagree.[4]

This defence has the potential to overcome not only the criticisms of section 33 made by Charter supporters, but also the objections of those who oppose the Charter on the ground that it is undemocratic. That is not surprising. Section 33 has been described as a uniquely Canadian compromise of two rival constitutional models: the American model of strong judicial review, and the British model of parliamentary sovereignty.[5] Whether it is a genuine compromise is, of course, open to question. Geoffrey Marshall has protested that 'It is not so much a compromise as a capitulation' of proper rights-protection to parliamentary sovereignty.[6] Others take the opposite view, complaining that in practical terms it has not succeeded in curbing the undemocratic supremacy of the courts.[7] Perhaps the fact that it has satisfied neither side indicates that it is, indeed, an effective compromise.

Ideally, such a compromise would combine the most attractive features of both models, while discarding their most objectionable features.[8] For example, the most powerful and popular argument against the judicial enforcement of constitutional rights maintains that it is undemocratic for unelected judges to invalidate laws enacted by a democratically elected legislature. But given section 33, judicial enforcement of the Charter can be argued to add a further check or balance to the political process without diminishing its fundamentally democratic character. On this view, section 33 is part of a broader constitutional scheme that encourages a 'dialogue' between legislatures and courts, in which the latter are rarely guaranteed the 'final say'.[9] The Charter permits an appeal from the rough-and-tumble of politics to a 'forum of principle', but section 33

[3] L. E. Weinrib argues that the purpose of s 33 is to enable legislatures to override rights when this cannot be justified under section 1: 'Learning to Live with the Override', (1990) 35 *McGill Law Journal* 541, 567–9. But any use of s 33 that could not in principle (leaving aside judicial versus legislative judgment) 'be demonstrably justified in a free and democratic society', as required by s 1, would be very difficult to justify at all.

[4] See, for example, P. H. Russell, 'Standing Up for Notwithstanding', (1991) 229 *Alberta Law Review* 293. This justification of s 33 is admittedly difficult to reconcile with its wording: see n. 57 below, and T. Kanaha, 'Understanding the Notwithstanding Mechanism', (2002) 52 *University of Toronto Law Journal* 221, 233–6.

[5] Ibid. 294.

[6] G. Marshall, 'Taking Rights for an Override: Free Speech and Commercial Expression', [1989] *Public Law* 4, 11.

[7] F. L. Morton and R. Knopff, *The Charter Revolution and the Court Party* (Peterborough, Ont.: Broadview Press, 2000).

[8] Russell, n. 4 above.

[9] P. W. Hogg and A. A. Bushell, 'The Charter Dialogue Between Courts and Legislatures', (1997) 35 *Osgoode Hall Law Journal* 75. For further discussion, see Williams, Ch. 12 above. See also Kanaha, n. 4 above.

confers a right of final appeal back to a consequently more informed and conscientious legislature.[10] What objection could be made, if the legislature retains the final say? As Peter Hogg has concluded, 'So long as the last word remains with the competent legislative body... much of the American debate over the legitimacy of judicial review is rendered irrelevant.'[11]

One purpose of this chapter is to ask if Hogg is right. But even if he is, his claim is not that section 33 completely disarms critics of the Charter. Another, equally important purpose of the chapter is to ask how much of the American debate is rendered irrelevant. This requires distinguishing between different objections that have been made to the judicial enforcement of constitutional rights, and asking which of them applies notwithstanding a notwithstanding clause. In particular, it requires distinguishing rights-based from consequentialist justifications of democracy, and corresponding objections to the judicial enforcement of rights. It is possible that a clause such as section 33 overcomes rights-based objections, because it preserves the democratic right to make the final decision, but does not overcome consequentialist objections.

The rights-based objection to constitutional rights

A leading contemporary critic of constitutional rights is Jeremy Waldron. His main criticism has consistently been that the judicial enforcement of such rights is inconsistent with the democratic right of ordinary people to participate on an equal basis in public decision-making. Waldron describes this right of participation as 'the right of rights', because it is the rights theorists' solution to the problem of authoritatively resolving disputes about rights.[12] He describes his critique as 'rights-based' because it is ultimately based on this 'right of rights'.[13]

Waldron himself has summarized his critique as follows:

> If we are going to defend the idea of an entrenched Bill of Rights put effectively beyond revision by anyone other than the judges, we should try and think what we might say to some public-spirited citizen who wishes to launch a campaign or lobby her MP on some issue of rights about which she feels strongly... we have to imagine ourselves saying to her: 'You may write to the newspaper and get up a petition and organize a pressure group to lobby Parliament. But even if you... orchestrate the support of a large number of like-minded men and women, and manage to prevail in the legislature, your measure may be challenged and struck down because your view of what rights we have does not accord with the judges' views. When their votes differ from yours, theirs are the votes

[10] See, for example, R. Knopff and F. L. Morton, *Charter Politics* (Scarborough, Ont.: Nelson Canada, 1992), ch. 8, esp. pp. 205–6 and 225–33.

[11] P. W. Hogg, *Constitutional Law of Canada* (Scarborough, Ont.: Carswell, 1997), 36.10–36.11.

[12] J. Waldron, *Law and Disagreement* (Oxford: Clarendon Press, 1999), 254.

[13] J. Waldron, 'A Right-Based Critique of Constitutional Rights', (1993) 13 *Oxford Journal of Legal Studies* 18; Waldron, n. 12 above, 214–25, 249–54.

that will prevail.' It is my submission that saying this does not comport with the respect and honour normally accorded to ordinary men and women in the context of a theory of rights.[14]

Waldron's argument is explicitly based on a premiss that is inapplicable to most of the Canadian Charter.[15] He is concerned only with rights that are 'put effectively beyond revision [that is, amendment] by anyone other than the judges'. In *Law and Disagreement* he puts the point in this way: 'a constitutional constraint is less unreasonable . . . the greater the opportunity for altering it by processes of constitutional amendment. We need to bear in mind, however, that such processes are usually made very difficult; indeed, their difficulty . . . is precisely definitive of the constraint in question.'[16] This is not quite right, because section 33 shows that there can be other ways of overcoming or relaxing constitutional constraints than by constitutional amendment. Section 33 does not give Canadian legislatures any power to amend the Charter, but does enable them to free themselves from most of its constraints. Consequently, where those constraints are concerned, it is not the case that when the judges' votes differ from those of the public-spirited citizen and her like-minded supporters, the judges' votes necessarily prevail. We should not say to her: 'When their votes differ from yours, theirs are the votes that will prevail.'[17] The public-spirited citizen can get up a petition, and lobby the legislature to override the judges. She only needs to persuade a majority of legislators to do so. And her ability to do so will depend mainly on her ability also to persuade a majority of her fellow citizens to strongly endorse her views. In Canada, after the Supreme Court invalidated the statutory prohibition of abortion, 'the aroused and losing group went immediately to the parliamentary lobby to press for legislative redress'—but it found that there was insufficient 'inclination on the part of the politicians to use the override'.[18]

Consider another of Waldron's arguments. Discussing the popular thesis that judicial enforcement of constitutional rights can enhance the quality of public debates about those rights, and therefore the character of democratic politics, he replies:

The idea that civic republicans and participatory democrats should count this as a gain is a travesty. Civic republicans and participatory democrats are interested in *practical political deliberation*, which is not just any old debating exercise, but a form of discussion among

[14] Waldron, 'A Right-Based Critique of Constitutional Rights', n. 13 above, 50–1. Note that all the main arguments made in *Law and Disagreement* were prefigured in this article.

[15] Earlier in the same article Waldron makes it clear that he is concerned with constitutionally 'entrenched' rights, which are 'immune' from legislative change, and therefore 'disable' the legislature and the citizens it represents; ibid. 27. He also notes that his concern is with 'American-style' judicial review; ibid. 19.

[16] Waldron, n. 12 above, 275.

[17] Waldron, 'A Right-Based Critique of Constitutional Rights', n. 13 above, 50–1.

[18] P. H. Russell, 'Canadian Constraints on Judicialization from Without', (1994) 15 *International Political Science Review* 165, 171, quoted in M. Tushnet, 'Policy Distortion and Democratic Debilitation: Comparative Illumination of the Counter-majoritarian Difficulty', (1995) 94 *Michigan Law Review* 245 n. 151.

> those who are about to participate in a binding collective decision. A star-struck people may speculate about what the Supreme Court will do next on abortion or some similar issue; they may even amuse each other, as we law professors do, with stories about how we would decide, in the unlikely event that we were elevated to that eminent tribunal. The exercise of power by a few black-robed celebrities can certainly be expected to *fascinate* an articulate population. But that is hardly the essence of active citizenship. Perhaps such impotent debating is nevertheless morally improving . . . But independent ethical benefits of this kind are . . . not the primary point of civic participation in republican political theory.[19]

This reply is based on the assumption that public discussion of judicial decisions concerning constitutional rights is politically impotent: since a constitutional amendment is rarely politically feasible, those decisions are usually conclusive for practical purposes. But if section 33 of the Charter can be invoked, that assumption is simply inoperative. Public discussion is not politically impotent.

Opponents of judicial review usually respond by pointing out that section 33 is very rarely used, because it is too politically dangerous. But the most likely reason for legislators not using the override is that the electorate is unlikely to trust their judgment about constitutional rights more than judges' judgment. And surely that is the electorate's democratic prerogative, which Waldron would be bound to respect. It would not be open to him to object that an ingenuous electorate is likely to be deceived by the specious objectivity of constitutionalized rights, or dazzled by the mystique of the judiciary—by a naive faith in judges' expert legal skills, superior wisdom, and impartiality. That objection would reflect precisely the same lack of faith in the electorate's capacity for enlightened self-government that motivates proponents of constitutionally entrenched rights. They fear that a majority of voters, motivated by ignorance, prejudice, or passion, might trample on the rights of minorities or individuals. Waldron objects that ordinary people should not be presumed to be ignorant, prejudiced, or intemperate, because that would be inconsistent with the basis of their having rights in the first place. '. . . since the point of any argument about rights has to do with the respect that is owed to [the ordinary] person as an active, thinking being, we are hardly in a position to say that our conversation takes his rights seriously if at the same time we ignore or slight anything he has to say about the matter.'[20] But if a majority's opinions about the rights even of minorities and individuals are entitled to respect, surely their opinions about the exercise of one of their own rights—to political participation—is entitled to even more respect, because in that case there is even less danger of ignorance or prejudice. We are concerned here with the 'right of rights' of a majority of ordinary people collectively to make final decisions about rights, if necessary by endorsing a use of the override clause. It would be inconsistent for Waldron to base the right to political participation on the capacity of ordinary people for intelligent and conscientious moral deliberation, but then to doubt that capacity when it comes to deliberating about the use of an override clause. If a majority of ordinary

[19] Waldron, n. 12 above, 291.

[20] Ibid. 251.

people strongly prefer that an override not be used, because in relation to rights they trust judges more than legislators—or perhaps even more than themselves—how can the rights-based theorist say they are wrong?

This question, incidentally, touches on the new Human Rights Act 1998 (UK), which authorizes judges to declare legislation to be incompatible with protected rights, but not to invalidate it. The government and Parliament will be legally free to decide whether or not the legislation should consequently be amended or repealed. It is sometimes suggested that this freedom will prove to be illusory, because it will not be politically feasible to ignore a judicial declaration of incompatibility. Only time will tell. But even if this proves to be the case, it will not follow that the judiciary has been given power to trump the democratic process. The democratic process will determine what is or is not politically feasible.

Someone might be tempted to respond to this argument along much the same lines that Waldron takes in refuting a very different argument. That different argument is this: if a bill of rights has been adopted democratically, with the support of a majority of the people, then judicial invalidation of statutes for violating those rights is perfectly democratic because the people have authorized it. Waldron replies that if the people chose to establish a dictatorship, it would not follow that the dictatorship was democratic—it would only follow that democracy had been extinguished democratically. He suggests that the democratic adoption of a bill of rights 'amounts to exactly that: voting democracy out of existence, at least so far as a wide range of issues of political principle is concerned'.[21] Could a similar reply be made here—that a routine reluctance to use an override clause to trump judicial decisions is in effect a democratic abdication of democratic rights?

There is clearly a difference between relinquishing or disabling one's power to make certain kinds of decisions, and declining—even routinely—to exercise it. For example, in constitutional law there is a crucial difference between, on the one hand, a legislature irrevocably transferring its powers to another body and, on the other, its delegating those powers while retaining its ability at any time to override its delegate or even cancel the delegation. It is possible to distinguish between many different arrangements, including: (1) the permanent surrender of power; (2) the indefinite surrender of power, subject to the possibility of reclaiming it by onerous means such as a constitutional amendment; (3) the temporary surrender of power to a delegate for a fixed period, followed by its resumption or fresh delegation to the same or some other delegate; and (4) the delegation of power, whether indefinite or temporary, subject to the retention of power at any time to override the delegate and/or cancel the delegation by non-onerous means.

Democracy is surely compatible with arrangements (3) and (4), even if this is doubtful in the case of (2). Indeed, modern representative democracies

[21] Waldron, 'A Right-Based Critique of Constitutional Rights', n. 13 above, 46.

resemble (3): the electorate confers legislative power on elected officials for more or less fixed periods, retaining only the power occasionally to decide whether to extend their terms or replace them.[22] We do not generally regard this as undemocratic. Nor do we regard as undemocratic the delegation of extensive law-making power to unelected officials, provided that elected officials retain the power to override them. Much modern law-making consists of regulations made by executive governments, which elected legislatures can scrutinize before they come into operation, and disallow if they see fit. Even if it were the case that legislatures seldom disallow such regulations, that would not in itself demonstrate a diminution of democracy.

It follows that we regard democracy as based on a *right* to participate *indirectly*, rather than a *duty* to participate *directly*, in public decision-making.[23] A right, by definition, does not have to be exercised; otherwise, it would be a duty rather than a right.[24] Of course, a right can be accompanied by a duty to exercise it. In Australia, for example, voters have a legal duty to exercise their right to vote. But a rights-based theorist should surely argue against the imposition of such duties. Rights are maximized if they coexist with rights *not* to exercise them. In countries where voters do not have a duty to vote, for example, some voters deliberately refuse to vote in order to express their disapproval of the candidates or the political process. Their right not to vote reflects a broader freedom not to participate in processes they find distasteful. It follows from all this that a rights-based theorist is not well placed to object to the infrequent exercise of a democratic right to override judicial decisions.

So an override clause is not subject, merely because it is rarely used, to an objection similar to Waldron's rebuttal of the 'democratic' justification of entrenched constitutional rights. This point can be taken one step further. The existence of an override clause rebuts Waldron's rebuttal. He objects that judicial enforcement of a bill of rights is undemocratic even if the bill was adopted democratically. His objection assumes that by adopting a bill of rights, the democratic process more or less permanently transferred to the judiciary the power of ultimate decision-making with respect to those rights. But to the extent that judicial decisions can be overridden, that assumption is inapplicable, and the objection therefore baseless. The transfer of power to the judges is more like a delegation of power to make decisions that can be overridden by the legislature, just as it can override the exercise of powers it has delegated to the executive. The 'democratic' justification of entrenched constitutional rights then stands undefeated.

[22] This resembles (3) because the electorate is usually unable to exercise legislative power itself, and therefore cannot resume the power. Electors are restricted to choosing those who will exercise the power on their behalf.

[23] Except in Australia, where compulsory voting in both elections and constitutional referenda in effect imposes a duty to participate both indirectly and directly in different decision-making processes.

[24] Of course, a right can be accompanied by a duty: in Australia the right to vote is accompanied by a duty to exercise it.

Goal-based objections to constitutional rights

According to Waldron, 'If there is a democratic objection to judicial review, it must also be a rights-based objection.'[25] But that is surely wrong. Democracy has been defended on many grounds other than rights, such as perfectionist and consequentialist grounds (which I will collectively call goal-based grounds). For example, it has been argued that widespread participation in public debate and decision-making, in which all are treated as equals, helps develop important civic virtues: it lessens feelings of powerlessness, and improves self-confidence and self-respect; it promotes education, a broadening of horizons, and an appreciation of other points of view; and by doing so, it fosters cooperation and compromise, a sense of responsibility to the community, and a more willing acceptance of group decisions.[26]

Representative democracy may be more conducive to the realization of these benefits than direct democracy. A system in which decisions can only be made by representatives of the people, after debating contentious issues face to face, rather than by the people themselves in a mass plebiscite, encourages due deliberation before decision-making. The presence of legislators representing all affected interests makes it more likely that pertinent information will be duly considered, and participation in debate requires legislators to listen carefully to one another, even if only to sharpen their rebuttals. Since prejudice and intolerance tend to diminish when people engage in dialogue with one another, representative democracy is thought to promote mutual respect, moderation, and compromise.[27] Moreover, legislators must build coalitions with one another if they are to be effective: all majorities are groupings of minorities that have joined forces in either a political party, a coalition of parties, or a temporary alliance. It is taken for granted that political power is impermanent, and that opponents defeated today might turn the tables tomorrow. This adds to the impetus towards moderation, for two reasons: first, the frequent necessity to sacrifice parochial and extreme demands in order to build the necessary coalitions; and secondly, the fear of backlash if one's temporarily defeated adversaries should gain the upper hand in the future.[28] As Martin Diamond has put it,

> The discovery that one's grossest demands are absurdly impossible of achievement can lead to an enlightened kind of self-interest, a habitual recognition of the indisputable needs of others and a general sobriety about the general requirements of society. And

[25] Waldron, n. 12 above, 282.

[26] For a critical discussion of arguments of this sort, see W. Nelson, *On Justifying Democracy* (London: Routledge & Kegan Paul, 1980), ch. 3.

[27] This may seem to be belied by the frequent angry and contemptuous exchanges between legislators in Australian parliaments. But it is often surmised that these are histrionics, because outside the media limelight the same legislators are respectful and even friendly towards one another.

[28] I owe the ideas in this paragraph to R. Knopff, 'Populism and the Politics of Rights: The Dual Attack on Representative Democracy', (1998) 31 *Canadian Journal of Political Science* 683, 689–94.

something still worthier can happen. As the extremes of selfishness are moderated, the representative can become free to consider questions affecting the national interest on their merits.[29]

It is sometimes argued that the realization of these benefits is jeopardized when politics is 'judicialized' by the enforcement of constitutional rights through litigation. 'Democratic debilitation', a term coined by Mark Tushnet, is a useful label for many ways in which, it has been alleged, such litigation might damage both the process and spirit of representative democracy.[30] Democratic debilitation can affect either legislatures, the electorate, or both. Moreover, predictions of debilitation are sometimes difficult to reconcile with one another. For example, some expect the judicialization of politics to engender apathy and irresponsibility among legislators and the electorate, whereas others anticipate an aggravation of political extremism and intolerance, which is hardly a symptom of apathy.

The argument for apathy and irresponsibility goes something like this. First, legislators might be inclined to devote less attention to the compatibility of proposed legislation with protected rights if the matter is likely to be litigated in the courts anyway. They might become reckless as to compatibility or, worse still, 'pass the buck' to the courts, and shirk responsibility for unpopular decisions they would otherwise have to make. Secondly, frequent resort to litigation to advance claims of rights might divert vital funds and energies from grass-roots political mobilization, and even victory in the courtroom could engender political impotence because of complacency. Constitutional challenges are 'conducted via technocratic representation, i.e. lawyers, who only demand fund-raising from their clientele, not advice, not meetings, marches or votes. A victory in the courts may still leave a broke and apathetic rump organization behind, not one capable of moving forward any further.'[31] Thirdly, if political debate is subsumed by constitutional debate, couched in legalistic jargon and formulas, laypeople (including legislators) may come to be regarded, and to regard themselves, as incompetent to participate.[32] Consequently, they might lose interest in the debate. Fourthly, the loss of ultimate responsibility for how questions about rights are decided might make the electorate more politically enervated, apathetic, or even irresponsible. James Bradley Thayer famously urged judicial restraint partly because an excessive readiness to

[29] M. Diamond, *The Founding of the Democratic Republic* (Itasca, Ill.: Peacock, 1981), 78, quoted in Knopff, n. 28 above, 691.

[30] Tushnet, n. 18 above.

[31] H. Glasbeek, 'A No-Frills Look at the Charter of Rights and Freedoms, or, How Politicians and Lawyers Hide Reality', (1989) 9 *Windsor Yearbook of Access to Justice* 293, 344. For strong evidence of this in the United States, see G. Rosenberg, *The Hollow Hope: Can Courts Bring About Social Change?* (Chicago: University of Chicago Press, 1991), 12, 282, 313–14, and 339–41. On the other hand, Rosenberg also reports that courtroom victories can galvanize the opposition into strenuous political efforts to overturn them; ibid. 155–6, 138–9, and 341–2.

[32] This may also impoverish political debate by confining it to a procrustean bed of constitutional formulas. As Waldron suggests, it is healthier to discuss issues of principle directly and freely, 'rather than having to scramble around constructing those principles out of the scraps of some sacred text, in a tendentious exercise of constitutional calligraphy'; Waldron, n. 12 above, 220, 289–90.

overrule the legislature might gradually diminish 'the political capacity of the people' and its sense of moral responsibility.[33]

The argument for extremism and intolerance has been put most eloquently by the leading Charter critics F. L. Morton and Rainer Knopff. They argue that when judges can enforce rights, political antagonists become more inclined to resolve disagreements through litigation, rather than respectful discussion with one another in a search for compromise. This aggravates and polarizes disputes, by inflating policy claims that are open to reasonable disagreement, into moral absolutes that brook no opposition. The rhetoric of rights encourages the assumption that there is a single, correct answer to contentious questions of social policy, resistance to which is wrong or even illegitimate, and should therefore be permanently overridden. 'The courtroom process is inescapably about claiming the uncompromisable trumps known as rights, and it thus encourages participants to speak the language of extremism both in and out of the courtroom.'[34] Morton and Knopff summarize their objection to the Charter as follows:

> To transfer the resolution of reasonable disagreements from legislatures to courts inflates rhetoric to unwarranted levels and replaces negotiated, majoritarian compromise politics with the intensely held policy preferences of minorities. Rights-based judicial policy-making also grants the policy preferences of courtroom victors an aura of coercive force and permanence that they do not deserve. Issues that should be subject to the ongoing flux of government by discussion are presented as beyond legitimate debate, with the partisans claiming the right to permanent victory. As the moralist of rights displaces the morality of consent, the politics of coercion replaces the politics of persuasion. The result is to embitter politics and decrease the inclination of political opponents to treat each other as fellow citizens . . .[35]

Although these two arguments, for apathy and irresponsibility, and for extremism and intolerance, are not obviously compatible, they are reconcilable. It might be hypothesized that the majority of legislators and citizens—who occupy the broad 'middle ground' of politics—will become more apathetic and irresponsible, while those closer to the ends of the political spectrum will become more zealous and intolerant of their opponents. This might happen if a policy status quo, established by the moderate majority, strikes a compromise between two passionately opposed minorities. If one minority persuades a court to overturn that status quo in its favour, members of the moderate majority might not think it worth the effort required to overturn the judicial decision, given that their views were not passionately held in the first place. Their reluctance to do so might be reinforced by lack of confidence in their competence to dispute the complex legalistic reasoning of judges presumed to possess special expertise about constitutional rights. On the other hand, the opposed minority, outraged by their adversaries' courtroom victory, might mount a furious effort to reverse it, escalating the political struggle between these groups and aggravating their

[33] See J. B. Thayer, *John Marshall* (Chicago: University of Chicago Press, 1967), 85–6.

[34] Knopff, n. 28 above, 702.

[35] Morton and Knopff, n. 7 above, 166.

mutual animosity. According to Mary Ann Glendon, this was precisely what happened in the aftermath of the abortion decision in *Roe v Wade*:[36]

American experience suggests that the real danger represented by regular invalidation of legislation on constitutional grounds is not that elected representatives will rise up in anger against the courts. On the contrary, legislators are often relieved at being able to say that their hands are tied by the courts, especially where controversial matters are concerned. One danger is, rather, of atrophy in the democratic processes of bargaining, education, and persuasion that takes place in and around legislatures. Another is that by too readily preventing compromise and blocking the normal political avenues for change, courts leave the disappointed majority with no legitimate political outlet... Public debate about abortion in Europe has not put an end to controversy. But it is not marked by the degree of bitterness, desperation, and outrage that occasionally erupts into violence in the United States.[37]

Although Canadian legislatures can override judicial decisions, they may fail to do so for the very reasons just described. Apathy or political inertia on the part of the moderate majority, and the increased intransigence of the opposed minorities, can make it impossible to assemble the necessary numbers. That is how Morton and Knopff explain the failure of Canadian legislatures to make better use of section 33 to override unpopular judicial decisions.[38] But their argument also suggests that on the odd occasions when legislatures do employ section 33, the political process is likely to be further embittered by howls of outrage from the defeated minority, whose self-righteousness would have been inflated by vindication in the courts.[39] Whatever the outcome, on this view, the flames of extremism are likely to be fanned.

Morton and Knopff's analysis is contested by Peter Hogg, who claims that in Canada judicial enforcement of rights has generated a 'dialogue' between courts and legislatures that has actually enhanced the democratic process.[40] He has systematically examined legislative responses to judicial decisions invalidating legislation under the Charter, and concludes that in most cases new legislation was passed that accomplished the legislature's original objective consistently with the courts' interpretation of relevant Charter rights.[41] If so, then at least in these cases, the claim that Charter successes tend to induce defeatism and apathy among moderate majorities, and thereby entrench the views of extremist minorities, would seem to be falsified.[42] Morton and Knopff concede that legislatures often

[36] 410 US 113 (1973).

[37] M. A. Glendon, '*A Beau Mentir Qui Vient De Lion*: The 1988 Canadian Abortion Decision in Comparative Perspective', (1989) 83 *Northwestern University Law Review* 569, 588.

[38] Morton and Knopff, n. 7 above, 163 and 165.

[39] See ibid. 155–7 on the 'moral inflation' encouraged by the rhetoric of rights.

[40] See P. W. Hogg, 'The *Charter* Revolution: Is It Undemocratic?', (2001–2) 12 *Constitutional Forum* 1. Hogg's 'dialogue theory' is discussed at greater length by George Williams, Ch. 12 above.

[41] See P. W. Hogg and A. A. Bushell, 'The Charter Dialogue Between Courts and Legislatures', (1997) 35 *Osgoode Hall Law Journal* 75.

[42] Hogg goes so far as to suggest that Morton and Knopff's two examples of legislative inertia are in fact examples of dialogue; n. 40 above, 6–7; contra, Morton and Knopff, n. 7 above, 162–5.

fail to respond to Charter decisions because they concern moral questions that are 'not a priority for the government, the opposition parties, or the majority of voters', and that 'When the policy is central to the government's program, the government should have little difficulty mustering the political will to respond effectively.'[43] This suggests that the main stumbling block to effective legislative responses is not general political apathy caused by the Charter, but relative indifference about particular issues that is independent of it. Moreover, legislators would surely be more willing to use section 33 if they did not fear that doing so would be unpopular with voters. Carefully designed surveys of public opinion in Canada indicate that in the abstract, more than two-thirds of the Canadian public prefer the courts, rather than legislatures, to have the final say in relation to Charter rights. This proportion declines, particularly among Francophones, when people consider the question in the context of specific issues such as laws controlling trade unions or assisting poor people; but it remains over 50 per cent.[44] This has been attributed partly to the diminished moral authority of Canadian legislatures, due to their lack of adequate internal checks and balances.[45] This does not suggest apathy among voters, but rather, a positive distrust of their elected legislators. And who can confidently say that this distrust is undeserved?

Hogg's 'dialogue' theory, and analysis of legislative responses to judicial decisions that underlies it, have been challenged.[46] It is beyond the scope of this chapter to attempt to settle that debate, or the broader question of the impact of judicial enforcement of Charter rights on Canadian political culture. That would require gathering and interpreting empirical evidence of changes in the behaviour and motivations of citizens and legislators throughout the country, involving very difficult questions of cause and effect. For present purposes, the important point is that when a bill of rights includes a comprehensive override clause, it survives Waldron's rights-based objection. The question of its compatibility with democratic values then depends on sociological evidence that is inevitably impressionistic and contestable.

The desuetude of section 33

Even if Morton and Knopff are right, it is natural to ask why section 33 has not been effective in preventing or at least minimizing the democratic debilitation

[43] Morton and Knopff, n. 7 above, 164 and 165.

[44] Predictably, politicians are much more inclined to favour legislatures, and lawyers to favour courts. See P. M. Sniderman, J. F. Fletcher, P. H. Russell, and P. E. Tetlock (eds.), *The Clash of Rights, Liberty, Equality, and Legitimacy in Pluralist Democracy* (New Haven: Yale University Press, 1996), 163–7.

[45] Knopff and Morton, n. 10 above, 232.

[46] See, for example, C. Manfredi and J. B. Kelly, 'Six Degrees of Dialogue: A Response to Hogg and Bushell', (1999) 37 *Osgoode Hall Law Journal* 513, 513–17; C. Manfredi, *Judicial Power and the Charter: Canada and the Paradox of Liberal Constitutionalism*, 2nd edn. (Toronto: Oxford University Press, 2001), 177–9; P. Hogg and A. A. Thornton, 'Reply to "Six Degrees of Dialogue"', (1999) 37 *Osgoode Hall Law Journal* 513, 536–9.

that they report. When judicial interpretations of rights are conclusive (subject only to constitutional amendment), it is easier to appreciate how democracy might be debilitated. But the whole point of an override clause is to ensure that the judges do not have the final word. Precisely because it enables them to be overridden, such a clause has the potential to stimulate robust and potent political debate, among both legislators and the electorate, about questions of rights that may be or have been decided by judges. In doing so, it could 'encourage a more politically vital discourse on the meaning of rights and their relationship to competing constitutional visions than what emanates from the judicial monologue that exists in a regime of judicial supremacy'.[47]

There is general agreement that section 33 has failed to fulfil that potential in Canada. This is partly because it is widely believed that the clause has been used only once outside Quebec, and not at all since 1988.[48] In a recent thorough study Tsvi Kanaha has demonstrated that it has in fact been used more often than this, but the fact remains that it has been used very rarely.[49] Kanaha also shows that the use of the clause has often failed to generate, among the electorate, the 'politically vital discourse on the meaning of rights' that its supporters had anticipated, although she fails to consider the extent to which legislators have engaged in such discourse before using it.

The clause has been invoked so rarely that arguably 'Something like a convention against its use may have emerged, precisely because the political costs of invoking the power turned out to be too great.'[50] Just as conventions develop through regular practice evolving into prescriptive custom, the less section 33 is used, the more its use is likely to be disapproved of.[51] In 1998 the premier of Alberta withdrew a proposal to use section 33, explaining that 'It became abundantly clear that to individuals in this country the Charter of Rights and Freedoms is paramount and the use of any tool . . . to undermine [it] is something that should be used only in very, very rare circumstances.'[52] This attitude apparently extends to many legislators. Michael Mandel reports that when Prime Minister Mulroney condemned section 33, after Quebec's perceived abuse of it, his speech 'led to the usual declarations by opposition members of their sincere hatred for the clause, and even a challenge to the Prime Minister to abolish it'.[53]

It is not clear why section 33 has been so rarely used. Morton and Knopff's explanation has already been discussed.[54] Howard Leeson hypothesizes that it is the result of a combination of factors: the unwillingness of legislators to 'take on' the judiciary because of its superior popularity among the general public; the

[47] Manfredi, n. 46 above, 191.

[48] Ibid. 5.

[49] T. Kanaha, 'The Notwithstanding Mechanism and Public Discussion: Lessons from the Ignored Practice of Section 33 of the Charter', (2001) 44 *Canadian Public Administration* 255.

[50] Tushnet, n. 18 above, 296, citing A. Heard, *Canadian Constitutional Conventions: The Marriage of Law and Politics* (Toronto: Oxford University Press, 1991), 147.

[51] H. Leeson, 'Section 33, the Notwithstanding Clause: A Paper Tiger?', (2000) 6 *Choices* 20 (Institute for Research on Public Policy).

[52] Quoted in Manfredi, n. 46 above, 187–8.

[53] Mandel, n. 2 above, 95.

[54] Text accompanying n. 38 above.

professionally ingrained and career-oriented tendency of government lawyers, who advise the responsible minister, to recommend deference to the courts; a preference for less drastic legislative responses of the kind discussed by Hogg, with override relegated to weapon of last resort; and a sense of futility given that an override expires after five years unless it is renewed.[55] But two other reasons, not mentioned by Leeson, are often suggested.

One is the wording of section 33. It authorizes Canadian legislatures to declare that their enactments 'shall operate notwithstanding a provision included in [the specified sections] of this Charter'. The power is thus posed as a power to override the Charter itself, rather than disputed judicial interpretations of the Charter. This must make its use very difficult to justify. When the judiciary disagrees, or is expected to disagree, with the legislature as to the 'true' meaning and effect of Charter provisions, the legislature cannot ensure that its view will prevail without appearing to override the Charter itself. And that is vulnerable to the politically lethal objection that the legislature is openly and self-confessedly subverting constitutional rights.

There is surely no need for an override clause to convey that impression, which, at least from the legislature's point of view, is erroneous. Section 33 has always been defended on the ground that, since rights are not absolute, but must often give way to other rights and interests, what they require in particular cases is often a subject of reasonable disagreement; and that there is no good reason to assume that when judges and legislators disagree, the former are necessarily correct.[56] It is unfortunate that this justification is not reflected in the wording of the section itself. Knopff and Morton complain that 'It is surely eloquent testimony to the power of legalism that the Charter provision most obviously embodying non-legalistic scepticism of judicial power was phrased in legalistic language. The form and content of section 33 are mutually contradictory, and the former symbolically undermines the latter!'[57] But an override clause could be drafted differently, to authorize the legislature to declare that a statute or statutory provision shall be deemed by the courts to be consistent with specific, nominated rights. In a healthy democracy, responsible legislators would feel free to override actual or anticipated judicial interpretations of constitutional rights that, after careful and conscientious reflection, they do not agree with. That, after all, is a power exercised by the judges themselves, when they overrule previous judicial decisions that they have come to regard as erroneous. They do not treat their predecessors, or expect their successors to treat them, as infallible oracles.

A related obstacle inherent in the wording of section 33 is its limitation of any override to renewable five-year periods.[58] Overrides are thereby treated as short-term expedients, no doubt because they are described as overriding the Charter itself. If judicial interpretations of rights, rather than the rights themselves, were

[55] Leeson, n. 51 above, 18–19.
[56] See Russell, n. 4 above.
[57] Knopff and Morton, n. 10 above, 179–80.
[58] I am grateful to Grant Huscroft for emphasizing this point in comments sent to me.

treated as overridden, there would be less reason to impose such a limit. That would remove an additional disincentive to using the clause. It is difficult enough for a legislature to summon the political will to use it once, let alone twice or thrice, and a one-off use may not seem worth the effort.

A second reason for the apparent desuetude of section 33 concerns the history of its use. It was first used by the Quebec legislature to insert a notwithstanding clause into all of its statutes then in force. This sweeping and indiscriminate use of the clause was upheld by the Supreme Court of Canada in *Ford v Quebec (Attorney-General)*,[59] notwithstanding contrary expectations about its proper use, and respectable arguments in favour of a narrower interpretation.[60] This confirmed the worst fears of those who had originally objected to the clause,[61] although Hiebert observes that it 'did not evoke widespread public condemnation'.[62] The section was next used by the legislature of Saskatchewan, to protect a statute ordering public employees to end a strike, which was vulnerable to challenge on the ground that it violated freedom of association. This use of section 33 did not incur any voter backlash, and may even have assisted the government's successful bid for re-election.[63] But subsequently Quebec used the section to protect a law prohibiting the use of English in public signs. This was extremely unpopular throughout the rest of Canada, and probably sabotaged the Meech Lake Accord, which was being negotiated at the time.[64] Quebec's use of the section was widely interpreted as subordinating individual rights (of Anglophones) to majoritarian preferences (of Francophones), which seemed to confirm the view that the protection of individual rights could be safely entrusted only to the courts. Prime Minister Mulroney immediately condemned section 33 as a 'fatal flaw' that made the Charter 'not worth the paper it was written on'.[65] As a result, it 'became virtually impossible to defend the use of section 33 outside of Quebec';[66] 'section 33 has now, except for the francophone majority in Quebec, generally assumed the mantle of being constitutionally illegitimate'.[67]

This was arguably the result of fortuitous events in Canadian history, rather than a general law of political dynamics. Quebec's perceived abuse of the section made section 33 virtually unusable before it had been given a 'fair go'. 'The opposition to any use of the notwithstanding clause', argues Manfredi, 'is [partly] the product of historical accident... Canadians experienced a use of section 33 that they found objectionable before the Supreme Court rendered a politically unpopular Charter decision.'[68] Moreover, section 33 could have been either drafted so as to deter Quebec's perceived abuse of it, or interpreted in the

[59] [1988] 2 SCR 712 (Can.).
[60] Manfredi, n. 46 above, 184.
[61] Ibid. 184.
[62] J. Hiebert, *Limiting Rights: The Dilemma of Judicial Review* (Montreal: McGill–Queen's University Press, 1996), 139.
[63] Knopff and Morton, n. 10 above, 30.
[64] Hiebert, n. 62 above, 140–1; Mandel, n. 2 above, 92.
[65] Quoted in W. A. Bogart, *Courts and Country: The Limits of Litigation and the Social and Political Life of Canada* (Toronto: Oxford University Press, 1994), 311.
[66] Manfredi, n. 46 above, 187.
[67] Hiebert, n. 62 above, 139.
[68] Quoted in Tushnet, n. 18 above, 296.

Ford case so as to invalidate that abuse.[69] In either case, section 33 might have been saved from its ignominious fate.

Conclusion

If a bill of rights includes a comprehensive override clause, the question of its compatibility with democratic values cannot be settled by appealing to Waldron's 'right of rights'—the right to participate on an equal basis in the final determination of public policy. This is because the override clause preserves that right. Instead, the question is whether, despite the existence of the override clause, judicial enforcement of constitutional rights corrodes 'the habits and temperament' that are necessary for democracy to thrive.[70] This can only be resolved by sociological evidence of differences in political culture that is extremely difficult both to collect and to interpret.

In principle, an override clause such as section 33 should help legislators resist the democratic debilitation that might otherwise attend the legalization of rights. The failure of Canadian legislatures to make more frequent use of their override clause is something of a puzzle. It may be due to factors peculiar to Canada, especially the ways in which the clause was drafted, interpreted, and allegedly abused by Quebec. Amendments to section 33, which cannot be discussed here, have consequently been proposed in the hope of reinvigorating it.[71] If, even in Canada, there is still hope that a differently worded override clause might be put to better use, the same must be true of other countries. In Australia the Constitutional Commission observed in 1988 that 'Canadian experience in the use of such a power is no safe guide to how such a power might be used in Australia . . . There is no knowing how Australian governments might seek to utilise a legislative override power.'[72]

On the other hand, it is possible that the drafting and early usage of section 33 were not the crucial factors, and that no override clause would have proven politically usable. The major obstacle to the more frequent use of the clause might lie 'less in the existing section 33 than in the perspective of oracular legalism. To the extent that judicial pronouncements are seen as the very embodiment of the constitution, rather than as debatable interpretations of it, the use of section 33 will be seen as illegitimate.'[73]

On this view, legislators, the electorate, or both are the victims of a kind of false consciousness. They are deluded by the specious objectivity of constitutional rights and a naive faith in judges' capacity to discern their true import by virtue of superior legal expertise, wisdom, and impartiality.

[69] Quoted in Tushnet, n. 18 above, 299

[70] Morton and Knopff, n. 7 above, 149 and 151.

[71] See, for example, Manfredi, n. 46 above, 192–3, and Hiebert, n. 62 above, 142.

[72] *Final Report of the Constitutional Commission* (Canberra: Australian Government Publishing Service, 1988), vol. i, p. 494, para 9.222, and p. 495, para 9.224.

[73] Knopff and Morton, n. 10 above, 231.

It is beyond the scope of this chapter to assess this claim, which, in the absence of careful empirical research into public attitudes, presumably rests on anecdotal and impressionistic evidence. Legislators and voters show little sign of being overawed by 'oracular legalism' when seemingly lenient sentences imposed by judges on criminals are subjected (as they often are) to voluble public criticism. But perhaps matters are different where constitutional rights are concerned. In the absence of sufficient evidence to assess the claim, some general points can nevertheless be made.

As previously observed, there are two obstacles to rights-based democrats making such a claim. First, even if legislators and the electorate are deluded, their democratic right to the final say remains intact. Secondly, alleging such a delusion is difficult to reconcile with the basis of that right: namely, the presumption that ordinary people are sufficiently intelligent, knowledgeable, and virtuous to deserve it.[74]

The first of these obstacles does not prevent goal-based democrats from alleging that legislators or the electorate are deluded in this way. From their perspective, the mere preservation of the democratic right to the final say is not the crucial issue. More important are the beneficial consequences that flow from its frequent exercise, and these may be jeopardized if—for whatever reason—it is exercised rarely.

But the second obstacle is not so easily avoided. Goal-based democrats regard the cultivation of intelligence, knowledge, and virtue throughout the community as one of the main beneficial consequences of democracy. Nevertheless, democracy would not be viable unless there was a considerable fund of these qualities to start with. Therefore, even goal-based democrats should have considerable faith in the inherent intelligence, knowledge, and virtue of the electorate. Two points follow. First, if there are two explanations for a popular opinion, one dismissing it as a delusion and the other accepting it as reasonable and possibly even justified, then goal-based democrats should accept the second explanation unless there is very clear evidence of the alleged delusion. Secondly, they should also be confident that their fellow citizens have sufficient intelligence to enable any delusion to be readily dispelled by the dissemination of accurate information. Both points apply to the apparent opinions of ordinary Canadians that their rights are better protected by judges than by legislators, and that the override clause should rarely be used.

It is dangerous for any democrat to allege that the electorate is deluded in this way. If the electorate can be duped by the claim that a small group of people possess superior expertise or wisdom, and persuaded to defer unquestioningly to the judgments of that group, then perhaps they might defer as readily to demagogues as to judges.[75] But that would strengthen the case in favour of constitutional rights.

[74] See text to n. 20 above.

[75] I owe this way of putting the point to Kristen Walker.

14

Addressing Homelessness: Does Australia's Indirect Implementation of Human Rights Comply with its International Obligations?

DIANNE OTTO

Successive Australian governments have chosen, in the main, not to *directly* incorporate Australia's international human rights obligations into domestic law. That is, with some important exceptions, they have not taken the path of adopting legislation, or promoting constitutional change, which would bring international human rights law directly into Australian law and make it amenable to judicial enforcement.[1] Nor have Australian governments followed the lead of their Commonwealth compatriots by adopting some form of intermediate approach, which would empower courts to interpret legislation consistently with its international human rights obligations while retaining parliamentary supremacy, as in Canada,[2] New Zealand,[3] and the United Kingdom.[4] While it is true that *some* human rights are directly protected by the Australian Constitution,[5] by

[1] The Australian government has the option of indirect implementation because treaties are generally non-self-executing in Australia, which means that constitutional amendment or legislation is necessary before treaty obligations are directly applicable in domestic law.

[2] Canadian Charter of Rights and Freedoms 1982, s 33, empowers provincial and federal legislatures, by ordinary majority, to override Charter rights for a renewable period of five years ('notwithstanding' provision).

[3] Bill of Rights Act 1990 (NZ), s 6, requires that courts, wherever possible, prefer an interpretation of legislation that is consistent with the legislatively enacted Bill of Rights over any other interpretation, while s 4 provides that the Bill of Rights cannot invalidate inconsistent legislation.

[4] The Human Rights Act 1998 (UK), s 3, requires that courts read and give effect to legislation in a way that is consistent with the European Convention for the Protection of Human Rights and Fundamental Freedoms 1950, while s 4 empowers the courts to declare legislation incompatible with the Convention, but only the Parliament is able to invalidate such legislation by amendment or repeal.

[5] The express rights in the Commonwealth Constitution include the prohibition of laws limiting the free exercise of religion (s 116), a largely formal right to trial by jury for federal indictable offences (s 80), protection against discrimination on the basis of residence in one state rather than another (s 117), a guarantee that compulsory acquisition of property takes place on just terms (s 51(xxxi)), and a guarantee that interstate trade, commerce, and intercourse be absolutely free (s 92). For a more expansive reading of express rights in the Australian Constitution, see P. Bailey, *Human Rights:*

legislation,[6] and by way of the common law,[7] and that international human rights law can in certain circumstances influence statutory interpretation, the development of the common law, administrative decision-making, and constitutional interpretation,[8] the coverage falls a very long way short of being either systematic or comprehensive when measured against Australia's international human rights obligations.

Instead, Australian governments have relied on the *indirect* effects of legislation and government policies and programmes to ensure the enjoyment of many human rights, including civil and political rights such as freedom of speech, the right to vote and the right to peaceful assembly, and most economic and social rights. As explained in its recent periodic report to the UN Committee on Economic, Social and Cultural Rights (CESCR), the Government believes that 'In many cases, rights are more readily promoted by less formal processes [than traditional legal sanctions], often associated with inquiry, conciliation and report.'[9] This indirect approach is justified as being consistent with the institution of responsible government in a democracy, whereby human rights are best articulated and protected through democratic rather than judicial processes.[10] Indeed, proponents of this argument urge that the right of everyone to be equally involved in decision-making about rights guarantees is itself a fundamental human right.[11] Various other rationales for the Australian approach have included deference to federal constitutional arrangements, the fear of legalizing politics by attributing too much power to an unelected and

Australia in an International Context (Sydney: Butterworths, 1990), 84–6. The High Court of Australia has also recognized implied constitutional rights to freedom of political communication, movement, and association, and to procedural due process in the exercise of judicial power. For a comprehensive discussion of implied constitutional rights, see G. Williams, *Human Rights Under the Australian Constitution* (Melbourne: Oxford University Press, 1999).

[6] The Racial Discrimination Act 1975 (Cth), Sex Discrimination Act 1984 (Cth), Human Rights and Equal Opportunity Commission Act 1986 (Cth), Disability Discrimination Act 1992 (Cth), and Crimes (Torture) Act 1998 (Cth) all directly implement, but in a more or less limited way, some of Australia's international human rights obligations. Further, the Human Rights (Sexual Conduct) Act 1994 (Cth) and the Privacy Act 1988 (Cth) partially implement the right to privacy, Art 17 of the International Covenant on Civil and Political Rights 1966. Many of these protections can also be found in state and territory legislation. Some of Australia's international human rights obligations are also directly implemented through industrial relations legislation.

[7] See *Dietrich v The Queen* (1992) 177 CLR 292, recognizing that the common law requirement of a fair trial requires, in most cases, that an indigent be provided with representation at public expense. But the human rights protections offered by the common law are limited, especially in relation to social and political equality and non-discrimination. See, for example, *Leeth v Commonwealth* (1992) 174 CLR 455; and *Kruger v Commonwealth* (1997) 146 ALR 126.

[8] K. Eastman and C. Ronalds, 'Using Human Rights Law in Litigation: A Practitioner's Perspective', in D. Kinley (ed.), *Human Rights in Australian Law* (Sydney: Federation Press, 1998).

[9] *Third Periodic Report: Australia*, 23/07/98, E/1994/104.Add/22, para 21.

[10] Sir Robert Menzies, former Australian prime minister, gives a classic exposition of this view in *Central Power in the Australian Commonwealth* (Charlottesville: University Press of Virginia, 1967), 54. For a more sophisticated defence of democratic promotion and protection of human rights, see T. Campbell, 'Democracy, Human Rights and Positive Law', (1994) 16 *Sydney Law Review* 195.

[11] J. Waldron, 'A Right-Based Critique of Constitutional Rights', (1993) 13 *Oxford Journal of Legal Studies* 18.

politicized judiciary, and an enduring commitment to utilitarianism.[12] Even with respect to economic and social rights, the Australian argument has been more about the appropriate means of articulating and enforcing them than about their justiciability per se.

This chapter explores whether the Australian approach to implementing human rights, indirectly through democratic political processes rather than directly through judicial enforcement, fulfils Australia's obligations under international law to ensure that all Australians enjoy the human rights enumerated in the human rights treaties to which it is a party. Using the national Supported Accommodation Assistance Program (SAAP)[13] as a case-study, I argue that the Australian system, in its present form, does not adequately implement Australia's international obligations because it does not, on its own terms, provide adequate non-judicial accountability mechanisms that would ensure 'effective remedies' for any violations. Ultimately, I am asking how Australians want to treat the most vulnerable and disadvantaged members of the community, and, in the expectation that the response will embrace the universal standards of human rights, I conclude that a revised mix of legal and political mechanisms that strengthens democratic debate and non-judicial enforcement, while also giving more power to courts than they currently enjoy yet maintaining parliamentary supremacy, will best achieve that humane, just, equitable, *and* democratic society.

What are Australia's international human rights obligations?

My discussion will focus on the implementation of the International Covenant on Economic, Social and Cultural Rights 1966 (ICESCR),[14] which is undoubtedly the most neglected human rights treaty in the Australian political and legal landscape. Until the end of the cold war this could be said to parallel a more general neglect of economic and social rights internationally, due partly to cold war ideological disputes about the proper limits of state power and partly to disputes within liberalism about the justiciability of economic and social 'rights'.[15] The legacy of this era was a lack of normative development of many

[12] H. Charlesworth, 'The Australian Reluctance About Rights', in P. Alston (ed.), *Towards an Australian Bill of Rights* (Canberra: Centre for International and Public Law, 1994), 21, 22.

[13] SAAP was the first nationally coordinated approach to addressing homelessness in Australia, commencing in 1985.

[14] International Covenant on Economic, Social and Cultural Rights 1966 (ICESCR), UN GA Res 2200A(XXI) (16 Dec. 1966).

[15] See E. W. Vierdag, 'The Legal Nature of the Rights Granted by the International Covenant on Economic, Social and Cultural Rights', (1978) 9 *Netherlands Yearbook of International Law* 69; M. Cranston, *What Are Human Rights?* (New York: Taplinger, 1973), 65–71; contra G. J. H. van Hoof, 'The Legal Nature of Economic, Social and Cultural Rights: A Rebuttal of Some Traditional Views', in P. Alston and K. Tomasevski (eds.), *The Right to Food* (The Hague: Martinus Nijhoff, 1984), 97, 98–102; K. D. Ewing, 'Social Rights and Constitutional Law', [1999] *Public Law* 104.

of the rights enumerated in the ICESCR and a dearth of national institutions specifically committed to the promotion of economic and social rights.[16] The Australian Human Rights and Equal Opportunity Commission (HREOC), the most important of the Government's 'less formal' measures to promote human rights, is a prime example of the ambivalence towards economic and social rights at that time. The HREOC Act 1986 (Cth) failed to include the ICESCR in its scheduling of human rights instruments, which define 'human rights' for the purposes of the Act.[17] This means that ICESCR rights are not even subject to the limited oversighting and conciliation functions of HREOC. While some of the rights enumerated in the ICESCR are nevertheless included by way of the other instruments listed in the Schedule,[18] a large gap remains.

Since the end of the cold war, ambivalence about economic and social rights has altered significantly, with the inclusion of economic and social rights in many national constitutions, the adoption of a Collective Complaints Protocol to the European Social Charter 1961, and the tireless normative work of the CESCR, which was established in 1985 to monitor the implementation of the ICESCR.[19] At the centre of this changing landscape is a rejection of the earlier cartography that drew a distinction between rights according to whether they involved negative or positive implementation obligations.[20] The misleading dualistic conceptualization has been superseded by a four-part typology of duties, which is applicable to all human rights.[21] The typology layers state responsibility to fully realize *every* human right into four separate, yet interconnected, obligations

[16] P. Alston, 'The Committee on Economic, Social and Cultural Rights', in P. Alston (ed.), *The United Nations and Human Rights: A Critical Appraisal* (New York: Oxford University Press, 1992), 473, 474.

[17] The exclusion of the ICESCR was despite its entry into force for Australia, without reservation, on 10 Mar. 1976.

[18] All the scheduled instruments contain some economic and social rights: the International Covenant on Civil and Political Rights 1966 (ICCPR), UN GA Res 2200A(XXI) (16 Dec. 1966); the Convention Concerning Discrimination in Respect of Employment and Occupation 1958 (ILO Convention no. 111); the Convention on the Rights of the Child 1989, UN GA Res 44/25 (20 Nov. 1989); the Declaration on the Rights of the Child 1959, UN GA Res 1386 (XVIV) (29 Nov. 1959); the Declaration on the Rights of Disabled Persons 1975, UN GA Res 3447 (XXX) (9 Dec. 1975); the Declaration on the Rights of Mentally Retarded Persons 1971, UN GA Res 2856 (XXVI) (20 Dec. 1971); and the Declaration on the Elimination of All Forms of Intolerance and of Discrimination Based on Religion or Belief 1981, UN GA Res 36/55 (25 Nov. 1981).

[19] Unlike the other main human rights treaties, the ICESCR did not establish a treaty-monitoring committee, but instead left this task to the Economic and Social Council (ECOSOC). ECOSOC established the CESCR as a subsidiary organ to fulfil this role in ECOSOC Res 1985/17, 1985 UN ESCOR Supp (no. 1) at 15, UN Doc E/1985/85 (1985). The CESCR consists of eighteen experts serving in their personal capacity for four-year terms. They are elected by ECOSOC from candidates nominated by states parties.

[20] H. Shue, *Basic Rights: Subsistence, Affluence and US Foreign Policy* (Princeton: Princeton University Press, 1980).

[21] Building on Henry Shue's work, ibid., the typology was developed by van Hoof, n. 15 above, 106–8. It was embraced in the Limburg Principles on the Implementation of the International Covenant on Economic, Social and Cultural Rights, UN Doc E/CN.4/1987/17, Annex, repr. in (1987) 9 *Human Rights Quarterly* 122. The typology was recently further elaborated in the Maastricht Guidelines on Violations of Economic, Social and Cultural Rights, set out in (1998) 20 *Human Rights Quarterly* 691.

or duties: to respect, protect, promote, and fulfil.[22] The typology demonstrates that economic, social, and cultural rights share the same basic qualities as other human rights and, in particular, it indicates that they are equally capable of being incorporated into national and international legal systems. As the CESCR has emphasized, every ICESCR right has 'at least some significant justiciable dimensions' which, if violated, are appropriately resolved by courts.[23] However, the Australian approach has remained mired in its own mythologies and, outside the anti-discrimination framework, resists even quasi-judicial approaches to incorporating economic and social rights into Australian law.

The specific legal obligation to implement the ICESCR is set out in Article 2(1) as follows:

> Each State Party to the present Covenant undertakes to take steps, individually and through international assistance and cooperation, especially economic and technical, to the maximum of its available resources, with a view to achieving progressively the full realisation of the rights recognized in the present Covenant by all appropriate means, including particularly the adoption of legislative measures.

When considering implementation in a federated state like Australia, Article 28 is also important because it reiterates the general rule of international law that the Federal Government's international obligations are not limited by the division of powers between different levels of government:[24] 'The provisions of the present Covenant shall extend to all parts of federal States without any limitations or exceptions.'

Therefore, the Federal Government must ensure that state[25] governments play their part to the extent that implementation falls within their respective constitutional powers, which may be considerable. While the Federal Government theoretically has the constitutional power to legislate to implement its international treaty obligations under the external affairs power,[26] in keeping with their general antipathy to incorporation, successive governments have instead relied on the cooperation of the states.[27] Implementation that relies on

[22] Briefly, the duty to *respect* refers to a state's obligation to refrain from acting in ways that would deprive people of their rights or impair their enjoyment of them, and is immediately applicable. The duty to *protect* requires states to act to ensure that third parties (private actors) do not violate human rights. The duty to *promote* includes ensuring human rights education at all levels of society. The duty to *fulfil* obliges states to take positive action to ensure that rights are realized or made accessible to everyone.

[23] 'The domestic application of the Covenant: 03/12/98', *CESCR General Comment 9*, E/C.12/1998/24, 3 Dec. 1998, para 10, in *Compilation of General Comments and General Recommendations Adopted by Human Rights Treaty Bodies*, HRI/GEN/1/Rev.5, 26 Apr. 2001 (hereafter *Compilation of General Comments*).

[24] Vienna Convention on the Law of Treaties 1969, Art 27: '[A] party may not invoke the provisions of its internal law as justification for its failure to perform a treaty.'

[25] References to 'states' include the Northern Territory and the Australian Capital Territory.

[26] See *Koowarta v Bjelke-Petersen* (1982) 153 CLR 168; *Commonwealth v Tasmania* (*Tasmanian Dam* case) (1983) 158 CLR 1.

[27] D. Williams, 'Australia's Treaty-Making Processes: The Coalition's Reform Proposals', in P. Alston and M. Chan (eds.), *Treaty-Making and Australia: Globalization Versus Sovereignty?* (Sydney: Federation Press, 1995), 185.

intergovernmental consultation and cooperation will always be vulnerable to political exigencies, which will tend to be incompatible with human rights norms, in the absence of effective mechanisms of human rights accountability and a strong human rights culture. These absences are a major weakness in the Australia system of indirect implementation, as will be illustrated by the case-study.

Article 11(1) of the ICESCR, largely repeating the text of Article 25 of the Universal Declaration of Human Rights 1948,[28] sets out the right to an adequate standard of living in the following terms:

> The States Parties to the present Covenant recognize the right of everyone to an adequate standard of living for himself [*sic*] and his family, including adequate food, clothing and housing, and to the continuous improvement of living conditions. The States Parties will take appropriate steps to ensure the realisation of this right, recognising to this effect the essential importance of international cooperation based on free consent.

Under this article the Government commits itself to 'recognise' that *everyone* within its jurisdiction, not just male-headed households as suggested by the text,[29] has the right to adequate food, clothing, and housing, and to living standards that are continuously improved. Fully implementing Article 11(1) involves recognizing that it depends on a complex interplay of economic and social conditions and the enjoyment of other rights, including many civil and political rights.[30] Despite this complexity, the CESCR has adopted three General Comments,[31] which identify specific obligations relating to Article 11(1) and help to make the task of implementation more tangible.[32] In the first of these the CESCR rejects the view that the right to adequate housing is satisfied by the mere presence of a roof over one's head, insisting instead that it involves 'the right to live somewhere in security, peace and dignity'.[33] The General

[28] UN GA Res 217A(III), 10 Dec. 1948.

[29] 'The Right to Adequate Housing', *CESCR General Comment No. 4* (6th Sess. 1991), para 6: 'While the reference to "himself and his family" reflects assumptions as to gender roles and economic activity patterns commonly accepted in 1966 when the Covenant was adopted, the phrase cannot be read today as implying any limitations on the applicability of the right to individuals or to female-headed households or to other such groups.' See, further, 'The Right to Adequate Food', *CESCR General Comment No. 12* (20th Sess. 1999), para 1, *Compilation of General Comments*, n. 23 above.

[30] *CESCR General Comment No. 4*, n. 29 above, para 9. See, further, L. Farha, 'Women and Housing', in K. D. Askin and D. M. Koenig (eds.), *Women and International Human Rights Law*, i (Ardsley, NY: Transnational Publishers, 1999), 483, 494.

[31] The purpose of General Comments is to consolidate the experience that has been gained from examining states' periodic reports and make it available to assist and encourage the further implementation of the ICESCR by all states parties. See, further, 'Reporting by States Parties', *CESCR General Comment No. 1* (1989), para 3, *Compilation of General Comments*, n. 23 above. Many General Comments provide authoritative interpretations of the Covenant's provisions, which make important contributions to the normative development of the Covenant rights.

[32] *CESCR General Comment No. 4*, n. 29 above; 'The Right to Adequate Housing: Forced Evictions', *CESCR General Comment No. 7* (16th Sess. 1997), *Compilation of General Comments*, n. 23 above; and *CESCR General Comment No. 12*, n. 29 above.

[33] *CESCR General Comment No. 4*, n. 29 above, para 7. At para 8 the CESCR identifies various requirements of the concept of 'adequacy', including legal security of tenure, availability of services and infrastructure, affordability, habitability, accessibility, location, and cultural adequacy.

Comment also notes that homelessness and inadequate housing are significant problems in some of the most economically developed countries.[34]

Appraising the Australian Government's compliance with its obligations under Article 11(1), in relation to homeless people, requires assessing the measures the Government has adopted to address homelessness against the four main requirements of Article 2(1). The first, that the Government must 'take steps' towards realizing the right, is an obligation of conduct. Although the wording falls short of requiring that the right to an adequate standard of living be 'guaranteed', it is a positive undertaking. Therefore, the Government cannot be inactive, or just refrain from taking steps that would result in an increase in homelessness, but must immediately act to adopt measures aimed at achieving the 'full realisation' of Article 11(1).[35] The steps taken 'should be deliberate, concrete and targeted as clearly as possible towards meeting the obligations recognised in the Covenant'.[36] Among the steps envisaged by the CESCR are adopting a national housing strategy,[37] giving due priority to addressing the housing needs of disadvantaged groups,[38] and effectively monitoring the full extent of homelessness and inadequate housing.[39]

The second requirement is that the steps taken must be 'with a view to achieving progressively the full realisation of the rights recognised'. Implicit in this wording is the acceptance that states parties may need some time to fully realize economic, social, and cultural rights. However, the CESCR has emphasized that the obligation requires movement 'as expeditiously and effectively as possible towards the goal [of full realisation]'.[40] Therefore, for example, the Government would be expected to achieve, over time, a decrease in the number of homeless people in Australia. Of particular importance is that the obligation does not allow any retrogressive measures, except in the narrowest of circumstances. The CESCR has cautioned that such measures 'would require the most careful consideration and would need to be fully justified by reference to the totality of rights provided for in the Covenant and in the context of the full use of the maximum available resources'.[41] The CESCR has also stressed that there are immediately realizable aspects of every Covenant right, including the obligation to ensure non-discrimination in the enjoyment of all ICESCR rights, as provided for in Articles 2(2) and 3.[42]

The third requirement of Article 2(1) is that the Government take steps 'to the maximum of its available resources'. While resource distribution is primarily a political determination, states parties do not have complete discretion. The

[34] Ibid., para 4.

[35] P. Alston and G. Quinn, 'The Nature and Scope of States Parties' Obligations Under the International Covenant on Economic, Social and Cultural Rights', (1987) 9 *Human Rights Quarterly* 156.

[36] 'Article 2, para. 1: the nature of States parties obligations', *CESCR General Comment No. 3*, para 2 (1990), *Compilation of General Comments*, n. 23 above.

[37] *CESCR General Comment No. 4*, n. 29 above, para 12.

[38] Ibid., para 11.

[39] Ibid., para 13.

[40] *CESCR General Comment No. 3*, n. 36 above, para 9.

[41] Ibid.

[42] Ibid., para 5.

Covenant envisages that budget allocations are reviewable as against the country's 'real' resources, which obliges states parties to show that they have given adequate consideration to their obligations in the budget process.[43] The CESCR has also taken the view that the obligation involves the satisfaction of a 'minimum core' of each of the rights, which includes, *inter alia*, the provision of basic housing.[44] In a developed state like Australia, the concept of a minimum core obligation is not a very useful yardstick, as the resources available should enable the Government to come very close to fully realizing the rights in the ICESCR.[45]

The fourth requirement is implementation by 'all appropriate means'. While Article 2(1) expresses a preference for legislative measures, other means are clearly acceptable. In taking a 'broad and flexible approach',[46] the Covenant leaves considerable scope for states parties to determine the measures they adopt; it is the result of 'progressive movement towards' full realization that is of primary importance, rather than the means of its achievement. However, while the means will be appropriate if they produce the result of progressive realization,[47] the CESCR is also of the view that 'the norms must be recognised in appropriate ways within the domestic legal order'.[48] Consequently, a failure to incorporate a Covenant right directly into the domestic legal system is not necessarily a violation of Article 2(1), but the state party would need to be able to justify its indirect measures in terms of their appropriateness.[49]

Concomitant with the obligation to implement rights by all appropriate means is the obligation to provide appropriate mechanisms for remedying violations of ICESCR rights and ensuring governmental accountability.[50] Therefore, the ICESCR will not be fully implemented in the absence of 'effective remedies' enabling individuals and groups to enforce the rights guaranteed in the ICESCR.[51] In particular, the CESCR is concerned that states parties provide sufficient access to judicial remedies where the rights are capable of immediate application.[52] In relation to the right to adequate housing, the CESCR has said that many components of the right lend themselves to the provision of legal remedies, such as protecting against forced evictions,[53] even to some extent in

[43] Alston and Quinn, n. 35 above, 180.

[44] *CESCR General Comment No. 3*, n. 36 above, para 10.

[45] For consideration of how to make this assessment, see R. Robertson, 'Measuring State Compliance with the Obligation to Devote the "Maximum Available Resources" to Realizing Economic, Social and Cultural Rights', (1994) 16 *Human Rights Quarterly* 693.

[46] *CESCR General Comment No. 9*, n. 23 above, para 1.

[47] Ibid., para 5. The CESCR has interpreted the use of the term 'appropriate' in Art 2(1) to require that 'the means used should be appropriate in the sense of producing results which are consistent with the full discharge of its obligations under the Covenant'.

[48] *CESCR General Comment No. 9*, n. 23 above, para 2.

[49] Ibid., para 3.

[50] Ibid., para 2.

[51] Ibid., para 9.

[52] *CESCR General Comment No. 3*, n. 36 above, para 5. The CESCR has emphasized the appropriateness of judicial remedies for some obligations, such as (but not limited to) those guaranteeing the non-discriminatory enjoyment of ICESCR rights. See *CESCR General Comment No. 9*, n. 23 above, para 9.

[53] *CESCR General Comment No. 4*, n. 29 above, para 17; and *CESCR General Comment No. 7*, n. 29 above, para 9, whether by public or private persons or bodies.

emergency housing situations.[54] But the term 'effective remedy' is not limited to judicial remedies and the CESCR accepts that administrative remedies will often be appropriate.[55] Thus, remedies may be provided by independent statutory bodies established by parliaments, such as ombuds offices and human rights commissions, like HREOC, or by other forms of alternative dispute resolution. In addition, remedies may be policy-based, such as developing a plan for implementation, establishing benchmarks and time-frames, or explicitly articulating human rights principles to guide programme development. Yet while a wide range of non-judicial measures can play an important role, their adequacy in providing effective remedies must be seriously questioned.

In sum, it is clear from the text of the ICESCR, and from the authoritative interpretations developed by the CESCR, that the obligation to implement the Covenant gives governments wide discretions to determine measures that are consistent with the particularities of their legal, political, and administrative systems. Remedies too may be very diverse, ranging from judicial enforcement to the setting of benchmarks against which the effectiveness of policies can be assessed. Article 2(1) balances the relationship between politics and law by forefronting government policy-making when it comes to determining the 'maximum available resources', while giving particular emphasis to legislative measures in implementation. As the case-study will show, one consequence of the Australian preference for indirect implementation and the traditional 'reluctance' about legal rights[56] is a lack of effective remedies for violations of ICESCR rights. This casts doubt on Australia's present capacity to fulfil its international obligations, despite the Government's claim that it is 'fully committed to protecting each right guaranteed by the Covenant'.[57]

The Case-Study: The Supported Accommodation Assistance Program

The SAAP provides services and support to some of the most disadvantaged and marginalized people in Australia: the homeless population of elderly people, mainly men; women and children who are escaping domestic violence; unemployed and/or abused young people; and families living in poverty.[58] Those supported by SAAP include Aborigines and Torres Strait Islanders[59] and people

[54] *CESCR General Comment No. 4*, n. 29 above, para 8(a).

[55] In the case of administrative remedies, an effective remedy means one that is 'accessible, affordable, timely and effective'; *CESCR General Comment No. 9*, n. 23 above, para 9.

[56] Charlesworth, n. 12 above.

[57] *Third Periodic Report: Australia*, n. 9 above, para 7.

[58] Australian Institute of Health and Welfare, *SAAP National Data Collection Annual Report 2000–01* (Canberra: AIHW, 2001), estimates SAAP services supported 91,200 clients during the twelve-month period. This figure does not include accompanying children. The main reasons for seeking assistance were domestic violence (23 per cent), eviction or end of previous accommodation (11 per cent), relationship breakdown (10 per cent), and financial difficulty (10 per cent).

[59] Ibid. During 2000–1 Aborigines and Torres Strait Islanders comprised 16 per cent of SAAP clients, yet their representation in the population is under 2 per cent.

from many different ethnic backgrounds including, increasingly, asylum-seekers awaiting determination of their immigrant status. The programme is jointly funded by the federal and state governments and administered by the states within a legislated national policy framework. It provides financial assistance to non-government organizations and local government authorities that provide a range of supported accommodation and related support services to people who are temporarily or permanently homeless.[60] It is the first coordinated national approach to addressing the complex and multifaceted problems of homelessness in Australia.[61] As the Government reported to the CESCR in its 1990–7 periodic report, SAAP 'is one of the primary Government responses to homelessness' and, as such, it constitutes an important measure towards implementing Article 11(1).[62]

The SAAP is given effect through Commonwealth–state Agreements of five years' duration. The objective of the programme, identified in the first Agreement 1985–9 (SAAP I), is to assist those who need housing support 'to move towards independent living, where possible and appropriate'.[63] To this end, the programme aims to fund services that encourage self-help in a non-institutionalized setting.[64] While SAAP's significance in the context of International Youth Year (1985) and the International Year of Shelter for the Homeless (1987) was noted in the Second Reading Speech, no mention was made of its relationship to Australia's international human rights obligations.[65]

However, successive SAAP agreements have paid increasing attention to recognizing the 'rights' of the homeless people who use SAAP services. The second Agreement 1990–4 (SAAP II) emphasized the importance of providing support that recognizes clients' independence, dignity, and self-esteem,[66] and aimed to 'establish a framework for the protection of the rights of users of services'.[67] Specifically, the Agreement required the development of principles and strategies for the protection of user rights, and the establishment of internal grievance procedures within each SAAP-funded service and external review procedures 'by government officials or other independent review'.[68] The SAAP II also indicated that user rights 'may include such matters as participation in decision making,

[60] Second Reading Speech, Supported Accommodation Assistance Bill 1985, House of Representatives, 27 Mar. 1985, *Hansard* 1020.

[61] The SAAP was preceded by the Homeless Persons Assistance Act 1974 (Cth), which was the first legislation to recognize that the provision of assistance to homeless people was a responsibility of the national government.

[62] *Third Periodic Report: Australia*, n. 9 above, para 219.

[63] Supported Accommodation Assistance Act 1985 (Cth) (SAAP I), Schedule, para 6.

[64] Minister for Community Services, Second Reading Speech, n. 60 above.

[65] Ibid.

[66] Supported Accommodation Assistance Act 1989 (Cth) (SAAP II), Schedule 1, Form of Agreement. The new Agreement was informed by the report of the National SAAP Evaluation Steering Committee, 'Homes Away from Home: National Evaluation of the Supported Accommodation Assistance Program', prepared by Colleen Chesterman (1988).

[67] SAAP II, ibid., para 7(1)(f). The SAAP II also emphasized non-discrimination as a programme principle, and explicitly noted that services should be designed to provide equitable access for Aboriginal people and people from non-English-speaking backgrounds; see para 6(1)(d).

[68] Ibid., clause 15.

information about available assistance, and security and freedom from abuse',[69] making it clear that user rights were internal to SAAP services, as between users and service providers, rather than rights that could be exercised against the state with respect to the standard of living of service users.

Five years later the national evaluation of SAAP II found that only 'some progress' had been made in the development and implementation of user rights policies, in the process of developing SAAP minimum service Standards.[70] The evaluation found variations between states in the scope of the Standards and in their progress towards implementation.[71] It recommended that the ongoing implementation of a national user rights policy be given a high priority and also that nationally consistent minimum standards of service delivery be developed and incorporated into funding agreements with SAAP providers.[72] With regard to internal grievance procedures, the evaluation found that most states were still in the process of implementation. Even more troubling, external complaints and appeals mechanisms were only in place in New South Wales,[73] where a Community Services Commission was established in 1994 to consider complaints from users of any community service, including those funded by SAAP.[74] The evaluation noted the particular difficulties of implementing user rights policies in SAAP 'where many users have low self esteem, limited coping skills and often use services for relatively short periods'.[75] It also noted that some service providers were concerned 'about the possible consequences for them (and indeed for other SAAP users) of the irresponsible exercise of user rights policies by individual clients'.[76] Understanding rights as encouraging and condoning 'trouble-making', in this way, is one commonly heard expression of the Australian 'reluctance' about rights. The national evaluation of SAAP II also found that 'the most intractable problem facing SAAP is the lack of suitable, affordable housing for SAAP users when they leave SAAP services'.[77] Consequently, the primary objective, to provide *transitional* support and move clients as quickly as possible to independent living, was thwarted by a lack of 'exit points',[78] and

[69] Ibid., para 15(a).

[70] National SAAP Evaluation Steering Committee, *Moving Forward: Report of the National Evaluation of SAAP*, prepared for the Steering Committee by Mary Lindsay (1993), 71.

[71] Ibid. 73–4.

[72] Ibid. 82.

[73] External complaints mechanisms were also available, to a very limited extent, in the Australian Capital Territory, with the establishment of the Office of the Community Advocate in 1992. However, the role of the Community Advocate is restricted to protecting the rights of children under 18, adults with a disability, people with a mental dysfunction and involved in the criminal justice system, and people with a physical, mental, psychological, or intellectual condition which necessitates protection from abuse, neglect, or exploitation, which would by no means cover all SAAP clients. See *Moving Forward*, n. 70 above, 72.

[74] The legislation establishing the Community Services Commission was the Community Services (Complaints, Appeals and Monitoring) Act 1993 (NSW), since renamed the Community Services (Complaints, Reviews and Monitoring) Act. Priority is given to vulnerable groups, which are identified as children and young people, people with disabilities, consumers of home care services, and consumers of SAAP services. Of the 1,106 complaints finalized by the Commission in the year 2000–1, only 3 per cent involved SAAP services. See <http://www.csc.nsw.gov.au>.

[75] *Moving Forward*, n. 70 above, 71.

[76] Ibid. 72.

[77] Ibid. 107.

[78] R. Fopp, 'No Where to Go: An Analysis of the Supported Accommodation Assistance Program', (1996) 31/2 *Australian Journal of Social Issues* 209, 212.

some SAAP users were forced to 'remain in SAAP services when their need for support has passed'.[79] This, in turn, led to the high turn-away rate of potential SAAP users, exacerbating their housing crisis.

It was not until the third Agreement 1995–9 (SAAP III)[80] that an explicit connection with Australia's international human rights obligations was made in the legislation. The preamble to the Act referred to Australia's recognition of 'international standards for the protection of universal human rights and fundamental freedoms' as one of the considerations that had informed the legislation. Six international instruments were listed, with the ICESCR first among them.[81] In addition, the preamble recognized the need to 'redress social inequalities and to achieve a reduction in poverty' and declared the right of homeless people 'to an equitable share of the community's resources'.[82] The preamble also stated that the Federal Government intended to work cooperatively with the state governments to ensure that the 'universal human rights [of SAAP clients] are not prejudiced by the manner in which services are provided to them'.[83] These commitments seemed to promise, in addition to user rights, the recognition of a broader range of rights, involving substantive claims on community resources to ensure an adequate standard of living for homeless people. However, the minister in his Second Reading Speech made it clear that 'the rights of people who are homeless, to housing and to the other essential elements of a decent quality of life' would be realized by paying more attention to linking people to a range of other services, thereby 'maximising people's chances to participate',[84] rather than by guaranteeing substantive rights. While the need to improve the internal protection of user rights within SAAP services is an important goal,[85] rights limited to the service delivery arena do nothing to address the problem of the shortage of adequate housing options.[86]

Although guided by national principles,[87] the responsibility for developing service standards and practices remained with the state governments, paving the

[79] *Moving Forward*, n. 70 above, 107.

[80] Supported Accommodation Assistance Act 1994 (Cth) (SAAP III).

[81] Ibid., Preamble, para 4. The other instruments referred to were the International Convention on the Elimination of All Forms of Racial Discrimination 1965, the Convention on the Elimination of All Forms of Discrimination Against Women 1979, the Convention on the Rights of the Child 1989, the Universal Declaration of Human Rights 1948, and the Declaration on the Elimination of Violence Against Women 1994.

[82] SAAP III, n. 80 above, Preamble, paras 2 and 5.

[83] Ibid., para 7.

[84] Second Reading Speech, House of Representatives, *Hansard*, 10 Nov. 1994, 3013.

[85] SAAP III, n. 80 above, s 5(4)(f) states: 'SAAP is to safeguard clients' rights and deal with clients' responsibilities through measures including, but not limited to (i) the development of grievance and appeals procedures; and (ii) the development of charters of clients' rights and responsibilities.'

[86] *CESCR General Comment No. 4*, n. 29 above, para 8, defines adequate housing as including security of tenure, availability of services infrastructure, affordability, habitability, accessibility, location, and cultural adequacy.

[87] B. Grigson, 'The Supported Accommodation Assistance Program—Client Rights and Participation', (1998) 11/3 *Parity* 5. The principles are: to ensure user rights, participation, and choice, complaints and dispute resolution, safety and security, access to services, information and consultation, privacy, confidentiality, and access to personal information, efficient and effective management, coordinated, planned, and reliable service delivery, and responsiveness to all clients.

way for the development of seven different sets of standards. In Victoria the SAAP Standards of Service Delivery[88] identified five standards relating to the service environment[89] and seven relating to user rights.[90] Responsibility for implementing the Standards is devolved further to the nine regions in Victoria. At this level they are incorporated into the funding agreements, which are negotiated between individual SAAP services and regional SAAP advisers, who also provide advice to services on the implementation of the Standards. In Victoria all 330 SAAP services commit, through their funding negotiations, to implement the Victorian SAAP Standards and to have in place an internal grievance procedure. These commitments are then further translated into service practices within each individual service, usually in the form of internal policies and procedures manuals.

In order to make an assessment of the progress towards protecting the rights of service users, the two workers at the Support and Accommodation Rights Service (SARS) were interviewed in Melbourne on 17 July 2001.[91] The SARS, which opened in January 1994, is funded by SAAP under the auspices of the Council to Homeless Persons, a peak body to many of the SAAP-funded services in Victoria. The SARS offers an advocacy service for SAAP clients, or potential SAAP clients, when they come into conflict with a service.[92] According to SARS publicity about its service, those seeking or using SAAP services have rights

[88] Health and Community Services (H & CS), *SAAP Standards of Service Delivery* (Melbourne: H & CS, 1994); H & CS, *SAAP Standards Implementation Guide*, researched and written by David Aarons (Melbourne: H & CS, 1994).

[89] Included in this category are: a service culture sensitive to the problems of homelessness, domestic and family violence, and personal crisis; a non-institutionalized, safe, and appropriate physical setting which provides for individual needs; an environment that is healthy and safe for employees, volunteers, and service users; suitably skilled and/or experienced staff who receive ongoing training; and ongoing supervision and support for staff from management.

[90] The standards relating to user rights were: autonomous decision-making, assessment, and referral, service information, privacy and confidentiality, non-threatening environment, support and participation in service management. The standards are augmented by other policies including Department of Human Services Victoria (HSV), *Information Privacy Principles* (Melbourne: HSV, 1999), which sets out twelve principles to guide the collection of personal information by HSV and SAAP service providers, accompanied by extensive explanatory notes; and HSV, *Quality Improvement in Case Management* (Melbourne: Homeless and Family Violence Services Unit, HSV, Jan. 1999).

[91] Interview with Paula Marsh and Andrea Stanlake, Supported Accommodation Rights Service, Melbourne (SARS), 17 July 2001 (hereafter SARS Interview) (copy on file with author).

[92] G. Wettenhall, M. Howie, and A. Howie, *What's in a Name? How the SAAP Advocacy Service Became the Supported Accommodation and Rights Service* (Melbourne: Waalima Publications, Mar. 1995), 9. Interestingly, the SARS was initially called the SAAP Advocacy Service, but the name was changed in 1995, as recommended by consultants, who found that almost none of the forty-six service users in their study knew what either 'SAAP' or 'advocacy' meant. While they found that younger service users understood the concept of 'rights' and felt comfortable with it, they found that older people preferred a 'softly softly' approach. While they concluded that in the longer term it may be necessary to provide different information for young and old service users, they opted for the use of the term 'rights' in the name of the service because of the particular vulnerability of young people. The view of the older service users would appear to reflect the traditional suspicion about rights discourse in popular Australian culture.

to freedom, privacy and safety... to have whatever is necessary so that you are not hungry, are not cold, have a house, and are looked after when you are ill... to be protected if someone wants to force you to change the way you are, what you think or write... nobody can enter your house without a reason... [to] be protected in the same way, everywhere and like everyone else.[93]

The source of these rights is identified as the Universal Declaration of Human Rights, but this is misleading. The reality is that the SAAP Standards define the rights that are to be enjoyed by SAAP users, and SARS advocacy is limited to the Standards. There is no right to 'have a house' in the Standards and there is no guarantee that a homeless person will have access to a SAAP service. Further, the procedures for conflict resolution are defined by each service's internal grievance procedure, which may also restrict the extent of advocacy that is possible.[94]

The most common complaints that SARS receives are about being evicted from a SAAP service or the withdrawal or denial of a service.[95] If the client is being evicted for behaviour that the client knew would lead to eviction, there is really nothing that SARS can do to assist them.[96] This raises the thorny issue of the relationship between user rights and responsibilities, which is also related to the fear that rights will be exercised irresponsibly. The SAAP Standards require that within twenty-four hours of being in the service, a service user must be provided with information about user rights and responsibilities.[97] According to SARS, the list of responsibilities (often merged with service rules) is usually much longer and more involved than the list of rights.[98] It is a common occurrence that a service provider withdraws rights because responsibilities are not fulfilled or rules are broken. One example given by SARS is that services users are frequently evicted because of 'violence', yet there are many unresolved issues about what constitutes violence, and middle-class workers can have a very different view from, for example, a young woman who has been subjected to violence all her life.[99] In the event of eviction from a SAAP service, it is not uncommon, in the experience of SARS, that the service provider will also refuse to refer the evicted person on to another service; the view is taken that 'well if you can't be responsible, then I'm not going to give you a right'.[100]

The SARS has also found that many workers in the sector have never seen the SAAP Standards and do not know that they are binding. While workers have 'dutifully' read the service's policy manual, they are often not aware that it is based on the Standards, 'which usually sit on the manager's bookshelf, in their office'.[101] The service policies develop 'like a game of whispers', starting off consistent with the SAAP Standards but changing, over time, as the service

[93] Support and Accommodation Rights Service, pamphlet, n.d., available from <http://www.chp.org.au/sars>.

[94] SARS Interview, n. 91 above, 10.

[95] Ibid. 28. Other common complaints to SARS have been about lack of confidentiality and lack of support.

[96] Ibid. 24–5.

[97] *SAAP Standards*, n. 88 above, 8.

[98] SARS Interview, n. 91 above, 22.

[99] Ibid. 23.

[100] Ibid. 22.

[101] Ibid. 10.

changes direction or faces different challenges.[102] Further, SARS has found that, on occasion, when asked about their internal grievance procedure, a worker will say they 'just can't find it', despite the requirement in the Standards that they provide a copy to new clients within twenty-four hours.[103]

During the 1999/2000 financial year SARS assisted 350 service users who required information, referral, and advice, and provided advocacy for more than seventy others who entered into formal grievance procedures with SAAP services. Needless to say, despite the best efforts of the two SARS workers, it is impossible for such a small unit to provide adequately a state-wide advocacy and advice service for over 27,000 service users annually with over 12,000 accompanying children,[104] let alone for the overwhelming number of people whose requests for assistance cannot be met by SAAP.[105] Further, SARS is by definition concerned only with advocacy for clients in processes that are internal to services. SARS does not play a mediation or adjudicative role, nor does it have any investigative or community visiting powers. If a dispute remains unresolved, the only option is to take it to the regional SAAP adviser, which, in the experience of SARS, has not been helpful.[106]

In sum, there is no mechanism for effectively monitoring services' compliance with the SAAP Standards or the operation of internal grievance procedures. Apart from occasional internal scrutiny when an individual client makes a complaint, there is only the annual process of renewing Funding Agreements with the regional SAAP adviser, which is a highly formal process that is usually satisfied by the mere existence of a user rights policy and an internal grievance procedure.[107] It does not matter, for example, whether the internal grievance procedure is 'a little quarter page diagram' or 'sixteen pages of legalese', as the form of the procedure is at the discretion of the service provider.[108] Further, except in New South Wales, there is no external, independent review or appeals mechanism. The lack of accountability, especially in the context of devolution, leads to a lack of uniformity in the 'rights' ostensibly enjoyed by service users, divergent interpretations of those rights, confusion about the relationship between rights and responsibilities, and uneven implementation. This leads to a great deal of confusion for clients and does not engender the respect for user rights that the SAAP programme has so keenly promoted at the national policy level.

This brings us to the heart of the Australian debate about rights and the best way to implement them. The SARS workers preferred a non-judicial approach. They thought the 'legal' approach was problematic because it did not leave room

102 Ibid. 10–11.

103 Ibid. 5.

104 Department of Human Services (Victoria), *Review of Services, Programs and Directions in SAAP III* (Melbourne: KPMG Consulting, 1998), records statistics from the SAAP National Data Collection Agency, 1997–8, for Victoria. They indicate that 10,924 men and 16,141 women were SAAP clients during that period. These numbers exclude clients whose sex was unknown, and also exclude any dependent children of SAAP clients.

105 Ibid. 37. Unmet requests for assistance in Victoria in 1997–8 numbered over 45,000.

106 SARS Interview, n. 91 above, 10.

107 Ibid.

108 Ibid. 35.

for 'more ethical concerns'[109] and worked against the approach of 'honestly talking things through' because workers would take the view that 'I'm not admitting anything if I think you're going to have me in court in the witness box.'[110] They thought that, in the event of extreme abuse, existing civil and criminal laws were sufficient. The SARS workers saw the solution to the present lack of accountability lying in a scheme of independent investigators able to follow up complaints by being able to 'walk into that service, check it out, see what was really happening, make a report, make a finding and then tell the Department "You need to act... on this, because while they might have the policies, they're actually not abiding by them."'[111] They also liked the idea of a 'community visitor' scheme that would involve unscheduled visits to 'check out with the clients how it's going and what their views of the service are' and report on their findings 'in a way that's a bit anonymous (for the client) and actually might have some impact'.[112] While they observed that 'the services would go nuts', they thought that investigation by a disinterested party would fill the current gap in service accountability.[113]

The Victorian evaluation of SAAP III was also critical of the limited capacity of the Funding Agreement process to monitor adherence to the SAAP Standards. It suggested a range of strategies that would provide incentives for best practice and disincentives for poor practice and recommended the establishment of more rigorous monitoring and review mechanisms both within services and externally through accreditation and/or auditing processes.[114] Yet there were no new developments in the SAAP IV Agreements that addressed the issues of accountability any differently.[115] Further, while the programme remains committed to the improvement of the quality of SAAP service delivery, the lack of any guarantee of access to SAAP services for large numbers of eligible homeless people also remains unaddressed, and the critical shortage of adequate long-term housing options for those SAAP clients who no longer need supported accommodation remains outside the scope of SAAP.

Can indirect measures of implementation fulfil Australia's international obligations?

As a coordinated national response to homelessness, SAAP provides a means for the Federal Government to fulfil some of its implementation obligations

[109] The view that 'rights' are antithetical to ethical values like happiness and empathy is, as Campbell argues, a common assumption in political ideology. See Campbell, n. 10 above, 198, citing C. Sypnowitch, *The Concept of Socialist Law* (New York: Oxford University Press, 1990).

[110] SARS Interview, n. 91 above, 37.

[111] Ibid. 38.

[112] Ibid. 39.

[113] Ibid.

[114] Ibid. 8.

[115] SAAP IV Agreements were negotiated, for the first time, on a bilateral basis between the Commonwealth and each state government, under the provisions of the Supported Accommodation Assistance Act 1994 (Cth) (SAAP III) and according to the Memorandum of Understanding for the SAAP Program 2000–05 endorsed in principle by the Commonwealth and state governments on 5 Aug. 1999, and thereafter signed by the individual states on various dates.

under the ICESCR, particularly aspects of its obligation to recognize the right of everyone to an adequate standard of living (Article 11(1)). Successive SAAP Agreements have strengthened the programme's emphasis on providing support towards independent living, on service user rights, and on the establishment of grievance procedures within services, drawing increasingly on international human rights standards for guidance. The programme clearly aims to empower people who are among the most vulnerable and disadvantaged in the Australian community by promoting the core human rights principles of dignity, autonomy, and participation. It provides an illustration of how international human rights instruments are contributing a new language of rights, and a framework for expressions of human dignity, to the Australian political and legal landscapes. While SAAP is only one of a complex range of measures required to fully implement Article 11(1), it nevertheless provides a useful case-study of the benefits and problems associated with indirect forms of implementation.

In order to assess the extent to which SAAP implements Article 11(1), we need to consider the requirements of Article 2(1) in light of the case-study. The first of these, the requirement that the Government 'take steps' towards realizing the right, has no doubt been satisfied. The Government has not been inactive in addressing homelessness, and the development of SAAP is a positive measure towards that end. The programme seeks to give 'due priority' to those who are living in unfavourable conditions,[116] and is 'deliberate, concrete and targeted' towards the primary goal of supporting clients to attain independent living, which would realize at least some aspects of the right to an adequate standard of living. Further, the SAAP definition of 'homelessness' is broadly framed as 'inadequate access to safe and secure housing',[117] which is consistent with the CESCR's view that 'adequate housing... should be seen as the right to live somewhere in security, peace and dignity'.[118] Nevertheless, the case-study reveals that other 'steps' need to be taken, like ensuring that there are more long-term housing options available to SAAP clients when they are ready to leave SAAP services. Such steps would include, as strongly recommended by the CESCR, that the Federal Government develop a national housing strategy that

[116] *CESCR General Comment No. 4*, n. 29 above, para 11.

[117] SAAP III, n. 80 above, s 4(2) states:

> For the purposes of this Act, a person is taken to have inadequate access to safe and secure housing if the only housing to which the person has access:
>
> (a) damages, or is likely to damage, the person's health; or
> (b) threatens the person's safety; or
> (c) marginalizes the person through failing to provide access to:
>   (i) adequate personal amenities; or
>   (ii) the economic and social supports that a home normally affords; or
>
> places the person in circumstances which threaten or adversely affect the adequacy, safety, security and affordability of that housing.

[118] *CESCR General Comment No. 4*, n. 29 above, para 7.

is consistent with Australia's obligations under the ICESCR, and ensure that state and territory governments do likewise.[119]

The second requirement of Article 2(1) is to achieve 'progressively' the full realization of the recognized right, as 'expeditiously and effectively as possible'. In the context of SAAP, this could mean achieving a reduction in the number of people needing SAAP services, a decrease in the number of people turned away because SAAP services are full, and/or a decrease in the number of SAAP clients forced to remain in SAAP beyond when their need for support has passed. Yet despite the five-yearly reviews of the programme that assess its progress towards fulfilling national objectives, and annual national data collection that should enable new problems and trends to be identified and addressed quickly, progress has not been achieved according to any of these measures.[120] The CESCR drew attention to this issue after its initial review of Australia's last periodic report, asking why the Government had failed to address the rising number of homeless people and requesting that comparative statistics covering the previous five years be provided on the number of people who are homeless and the number who have access to public housing.[121] The CESCR also requested information on the access of homeless people, among others, to adequate food.[122] These requests indicate that the Government provided inadequate information for the monitoring purposes of the CESCR, indicating a failure to fulfil its reporting obligations, and leaving open the possibility that there was in fact a regressive movement, which the CESCR has said would need to be 'fully justified'.

The third requirement of Article 2(1) is that the Government devote the 'maximum of its available resources' towards progressively realizing ICESCR rights. As Australia's economy grew consistently through the 1990s, anything less than full enjoyment of an adequate standard of living raises fundamental questions about resource allocation. While the Government has progressively increased its expenditure on SAAP,[123] there is clearly a serious shortage of long-term housing options of the sort that are required by those who use SAAP services; low-rental housing, suited to a range of household configurations, located close to services and public transport. This is despite the Commonwealth–State Housing Agreement, which aims to 'assist every Australian with access to housing that is affordable, secure and appropriate to his or her needs' and a Rent Assistance Program administered through the social

[119] *Concluding Observations of the Committee on Economic, Social and Cultural Rights: Australia. 01/09/2000*, E/C.12/1/Add.50, 1 Sept. 2001, para 34.

[120] *SAAP National Data Collection 2000–1*, n. 58 above, 59. The data collected shows that in 2000–1 SAAP services supported an estimated 91,200 clients, which was an increase over the previous year's estimate of 90,000, although this was a decrease from the 1997–8 figure of 94,100. See <http://www.aihw.gov.au/publications/hou/saapndcar 00-01>

[121] *List of Issues: Australia. 23/05/2000*, E/C.12/Q/AUSTRAL/1, 23 May 2000, para 25.

[122] Ibid., para 28.

[123] Recurrent expenditure for SAAP increased by 22 per cent in the five years from 1996–7 ($219.8 million) to 2000–1 ($268.5 million), which in real terms amounts to an increase of 10 per cent; *SAAP National Data Collection 2000–01*, n. 58 above, 59.

security system.[124] The failure of the Government to provide the CESCR with comparative statistics showing expenditure on public housing over the previous five years[125] also suggests that it had reason to avoid scrutiny of the level of resources it had devoted to low-income housing.[126]

The fourth requirement, which is the primary focus of my inquiry, is that the Government take 'appropriate' measures in the sense that they produce the result of progressive realization. The ICESCR clearly places emphasis on legislative measures, and the CESCR has said that a state party would need to justify non-legislative (indirect) measures in terms of appropriateness. There are many questions associated with the adequacy of the legislative measures that have been adopted by Australian governments,[127] which directly implement some incidents of Article 11(1) by prohibiting discrimination by landlords and protecting landlord–tenant rights and obligations, but they must be put aside to maintain my focus on indirect implementation. There are two concomitant obligations involved in taking appropriate implementation measures, which apply to indirect as well as direct measures: first, the obligation to recognize the right in the most appropriate form; and secondly, the obligation to provide mechanisms for remedying or redressing violations of the right.

With respect to the first of these obligations, the SAAP legislation provides for the identification and protection of the rights of SAAP clients as service users, which is understood as a way of assisting them towards independent living. User rights are not 'legal' rights, which entail a correlative and enforceable legal duty that they be respected or enjoyed. Nor are they 'human rights' in the sense of being inherent. Although informed in a general way by human rights principles, user rights are defined by policy processes at the state level, implemented through SAAP Funding Agreements, and enjoyed by service users as the result of an unenforceable 'contract' with the service provider that specifies rights in the context of user responsibilities. Conditioning the enjoyment of user rights on the performance of responsibilities is consistent with the Federal Government's embrace of 'mutual obligation' as the cornerstone of its welfare policies, in its move away from welfare 'entitlements'.[128] Under this policy, the Government ostensibly provides basic necessities, such as income support and job-search

124 *Third Periodic Report: Australia*, n. 9 above, paras 217–18.

125 *List of Issues*, n. 121 above, para 25.

126 In fact, Australian governments over the past decade have decreased expenditure on public housing while increasing expenditure on rental subsidies in the private rental market. This move towards greater reliance on the private market has failed to deliver affordable housing to the poorest Australian households, who are spending a mean of 66 per cent of their income on housing. See Australian Social and Economic Rights Project (ASERP), *Australia's Compliance with the UN Covenant on Economic, Social and Cultural Rights: Community Perspectives*, submission to the UN Committee on Economic, Social and Cultural Rights (Melbourne: Victorian Council of Social Service, Apr. 2000), 40–1.

127 Ibid. 39 and 41. Concerns include reports of widespread discrimination and the lack of minimum housing standards in the private rental market.

128 J. Newman, 'The Future of Welfare in the 21st Century', National Press Club, 29 Sept. 1999, Canberra. See <http://www.facs.gov.au/internet/>.

assistance for unemployed people, in exchange for undertakings that they engage in various activities aimed at increasing employability. Access to basic needs is denied, as in the SARS example,[129] if the obligations are not met, without any reference to the capacity of the person to fulfil the obligation or to human rights principles. Such an approach to 'rights' is a thinly veiled exercise in coercive social control of those who are dependent on the community to provide basic social and economic goods.[130] Although detailed discussion of the policy of 'mutual obligation' is beyond the scope of this chapter, it appears to be inconsistent with Australia's international human rights obligations, and its influence on the conditionality of user rights in SAAP services may violate the ICESCR.

The rights available to SAAP clients are more aptly described as 'privileges' in the Hohfeldian sense of being available to the rights-holder on a contingent basis rather than as a legal entitlement.[131] Unlike legal rights, which are referred to as 'claim rights' by Hohfeld,[132] there is no express legal obligation on the state to honour 'privileges'.[133] Indeed, the privatization of many services that were previously provided directly by the government has eroded the limited legal protection of welfare privileges previously provided by administrative law, because administrative review does not extend to 'contracts' between non-governmental case managers and clients.[134] Only the direct implementation of Article 11(1) would create claim rights, like those identified in the SARS publicity, to have 'whatever is necessary so that you are not hungry, are not cold, have a house, and are looked after when you are ill'. Further, only direct incorporation would give legal force to the 'right' of homeless people to an equitable share of the community's resources, referred to in the preamble to the SAAP III legislation, and create a cause of action in relation to the lack of 'exit points' for SAAP clients. As a privilege, enjoyment of the right to an adequate standard of living is solely dependent on political processes to determine its scope.

The appropriateness of recognizing an ICESCR right in the form of a privilege depends on fulfilling the second obligation associated with implementation, which is to ensure that there are effective 'remedies' in the event of a violation and independent mechanisms for ensuring government accountability.[135]

[129] See discussion in text at n. 100 above.

[130] P. L. Kinnear, 'Mutual Obligation: A Reasonable Policy?', Paper presented at the National Social Policy Conference, University of New South Wales, 4–6 July 2001 (copy on file with author).

[131] W. N. Hohfeld, *Fundamental Legal Conceptions as Applied in Judicial Reasoning*, ed. W. W. Cook (New Haven: Yale University Press, 1919), 38–9.

[132] Ibid. 36–8.

[133] This was confirmed by a single judge of the High Court in *Green v Daniels* (1997) 51 ALJR 463. Stephen J found that unemployment benefits provided through the Social Securities Act 1947 (Cth) were 'no more than a gratuity', which was not enforceable at law. See, further, P. Bailey, 'The Right to an Adequate Standard of Living: New Issues for Australian Law', (1997) 4 *Australian Journal of Human Rights* 25.

[134] T. Carney and G. Ramia, 'From Citizenship to Contractualism: The Transition from Unemployment Benefits to Employment Services in Australia', (1999) 6 *Australian Journal of Administrative Law* 117.

[135] See, further, D. Otto and D. Wiseman, 'In Search of "Effective Remedies": Applying the International Covenant on Economic, Social and Cultural Rights to Australia', (2001) 7 *Australian Journal of Human Rights* 5.

Remedies and accountability mechanisms can be very diverse and are by no means limited to the judicial sphere. In SAAP the non-judicial remedial apparatus designed to protect user rights (privileges) consists of internal grievance procedures, appeals to regional SAAP advisers, and, in theory except in New South Wales, independent external review. Given the vulnerability of SAAP clients, and the real possibility of eviction if a dispute is unresolved, the absence of comprehensive, independent, and publicly accountable external review mechanisms is a serious shortcoming of the SAAP scheme. The operation of such mechanisms would seem to be indispensable to ensuring effective remedies for individual service users, in the event that privileges are denied in a way that is inconsistent with the programme's policy and/or its legislated aims. Further, external review mechanisms could serve the related functions of raising broader human rights concerns and drawing attention to systemic problems that may require changes in policy or resource allocation, like the shortage of housing options for people on low incomes.

In the absence of the mechanisms envisaged in the SAAP legislation, the options for seeking an individual remedy are few indeed. There is limited recourse to HREOC, which is only empowered to reach a conciliated settlement of human rights complaints and, in any event, is confined to a definition of 'human rights' that does not include the ICESCR. The Ombudsman (*sic*), whose powers of review are broadly framed so as to cover human rights concerns in a general way,[136] is similarly limited to the review of prescribed public authorities. In any event, generic options for administrative review are limited in their capacity to protect the rights of disadvantaged and marginalized groups, such as homeless people, because of formality and costs. Finally, there is the 'remedy' of democratic politics, which is also unlikely to be effective for groups who exercise little political power.[137] This conclusion highlights the present importance of the ability to seek a remedy from an international body, particularly for disadvantaged Australians, once domestic options have been exhausted. Even though the 'views' of an international human rights treaty committee are not binding, and thus any governmental response to their views will also rely on political processes, at least such avenues provide independent review and the possibility of engaging the world community in shaming the Government into action.[138] While there is, as yet, no individual complaints mechanism attached to the ICESCR, there is some scope for complaints about violations of economic and social rights to be considered by other treaty

[136] J. McMillan and N. Williams, 'Administrative Law and Human Rights', in D. Kinley (ed.), *Human Rights in Australian Law* (Sydney: Federation Press, 1998), 63, 66. See the Ombudsman Act 1976 (Cth), s 15. All Australian states and territories have legislated for an office to perform similar functions to those of the Commonwealth Ombudsman.

[137] K. Walker, 'Who's the Boss? The Judiciary, the Executive, the Parliament and the Protection of Human Rights', (1995) 25 *Western Australian Law Review* 238, 250.

[138] The Government's response to the Human Rights Committee's views in *Toonen v Australia*, CCPR/C/50/D/488/1992, provides an example of the mixed success of this strategy. See W. Morgan, 'Protecting Rights or Just Passing the Buck? The Human Rights (Sexual Conduct) Bill 1994', (1994) 1 *Australian Journal of Human Rights* 1.

committees.[139] The present antipathy of the Australian Government to these bodies is deeply regrettable,[140] especially since they play such a key role in attending to some of the remedial deficiencies of the present system of implementation. Needless to say, in the absence of the availability of effective domestic remedies, it is unlikely that Australia's indirect forms of implementation comply with its international obligations.

This conclusion is consistent with the view of the CESCR, which has, like every other human rights treaty committee,[141] regularly raised questions about Australia's lack of direct implementation of human rights. In 2000 the CESCR asked the Government to discuss the extent to which the ICESCR was incorporated into domestic law and to explain why it was excluded from the HREOC system.[142] It also asked the Government to cite specific examples of its claim that human rights can in many cases be 'more readily promoted by less formal processes often associated with inquiry, conciliation and report'.[143] Clearly dissatisfied with the responses it received, the CESCR concluded that the lack of legal status of the Covenant was 'impeding the full recognition and applicability of its provisions',[144] and 'strongly' recommended that it be incorporated legislatively in order to ensure its applicability in domestic courts.[145]

Despite the CESCR's clear preference for direct incorporation of human rights into Australian law, there are many ways in which the Government could make its indirect measures of implementation more effective. If it did so, it would be in a better position to respond to questions about how the processes of inquiry, conciliation, and report are being used to meet the Government's obligations under the ICESCR, and to justify its use of indirect measures in terms of

[139] Discrimination in the enjoyment of ICESCR rights will violate Art 26 of the ICCPR, which guarantees equal protection of the law. Further, racial discrimination in the enjoyment of economic, social, and cultural rights violates Art 5(e) of the International Convention on the Elimination of All Forms of Racial Discrimination 1965. Both of these instruments have individual complaints mechanisms that have been ratified by Australia.

[140] See, further, D. Otto, 'From "Reluctance" to "Exceptionalism": The Australian Approach to Domestic Implementation of Human Rights', (2001) 26/5 *Alternative Law Journal* 219.

[141] See *Concluding Observations of the Committee on the Elimination of Discrimination Against Women: Australia.* 22/07/97, A/52/38/Rev.1, Part II, para 398; *Concluding Observations of the Committee on the Rights of the Child: Australia.* 10/10/97. CRC/C/15/Add.79, 10 Oct. 1997, para 24; *Concluding Observations by the Committee on the Elimination of Racial Discrimination: Australia.* 19/04/2000. CERD/C/304/Add.101, 19 Apr. 2000, para 6; *Concluding Observations of the Human Rights Committee: Australia.* 28/07/2000. A/55/40, paras 498–528, 28 July 2000; and *Conclusions and Recommendations of the Committee Against Torture: Australia.* 21/11/2000. CAT/C/XXV/Concl.3, 21 Nov. 2000, paras 7(a) and (b).

[142] *List of Issues*, n. 121 above, para 7.

[143] Ibid., para 9, referring to *Third Periodic Report: Australia*, n. 9 above, para 21.

[144] *Concluding Observations: Australia*, n. 119 above, para. 13.

[145] Ibid., para 24. The CESCR also encouraged the Government to follow the view of the High Court in *Minister for Immigration and Ethnic Affairs v Teoh* (1995) 183 CLR 237, that the ratification of an international human rights treaty gives rise to a legitimate expectation that administrative discretions will be exercised consistently with its terms.

their appropriateness. With respect to SAAP, this would require establishing independent external mechanisms able to review the implementation of SAAP standards, as envisaged by the legislation. The Community Services (Complaints, Appeals and Monitoring) Act 1993 (NSW) established a watershed legislative framework, which could be emulated by other states.[146] One of the bodies created was the Community Services Commission (CSC), which takes a multidimensional approach to ensuring that community services safeguard the rights and interests of consumers, including dealing with individual complaints.[147] Yet even this progressive approach was, until recently, compromised by the CSC's inability to make decisions or recommendations that are inconsistent with government policy or resource allocation.[148] As the 1999 review of the CSC by the New South Wales Law Reform Commission pointed out, this prevented the CSC from observing its primary guiding principle, which is to act in the best interests of the service user concerned.[149] This restriction is an inappropriate means of providing for what the Second Reading Speech described as 'the primacy of the elected representatives of the people for policy determination and resource allocation',[150] because it prevents any criticism of government policies, which surely contradicts the democratic rationale of indirect forms of implementation. This situation was remedied in December 2002 by amendments which made the CSC a statutory division of the New South Wales Ombud's Office. This change had the effect of removing the restriction on criticizing government policies or resource allocation and has, in some other regards as well, strengthened the powers of the CSC.[151] This example highlights the inherent conflict of interest in the government establishing 'independent' mechanisms that are able to review its decisions and those of Government-funded service providers. It suggests, as the CESCR has urged, that access to judicial remedies (direct implementation) may at some point be necessary to ensure the effectiveness of indirect forms of implementation and the result of progressive realization[152] because, ultimately, the courts provide the best guarantee of independent monitoring and of effective remedies.

[146] The legislation established four bodies: the Community Services Commission (CSC), the Community Visitors Scheme, the Community Services Review Council, and the Community Services Appeals Tribunal, which was reconstituted as the Community Services Division of the Administrative Decisions Tribunal in 1999.

[147] The CSC may also conduct reviews and inquiries, monitor standards, make recommendations about systemic issues, support the development of advocacy services for consumers, and play an educational role in relation to service providers and consumers.

[148] Community Services (Complaints, Appeals and Monitoring) Act 1993 (NSW), s 5(c).

[149] NSW Law Reform Commission, *Report 90 (1999)—Review of the Community Services (Complaints, Appeals and Monitoring) Act 1993 (NSW)*, para 2.35.

[150] New South Wales, *Parliamentary Debates (Hansard)*, Legislative Assembly, 11 Mar. 1993, the Hon. J. Longley, Minister for Community Services, Second Reading Speech, 768.

[151] Community Services Legislation Amendment Act 2002 (NSW). At the same time amendments were also made to the Ombudsman Act 1974 (NSW).

[152] *CESCR General Comment No. 9*, n. 23 above, para 3.

Conclusions

The Australian Government is in a unique position to develop, promote, improve upon, and extend the use of indirect measures of human rights implementation, given its singular resistance to legislative or constitutional entrenchment. Therefore, it might be expected that the Government's record in enhancing democratic participation in the implementation of rights, by promoting informed community debate about human rights in general and the distribution of social and economic goods in particular, would be exemplary. It might also be expected that substantial monitoring roles would be undertaken by a range of watchdog mechanisms, like human rights commissions, ombuds offices, policy coordination networks, and the like, which are particularly important for the protection of economic and social rights[153] and also create opportunities for grass-roots engagement in 'dialogue' about rights.[154] Yet, paradoxically, government funding of HREOC has been drastically reduced since 1996, and many of the national machineries that enhanced the ability of disadvantaged groups to participate in national policy development have been dismantled, most notably those that engaged indigenous people[155] and women.[156] Further, it is hard to understand why the ICESCR has not been scheduled to the HREOC Act 1986 (Cth),[157] and why there is a dearth of benchmarks against which the Government's performance in delivering social and economic goods can be measured.[158] It is difficult to take the Government's stated commitment to human rights seriously when there are such fundamental problems with its preferred approach to implementation, many of which have relatively easy solutions that are entirely consistent with democratic responsible government. In addition, the absence of appropriate remedial and accountability mechanisms places an unjustifiable burden on already overstretched international monitoring mechanisms.

[153] B. von Tigerstrom, 'Implementing Economic, Social and Cultural Rights: The Role of National Human Rights Institutions', in I. Merali and V. Oosterveld (eds.), *Giving Meaning to Economic, Social and Cultural Rights* (Philadelphia: University of Pennsylvania Press, 2001), 139; M. Gomez, 'Social Economic Rights and Human Rights Commissions', (1995) 17 *Human Rights Quarterly* 155, 163.

[154] J. Nedelsky and C. Scott, 'Constitutional Dialogue', in J. Bakan and D. Schneiderman (eds.), *Social Justice and the Constitution: Perspectives on a Social Union for Canada* (Ottawa: Carleton University Press, 1992), 59.

[155] See *Concluding Observations by the Committee on the Elimination of Racial Discrimination: Australia* 24/02/2000, CERD/C/56/Misc.42/rev.3, para 11.

[156] See, for example, M. Sawer, 'The Watchers Within: Women and the Australian State', in L. Hancock (ed.), *Women, Public Policy and the State* (South Yarra: Macmillan Education Australia, 1999), 36.

[157] 'The Role of National Human Rights Institutions in the Protection of Economic, Social and Cultural Rights', *CESCR General Comment No. 10*, para 3: 'It is essential that full attention be given to economic, social and cultural rights in all of the relevant activities of these institutions.' *Compilation of General Comments*, n. 23 above.

[158] For example, in response to Australia's last periodic report the CESCR recommended that an official poverty line be established 'so that a credible assessment can be made of the extent of poverty in Australia'; *Concluding Observations: Australia*, n. 119 above, para 33.

However, even with the best systems of indirect implementation in place, it is likely that some questions will still remain about the appropriateness of Australia's primary reliance on indirect methods, especially in relation to independent review and the adequacy of remedies provided by political and administrative mechanisms.[159] Consequently, there may still be a need for some form of direct implementation, especially in protecting the human rights of the most vulnerable groups in Australian society.[160] While it is important to distinguish properly between the functions of courts and parliaments, and to respect parliamentary supremacy in a system of representative and responsible government, legal processes can nevertheless play an important role in implementing human rights. Legal forms of implementation need not insulate the interpretation and application of human rights from the political sphere, as the examples of Canada, New Zealand, and the United Kingdom show. The Australian optimism about the ability of democratic processes to protect human rights could lead to the development of a uniquely Australian system of 'dialogue' between the judicial and political arms of government, whereby the courts contribute to the public debate by giving human rights values more prominence than they would otherwise enjoy, as suggested by the Canadian experience.[161] But first the dichotomizing of direct and indirect forms of implementation, between political and legal means of protecting rights, needs to be rejected. Once this is rejected, the question becomes one of the appropriate balancing of involvement of the two arms of government. A system that provides judicial review while still protecting parliamentary supremacy would, in my view, optimize the realization of outcomes that are consistent with Australia's international human rights obligations.

The monitoring of Australia's compliance with its international legal obligations under the ICESCR is of critical importance, as there is the real possibility that government policies of economic liberalization and the privatization of social services have resulted in a diminution of economic and social rights protections. While political processes are crucial to achieving effective and informed public participation in social policy formulation and economic decision-making that is consistent with Australia's international human rights obligations, legal processes can provide an essential check on the reasonableness or justifiability of governmental action in light of its effects on human well-being,

[159] See, for example, the limited remedies available to conciliated disputes under federal anti-discrimination legislation; P. Bailey and A. Devereux, 'The Operation of Anti-Discrimination Laws in Australia', in D. Kinley (ed.), *Human Rights in Australian Law* (Sydney: Federation Press, 1998), 292, 305.

[160] B. Burdekin, 'The Impact of a Bill of Rights on Those Who Need it Most', in P. Alston (ed.), *Towards an Australian Bill of Rights* (Canberra: Centre for International and Public Law and HREOC, 1994), 147, 153.

[161] P. W. Hogg and A. A. Bushell, 'The *Charter* Dialogue Between Courts and Legislatures (Or Perhaps the Charter of Rights Isn't Such a Bad Thing After All)', (1997) 35 *Osgoode Hall Law Journal* 75.

and ensure that fundamental guarantees of human dignity are safeguarded. Until both systems are working more effectively, and in dialogue with each other, it is wrong for the Australian Government to claim, as it does, an exemplary record in fulfilling its international human rights obligations.

15

Indigenous Rights

STEVEN CURRY

Introduction

Indigenous minorities within industrialized liberal democracies have a legitimate claim to rights other citizens of these states do not share. This proposition is contentious, largely because it is taken to be incompatible both with contemporary liberal rights theory and with the doctrine of popular sovereignty. Further controversy will arise from my claim that one of these rights is the right to promote and enforce traditional indigenous law and have this law apply to non-indigenous citizens. Such a right would appear to undermine the rule of law and the ideal that citizens should be the authors of the laws that govern them.

My primary purpose in this chapter is to argue that indigenous citizens ought to be accorded a set of special group rights by virtue of their being indigenous. I will attempt to sketch these rights. To the extent that the list I provide is incomplete and indicative I will at least have explained by what method we can deduce what the full set of rights ought to be.

In the process of developing this explanation of indigenous rights I will also attempt to defend them against the serious objections described above. By explaining the basis for these special rights I will be able to explain how these rights are compatible with the fundamental moral commitments of a liberal democratic state governed by the rule of law. It is my belief that these rights, alongside a fuller expression of universal human rights and general democratic rights, allow the fullest expression of our basic moral commitments, and so the fullest protection of and respect for our common dignity and worth as human beings. In this sense recognition of indigenous group rights is an essential element of democratic life, not an exception to it.

Debate concerning indigenous rights takes place within the context of the continuing oppression of indigenous minorities within otherwise advanced and prosperous industrialized nations. I will avoid talking about 'post-colonial' states, despite the succession to independence of most one-time colonies, because

Previous versions of this chapter were read at a workshop hosted by the editors of this volume at the Novotel, St Kilda, Melbourne, which was funded by the Australian Research Council, and at a seminar at Charles Sturt University, Wagga Wagga, which was run with the assistance of the Centre for Applied Philosophy and Public Ethics. The feedback I received from participants at both events substantially improved this chapter and clarified its direction. I wish to thank the organizers of both events, the participants, and the funding bodies.

states that do not recognize the full range of indigenous rights described here are not post-colonial, but are successors to the colonial era legal, political, and economic relations that created and sustain indigenous oppression. I will therefore talk about 'successor states', and will define a post-colonial state as one that has achieved a constitutional settlement between indigenous and colonial civilizations.[1]

Universal and group-differentiated rights

Until comparatively recently, theorists, influenced by Immanuel Kant, assumed that all rights are universal. This is because of the way that Kant established rights as products of reasoning about the common moral status of persons. Morality was reduced to deduction of moral rules or laws from the demand that we be consistent in our treatment of relevantly similar things. If I would not wish to be lied to (as this would reduce my capacity to live my life in accordance with my own reason) then I ought not to lie to others. This is an absolute prohibition against lying (or so Kant thought) and gives rise to a right not to be lied to, a right shared by all rational beings.[2] J. S. Mill used a similar form of reasoning to establish a basic set of universal liberal rights, such as the right to freedom of conscience, to freedom of speech, and freedom of movement.[3]

As the domain of rights talk expanded into the civil and political realms, each step was based upon appeal to the same universal moral status of persons. Women based their claim to equal political rights on the assertion that women are persons equal to men, possessing the same rationality and capacity for autonomy.

This view of rights is inhospitable to the idea that some rights are partial or sectional. If one person enjoys the capacity to do something, or to be exempted from something, that is denied to others, then this capacity is a privilege not a right, and is an exception that demands a very strong, usually pragmatic, justification. A theory of rights of this sort would tend to deny that claims advanced by indigenous minorities could count as rights. In fact it would tend to reduce them to the level of special pleading. This would tend to delegitimize

[1] The statistical expressions of indigenous disadvantage paint a stark picture of continuing dispossession and oppression. In Australia, for instance, Aboriginal and Torres Strait Islander birth rates are about 50 per cent higher than non-indigenous Australians, their infant mortality is 15.2 per 1,000 live births (over three times the rate for other Australians), and their median life expectancy is 50 years compared to the 77 years other Australians can expect (Australian Bureau of Statistics, Publication 3302.0; these figures are based on 1998 data). Unemployment among Australia's indigenous people is 23 per cent. A further 17 per cent undertake a form of work-for-the-dole scheme (Australian Council of Social Services web site: <http://www.acoss.org.au/ info/2000/info214.htm>

[2] See, in particular, I. Kant, *Groundwork of the Metaphysics of Morals* (Cambridge: Cambridge University Press, 1998), esp. sect. 2.

[3] See both J. S. Mill, *On Liberty* (London: J. M. Dent, 1960), esp. chs. IV and V, and J. S. Mill, *Representative Government* (London: Longman, 1865), esp. chs. VII and VIII.

claims to exemption from ordinary criminal proceedings or from laws restricting the hunting of protected species.

Under pressure to provide an account of indigenous rights, contemporary liberal theorists have developed a view of rights that will allow for what are sometimes called 'group-differentiated' or simply group rights. These rights are described in terms of the goods of community, cultural membership, and self-determination. The underlying idea is that persons do not flourish in a vacuum. Critics of liberalism have often claimed that it treats persons as atoms unburdened by significant relations and free from formative influence. In responding to this criticism liberals have recognized that persons flourish within communities, and that the communities they develop in are linguistic communities within which a person's speech has meaning, lifeworlds in which goals and values are formed, networks which enable the formation and achievement of what liberals often like to call 'significant projects'. Recognizing that community is not just a good, but a necessity for human flourishing, liberals have recognized that significant rights, such as preservation of languages, autonomy to teach and learn, and access to a relevant economic basis for autonomy, are just as significant as individual liberties such as the right to speech. After all, without a shared linguistic community in which to speak meaningfully, the right to speak as such is pointless.[4]

These are called group rights because they depend on the good of group membership, and require group membership to operate. They can be roughly divided into two types. The first type, group-differentiated rights, still belong to individuals. A person might have a right to take whalebones from beaches for carving. In New Zealand the law forbids the taking of any natural item, such as sand or stone and natural flotsam, in order to preserve the ecosystem. However, persons of Maori descent may take whalebone because it is essential for carving, an ancient art form of spiritual as well as aesthetic importance. Each Maori person possesses the right individually. They depend upon their membership of the group for the right, but possess and exercise it individually. The second group of rights are more particularly group rights. They are the rights of groups. An individual cannot preserve and use a language. Only a linguistic community can do this. The community has a right to preserve, use, and teach its language.[5]

The ontological status of these rights-possessing groups is a matter of some controversy, but we need only accept that groups can be the source of rights, and that some rights are exercised by persons in common and cannot be exercised severally.

This contemporary rights theory still has a universalizing aspect. I take it that to the extent that there are universal group and group-differentiated rights they

[4] Important recent works on group rights include W. Kymlicka, *Multicultural Citizenship* (Oxford: Clarendon Press, 1995); D. Miller, *On Nationality* (Oxford: Clarendon Press, 1995); P. Pettit, *Republicanism* (Oxford: Clarendon Press, 1997); and R. Poole, *Nation and Identity* (New York: Routledge, 1999).

[5] Kymlicka, n. 4 above, 76–80, 82–93.

are not generally controversial. They retain their universal character, and rely on a view of human beings as products of cultures and relying on practices to give their lives meaning. We can all lay claim to rights to speak our own language and to access arts and practices that express our deeply held convictions and worldviews. Our view of ourselves as complex beings with rich intellectual, emotional, and spiritual lives is enhanced by this sort of rights theory. It helps to make sense of the shared good of multicultural societies, tolerance, and a community of nations.

One way to make sense of this modern approach to rights is to regard rights as arising from interests. This approach has its roots in Kant's original method, which relied upon claims about what is necessary for a person to flourish as a rational being. A fuller expression of this idea can be found in Joseph Raz's *The Morality of Freedom*.[6] In that work Raz develops an analysis of rights as expressions of fundamental human interests. If a person has a need that is essential to their well-being or flourishing as a human person, then that need may give rise to demands upon others to do or not to do certain things. This need, at its most fundamental level, will probably be shared by all persons at all times, but it will need to be protected and promoted in different ways depending upon the material circumstances and cultural context of the person concerned, their particular physical, psychological, and emotional capacities, life stage, and so on. For instance, every person needs education. We require information, instruction, and opportunities for reflection if we are to develop our capacities, learn skills, and perfect our abilities. This is a fundamental human need that can be met in a wide variety of ways, depending upon the resources available, the social context of the knowledge we need, and the use to which we will put it. A member of a hunter-gatherer society, living in a small, close-knit community, will need access to the special skills of her elders and a chance to engage with them in a relationship of pupillage. If she is denied the resources to feed and clothe herself during this time, or is denied access to teachers without a relevant reason, then she has been done an injustice. Exactly the same injustice is done to an inhabitant of a complex industrial society if he cannot access an institution of higher education. An indigenous citizen of a modern state is harmed if access to both these forms of education is not available. At the very least she should not be denied relevant opportunities to engage economically, politically, and socially with either cultural world or both worlds if she should choose to do so. This harm lies in the denial of opportunities to develop as a person in ways relevant to her conception of her own good. It does not matter that it will be impossible for practical reasons for her to embrace all of the opportunities offered by both.[7] Rights emerge from moral reflection upon the claims we can legitimately make against others, either for their forbearance (negative rights) or assistance (positive rights) in meeting our fundamental needs, subject to the cultural expression of those needs, their importance relative to the needs of others, and the capacity

[6] (Oxford: Clarendon Press, 1986).

[7] I am indebted to Bindi Bennett for this example.

of others to respond. Rights can therefore be regarded as human artefacts, but not accidental ones. They are properly subject to consideration of genuine moral weight, and to a process of shared debate and deliberation.[8]

Raz's approach treats rights as moral constraints and imperatives that arise from moral reflection at the intersection of fundamental human needs, developing capacities to respond to those needs, and historical contingency. They emerge from particular circumstances and can be expected to change over time, and to attach to different persons. It is analytically necessary that a right should give rise to obligations. Therefore, one of the contingencies that affects the emergence of rights is the presence of definite persons with particular capacities to respond to needs in particular ways. Changes in social structures and material wealth will create new ways to respond to old problems, and so new rights may emerge.

In the case of indigenous rights, moral responsibility on the part of non-indigenous citizens arises in two ways. First, colonization created the absolute and relative poverty of indigenous communities, while simultaneously creating the wealth enjoyed by non-indigenous citizens. We have the wealth to respond to indigenous poverty, and a historical connection with the causes of that poverty. Therefore, a morally weighty responsibility can easily be thought to arise on the part of non-indigenous citizens of successor states. So it is possible to talk of an indigenous right to special remedial action to alleviate poverty. Secondly, the concept of indigenous rights is only possible within a colonial context, because indigeneity as a category is only possible when one group of people is to be distinguished from another group who arrived later. If a group of people is not marginalized in what was their own country, the category of indigenous persons does not arise. Indigenous citizens are marked out as a distinct group only because of their colonial dispossession. When I was growing up in New Zealand, we often talked about indigenous Fijians (despite their being a majority in Fiji) but not about indigenous Tongans (they were simply called Tongans). Having marginalized and marked out a group in the process of their dispossession it would be rank moral hypocrisy to deny them special remedial measures on the grounds that making distinctions between groups of citizens is unfair or undemocratic.

Indigenous Rights as Group Rights

Having just claimed that we cannot deny a special category of indigenous group rights on the excuse that such rights are 'undemocratic', I must now show just how we can recognize such group rights without abandoning democratic principle.

There is a trivial and somewhat quick response available to the objection that special group rights are anti-democratic. We might simply claim that individual interests properly mitigate democracy. The concept of liberal democracy

[8] Raz, n. 6 above, ch. 7.

contains an implicit limitation on democratic government. A liberal state is one that promotes and protects individual rights, and allows maximal freedom for citizens to pursue their own good as they see fit. This liberal element imposes a definite limit on the scope of majoritarian decision-making and is widely regarded as a necessary balance against the possibility of a 'tyranny of the majority'. If a liberal democratic state already embodies limits of democracy arising from recognition of some rights, why should recognition of further rights be problematic?

I am dissatisfied with this response because, while it is true up to a point, it misses a significant difference between the liberal protection of individual rights and the recognition of special group rights. In general, the sorts of group rights recognized by the modern liberals are ones that are shared by all citizens; we all have a need for and a right to a cultural identity and linguistic community. However, special indigenous rights are different. I have in mind rights to things other than general categories of goods, but to specific things that, by their nature, would be denied to other citizens. An example I have used previously is the right to hunt endangered species. There will be some specific justification for this right that relies upon indigeneity and not a more general need alone. If there are such rights (and I will argue soon that there are), then these mark out indigenous citizens as a group with claims nobody else can advance that will place limits on majority decisions that no other citizen can make. It would be as if indigenous citizens counted twice: once as citizens who may engage in political action like everyone else and again as a class of persons having privileges, exemptions, and even vetoes. This is clearly a challenge to democratic rule that cannot be explained away simply by reference to a standard doctrine of balance between rights and majoritarianism.

If indigenous rights are to have a secure foundation, they must rest in democratic theory and not be regarded as exceptions to it. The way out of the problem is to locate indigenous rights within the practice of justification of political authority. Political philosophers often talk about the problem of justification of state power and the origins of a supposed duty to obey the law and legal authority. They regard democracy as a special form of government because it is uniquely able to secure the consent of the governed and so provide a proper moral basis for legal authority. I will call this the problem of legitimacy. A state is legitimate if and only if it can secure the consent of the governed. Indigenous people have historically not been asked for their consent, a particularly acute problem because the colonial state was erected over the top of their own nations. Even where treaties were signed they were never regarded as necessary before Europeans established their colonies (they built the colonies first and signed treaties later), and in any case they were almost always dishonoured.[9]

[9] D. Brown, *Bury My Heart at Wounded Knee* (London: Book Club Associates, 1972); S. L. Harrington, *Crow Dog's Case: American Indian Sovereignty, Tribal Law and US Law in the Nineteenth Century* (Cambridge: Cambridge University Press, 1994).

Indigenous rights will lack a strong moral basis if they are regarded either as compensation for past harms or as concessions made for the sake of securing consent in the present. Compensation for past harms is a weak basis for rights because compensation demands that those harmed get back either what they should have had all along, or something of equal value. Compensation in this sense is a material one, having regard to the value of lost resources, but will not be of much use in securing intangibles such as a lost nation, or cultural rights that must be enjoyed in a much different context.[10] Indigenous rights will also not be equivalent to concessions made by a successor state in order to secure indigenous consent in the present. This is simply because such 'rights' would arise from negotiation and would consist of whatever the state had to give over in order to get an agreement. Indigenous rights, if there really are rights to speak of, have a much deeper and therefore stronger moral basis.

The only conceivable basis for special indigenous group rights within a democratic setting lies in a counterfactual analysis of the rights indigenous people would have had if the successor state had arisen from an open negotiation for the coming together of free and independent nations into a new federated constitutional state. This is a complicated way of saying that we should imagine what would have happened if the colonizers had refused to establish colonies without the genuine consent of the previous inhabitants, and had kept their word. At some point, either straight away or over time, these new neighbours would come together to form a new state for them all to live in so as to share the land and its resources, pool their knowledge bases and technologies, and so flourish. In order for this to happen the various parties would have had to sit down as equals and negotiate the form of the new constitution. The resulting state would have been governed by a mixture of the institutions and laws of all those coming together to form it. No single system of laws would have been imposed on the other parties since they would never agree to be sucked into a completely alien way of life. This is what consent actually demands, the establishment of a post-colonial state that approximates to the state that would have been built by genuinely free and equal partners.

This is because consent requires the chance to dissent—not to be in the position jokingly offered by Henry Ford that customers could choose to have their new Model T car in any colour they liked... as long as it was black. If a state's legitimacy rests on consent, then there must be a process by which citizens may withhold their consent or transfer it elsewhere. This is why the rights recognized in liberal democratic theory and in international conventions include the right to leave a state, and the right to choose the government by free election.[11] Indigenous people face a special problem in this respect. Their incorporation into the state was coerced in the first instance. Unlike other citizens

[10] An excellent discussion of the problems inherent in compensatory justice can be found in A. Corbo Crehan, 'Compensating for Historical Injustice: Three Important Issues', (1999) 1 *Australian Journal of Professional and Applied Ethics* 2.

[11] See the Universal Declaration of Human Rights, Arts 13 and 21.

they cannot decide to 'love it or leave it', since to leave the country in protest is to give up whatever chance they have of recovering what was lost. It is to lose their country twice. So the ordinary standards of consent are inadequate.[12] The only way to secure genuine consent is to engage in a process of discussion which will reveal just what conditions would match indigenous requirements for recognition of their status as first nations, and then to incorporate these into the constitutional framework of the state. Naturally some compromise will be necessary, but compromise would have been necessary in any uncoerced act of union.

This will still mean that indigenous citizens have some group rights denied to others, but it will limit the extent to which these rights privilege indigenous citizens or count them twice. In the penultimate section I will explain in more detail how constitutional recognition of first nations as partners in a federal system will work. For now I want to point out that citizens are equal to the extent that they are treated equally under a system of law that applies to everyone. This is what the rule of law demands. This equality is not diminished if the law is at least partly derived from older systems of law that are in some sense alien to the individual's own cultural heritage. Anyone who would deny this will have to deal with the consequence that only members of the dominant culture can ever be genuinely free, and only if they deny any measure of freedom to members of minority cultures who will live under laws entirely alien to them, which is largely the position of indigenous citizens in most successor states now. A system that rests on the consent of all the citizens, and which respects the rule of law, requires a system that can apply to everyone without alienating anyone. This, of course, does not require that every culture get specific cultural recognition. However, this requirement suggests that if we must give special consideration to the unique problem of consent facing indigenous minorities, then we should aim for a system of law, especially at the constitutional level, that reflects indigenous law and tradition to the extent that it must do so to meet the counterfactual condition I have just described. This is not the same as establishing an entirely separate system of law for indigenous people, but rather a single system of law derived from a number of sources that everyone will live under. It means that, to some extent, non-indigenous citizens should be subject to indigenous law, or laws derived from indigenous law.

This proposition lies at the heart of the continuing challenge facing liberal democratic states. In virtually all the states that face this challenge, those that are liberal democratic constitutional democracies with indigenous minorities, indigenous communities enjoy some level of local autonomy and have some set of group rights. In Australia land councils and local government allow indigenous communities a modicum of self-government. Native Title has secured much greater access to sacred sites, camping and hunting grounds, ceremonial sites,

[12] R. Poole, 'National Identity, Multiculturalism and Indigenous Rights: An Australian Perspective', in J. Couture, K. Nielsen, and M. Seymour (eds.), *Rethinking Nationalism* (New York: Berg, 1997).

and traditional resources. Native Title has been used to provide legal support for hunting and fishing rights.[13] In some jurisdictions indigenous defendants in minor criminal cases can be subject to traditional law as an adjunct to state law. However, indigenous people have no power to exclude non-indigenous people from their lands or to prevent access to their resources (except where state laws impose restrictions on access to some reserve lands) and cannot veto resources use, vet laws, or in any other way hold non-indigenous people to account for their breaches of indigenous law.[14]

Even in Canada and the United States, where treaties have secured some jurisdictional rights in indigenous communities, local law is subject to overarching state and federal laws, or does not apply to non-indigenous people at all. In every case local autonomy is limited by constitutional supremacy that lies with a system of law entirely alien to indigenous law. In this crucial respect these countries still fail the counterfactual test for consent required for real legitimacy.

As a result of these developments, we now face the curious situation in which states actually recognize indigenous rights as privileges not enjoyed by other citizens, but will not recognize indigenous rights where these involve incorporating indigenous citizens and their concerns into the body politic as an integral part.

Indigenous rights as universal rights

'Mr Neal is entitled to be an agitator.' With these words Justice Lionel Murphy of the Australian High Court embraced the liberal doctrine that political dissent is a fundamental right, and embedded it in Australian jurisprudence.[15] It is one of Murphy's more famous acts during a distinguished, if controversial, career as a politician and magistrate. Mr Neal was chairman of the Yarrabah community council. He had been convicted of assault in the Queensland magistrates' court after he spat on a white official during an argument. He appealed the severity of his sentence to the Court of Appeal (the Supreme Court of Queensland). However, that Court decided to ignore the grounds upon which the appeal was brought, choosing instead, entirely of its own volition, to increase the sentence on the grounds that it was inadequate. In deciding to increase the sentence, the Court implicitly accepted comments made by the original magistrate that Mr Neal was liable for severe punishment because he was the sort of malcontent responsible for stirring up trouble on reserves and upsetting the 'happy lives' of the 'genuine Aborigines' who were content with white authority. Mr Neal was sentenced for being a troublemaker.

[13] See *Yanner v Eaton* (1999) 201 CLR 351.

[14] See, for instance, the so-called *Sea Rights* case (*Commonwealth v Yarmirr; Yarmirr v Commonwealth* (2001) 184 ALR 113), in which the High Court of Australia found that indigenous law was not a sufficient ground for asserting any exclusive rights in, or authority over, maritime resources.

[15] See Murphy J's dicta in *Neal v The Queen* (1982) 149 CLR 305, 316.

Murphy J made it clear that he regarded the sentence as a deliberate attempt to silence an Aboriginal critic of the reserve system. In fact, while deploring any occasion of assault, Murphy would have released Mr Neal without a sentence if the original conviction itself had been appealed to him. This case is a very clear example of the sort of struggle that indigenous people have with an alien legal system. It is difficult to imagine a white defendant being sentenced to six months' jail with hard labour for spitting on an opponent during a political dispute. Mr Neal's problem had two aspects. First, old-school jurists who clearly still regarded it as their job to defend the colonial system from attack racially discriminated against him. Secondly, his struggle to wrest control of his community from officials of the Department of Aboriginal Affairs was regarded as illegitimate. This illegitimacy was caused by the relationship between indigenous communities and the state power that supervened them. This relationship is characterized by a hierarchical and unidirectional flow of authority. Indigenous communities are strictly subject to overarching state power, so that whatever authority or executive control they might exercise—even over themselves—is derived from the legal authority exercised by the state and delegated to them. On a grander scale all claims to indigenous self-government or self-determination have this character.

Chief Justice John Marshall of the United States Supreme Court developed the clearest legal expression of this relationship. In 1823 the Supreme Court was asked to adjudicate between conflicting claims to the same area of land. Two parties claimed to have purchased the land from the local indigenous owners during the period of British colonial rule. They had not been able to take up their holdings because of the outbreak of the War of Independence. Later another party purchased the same land from the US Government. While sympathetic to the claim that the original inhabitants held the original title to the land and so those who bought it from them held the title, Marshall concluded that no US court could recognize this title against a title derived from the federal government. He reasoned that US law could not recognize any sovereignty in conflict with itself. Therefore, whatever status Indian tribes might have in US law, it could not be equal to the status of the United States itself as a sovereign power. He coined the term 'domestic dependent nation' to describe those Native American societies resident within the United States and having a treaty relationship with it. Because US law could not recognize indigenous sovereignty as equal to US sovereignty, but because Marshall could not go along with the convenient fiction that tribes had no sovereignty at all, he decided that the legal system could recognize tribal sovereignty, but only to the extent that recognition of this sovereignty was granted explicitly by the law or did not conflict with it. Under no circumstances could 'dependent nations' ever exercise an authority that would conflict with or limit the power of the United States.[16]

[16] See *Johnson and Graham's Lessee v William McIntosh* 21 US 543 (1823). Marshall later used this doctrine in his judgments in the *Cherokee Nation* cases: *Cherokee Nation v State of Georgia* 30 US 1 (1831) and *Worcester v Georgia* 31 US 515 (1832).

From the perspective of jurisprudence the relationship is logical, even necessary. If a court derives its authority to act from a particular constitutional relationship to a particular sovereign power, it cannot question the authority of that sovereign without also questioning its own authority to question that power to begin with. In his judgment in the *Mabo* appeal, Justice Brennan of the High Court stated that this limitation on the prerogatives of domestic courts was essential to the separation of powers between the judiciary and the executive. In defining the limited scope of Native Title as a 'burden on Crown sovereignty', not a competing sovereignty, he appealed to the Act of State Doctrine, which he defined as follows:

> 'The acquisition of territory by a sovereign state for the first time is an act of state which cannot be challenged, controlled or interfered with by the courts of that state.' This principle... precludes any contest between the executive and the judicial branches of government as to whether a territory is or is not within the Crown's Dominions.[17]

The only way that domestic courts in any state can give equal weight to the rights of indigenous communities or nations forcibly incorporated into that state is if the law somehow explicitly contains some body of rights and/or prerogatives that arise from this prior sovereignty, and which are taken to depend for their moral, if not their legal, force upon that prior sovereignty.[18]

The two aspects of the problem faced by Mr Neal and the Cherokee give rise to different aspects of the set of rights we might now care to impute to them. Our method for deriving rights discussed earlier is to find the ways in which basic interests of persons are threatened and might be protected or promoted in a certain set of circumstances.

There can be no doubt that any discussion of indigenous rights should begin with a reiteration of the civil and human rights of indigenous people. Mr Neale's case in particular illustrates just how badly indigenous people (like other marginalized groups) can be treated when the law falls more heavily on them because of the attitudes and presumptions of those (usually from a dominant group) who administer it. The Razian method I described earlier might even lead us to postulate certain indigenous rights just because they are necessary to counter the special vulnerability of indigenous people in this regard. We could easily justify indigenous civil rights such as the right to special categories of legal assistance and even to separate or adjunct legal processes. While these might be expressed as special indigenous rights, they ought properly to be regarded as unique expressions of common civil rights shared by all citizens.

The material and social disadvantage I alluded to above could easily give rise to especially urgent welfare or social rights. The form of these 'social rights' has been described in other chapters of this volume, particularly by K. D. Ewing

[17] *Mabo and Others v Queensland (No 2)* (1992) 175 CLR 1, 31. The quotation is from Gibbs J in *New South Wales v Commonwealth* (1975) 135 CLR 337, 388.

[18] A fuller discussion of the relationship between pre-colonial and colonial sovereignties may be found in S. Curry, 'Are Our Hands Tied? Acts of State and Indigenous Sovereignty', (2000) 2 *Australian Journal of Professional and Applied Ethics* 4.

(Chapter 16), so I will not plough this ground again. Suffice it to say that if we have a general commitment to social rights, then relative indigenous disadvantage ought to give rise to special (if hopefully temporary) indigenous rights to extra remedial assistance. Given the way this disadvantage (in both absolute and relative terms) impacts upon very fundamental human needs, it is easy to see how my Razian approach would establish these economic and social rights.

However, it is salutary to reflect that social rights of the sort advocated by Ewing rely heavily upon the idea that a democratic state ought to embrace 'equality' as a basic constitutional commitment.[19] Indigenous commentators have not always been satisfied with the contention that equality is the primary principle underpinning claims for justice in indigenous affairs. Some have argued that the pursuit of 'statistical equality', i.e. material equality, masks or even denies important elements of indigenous aspirations. This occurs because the concentration upon such equality implicitly assumes that justice for indigenous people is the same as the achievement of all the commodities and advantages of 'Western' civilization. It is therefore an assimilationist policy.[20]

This apparently inconsistent claim against efforts to rectify the injustice of indigenous disadvantage has its root in the problem of consent that is the motivation for this chapter. The explicit legal priority of the successor state's sovereignty, expressed by Marshall in *Johnson v MacIntosh* and the *Cherokee Nation* cases, is reflected in social reality. This reality involves the implicit assumption that the priorities of the good life in the dominant culture must be good for every citizen, when in fact they are less important, even irrelevant or pernicious, to the pursuit of goods valued by indigenous persons. Naturally an enlightened social policy could provide space and material support for these other priorities, but even then it would not wholly succeed in responding to the rights of indigenous persons. A residual inequality would remain. The full expression of indigenous culture demands recognition of a fundamental claim to land and resources that is not equivalent to 'ownership' in Western law, and for the exercise of legal powers and prerogatives derived from an alternative legal tradition.

For example, Australian Aborigines have a complex legal system, one that has a multitude of sources and a series of overlapping jurisdictions. One strand of this system is the Dreaming, a timeless, ontologically distinct realm, part history, part spiritual present, from which persons derive traditional responsibility for animal species, sacred places, and territories. An individual's identity is linked to a complex of familial ties, clan and tribal memberships, ceremonial groupings, custodial responsibilities, and a totemic connection to a powerful Dreaming

[19] See K. D. Ewing, 'Social Rights and Constitutional Law', (1999) *Public Law* 104, 115–16.

[20] See, for example, J. Chesterman and B. Galligan, *Citizens Without Rights* (Melbourne: Cambridge University Press, 1997); M. Mowbray, 'Mainstreaming as Assimilation in the Northern Territory', (1990) *Australian Aboriginal Studies* 20, 26; W. Sanders, 'Destined to Fail: The Hawke Government's Pursuit of Statistical Equality in Employment and Income Status Between Aborigines and Other Australians by the Year 2000', (1991) *Australian Aboriginal Studies* 13.

spirit. These spirits in turn are linked to animal and plant species as well as sacred sites. A person having, for instance, a Red Kangaroo Dreaming will have special responsibilities for and towards red kangaroos. He would then have either a special right to hunt or consume this species, or, as in the red kangaroo case, be banned from using the animal as food. Instead he will be responsible for regulating the hunting of this species, enforcing laws regarding when and where the animal can be hunted, to what extent, and by whom. In this way persons have legal authority for maintaining valuable resources, legal rights that cross other jurisdictions such as tribal boundaries. The hunting of kangaroo by non-indigenous peoples without reference to this authority violates indigenous law and harms the cultural integrity, even the physical health, of the Dreaming guardian. This does not mean that only indigenous people should hunt the kangaroo, but that all hunters should be subject to the regulations governing the activity as these are articulated by the guardian. To ignore this traditional authority is to deny the full expression of the cultural rights of the bearers of that authority (and also a valuable source of expertise in resource management).[21]

The full complement of indigenous rights must include these sorts of interests, interests that cannot be secured by the achievement of material equality, or by the securing of civil rights. It is my contention that a post-colonial constitution can address these interests without violating the essential democratic commitment to civil equality.

The Post Colonial Constitution

The full recognition of indigenous rights must be regarded as a multifaceted exercise. In the first instance we must recognize that indigenous people do suffer a significant material and social disadvantage. There must be a significant attempt to provide material restitution and support, both as reparations and as the fulfilment of general welfare rights. Furthermore, every effort must be taken to secure the civil liberties and procedural rights of indigenous citizens. These efforts demand that we be prepared to provide special group cultural rights (such as access to sacred sites and political self-government at the local level), special legal rights, and special social rights such as access to remedial material welfare.

None of these efforts will count for anything, however, unless indigenous people can deploy their cultural and material resources on their own account to fulfil their own unique priorities. Furthermore, indigenous people must be able to continue the development of their own communities and cultures within a state formation that embodies their own laws and traditions, and to which they have been able to consent. Otherwise the colonizing tendency of dominant cultures will continue even in the provision of welfare services.

[21] The example was offered to me by Jocelyn Davis.

The constitutional form of this post-colonial state will by necessity be a compromise. However, all constitutions embody compromise; it is in their nature to facilitate a common political life among people with disparate interests. While it is not possible or even desirable to presume upon the outcome of a political process, I can say that a successful post-colonial constitution will embody indigenous law and tradition in the following ways. Most importantly, it must give legal force to fundamental 'laws of the land' derived from indigenous legal systems, particularly those laws that apply to all persons on the land rather than those pertaining to members of specific clans or tribes, moieties, religious or other societies, or having specific totemic associations. Furthermore, it will have to recognize and empower those bodies having traditional authority to regulate access to sacred sites and other culturally sensitive matters. It will have to recognize the legal status of those groups that enjoy regional or self-government, and provide a specific legal instrument for recognizing rights of exclusive use or control of land or resources where this is deemed necessary by traditional owners. It will have to establish explicitly a system of land tenure that recognizes indigenous property forms. This can best be achieved by recognizing original indigenous radical or reversionary title and then specifying when and how this title has been alienated by grants of freehold and so forth. It should also specify what residual rights are left over from such alienation, and organize an acceptable compromise between the resource rights and other rights retained by sovereign states and those same rights claimed by indigenous sovereigns. I would suggest that this could be achieved by the underlying reversionary title claims of all parties being ceded to the post-colonial sovereign state, subject to agreements concerning indigenous vetoes over resource use, royalty payments, and tax-sharing. This will allow indigenous communities to prevent inappropriate use of minerals, animals, plants, and waters, and allow an equitable sharing of the benefits of the application of new resource extraction technologies. Finally, the constitution must explicitly abolish the presumption of colonial sovereignty, recognizing instead the equal sovereignty of all contracting parties, and ceding all these in turn to the new state form. Inasmuch as this form gives legal power, even priority in certain cases, to indigenous communities, it will ensure that this cession empowers indigenous people and opens the way for the continuing cultural and material development of these ancient cultures.

Conclusion

Indigenous rights are human rights. They are universal in that they promote and protect fundamental interests we all possess in virtue of our common humanity. However, they are also unique to indigenous people because they express these interests in ways required by the position of dispossessed first nations within the context of colonialism, a colonial process that creates the category of 'the indigenous' to begin with. These rights are not exceptions from the norms of democratic government, and ought not to be treated as privileges. They are democratic rights inasmuch as they secure free consent to government on the part of vulnerable citizens, protect civil rights, and enable the formation of truly post-colonial constitutions. This constitution in turn is fully democratic in that it reflects an act of federation between free and equal peoples, which is the only way that the democratic ideal of civic equality can be respected in colonial and successor states. This post-colonial constitution will preserve the ideal of the rule of law because nobody will be exempted from the law or be subject to a special, racially defined law. Everyone will live under one law reflecting the ideal of a reasonable consensus among free and equal citizens.[22] Even indigenous citizens without tribal or cultural connections will benefit simply from the inestimable value of having their heritage valued as a full contributor to their nation, and of having their civil and human rights promoted on the back of this recognition. Non-indigenous citizens will also directly benefit. They will benefit from access to ancient and proven systems for management of land and resources. More importantly, they will benefit from membership of a state that respects all rights and embodies freedom and equality in the fabric of its laws.

[22] J. Tully, *Strange Multiplicity: Constitutionalism in an Age of Diversity* (Cambridge: Cambridge University Press, 1995); J. Rawls, *Political Liberalism* (New York: Columbia University Press, 1993), esp. lectures I and IV.

16

The Case for Social Rights

K. D. EWING

Introduction

The case against entrenched bills of rights is strong and compelling, and has been cogently made by many authors drawing on the experiences of different countries. Yet it remains an unalterable truth that no country with a bill of rights has given it up, and none is likely to. Many countries because of war or revolution, or in the optimism born of independence, have discarded old constitutional clothes for new ones: but all have retained their commitment to, or have introduced, entrenched bills of rights. While in some cases this may have been as a result of external pressure by a victor in war or by a former colonial power, political maturity has not led to any desire in these countries for constitutional change of a kind which would lead them to live without entrenched rights. And not only is there no example of bills of rights being discarded: this is a movement that is growing. It was not post-war rebuilding, or the 1989 revolutions, or the ending of apartheid, which led to the entrenchment (quasi or otherwise) since 1982 of constitutional rights in Canada, New Zealand, Sweden, or the United Kingdom. But it is not only at the national level that we can point to the extraordinary growth of the faith in rights. A highly visible indicator of what is a global trend is the European Union Charter of Fundamental Rights concluded at Nice in December 2000. No one knows where the debates about the legal status and scope of this particular document will end.

These developments—which cannot be ignored—present a real difficulty for scholars and activists who are committed to the principle of self-government in a community of equals. The constitutional reformers of the nineteenth century were convinced that this would be achieved by universal suffrage, which would also help create the conditions of equality in which popular sovereignty could flourish. But these ambitions are frustrated by entrenched rights, as well as other constitutional arrangements which in a number of ways undermine the ambitions of early constitutional activists. A fault line thus runs through modern liberal democracies: democracy presumes a system of self-government in a community of equals which liberal democratic regimes have failed to create and indeed have erected constitutional barriers to prevent. Put another way, political rights require a framework of social rights if the former are to be of universal application, yet political rights impede the development of social rights. This chapter canvasses the counter-intuitive and paradoxical position for someone opposed to the constitutional entrenchment of rights, namely that the entrenchment of rights is incomplete without more rights: social and economic rights to complement civil and political rights.

WHAT ARE SOCIAL RIGHTS?

The first issue for examination is to determine what is meant by 'social rights'. Social rights complement civil and political rights, and are to be found expressed in a number of international treaties and national constitutions. At the international level, the main instruments are the International Covenant on Economic, Social and Cultural Rights of 1966 (ICESCR), complementing the International Covenant on Civil and Political Rights of the same year. Also at international level are the conventions of the International Labour Organization (ILO) that advised us in the Declaration of Philadelphia in 1944 with extraordinary prescience that 'poverty anywhere constitutes a danger to prosperity everywhere', and also that

> the war against want requires to be carried on with unrelenting vigour within each nation, and by continuous and concerted international effort in which the representatives of workers and employers, enjoying equal status with those of governments, join with them in free discussion and democratic decision with a view to the promotion of the common welfare.[1]

At the regional level important instruments include the Council of Europe's Social Charter of 18 October 1961 and its expanded Revised Social Charter of 3 May 1996, these complementing the European Convention on Human Rights (ECHR), by which they are overshadowed. There must now be added the European Union's Charter of Fundamental Rights concluded at Nice in December 2000, in many ways a path-breaking document which reflects many European national constitutions by including in the same text both civil and political rights on the one hand, and social and economic rights on the other, and for the time being conferring on the latter the same legal status as the former.

But these documents only tell us where to find social rights; they do not tell us what they do or what they are for. Here we find that different texts make different provision, with matters addressed in one text not covered by another. But this is not the place to draw comparisons between international treaties or to compare these treaties with the national constitutions of countries such as Italy, France, or Spain (to which we return), far less to highlight strengths and weaknesses of rival conceptions. Our immediate concern is simply to identify some core themes and goals to which these different texts are addressed. To this end we can identify at least two different kinds of social rights, a distinction which becomes important when the contested question of the justiciability of social

[1] ILO Constitution, Annex, Part 1(d).

rights is considered. The starting point, then, is what we may refer to as substantive rights; substantive in the sense that they are designed to ensure that a people's basic needs are met, and perhaps also to ensure that there is a fair distribution of resources in a particular community. Unlike civil and political rights, which generally (though not necessarily exclusively) confer rights that are protected from violation by the state, social and economic rights are altogether more wide-ranging and far-reaching, in so far as they confer rights that may be exercised against the bearers of private power, as well as by the state.

Social rights in this sense cover potentially the whole range of the citizen's social experience: education, health care, housing, work, income security during periods of interruption from work, and income security after retirement from work. The purpose of substantive social rights is to guarantee not only that provision will be made to deal with these different matters; but also by the introduction of minimum standards to regulate the terms on which that provision is made in the first place. So it is not enough for the state to seek to guarantee a right to work (as do the ICESCR, and the Council of Europe's Social Charter of 18 October 1961, and its Revised Social Charter of 3 May 1996), but necessary also to recognize the right to just conditions of work (including the regulation of working time); the right to safe and healthy working conditions; and the right to a fair remuneration (as again do the ICESCR and the Social Charters of the Council of Europe). And as expectations rise and values adapt, so these core rights expand: in the case of the Revised Social Charter, we now have new rights relating to protection in cases of termination of employment; dignity at work (addressed mainly at sexual harassment); and the needs of workers with family responsibilities.

Alongside these social rights of a substantive nature are what we might refer to as procedural rights. These are rights that facilitate participation in the social sphere where other rule-making institutions operate. This is one of the virtues—perhaps the principal virtue—of social rights, as identified by the French legal philosopher Georges Gurvitch, who wrote of the need for a Bill of Social Rights to supplement the Bill of Political Rights. In the view of Gurvitch:

> To supplement the Bill of Political Rights with a Bill of Social Rights means to proclaim the rights of workers, of consumers, and of common men as groups and as individuals to take part effectively in all aspects of life and of advancing civilization, in creative work, in security, in well-being, in education and culture, as well as to participate actively in all possible manifestations of jural autonomy, of democratic supervision and control by those concerned, of self-government and of judicial procedure. The Bill of Social Rights means (within the sphere of integration and participation) jural negation of all exploitation and domination, of all arbitrary power, of all inequality, of all unjustified limitation of liberty of groups, collectivities, and individuals. It means also the proclamation of rights of individuals, groups and collectivities to enjoy a pluralistic organization which alone under present conditions is able to save and to guarantee human freedom.[2]

[2] G. Gurvitch, *A Bill of Social Rights* (New York: International Universities Press, 1945), 71.

The key words here are 'integration' and 'participation', with the emphasis on the integrative function of social rights. Also fundamentally important is the sense that human rights are not necessarily individual rights, but are rights for empowering groups which may act collectively. So much is clear from Gurvitch's claim that

> the *Social Rights* proclaimed by the new bills must be *rights of participation by groups and individuals* in the autonomous and self-governing wholes in which they are integrated, rights guaranteeing the democratic character of these latter: rights of worker, consumer, and common man to participate in the national community and to co-operate within it on equal footing with the citizen; right of supervision and control over any power which arises, under whatever form, in any group or in any collectivity in which the people concerned are integrated; rights of all participants to make appeals to one group or collectivity against another group or collectivity in order to protect liberty whenever it becomes menaced by a whole; rights of freedom for groups, within groups, and among the plurality of groups.[3]

These rights of participation take place in different ways at different levels. There is the right through autonomous associations to take part in the making of rules that affect the social sphere: the right of the citizen as worker to take part through his or her trade union in the making of substantive social rights. But there is also the right of the worker or the consumer or the student to take part in the making of rules in the social sphere that govern enterprises or institutions. In the workplace this is recognized in the right of workers to form and join trade unions, not just as a desirable end in itself, but as a means of underpinning the right to engage in collective bargaining with their employer through the trade union to determine the rules by which the workplace is to be governed. Reinforcing this fundamental procedural right designed to expand the frontiers of rights of participation from the public to the private sphere is the right to strike, without which it is widely recognized collective bargaining cannot take place.[4] Although procedural rights are important as a means of ensuring participation in the social sphere, we should not overlook the importance of such participation as a means of raising standards and of enhancing the quality of substantive rights: organized workers are generally better paid than those who are unorganized.

State violations of social rights

Although it might thus be argued that social rights play an essential part as a precondition of democratic government, does it follow that such rights should be constitutionally entrenched? In an era of universal suffrage, why cannot such rights be secured and retained by ordinary legislation, which would be subject to

[3] G. Gurvitch, *A Bill of Social Rights* (New York: International Universities Press, 1945), 70–1; my emphasis. The discussion of Gurvitch draws on K. D. Ewing, 'Human Rights and Industrial Relations: Possibilities and Pitfalls', (2002) 40 *British Journal of Industrial Relations* 138.

[4] *Crofter Hand Woven Harris Tweed v Veitch* [1942] AC 435, 463 (Lord Wright).

the normal vagaries of the democratic process? The problem with the legislative process is not simply one of institutional capture (principally by business interests); it is also one of institutional failure. Legislation simply does not work as a means of securing and preserving even the most minimum standards set by international treaties. While this might be excusable on the part of developing nations or transitional democracies, it is wholly inexcusable when those responsible are advanced industrialized nations which for the most part have voluntarily agreed to be bound by the minimum standards which they now ostentatiously disregard. As global and national inequalities grow,[5] this is an epidemic from which few countries are immune, though it has to be said that the social democracies of continental Europe so far have a degree of resistance that is not evident in countries such as Australia,[6] the United Kingdom, or the United States.[7]

It is clearly not possible to reveal the full extent of legislative failure in advanced liberal democracies in relation to social rights. Let it be sufficient for the purposes of illustration to take the United Kingdom as an example, and examine its recent record under the Council of Europe's Social Charter of 18 October 1961.[8] This is the sibling of the much better-known European Convention on Human Rights, which was incorporated into British domestic law by the Human Rights Act 1998, which is considered below. Britain has accepted sixty of the Charter's seventy-two paragraphs (one of the lowest among EU member states; only Denmark has accepted fewer), which fall into two categories. The first are what are referred to disarmingly as the 'hard-core' paragraphs. These are Articles 1 (right to work), 5 (right to organize), 6 (right to bargain collectively), 12 (right to social security), 13 (right to social and medical assistance), 16 (right of the family to social, legal, and economic protection), and 19 (right of migrant workers and their families to protection and assistance). The hard-core articles constitute in total twenty-eight paragraphs, of which the United Kingdom has agreed to be bound by twenty-five. All these provisions were subject to supervision in the fifteenth cycle, which was completed in 2001.

The other category contains the 'non-hard-core' provisions, which make up the bulk of the Charter. (There are also substantive provisions in the Additional Protocol, but these need not detain us as the United Kingdom has not ratified it either.) Not all of the non-hard-core provisions were the subject of examination in the fifteenth cycle, which was confined to Articles 7 (the rights of children and

[5] See S. Haseler, *The Super-Rich: The Unjust New World of Global Capitalism* (Basingstoke: Macmillan, 2000).

[6] See B. Creighton, 'The ILO and the Protection of Human Rights in Australia', (1998) 22 *Melbourne University Law Review* 239.

[7] For an indictment of the position in the United States, see Human Rights Watch, *Unfair Advantage: Workers' Freedom of Association in the United States Under International Human Rights Standards* (New York, 2000). For a symposium and critique, see S. Friedman and S. Wood (eds.), (2001) 39 *British Journal of Industrial Relations* 585.

[8] The following account in this section is based on K. D. Ewing, 'The Council of Europe's Social Charter of 18 October 1961: Britain and the 15th Cycle of Supervision', (2001) 30 *Industrial Law Journal* 409.

young persons to protection); 8 (the rights of working women to protection); 11 (the right to protection of health); 14 (the right to benefit from social welfare services); 17 (the right of mothers and children to social and economic protection); and 18 (the right to engage in gainful occupation in the territory of other contracting states). These different provisions are contained in twenty-four separate paragraphs, of which the United Kingdom has accepted seventeen. This means that the United Kingdom was bound by forty-two of the fifty-two provisions that were subject to supervision in the fifteenth cycle. Supervision mirrors the ILO procedures, with the Social Charter supervised by the Social Rights Committee of the Council of Europe (to which Collective Complaints may now be made in relation to those countries that have ratified the Collective Complaints Protocol of 1995; these countries do not include the United Kingdom).

To recap (for emphasis): Britain is bound by 60 of the 72 numbered paragraphs in the Charter. In this cycle of supervision 42 of these 60 paragraphs were examined, and it was found that Britain was in full compliance with only 19. The Committee was unsure about another 8 (because of a lack of information), but found that Britain was in breach of 14 of these obligations. So far as the hard-core articles are concerned, the Committee found that the United Kingdom complies with only 10 of the 25 paragraphs with which we have agreed to be bound. In the case of 4 paragraphs, the Committee was unable to reach a conclusion without further information, and in the case of 10, British law was found not to be in conformity with the Charter. Of the 17 non-hard-core articles examined, the Committee found that the United Kingdom had fulfilled 9 of its obligations; that in the case of 4 of the obligations, the Committee needed more information to reach a conclusion; and that in the case of the remaining 4, 'the situation was not in compliance with the Charter'. This is worse than the fourteenth cycle of supervision, when Britain was found to be in breach of 13 obligations.

The position is in some respects even worse than these bald figures otherwise suggest, for in some cases the breach of a numbered paragraph is for several reasons. So in the case of the right to organize in Article 5 of the Social Charter, Britain was found to be in breach for five different reasons, and in the case of the right to strike in Article 6(4), the failings are equally comprehensive. But it is not only freedom of association guarantees that are wanting. We are still said to have problems with forced labour (sanctions on striking seafarers) and child labour (the employment of children during school holidays and the failure to extend the minimum wage to the under 18s), in breach of Articles 1(2), 7(3), and 7(5). The Committee also recorded breaches of Articles 13(1) and (4), 16, and 19(4). These deal respectively with the right to social and medical assistance, the right of the family to social, legal, and economic protection, and the rights of migrant workers and their families. Reference should also be made to the breaches of Article 8(1) (entitlement to at least twelve weeks' paid maternity leave), breached on two grounds; and Article 18(3), by which contracting parties undertake to 'liberalise, individually or collectively, regulations governing the employment of foreign workers'.

The Human Rights Act 1998

These violations of international human rights instruments in the United Kingdom (as elsewhere) paradoxically take place in the context of constitutional change ostensibly designed to secure the better protection of human rights. Among the important institutional reforms of recent times is the Human Rights Act 1998, which by incorporating the ECHR, places new judicially enforceable restraints on popular sovereignty. The ECHR is concerned principally with what we might refer to as civil and political rights, or first-generation rights. It deals with the right to life and prohibition against torture, slavery, and forced labour; the right to liberty and security of the person, as well as the right to a fair trial and protection against retrospective criminal laws; and, in addition, the right to privacy, conscience and religion, expression, and association and assembly. The protocols provide protection for private property, parental choice in education, free elections, and the abolition of the death penalty. But there is no protection in practice for social rights, except incidentally for those with a vivid imagination and unbounded faith in the virtue of the courts.

In this way, social and economic rights are subordinated to the civil and political rights that we find incorporated into domestic law by the Human Rights Act. The former must yield to the latter. Yet at first blush the Act seems almost benign, for unlike many bills of rights it does not empower the courts to strike down an Act of Parliament.[9] The courts are required simply to interpret legislation where possible consistently with the Convention (s 3), a duty which admittedly operates even where the construction in favour of Convention rights may not be the most obvious or the most reasonable construction.[10] It is only where it is not possible to construe legislation in a manner which is consistent with Convention rights that the High Court and superior courts (but not tribunals or inferior courts), after giving the Crown an opportunity to take part in the proceedings (s 5), may make a declaration of incompatibility (s 4(2)). But this 'measure of last resort' is stated not to be binding on the parties, and does not affect the validity or operation of primary legislation (s 4(6)). It has the effect only of inducing a political headache in government, which must decide whether or not to bring forward fresh legislation to remove the incompatibility.

[9] It is also possible to derogate from Convention rights by means of secondary legislation (ss 14–17). This has been done in relation to the Anti-Terrorism, Crime and Security Bill, which was published on 12 Nov. 2001. The derogation is to permit legislation authorizing the detention without trial of international terrorist suspects, in breach of Art 5 of the Convention. See SI 2001/No. 3644. The order was made on 11 Nov., laid before Parliament on 12 Nov., and brought into force on 13 Nov. It was not debated until 19 Nov. See *House of Commons Debates*, 19 Nov. 2001.

[10] *R v A* [2001] 3 All ER 1, 17 (Lord Steyn).

The powers of the courts in relation to primary legislation are thus limited, and the courts at the highest levels have so far expressed considerable deference to the need to ensure that 'decisions as to what the general interest requires are made by democratically elected bodies or persons accountable to them', and on another occasion to 'the decisions of a representative legislature and a democratic government within the discretionary area of judgment accorded to those bodies'.[11] Yet the powers of the courts are not to be underestimated. The new rule of construction has been rightly criticized as a significant limitation of Parliament's sovereign will,[12] which applies even where there is no ambiguity in legislation and which requires the courts to adopt an approach to construction 'which linguistically may appear strained'.[13] One of the first casualties of the new power was legislation designed to exclude sexual history evidence in rape cases.[14] And although it is true that a declaration of incompatibility does not affect the formal validity of legislation, it remains the case that a statute carrying such a declaration will be badly wounded, with the result that it would be difficult for a government to resist calls for amending legislation, just as it is currently difficult to resist legislation to implement a decision of the European Court of Human Rights.

The limited role of the Act in relation to legislation raises questions about precisely what it is the Act is designed to do. The answer lies in section 6, which provides that is unlawful for public authorities (including courts and tribunals) to act in a way that is incompatible with Convention rights. This means that government departments, local authorities, and regulatory agencies must exercise their powers in a manner that is consistent with Convention rights, unless primary legislation permits no other course of action.[15] It is at this point that we encounter the possibility that the Act may not only be benign but that it may also be useful, to the extent that it may have an impact horizontally to regulate not only the exercise of state power, but also the exercise of private power. This possibility arises by the inclusion of the courts and tribunals within the definition of public authorities, which means that courts and tribunals must conduct their affairs in a way that is consistent with Convention rights (such as the right to a fair trial (Art 6) and the right to freedom of expression (Art 10)). But it means much more, for it applies also to the remedies that a court may order. So it would not be possible for a court to issue an injunction if to do so would violate the

[11] See, respectively, *R (Alconbury Ltd) v Environment Secretary* [2001] 2 WLR 1389 (Lord Hoffman); and *Brown v Stott* [2001] 2 All ER 97 (Lord Bingham).

[12] T. Campbell, 'Incorporation through Interpretation', in T. Campbell, K. D. Ewing, and A. Tomkins (eds.), *Sceptical Essays on Human Rights* (Oxford: Oxford University Press, 2001), ch. 5.

[13] *R v A*, n. 10 above, 17 (Lord Steyn).

[14] *R v A*, n. 10 above.

[15] Public authorities are not defined in the Act. A number of early cases have suggested that the courts have adopted a wide approach: *Poplar Housing Association Ltd v Donoghue* [2001] 3 WLR 183 (housing association a functional public authority); *Marcic v Thames Water Utilities Ltd* [2001] 3 All ER 698 (privatized water company a public authority); and *Aston Cantlow PCC v Wallbank* [2001] 3 All ER 393 (parochial parish council a public authority because 'it possesses powers which private individuals do not possess to determine how others should act'; ibid. 402). But compare *RSPCA v Attorney General* [2001] 3 All ER 530 (RSPCA not a public authority).

Convention rights of the defendant; or to fail to issue an injunction if to do so would violate the Convention rights of the applicant.

In this way the Act may have implications for the common law and indeed for litigation between private parties. So although Convention rights are directly enforceable against only public authorities, it is impossible to rule out the likelihood that they could be enforced indirectly by one private party against another.[16] This question—the so-called horizontal status of the Convention—has given rise to a great deal of confusion.[17] The better view appears to be that (i) Convention rights may not be directly enforced by one private party against another; but that (ii) Convention rights may be relied upon in an established cause of action to extend the rights of either party. Any sense of triumph is diminished by the fact that in the most celebrated case so far, the Act was used effectively to settle a commercial dispute which seems far removed from the territory of human rights. In *Douglas v Hello!*[18] Michael Douglas and Catherine Zeta-Jones sought to restrain the publication of unauthorized photographs of their wedding, alleging that their privacy had been violated. Guided in part by the Human Rights Act, the court accepted that there was now an enforceable right to privacy rooted in the equitable doctrine of breach of confidence. In the first hearing of the case, the court openly asserted that it was not to be assumed that 'the law will never protect privacy which is being turned to commercial ends'.[19]

Constitutional protection of social rights

What we have then is a system of government in which two key principles are being further eroded. Both the principle of popular sovereignty (through representative government) and the principle of political equality are being diminished by a constitutional development that gives the courts the power to challenge, if not formally veto, social (and other) legislation. How do we move forward? Returning to Gurvitch, there is a need 'to liberate the dynamic driving force of democratic principles from becoming petrified by retarding symbolic formulas, techniques and institutions crystallized at the end of the 18th century'. A 'rejuvenated democratic enthusiasm, a new democratic creative inspiration, a reinforced democratic faith', he continued, are needed 'in order to be able to rebuild the world of tomorrow on the basis of the highest democratic value—that of human liberty'. The strongest obstacle to democracy, wrote Gurvitch, was in the economic sphere, where we find 'economic feudalism, private industrial autocracies and arbitrary technocratic powers'. True political democracy

[16] See, further, *RSPCA v Attorney General*, n. 15 above, 547 (Lightman J).

[17] See M. Hunt, 'The "Horizontal Effect" of the Human Rights Act', [1998] *Public Law* 423; R. Buxton, 'The Human Rights Act and Public Law', (2000) 116 *Law Quarterly Review* 48; W. Wade, 'Horizons of Horizontality', (2000) 116 *Law Quarterly Review* 217.

[18] [2001] 2 All ER 289.

[19] Ibid. 325 (Sedley LJ).

was not possible without parallel 'industrial', 'economic', and 'social' democracy, a necessary precondition of which was the elaboration, acceptance, and realization of a bill of social rights: 'a Bill of Rights of *workers* and *consumers*, complementing their rights as *citizens* and serving as a basis for economic democracy.'[20]

A survey of the constitutional arrangements of a number of western European social democracies reveals that many if not most have embraced ideas of this nature.[21] These constitutional arrangements fall into two categories, the first providing clearly that social rights are constitutional rights, with Italy and Spain perhaps making the most extensive provision. In the case of Italy, a title in the Constitution headed 'Economic Relations' deals with matters as diverse as vocational training (Art 35); an entitlement to wages 'sufficient to protect [the worker] and his family in a free and dignified existence' (Art 36); working time (including holiday pay) (Art 37); equal rights for women and entitlement to 'the same wages for the same work as male labour' (Art 37); and 'freedom in the organization of trade unions' (Art 39).[22] In similar terms the Spanish Constitution provides that all citizens have the right to 'sufficient remuneration for the satisfaction of their needs and those of their families' and that 'in no circumstances may they be discriminated against on account of their sex' (Art 35). There is also protection for collective bargaining and the right to strike, though the law must include safeguards for essential services (Art 37). Protection is also given to 'a public social security system' (Art 41); the protection of health (Art 43); and 'decent and adequate housing' (Art 47).

It is true that not all European states go anywhere near as far as this pair. Nevertheless, in France the Preamble to the Constitution of the Fourth Republic (founded on 'political, economic and social principles') is incorporated into the Constitution of the Fifth Republic. The former recognizes the right to work; guarantees health care, material security, rest, leisure, and social security; and promises equal access to education, professional training, and culture. There is also a constitutional right to join a trade union of one's choice and to take part in the activities of the union (though few, it seems, do either, with France having the lowest level of unionization in Europe). This is reinforced by the express constitutional recognition of the right to strike, albeit that it is a right that is heavily qualified in the sense that it is to be 'exercised within the framework of the laws' that regulate its use.[23] In Germany too—where there is otherwise little constitutional protection of social rights—the Constitutional Court has carved a right

[20] Gurvitch, n. 2 above, 9–11; my emphasis.

[21] The following four paragraphs draw heavily on K. D. Ewing, 'Social Rights and Constitutional Law', [1999] *Public Law* 104, 117–19. See also G. van Bueren, 'Including the Excluded: The Case for an Economic, Social and Cultural Rights Act', [2002] *Public Law* 456.

[22] For a full account, see M. Ainis and T. Martines, *Codice Costituzionale* (Rome: Editori Laterza, 2001), 235–335.

[23] See M. Forde, 'Bills of Rights and Trade Union Immunities: Some French Lessons', (1984) 13 *Industrial Law Journal* 40.

to strike (and determined its boundaries) from the constitutional guarantee that everyone has 'the right to form associations, to safeguard and improve working conditions'.[24] This protects both the individual worker and the trade union in its organizational capacity.

These examples contrast with the position in those countries that cast their constitutional arrangements in the form of duties. This is a feature of the Scandinavian jurisdictions in particular, though the form is not confined to such countries. In Norway the Constitution provides by Article 110 that it is 'the responsibility of the authorities of the State to create conditions enabling every person capable of work to earn a living by his work'. According to one authority, this provides a 'legal obligation' to do 'what is necessary to ensure full employment, by presenting "an injunction to the State to pursue an active employment policy when this is necessary to avoid unemployment": it implies a prohibition against unemployment being used as an instrument of economic policy'.[25] The same article imposes another duty by providing that 'specific provisions concerning the right of employees to co-determination at their workplace shall be laid down by law'. Similar obligations on public authorities are to be found in Denmark, where it is provided that 'in order to advance the public weal efforts should be made to afford work to every able-bodied citizen on terms that will secure his existence', though it is also provided in the same article that any person unable to support himself (*sic*) or his dependants shall be 'entitled to receive public assistance, provided that he shall comply with the obligations imposed by statute in such respect'.[26]

The Swedish Constitution provides in general terms that 'the personal, economic and cultural welfare of the individual shall be fundamental aims of public activity', and then specifies particular duties of the public administration 'to secure the right to work, housing and education, and to promote social care and social security and a good living environment'.[27] A similar approach is to be found in the Netherlands, where it is stated to be the 'concern' of the authorities 'to promote the provision of sufficient employment' (Art 19), 'to secure the means of subsistence of the population and to achieve the distribution of wealth' (Art 20), and to 'provide sufficient living accommodation' (Art 22). In the Swedish context these duties of the state are complemented by the right to freedom of association and an express provision that 'any trade union or employer or association of employers shall be entitled to take strike or lock-out action or any similar measure unless otherwise provided by law or arising out of an agreement'. In the Netherlands other social rights have been introduced through the direct enforceability of provisions of the Council of Europe's Social

[24] Basic Law, Art 9(3). Also see Art 1.

[25] M. T. Andenas and I. Wilberg, *The Constitution of Norway: A Commentary* (Oslo: Universitetsforlaget AS, 1987), 134.

[26] Constitution of the Kingdom of Denmark, Art 75.

[27] Instrument of Government (Sweden), Art 2.

Charter of 18 October 1961. In one particularly important case in 1986 it was held that the guarantees of the right to strike in Article 6(4) of the Charter could be directly enforced in the Dutch courts.[28]

The Human Rights Act 1998 as a template

The enforcement of Article 6(4) of the Council of Europe's Social Charter of 18 October 1961 by the Dutch courts raises interesting questions about whether the Human Rights Act could be used as a basis for the incorporation of the Social Charter into British law and other parliamentary systems. The Revised Social Charter proclaims the indivisibility of human rights; the Social Charters are the indivisible siblings of the ECHR, also a treaty of the Council of Europe. As we have seen, this is a perception that is recognized in other advanced European states, and also now by the European Union in the Charter of Fundamental Rights concluded at Nice in December 2000. As we have also seen, this wide-ranging document embraces both civil and political rights as well as social and economic rights, both with the same status, and each informed by the standards of other international treaties to which individual member states are party and from which the authors of the Charter draw inspiration. The Charter currently applies only to the European Union and its institutions, and to member states in so far as they are enforcing Community law. Yet in this way the Council of Europe's Social Charter is a potential source of restraint—albeit indirectly and collaterally—on British law, and the law of other EU member states. How could it be made more direct and universal in application?

In response to this question, the Human Rights Act provides an extraordinarily fortuitous precedent, not only because it attempts to preserve the sovereignty of Parliament, but also because it has a limited horizontal effect, and addresses relationships between private parties. As already indicated, so far this has added fresh arrows to the quivers of those aiming at commercial targets. But social rights are rather different: some are addressed directly at private power and seek to regulate its activities, as well as empowering those who bear such rights. But before dealing with this matter in greater detail, incorporation of the Social Charter along the same lines as the ECHR would mean that all legislation would have to be construed in a manner that is consistent with Charter rights. Herein of course lies a danger in the sense that the courts in the common law tradition are likely to read down social rights and to dilute their effect,[29] even before any question of balancing social rights against property rights arises whenever there is a clash. But this is a problem that can be addressed by following the precedent of the Human Rights Act, which by section 2 requires the domestic

[28] *NV Dutch Railways v Transport Unions FNV, FSV and CNV* [1988] 6 ILLR 1.

[29] For a classic example (relating to ILO Conventions 87, 98, and 151), see *Council of Civil Service Unions v Minister for Civil Service* [1984] IRLR 353 (CA); upheld [1985] AC 274 (HL).

courts to have regard to—though not be bound by—the jurisprudence of the European Court of Human Rights in the construction of Convention rights.

The importance of such a canon of construction can be seen in the social field in cases such as *Banks v Chief Adjudication Officer*,[30] a decision of the House of Lords in the neglected discipline of social security law (though there are a number of scholars whose important work keeps the subject alive as an intellectual force).[31] In the *Banks* case social welfare legislation was construed to deny benefit to a special needs assistant in a local authority school for the periods of the school holidays when he was unpaid. The withholding of benefit was upheld by the highest court as a matter of statutory interpretation on the basis of a 3:2 majority, in the course of which one of the minority made a compelling case for the applicant, but also—perhaps unwittingly—a powerful case for an interpretative obligation of the kind proposed here. In the words of Lord Scott of Foscote:

> Mr Banks' income from his employment as a special needs assistant was around £3,367 per annum. This is surely below poverty level. Mr Banks' attempts to supplement this inadequate income by working elsewhere in school holidays failed. This is not surprising. It is not easy to find short-term work. If school ancillary workers like Mr Banks are barred from claiming jobseeker's allowance by being treated as being engaged in work when in fact they are not, what are they to do? They can, I suppose, give up their work as ancillary workers and seek some form of alternative employment where they will not be caught by the construction of the regulations that will have trapped Mr Banks and, pending such re-employment, they can claim benefit. But how will schools and other educational establishments then attract ancillary workers? And if the ancillary work employment is still open to them their benefit claim may be barred on the ground that that employment is available to them and they are not actively seeking it. This is a 'poverty trap' sequence that the Social Security Act 1986 was intended to cure. If there had been some express provision in the regulations that made this result unavoidable, then your Lordships would be unable to avoid it.[32]

But in this case, Lord Scott held that such a construction was not unavoidable and that the regulations could be construed in order to ensure that benefit was payable. Indeed, he accused his colleagues of defeating the claim 'by implying into the regulations a statutory fiction that is not expressed'.[33] Here is evidence that an interpretative obligation would make a difference, however unpalatable the courts might find the decisions they were driven towards. In cases where there was a breach, the precedent of the 1998 Act would enable the courts to make a declaration of incompatibility and bat the matter back to the government to determine how to respond. A sovereign Parliament could choose to retain the legislation in breach of the Social Charter, though their electors may expect it to be changed. The other point of course—following the precedent of the 1998 Act—is that the social security authorities would also be bound to interpret their

[30] [2001] 4 All ER 62.

[31] See N. S. Harris, *Social Security Law in Context* (Oxford: Oxford University Press, 2000).

[32] [2001] 4 All ER 62, 87.

[33] Ibid.

powers and duties in a manner consistent with the Social Charter, which indeed would be directly enforceable against public authorities whose schemes would have to be adapted and tailored to meet Social Charter measures. The standards of social welfare set by the Charter would be minimum standards below which it ought not to be possible to fall.

The other major point about the Human Rights Act as a precedent relates to the implications it would have for an incorporated Social Charter in terms of disputes between private parties. Following the model of the 1998 Act, the Social Charter would not be directly enforceable in actions between private parties; but if, nevertheless, the courts were regarded as public authorities and bound by it, they would be unable lawfully to grant a remedy in legal proceedings which violated or failed fully to apply the terms of the Charter. In this way the terms of the Charter would inevitably become implied terms of the contract of employment: an irreducible minimum below which the parties could not 'agree'. This in itself would be highly significant given that the European decency threshold for determining a fair wage for the purposes of the Social Charter is set at 60 per cent of the national average male wage.[34] The incorporation of the Social Charter would also have huge implications for the law relating to collective bargaining and the labour injunction in trade disputes. It would not be possible for a court to grant an injunction which undermined the right to strike at least to the extent protected by the Charter. In this sense the incorporation of the Charter would have great implications for the common law: it would be nothing short of the *socialization* of the common law from the old-fashioned liberal values and undemocratic nature of which the community would be partially liberated.

Conclusion

The argument in this chapter can be summarized as follows: social rights serve an important constitutional function, in the sense that they bring life and give meaning to the constitutional principles of liberty and equality. Although it is possible that the securing of these rights could be achieved by ordinary legislation in the normal way, the entrenchment or quasi-entrenchment of civil and political rights subordinates social and economic rights to these entrenched civil and political rights: the latter may be introduced and may be sustained only if compatible with the former. (In some systems the predominant role of civil and political rights is another means of erecting constitutional barriers to social progress, by preventing the control of electoral power in the political process.[35]

[34] Council of Europe, *European Social Charter: Committee of Independent Experts; Conclusions XIV-2* (1999), vol. 1, pp. 49–54.

[35] Most famously in *Buckley v Valeo* 424 US 1 (1976). A similar position was taken by the Alberta courts in Canada, though it appears that the Supreme Court of Canada has set its face against the libertarian position of its American counterpart, and appears prepared to accept equalizing measures. See *Libman v Quebec* (1997) 151 DLR (4th) 385.

This has not yet been the British experience, though it may be.[36]) We are thus impaled on the horns of a dilemma: political equality and popular sovereignty are the preconditions of democracy, but they are principles that constitutional government is increasingly unable to deliver. One solution to these difficulties is to swim with the tide and to seek to rebalance the Constitution with what Gurvitch referred to as a 'Bill of Social Rights'.

Although in many ways the least desirable option, it is also one that does not seem easily achievable in the emerging constitutional environment. There are, however, two indications that further 'rights creep' is already under way and that social rights will emerge as more prominent players in the British constitutional structure. The first is in the work of the parliamentary Joint Committee on Human Rights, which scrutinizes proposed legislation for compliance with human rights standards. This body is emerging as a body of integrity and independence (if not yet influence[37]) and has indicated in one of its first reports that its examinations will extend to compliance not only with the ECHR but also with other international treaties, including in one case the ICESCR. At the other end of the scale is the EU Charter of Fundamental Rights of December 2000, a document with an uncertain but evolving legal status which has already been used in litigation against the British Government in a case concerning the failure properly to implement the EC Working Time Directive. The impact of social rights in constitutional debates and adjudication in these different ways will inevitably give rise to irresistible calls for their more effective incorporation and protection in national constitutional law. For those countries debating the introduction of a bill of rights, the task of rights activists and scholars is to fight for a comprehensive text that promotes and extends, rather than diminishes and undermines, the principles of democratic self-government.

[36] *R v Radio Authority, ex parte Bull* [1997] 2 All ER 561; [1996] QB 169 for a robust defence of the ban on political advertising on radio and television. The court defended these restrictions in the interests of political equality. But see now *Vgt Verein Gegen Tierfabriken v Switzerland*, Application No. 24699/94 (European Court of Human Rights). It is true that in *Bowman v United Kingdom* (1998) 26 EHRR 1 the European Court of Human Rights found that third-party limits violated Art 10 of the Convention (freedom of expression). But this was because at £5(!) they were too low. New restraints set the limit at £500: there is no suggestion that this is vulnerable to successful challenge.

[37] The Joint Committee called into question the legality of the derogation in respect of the Anti-Terrorism, Crime and Security Bill, but it seems to little avail, though its report may be useful in subsequent legal proceedings by someone challenging the legality of his or her detention. See HL 37; HC 372 (2001–2).

Index